COMING OF AGE IN SECOND LIFE ▶

COMING OF AGE IN SECOND LIFE

An Anthropologist Explores the Virtually Human

Tom Boellstorff

With a new preface by the author

PRINCETON UNIVERSITY PRESS

PRINCETON AND OXFORD

Published by Princeton University Press, 41 William Street,
Princeton, New Jersey 08540

In the United Kingdom: Princeton University Press, 6 Oxford
Street, Woodstock, Oxfordshire OX20 1TW
All Rights Reserved

First new edition paperback printing, with a new preface by the author, 2015
Paperback ISBN: 978-0-691-16834-0
Library of Congress Control Number: 2015940356

British Library Cataloging-in-Publication Data is available

This book has been composed in Minion Pro and Arial display

press.princeton.edu

10 9 8 7 6 5 4 3 2 1

TO NEVA COZINE, MY MOTHER, FOR VIRTUALLY EVERYTHING

••

TO CARTER WALLAR ULASZEWSKI, MY GODSON, FOR BECOMING ACTUAL

Contents

A STORY OF THREE ISLANDS

> *Where do you start when you want to tell a story?*
> *Answer: you just start. The rest will come along like a little lost sheep.*

ANTHROPOLOGISTS LIKE TO tell stories that take you to unexpected places. But where do you start when you want to tell a story?

I should not overthink it. Like it says above, just start and the rest will come along like a little lost sheep. Those lines were written by Fran, someone I worked with in my research and (as often happens) a friend. You will learn more about her soon.

This is the preface to the 2015 edition of my book *Coming of Age in Second Life*, which was originally published in 2008. A preface like this is an odd kind of thing, because on purpose it is written many years after the main text it introduces. I find it a bit like commenting on a book written by an earlier self. It is still me, but I have changed, grown, moved on to other things, and the world has changed too.

As is often the case for new editions like this, the main text of *Coming of Age in Second Life* is unchanged save for correcting a few typographical errors. This is an "ethnography," a study of a culture in a particular place and time. There would be no way to update the text without it becoming a whole new book. But there are things an author can address in a preface like this one, including developments since the book's original publication, ways the book has been discussed, and themes of lasting value. I did not meet Fran until after this book was first published, and so it is fitting that with these things in mind, Fran and I are going to tell a story together. It is a story of three islands, and we will go backwards in time, just like you will go backwards in time from this preface to the rest of *Coming of Age in Second Life*.

AN ISLAND DANCE

I first met Fran on Namaste Island, next to her daughter Barbie and some other friends in a cabin with wooden walls. It was a support group for people with Parkinson's Disease; I do not have Parkinson's myself, but was conducting research about illness and disability. That is why I found myself sitting in this circle with Fran as our leader, sharing troubles, joys, challenges. I will never forget when Fran said "I was diagnosed with Parkinson's Disease about six years ago. And when I got my diagnosis, it was like a punch in the gut." Yet Fran not only supported others, but kept active on Namaste Island: "I'll just walk around, go to the beach, even go horseback riding."

My first dance with Fran was on this island too. It was at the Phantom of the Opera Masquerade Ball, a benefit for Parkinson's Disease charities held in a high-ceilinged ballroom that was all chandeliers and marble, with a tiled fountain in the center. I bought a new tuxedo for the event and my shopping excursion meant I arrived a little late. Right away I saw Fran in her luxurious red ball gown, complete with long red gloves, a necklace glittering with red and white stones, hair done up in blond curls, and an elegant white-feathered mask. Next to her was Barbie, whose gown shimmered blue and violet, every bit as breathtaking. Fran and I spun around the ballroom, song after song. At one point she looked at me and said "It thrills me to see me dancing. This is who I am."

Did you already guess that Fran and I were dancing not in the physical world, but in Second Life, a virtual world (Figure P.1)? What you might not have guessed is that Fran was eighty-five years old when we first danced (Figure P.2). That is not the typical image of someone in a virtual world, and

FIGURE P.1. Fran and Tom in real life.

FIGURE P.2. Fran and Tom in real life.

Fran was not the average Second Life resident, but anthropologists know that "outliers" can teach us a lot about the norm. Think with me like an anthropologist for a moment. When Fran said "this is who I am" while describing her avatar, she was not in denial about her physical body. She was saying that her virtual and physical bodies were both real, each in their own way. In this regard Fran was not an outlier at all. Her views beautifully captured a set of beliefs and experiences I commonly encountered in Second Life and other virtual worlds, and that other scholars have described as well. We should thus listen carefully when Fran said that being in Second Life was:

> Greater than great, okay?…When I'm doing things like, I will dance… and I'll watch my legs, and while I'm sitting here [in the physical world], my legs will be doing what I'm doing there that I cannot do here. I would fall on my face if I were to do something like that….I watch myself and I get thrilled that I am dancing! You see, I don't think of me sitting in this chair: "me" is the person on the computer.

Her understanding of both virtual and physical bodies as real goes back to the first time she created her avatar with Barbie:

> I said to Barbie "make me blonde" and I am grey, and "make me young" and I'm old, and so I do not look like my avatar at all. But if I look at

her, I see Fran. I guess that's who I am if I take a zipper and pull her out of me, that's who I am.

The difference between Fran's physical body and avatar body was not about hiding anything, and she often talked about her "fabulous" life in the physical world. She was not denying her physical body and was certainly aware of her Parkinson's Disease every day. Instead, Fran was taking advantage of a virtual world to make a reality in which her physical body was not her only embodiment. Over and over, Fran insisted that Second Life was as real as the "real world." As she once put it, "Actually I feel like this is more real-world to me than my real world." Her experience of having an avatar body was real, the places in Second Life where she spent time were real, and her relationships and activities in Second Life were real. All these aspects of virtual world social interaction were distinct from the physical world, but there could be influence between them. Barbie, Fran's daughter offline, could be Fran's friend online and their shared experiences were real. In the other direction, people Fran met online could become real friends, whether they socialized only online (because the person might be thousands of miles from Fran's home) or met in the physical world (as happened, for instance, with me).

What we learn is that as with other Second Life residents, Fran's physical body and avatar body were both aspects of her reality. The avatar body made it possible to wear a ball gown and go to a virtual ball—on occasion, to be asked to dance by young men who might not have taken the time to get to know Fran had they met her only in the physical world. It allowed Fran to run a support group for people with Parkinson's Disease who were scattered across the physical world. If we pay careful attention we learn something else as well. What is important is not just the avatar body, but the virtual world that avatar body inhabits (Boellstorff 2011). It is not just the avatar body dancing, but a ballroom to dance in; not just a support group, but a wooden cabin on Namaste Island where the group can meet. This aspect of virtual worlds—that they are places—is a topic discussed at length in *Coming of Age in Second Life*. It is a great example of how not all aspects of online technologies are the same. You do not have this shared experience of place when texting on a mobile phone or emailing from a laptop, though both of these forms of communication are real in their own way.

Note that I do not contrast Second Life (or other aspects of the Internet) with the "real world." Instead I talk about the "physical world" (or the "actual world"). Why? Because things online can be real or unreal, and the same goes for things in the physical world. You can learn a language online, or make a friend, or lose money playing poker: all real. On the other hand, you can put on a costume and engage in play or fantasy without ever using the Internet! One topic I address in *Coming of Age in Second Life* is the reality of virtual world identities, relationships, and cultures—and what this tells us about the human journey in a digital age. Fran's conclusion that what she was doing in Second Life was real was consistently shared by others I met during my research. You did not always do "real things" in Second Life (you could pretend to be a dragon, for instance), but even such roleplaying and fantasy was only possible because the broader virtual world was real.

CHANGE, SIZE, RELEVANCE

The number one question I get asked about Second Life nowadays is "does anyone still use it?" This well-intentioned question is shaped by some worrisome assumptions about what digital technologies we should study, and why. When I began my research, Second Life had about 2,500 active residents, with a maximum of about 200 online at any point in time, and I was fine with that. I was surprised to see Second Life grow quickly to over a million active residents. Soon after *Coming of Age in Second Life* was published, the total number of active residents peaked. While it has gone up and down since then, at the time I write this preface Second Life had around 30,000–60,000 persons online at any point in time, meaning there were probably around a half million active residents, more than 150 times its size when I began my study (Voyager 2014). But when there are over a billion people on Facebook, why talk about Second Life at all?

Like any ethnographer, I know that careful attention to a particular place makes it possible to learn valuable things that can be used for generalization and comparison. And the fieldsite need not be big. Anthropologists do not just study China and India; many conduct research in small villages with only a few hundred members. One dangerous implication of the technology industry's "hype cycle" is the assumption that the only things worth studying are the large or newly released (Boellstorff 2014). Bravado stands in for reasoned analysis.

Second Life, then, is plenty big to learn from, and this includes gaining perspective on changes in digital culture. As noted above, one thing a preface like this can do is address developments since a book's original publication, and another question I am commonly asked is "how has Second Life changed since your book came out?" This is difficult to answer because, like any social context, Second Life has changed: new groups and places appear while others disappear, and also technical changes occur (for instance, the addition of new "mesh" clothing, or the ability to run Second Life from mobile devices). Yet many things have not changed: the overall population is about the same, as is the general range of activities, the way in which one controls avatars, builds and transforms land, and so on.

What is perhaps more useful for the reader of the new edition of *Coming of Age in Second Life* to consider is what this ethnography has to say about current developments in digital technology and society. An ethnography (or any text for that matter) reflects what the author was thinking at that point, in the context of the topics researched. It is shaped by the time of its writing, and times change. When the topic is technology, the change can seem so fast that the ground slips out from under one's feet. When I joined Second Life on June 3, 2004, World of Warcraft did not yet exist, Facebook had fewer than a million users, and Twitter was almost two years away from being created. The whole domain of online culture has transformed since this book was first published. To even attempt to summarize these changes would take up far more space than I have here; instead, I will note two particularly interesting changes, and how *Coming of Age in Second Life* might help provide tools for pondering their implications.

ANONYMITY AND SURVEILLANCE

Influenced by everything from the history of games and roleplaying to the Burning Man festival, the creators of Second Life decided at the outset to delink avatar accounts from physical world identities. I am Tom Boellstorff, but my Second Life avatar name is Tom Bukowski—not by choice, but because I was forced to select a last name from a predefined list. There are now ways to have one's physical world name visible (in your "profile," or as a kind of screen name), but the most common pattern remains one in which avatar names are not the same as physical world names.

Since *Coming of Age in Second Life* was first published, we have seen the rise of many platforms that depart from this framework, encouraging or even requiring (as best they can) that users have "screen names" clearly linked to their physical world identities. Social network sites like Facebook are perhaps the best-known examples of this phenomena. Persons representing such platforms sometimes criticize the very idea of anonymity, associating it with deception, hate speech, and even criminal activity. All of these negative possible consequences of anonymity deserve ongoing consideration. Like any aspect of technology, the impact of anonymity depends on what we do with it.

However, it is interesting to see how the use of physical world identities in digital contexts has taken on a new range of meanings. The goal of a seamless self, identical online and offline, is pivotal to emerging regimes of state surveillance, with political consequences. Many technology giants of our era rely on this goal as well. For these corporations, of which Google is the exemplar, profits come primarily from advertising that is customized for specific consumers. As many have noted, this is why services from companies like Google and Facebook are mostly free: the person using the service is not really a customer, but a product delivered to advertisers.

With regard to these debates, one valuable lesson from Second Life is that pseudonymity is not the same thing as anonymity. Even if, for argument's sake, no one in Second Life knows I am "Tom Boellstorff," they do know that I am "Tom Bukowski." That avatar name might have virtual land associated with it, even a business or a brand. And that avatar name has a reputation: Tom Bukowski could be known as a considerate or an offensive person, and as a person who participates in particular activities. This illustrates how the question of anonymity is about communities as well as individuals. If a Second Life resident is a member of various friendship networks and groups, that resident is not "anonymous" at a collective level. In many online communities, groups collaborate without knowing each other's physical world identities. As we move into a future of potentially ubiquitous tracking and surveillance, Second Life reminds us of the possibility for forms of digital collectivity and selfhood that use pseudonymity in creative and community-enhancing ways. Second Life can thereby help us think about what happens when data becomes part of social context: no longer a secondary commentary on human existence, but part and parcel of that existence (Boellstorff 2015).

Mobility and materiality

Like most virtual worlds before it, Second Life was created to be accessed via desktop or laptop computers, due to the demands of processing power and broadband connectivity. The first iPhone was released in June 2007, three years after I began my research and a year before *Coming of Age in Second Life* first appeared in print. Mobile devices represent the most quickly adopted new technology in human history. A majority of people worldwide now primarily go online using mobile devices; thanks to companies like Xiaomi and Samsung, "smartphones" and tablets are not the exclusive provenance of the well-to-do. Linked to this rise of mobile devices has been what some have termed the "Internet of things": the use of sensors and digital connectivity to allow appliances, homes, cars, and even clothing to access or be controlled or tracked online, and to communicate with each other. The material world is becoming part of digital worlds.

What these developing dynamics of mobility and materiality will mean for virtual worlds is uncertain, but there will clearly be multiple, divergent effects. Many virtual worlds (including Second Life) can now be accessed using tablets and other mobile devices. This does not eliminate the gap between the online and offline, but makes the online accessible anywhere in the physical world. The online can now share in our mobility, leading to new possibilities for the "overlay" of the digital and physical.

One reason movement and materiality will have multiple effects is that at the same time as mobile devices allow virtual worlds to be delinked from specific physical locations (like a living room where a desktop computer is located), devices like Oculus Rift goggles allow us to access virtual worlds with a three-dimensional richness. As I note in chapter 1, "virtual worlds" and "virtual reality" are distinct. Historically, for most virtual world residents social immersion has been far more meaningful than sensory immersion. Most virtual worlds have been accessed via screens that do not fill the field of vision; photorealism is sometimes valued, but often virtual worlds make no attempt at such realism (like Minecraft); they can even be entirely text-based. On the other hand, many virtual reality technologies have been used for things like flight simulators that may not be connected to the Internet at all (and are thus not virtual worlds).

NAMASTE TO NETTLES

When I introduced you to Fran, she was on Namaste Island in Second Life, leading a weekly support meeting for people with Parkinson's Disease. All of the changes I have just discussed were swirling around that virtual wooden cabin, shaping the lives of those within it. Yet when the seemingly always-changing topic of technology is being discussed, it is helpful to think not just about changes to come, but also about traces of the past in the living present.

Many years before that support group meeting, Fran had sat in another cabin, volunteering at a summer camp for children who had recently lost a parent. She wrote about having the children throw a ball of yarn back and forth in a circle, making a web "to make the point of how we were depending on one another." She wrote as well that "My most favorite compliment paid to me was when one of the children said, 'We love Miss Frances, she thinks we are people.'"

The orphaned children named their cabin the Dew Drop Inn. When Fran would talk to the group of people living with Parkinson's about supporting each other, I could almost see the Dew Drop Inn before me. Here as well, Fran was bringing people together, weaving a world wide web of pixels instead of yarn.

We so badly need ways to understand how virtual and actual worlds are both real, and in that regard Fran is teaching us something here. Orphaned children meeting in the physical world, persons with Parkinson's meeting in the virtual world: she recognizes "we are people," all of us human, online and offline.

As mentioned earlier, our Second Life cabin was on Namaste Island, not too far from a beach where Fran's avatar could walk or ride a virtual horse. However, Fran did not join Second Life and walk on that virtual beach until moving to California to be near her daughter Barbie. We were talking about beaches one day at a support group meeting when Fran exclaimed, "Oh, you have no idea about my memories of beaches. I lived 35 years on the beach in Florida, and all the rest of my life near beaches. So beaches do mean a lot to me." Before experiencing Namaste Island, Fran had lived on Nettles Island on the Florida coast, "in a fantastic resort with loads of friends." Barbie purposely designed the beach on Namaste Island to resemble Nettles Island. Fran noted that she would sometimes say "'Let's go to Nettles Island on Namaste'... And I wasn't missing Nettles Island, because I could go there."

Once again Fran is teaching us about virtual worlds and what is real: through Second Life, she could "go there" to a memory of Nettles Island made real by experiencing Namaste Island. And the connections between the two islands do not end with visual resemblance. It was on Nettles Island—nearly twenty years before she entered Second Life—that Fran, already in her sixties, fearlessly entered the world of computing. She recalled how it was while living on Nettles Island that "my son gave me his old computer. And I started to play around with it and I started to write books on it." Many of the quotes from Fran you are reading are excerpts from those books. You are hearing Fran's voice from two islands, one virtual and one physical, but both parts of her "real life."

CONVERSATIONS

This book was an experiment.

As an ethnographer, I spend time with people to understand how they think and act. There are ethnographers who study a single community their entire working lives; others seek out new fieldsites during their careers. Before studying virtual worlds I had already published my first book about sexuality in Indonesia, *The Gay Archipelago* (Boellstorff 2005). I remain interested in that fascinating country, but wanted to try something "completely different," in the words of the famous Monty Python comedy sketch. If I tried employing the approach I had used in Indonesia in Second Life, would I fall flat on my virtual face? I was thrilled to discover that it was both possible and immensely rewarding to conduct rigorous ethnographic research in a virtual world.

The dream of every scholar is to be read, and I am honored that *Coming of Age in Second Life* has been widely discussed, and also translated into Polish and French (Boellstorff 2012a, 2013b). Even when we write individually, scholars are never alone. Scholarship is about conversations between researchers, students, communities, and anyone who wishes to participate. However, respecting the legitimacy of those we study is necessary for those conversations to work.

The Gay Archipelago was one of the first book-length ethnographies of LGBT persons published before the author had received a permanent university position (for a classic earlier example, see Newton 1972). The pioneers who have published on this topic largely did so after the relative safety of tenure; regardless, most faced job discrimination. With virtual worlds I hoped such concerns would not apply: technology is a sexy topic, and not so self-evidently political, right?

Naïve me. I have been surprised to encounter more negativity toward the people I studied in Second Life than those I studied in Indonesia. Most readers of *Coming of Age in Second Life* have treated virtual world residents as fully human, with something to teach us about new frontiers in technology and society. However, there have also been misrepresentations of virtual world residents as lost in escapism or fantasy, addicted to the virtual, neglecting "real" friends and family. Persons making such assessments rarely have someone like Fran in mind. These assessments reveal a limited understanding of virtual worlds, and involve inaccurate or even willful misreading of the work of myself and other scholars.

Ethnographic attention to virtual worlds demonstrates the same range of human activity as on the Internet more broadly—or, for that matter, in the physical world. In Second Life (as on Twitter, a news website, or a physical world town) we find deception and abuse, but also kindness and community. It depends on what we do with the technology, not some fixed characteristic of the technology itself. The words and actions of Fran (and others I discuss in this book) prove that residents of virtual worlds are not failures in need of a "real life;" *they are living real lives, online and offline.* Virtual worlds are not some kind of ideal toward which everyone will converge in a Matrix-like future. Rather, they are one genre of digital culture, important to study for its own sake and for what it teaches us about the broader ecology of online social forms.

Linden Lab, the company that created and manages Second Life, first called it "Linden World." I sometimes wish they had kept that name. It aligns more clearly with the thousands of other virtual worlds that currently exist, like World of Warcraft, Minecraft, or Eve Online. While concepts from Christianity have shaped virtual worlds (see chapter 8), the Christian overtones of "Second Life," recalling the Second Coming, misrepresent these influences, for instance with regard to the idea that the immaterial will eventually become flesh. The phrase "Second Life" can imply an attempted additional life separate from the physical world, so that Second Life residents "need to get a first life." These judgmental conclusions are inaccurate. Residents who like "Second Life" often feel the name captures the richness of the virtual environment—with all its friends, communities, and activities—not because it is sealed off from the physical world.

One of the most central lessons virtual worlds teach us about the Internet is that there is a pivotal difference between "distinct" and "disconnected." A video game or website is in important ways distinct from the physical world (if you shoot someone in a video game, no blood is shed in the physical world). But these things are always connected to the physical world, more explicitly (an email about a meeting to take place in a physical office one hour later) or implicitly (a video game with dragons that draws concepts from myths found in physical world cultures). The virtual and physical are distinct yet connected, and what makes this connection possible is that *both the virtual and the physical are real.*

At the time I wrote *Coming of Age in Second Life*, I felt that the term "digital" was overused and unclear (see chapter 1). I have since developed a more precise theory of the digital, taking inspiration from the origins of the word in terms of "digits" on a hand—fingers. Without gaps between fingers, we would not have fingers at all. Without the gap between 1s and 0s, digital computing would be impossible and there could be no Internet. Fingers on either side of the gap between them are both real, and the two voltage states that the 1s and 0s of digital computing represent are both real. In my more extended writing on this topic I discuss how thinking of the "digital" in this way is empirically accurate and conceptually rich, because it gives us a way to think about how the virtual and physical are *connected through distinction* (Boellstorff 2012b).

This crucial insight that the virtual and physical are both real has methodological implications, because in its absence it is easy to assume that you cannot get "real data" from online ethnographic methods. This assumption has shaped some conversations regarding the question of studying virtual worlds "in their own terms."

Ethnographers face with particular clarity an issue that confronts all social science researchers: the question of discrete cultures. On one hand, there are clearly different cultures around the world, on many spatial scales. There is such a thing as Japanese culture, and something that New Yorkers share. On the other hand, it is just as clear that cultures do not have firm boundaries. Human beings have been on the move since our origins. Forms of migration, commerce, and travel have continued up through our contemporary era of globalization, taking blatantly oppressive forms (like colonialism) and other forms with more ambivalent consequences (like nationalism or transnational organizing). Furthermore, ideas, assumptions, and beliefs can move between cultures even if individuals do not: for instance, the spread of religions around the world can involve missionaries, but it can also involve the movement of ideas and texts. Finally, cultures are internally diverse. Not all Japanese people do the same thing; New Yorkers are not of one mind.

The notion of studying cultures "in their own terms" is one response to this issue. As I discuss in chapter 3, to study a culture "in its own terms" means describing it from the point of view of its members. If an ethnographer studies Thai culture, this does not mean ignoring that Buddhism originates in India, or that China has had an influential role in Thailand's history. It means that the ethnographer, spending an extended time with people in Thailand, would seek to understand these influences as they do: it is neither feasible nor necessary that the ethnographer also spend time in India and China (or the many other places around the world that shape contemporary Thai culture).

The phrase "in its own terms" is well-established in anthropology; like any concept, it can be used incorrectly. The famous anthropologist Clifford Geertz long ago noted "the catch phrase... [can] run the danger... of locking cultural analysis away from its proper object, the informal logic of actual life" (Geertz 1973b:17). Geertz and other anthropologists argued for treating cultures as systems of practice and meaning, and I hope to have contributed to this approach by showing that in addition to what Geertz termed "the informal logic of actual life," we can now study *the informal logic of virtual life*. To study a virtual world "in its own terms" is not to treat it as a domain set apart, but as a distinct, yet connected, real domain of human experience.

This principle of studying cultures in their own terms is easy for most people to understand, but even ethnographers sometimes have difficulty applying it to virtual worlds. Unlike "Thailand" and "China," "Second Life" and "China" can seem to be different kinds of things, to the extent that only one side of the equation is treated as real. But as Fran reminds us, Second Life is real, and this reality cannot be reduced to the physical world backgrounds of its residents. When sitting together, Fran and her friends might have been talking about Parkinson's, a disease affecting their physical world bodies and physical world lives, where they are scattered across the United States and beyond. But the words and emotions they shared in that virtual wooden cabin are real. The experiences they shared riding a virtual horse on a beach or dancing in a virtual ballroom are real as well—but you cannot fly to California or Ohio or London to put your finger on them.

This issue of understanding an online culture "in its own terms" might seem unique to virtual worlds, but it is relevant to all digital topics, including those of mobile devices and the "Internet of things" mentioned earlier. It is possible to study any of these phenomena on their own terms, compare multiple such phenomena, or examine relationships between online and offline contexts (Boellstorff 2010). It depends on your research questions: what are you trying to understand, and why? This is a question of methodology, and together with three colleagues I wrote an entire book to address it—*Ethnography and Virtual Worlds: A Handbook of Method* (Boellstorff, Nardi, Pearce, and Taylor 2012). But the legitimacy of virtual worlds research will be compromised if we require such research always involve meeting the people studied in the physical world. Such a requirement would not just be impractical—it would be conceptually mistaken, since the vast majority of those people are not meeting offline themselves. It would fundamentally misrecognize that among the vibrant range of ways people use the Internet, one way is to inhabit virtual worlds, and through that habitation people engage in social relations that are shaped by physical world contexts but cannot be directly inferred from them.

SAMOA TO BATH BEACH

This book's title pays homage to Margaret Mead's *Coming of Age in Samoa*. In her preface to the 1973 edition of that classic, Mead wrote:

This is the fourth time that I have written a preface to a different edition of this book, published originally in 1928....In each preface I discussed how long ago the book was written and how different the world of readers was for whom it would again be published. But in the contemporary world I find that readers pay little attention to dates, and some even read this account of a bygone style of life as if it were, indeed, an account of life in the more bustling and vastly more complicated Samoa of today, and fail to take account of the differences. (Mead 2001:xxiii)

Writing my preface for a book published only six years earlier, I nonetheless sympathize with Mead's concerns. Yet as the human journey continues to be transformed by digital technology, there is value in keeping in mind that not everything changes. The patterns of the past, the legacies of all that has been said and done, all shape the present and the unfolding future—even when technology is the topic of discussion.

In September 2014, as I began writing this preface, I spent a day with Fran in California. She talked about trying to explain Second Life in her retirement community:

I've had people say "Do you still play that game you were telling me about?".... "Are you still playing the paper dolls, where you put the clothes on your doll?" You see, I didn't tell them it was a doll, I said it was an avatar. And I can get clothes for it, and I might [have] explain[ed] what pretty clothes I have or something. They think the avatar has tabs on top and you put on clothes like a paper doll.

These misunderstandings frustrated Fran, but she could understand how people in their seventies and beyond might have difficulty comprehending what it means to have an avatar. When describing Namaste Island and Second Life at the retirement community, Fran could draw on her rich life experiences. She recorded many of these experiences in her autobiographical story *My Crazy Patchwork Quilt*, written many years earlier on another island, Nettles Island, where, as noted above, she had first learned to use a computer. But Fran's life on islands did not begin off the Florida coast. Her childhood memories are filled with experiences from a third island—Long Island, more specifically the New York borough of Brooklyn:

You don't know Brooklyn, can't talk about Brooklyn unless you were born there. I was born the sixth of seven children in 1927. Depression. Where only the fittest survived.

Even in such circumstances, children in Fran's neighborhood found ways to create imaginative worlds of play:

> There was no money for special toys, but I still remember the hours of sheer enjoyment of the paper dolls we could cut out from the Sunday funnies. We would design clothes for those dolls for hours.

When people in her retirement home misunderstood avatars as being like paper dolls, Fran could relate this to the arc of a life shaped by islands of technology. Even her childhood in 1930s Brooklyn had "online" aspects:

> Those were the heydays of radio entertainment. We would all gather around at night after homework was done and eagerly listen to our favorite stories. Jack Benny with his cheapskate manner who played the violin, George Burns and his laughable dippy side kick Gracie Allen who were side-splitting with their corny one-liners.

When dancing to music in Second Life with Fran, I would sometimes think about her family around the radio at night during the Great Depression. It is not just movement between virtual and physical; it is also movement between continuity and change. This is a key insight that I hope *Coming of Age in Second Life* will leave the reader. Recall Fran talking about how beaches have meant so much to her, including the virtual beach on Namaste Island in Second Life, made to resemble Nettles Island in Florida. I keep this continuity in mind when reading what Fran writes about how as a child on Long Island:

> The beach could be reached by Shank's mare [walking] or roller skates… overlooking the Narrows which was the route for the Queen Mary, Normandy, and the many gigantic luxury liners that were headed to Europe. They tooted past the Statue of Liberty…Those boat whistles are another sound of my yesterdays.

I could say so much more about Fran, about so many people I have met in Second Life. In every story there is a life and in every life a thousand tales to tell. But as an anthropologist, I see as well the shared ways of thinking, feeling, and acting that virtual world residents experience through their histories, online and offline.

The subtitle of this book is "An Anthropologist Explores the Virtually Human," and the word "anthropology" itself comes from *anthropos*, meaning "human." What does it mean to talk about "the human?" There are things we share as families, as members of communities and networks, even as citizens of nations. And then there are things we all share as humans, even when they take on local characteristics. For instance, all humans have language, but the languages we use—English, Indonesian, Korean—are the products of specific histories. Anthropologists should participate in debates regarding this question of what humans share, and also how we differ. The fact that anthropologists often focus on smaller communities—and even learn from the experiences of individuals, like Fran—does not disqualify us from participating in these debates. Instead, such local knowledge represents one way anthropologists can contribute to a better understanding of humanity.

One of the most important aspects of this book that has withstood the test of time is treating virtual worlds as part of what it means to be human. While the transformations we make in our lives through digital technologies have exciting and frightening aspects, these transformations take place on the terrain of the human. They expand the possibilities of what it means to be human, but do not make us unhuman. In this regard, we can look to the history of anthropology for inspiration, for anthropologists have long been interested in how being human is shaped by engagements with the nonhuman. This has included our relationships with plants, animals, and nature in the broadest sense, so as to rethink the binarism of "nature" versus "culture." It has also included considering how technology transforms human abilities, embodiment, experience, and society.

At the time I write this preface, a trend in some quarters of anthropology is to talk about nature or technology as taking us "beyond the human" or "posthuman." I think this is mistaken. While this might seem a radical move, it is actually very conservative, because the implication is that when nature or technology "come to town," we become less human. To think in this way, that we leave the human behind and go "beyond" the human, presumes a quite romantic and inaccurate view of humanity as being external to nature and technology. It also disturbingly echoes a history where anthropologists and others talked about some ethnic or geographical groups as less human than white Europeans.

The reason *Coming of Age in Second Life* has the subtitle "An Anthropologist Explores the Virtually Human" (and not "Explores Beyond the Human") is precisely to underscore this point that the virtual is not beyond the human. When Fran joined Second Life, she did not become posthuman or go beyond the human. Instead, she expanded her human social interactions, her human sense of selfhood, her human use of technology to address disability, something that goes back to the first time someone, at the dawn of our species, picked up a stick to use as a cane. As you read this book, you will encounter the stories and experiences of many other Second Life residents. Through my analysis of their lives, I hope to give you some ways to think about virtual worlds and online cultures more broadly, and what these new frontiers tell us about our possibilities as human beings who come to be through *techne*—the ability to craft realities of our own making.

I have crafted this preface through Fran's biography, to give one example of how a rich life intersects with the new possibilities of digital technology. Islands and beaches, shores of worlds through time on which we forge our hopes and dreams. And for Fran, these shores of possibility extend back to her earliest days, beyond her own memory. She wrote that when she was an infant, her sisters "would take the baby carriage filled with sandwiches" and "walk about two miles to a place then called Bath Beach." From Bath Beach on Long Island to the beaches of Namaste Island in a virtual world, her story unfolds. The story of our human experience of digital culture continues to unfold too, and my sincerest hope is that *Coming of Age in Second Life* will give you more questions than answers, more ideas than conclusions, and above all a sense of wonder at the power and promise of the human spirit.

April 2015
Long Beach, California

I use pseudonyms for the physical and screen names discussed in the main text of this book. However, with their permission in this preface I have used the real avatar names of Fran (Seranade) and Barbie (Alchemi). Namaste Island is part of Creations Park, a place in Second Life that supports people living with Parkinson's and works to raise awareness about the disease. If you are in Second Life, the Second Life url or "slurl" to get to this place is http://maps.secondlife.com/secondlife/Creations%20Park/89/162/39.

BIBLIOGRAPHY TO THE PREFACE

Boellstorff, Tom. 2010. "A Typology of Ethnographic Scales for Virtual Worlds." In *Online Worlds: Convergence of the Real and the Virtual*, ed. William Sims Bainbridge, 123–134. London: Springer.

———. 2011. "Placing the Virtual Body: Avatar, Chora, Cypherg." In *A Companion to the Anthropology of the Body and Embodiment*, ed. Frances E. Mascia-Lees, 504–520. New York: Wiley-Blackwell.

———. 2012a. *Dojrzewanie w Second Life: Anthropologia Człowieka Wirtualnego*. Kraków: Wydawnictwo Uniwersytetu Jagiellońskiego.

———. 2012b. "Rethinking Digital Anthropology." In *Digital Anthropology*, eds. Heather A. Horst and Daniel Miller, 39–60. London: Berg.

———. 2013b. *Un Anthropologue dans Second Life: Une Expérience de L'humanité Virtuelle*. Louvain-La-Neuve: Academia Bruylant.

———. 2014. "Trending Ethnography: Notes on Import, Prediction, and Digital Culture." *Culture Digitally*, (January 27). Available at: http://culturedigitally.org/2014/01/trending-ethnography-notes-on-import-prediction-and-digital-culture (accessed October 31, 2014).

———. 2015. "Making Big Data, In Theory." In *Data, Now Bigger and Better!*, eds. Tom Boellstorff and Bill Maurer, 87–108. Chicago: Prickly Paradigm Press.

Boellstorff, Tom, Bonnie Nardi, Celia Pearce, and T.L. Taylor. 2012. *Ethnography and Virtual Worlds: A Handbook of Method*. Princeton: Princeton University Press.

Mead, Margaret. 2001. *Coming of Age in Samoa: A Psychological Study of Primitive Youth for Western Civilization* (1973 edition). New York: HarperCollins Publishers.

Newton, Esther. 1972. *Mother Camp: Female Impersonators in America*. Chicago: University of Chicago Press.

Voyager, Daniel. 2014. "Second Life Grid Stats 2014." *Daniel Voyager's Blog*. Available at: https://danielvoyager.wordpress.com/sl-metrics/ (accessed October 31, 2014).

Acknowledgments

ONE OF MY FAVORITE THINGS about anthropology is the flexibility it offers in terms of research projects—in my case, from Indonesia to an online world. In adding virtual worlds to my portfolio of research competencies, I have relied on the scholarship and support of a range of thinkers inside and outside the academy. Without them this book would not have been possible.

Above all, I am grateful to my fellow residents of Second Life. I use pseudonyms throughout the body of this book to protect confidentiality and so cannot thank them by name, but it is their thoughts, actions, and dreams that are this book's inspiration. As in the case of my research in Indonesia, I am continually taken aback by the breadth and depth of human kindness, the willingness of persons to share their lives with me, taking my thinking in directions I could not have foreseen. I see my fellow Second Life residents as colleagues and interlocutors, not "informants" (a term I do not use in my writing).

Due to this research design of this project I did not conduct research in Linden Lab, the company that owns and manages Second Life. Nevertheless I encountered several Linden Lab staff inworld and am thankful for their support. I did briefly meet two Linden Lab staff in the actual world, Robin Harper and Cory Ondrejka; both expressed kind interest in my work.

Stefan Helmreich and Douglas Thomas read an early version of this book in its entirety as reviewers for Princeton University Press. Their generous and detailed comments helped enormously in the process of revision. I am deeply thankful for their assistance. Stefan has been an intellectual companion for many years and his own work helped motivate my interest in undertaking this project. Since getting to know Douglas Thomas after beginning this project, he has been an unflinching supporter of my work and I greatly appreciate his support. Paul Dourish read several chapters of the manuscript in its final stages and provided helpful comments as well. Several colleagues from Second Life read drafts of this book including Gwyneth Llewelyn, Prokofy Neva, and The Sojourner.

Thomas Malaby has been an important interlocutor during this project, whose research has been invaluable in shaping my understanding of virtual worlds. Our coorganized panel at the 105th Annual Meeting of the American Anthropological Association in November 2006, "Anthropology at the Crossroads of Digital Society," represented a fruitful opportunity to exchange ideas: I also thank our discussant, Michael Silverstein, for his support and insightful comments.

A range of conferences and departmental colloquia provided me with opportunities to present this work while in progress. Comments I received from these interactions played a crucial role in helping me refine the arguments of this book. Above all, the Digital Cultures faculty seminar, organized by the Annenberg Center for Communication at the University of Southern California, played a crucial role in providing me with an intellectual environment in which to develop many of the ideas discussed in this book, including a January 2007 discussion of an early version of chapter 1. I thank all participants in that group and particularly its organizer, Mizuko Ito, who since graduate school at Stanford University has been a valued colleague. I would like to thank the organizers of the Los Angeles Game Symposium at the University of Southern California (2006); the Informatics Seminar of the Department of Informatics, University of California, Irvine (2006); the organizers of the workshop "A Multi-Disciplinary Approach to Computer Games: Understanding the State of the Art in Academic Computer Game Research," California Institute for Telecommunications and Information Technology, University of California, Irvine (2006); the Semiotics Group, Department of Anthropology, University of Chicago (2006); the MASSIVE Conference on the Future of Networked Multiplayer Games, California Institute for Telecommunications and Information Technology, University of California, Irvine (2006); the Culture, Power, and Social Change Research Interest Group, Department of Anthropology, University of California, Los Angeles (2006); the Lively Capital 2: Techno-Corporate Critique and Ethnographic Method conference, University of California, Irvine (2006); and the "New Media Studies Meets STS" panel at the Society for the Social Studies of Science conference, Pasadena, California (2005).

The Intel Corporation was the only body to provide financial support to me during this research; their investment in my work and of the anthropology of technology more generally is greatly appreciated. Genevieve Bell has been a colleague since our days at graduate school together, and a vital interlocutor throughout this project. During the final stages of writing this book, I received helpful comments from several other researchers at Intel, including Maria Bezaitis, Ken Anderson, and Brooke Foucault.

My colleagues at the University of California, Irvine have been important sources of intellectual inspiration throughout this project: Victoria

Bernal, Mike Burton, Teresa Caldeira, Leo Chavez, Susan Coutin, Lara Deeb, Julia Elyachar, Susan Greenhalgh, Inderpal Grewal, Karen Leonard, George Marcus, Michael Montoya, Robert Nideffer, Simon Penny, Kristin Peterson, Kavita Philip, Mark Poster, Justin Richland, Lindsay Richland, Kaushik Sunder Rajan, Gabriele Schwab, Jennifer Terry, Roxanne Varzi, and Mei Zhan. In the Department of Informatics, Paul Dourish, Bonnie Nardi, David Redmiles, Walt Scacchi, Bill Tomlinson, and others provided a wonderful interdisciplinary environment in which I could develop my ideas. Barbara Dosher, Dean of the Social Sciences, was a constant source of support.

Fred Appel, my editor at Princeton University Press, showed an early and unwavering interest in this project. His enthusiasm has been crucial to this book. Heath Renfroe, associate production editor, and Maria Lindenfeldar, book designer, have also been incredibly helpful, as has Naomi Linzer, who has now been my invaluable indexer for three books. I held a contest in Second Life to select a resident image to be incorporated in the book's front cover. I thank Aino Korhonen, winner of that contest, as well as Tricia Aferdita (Tricia Griffith in the actual world), Xander Ruttan (Aaron Collins in the actual world), and Elektra Spark, all of whom helped me with the contest itself. Dena Dana took the wonderful image of my avatar that appears on the back cover.

My mother, Neva Cozine, has been my anchor of love and comfort in the world. The rest of my family—particularly, my sister, Darcy Boellstorff, my father, John Boellstorff, my stepfather, Daryl Hansen, and my "in-laws," Lisa Maurer, Maureen Kelly, William Maurer, and Cynthia Maurer, have always been there for me and I can never repay all I owe them. My neighbors and friends in Long Beach have provided me with an unmatched sense of home: I thank in particular Michelle Arend-Ekhoff, Christie Chu, Gemma Davison, Tom Douglas, David Hernandez, Dominic Lakey, and Michelle Marra. Brian Ulaszewski and Gina Wallar have been sources of comfort beyond measure. I dedicate this book to my mother and to Carter Wallar Ulaszewski, my godson.

The intellectual brilliance, devotion, and kindness of Bill Maurer, my partner and best friend, is the ultimate source of inspiration for this book.

PART I: SETTING THE VIRTUAL STAGE ▶

Chapter 1

THE SUBJECT AND SCOPE OF THIS INQUIRY

Arrivals and departures—Everyday Second Life—Terms of discussion—The emergence of virtual worlds—The posthuman and the human—What this, a book, does.

FIGURE 1.1. Arrival in Second Life (image by author).

ARRIVALS AND DEPARTURES.

Imagine yourself suddenly set down surrounded by all your gear, alone on a tropical beach close to a native village while the launch or dinghy which has brought you sails away out of sight (figure 1.1). You have nothing to do, but to start at once on your ethnographic work. Imagine further that you are a beginner, without previous experience, with nothing to guide you and no one to help you. This exactly describes my first initiation into field work in Second Life.

Many anthropologists will recognize the paragraph above as a famous passage, slightly altered, from Bronislaw Malinowski's *Argonauts of the Western Pacific*, published in 1922, describing the culture of the inhabitants of the Trobriand Islands north of Australia.[1] Despite his shortcomings, it was Malinowski more than any other anthropologist, and *Argonauts* more than any of Malinowski's books, that established the conviction that anthropologists should have extended experience in close proximity among those about whose lives they wished to speak: "it would be easy to quote works of high repute . . . in which wholesale generalizations are laid down before us, and we are not informed at all by what *actual* experiences the writers have reached their conclusion" (Malinowski 1922:3, emphasis added): "Living in the village with no other business but to follow native life, one sees the customs, ceremonies and transactions over and over again, one has examples of their beliefs as they are *actually* lived through, and the full body and blood of *actual* native life fills out soon the skeleton of abstract constructions" (Malinowski 1922:18, emphasis added).[2]

Malinowski speaks of "actual" experience, "actual" belief, "actual" life. In this book I take the methods and theories of anthropology and apply them to a *virtual* world accessible only through a computer screen. Because virtual worlds are so new, I will spend quite a few pages introducing some general issues to keep in mind, before plunging into the details of Second Life. I am an anthropologist whose previous and continuing research focuses on sexuality in Indonesia (Boellstorff 2005, 2007). *Coming of Age in Second Life* is an anthropological study of Second Life (abbreviated "SL" or "sl").[3] This is a virtual world owned and managed by a company, Linden Lab, where by the end of my fieldwork tens of thousands of persons who might live on separate continents spent part of their lives online.[4] To explore how anthropology might contribute to understanding culture in virtual worlds, I have departed from many previous studies of Internet culture by conducting fieldwork entirely *inside* Second Life, using my avatar Tom Bukowski and my home and office in Second Life, Ethnographia.[5] I went through standard human subjects protocols and engaged in normal anthropological methods including participant observation and interviews.

It might seem controversial to claim one can conduct research entirely inside a virtual world, since persons in them spend most of their time in the actual world and because virtual worlds reference and respond to the actual world in many ways. However, as I discuss in chapter 3, studying virtual worlds "in their own terms" is not only feasible but crucial to developing research methods that keep up with the realities of technological change. Most virtual worlds now have tens of thousands of participants, if not more, and the vast majority interact only in the virtual world. The forms of social action and meaning-making that take place do so within the virtual world, and there is a dire need for methods and theories that take this into account.

Another foundational conceit concerns the possibility of descriptive analysis, rather than the prescriptive modes of argumentation that characterize most discussions of virtual worlds, often due to legitimate interests in social implications and design. When studying gay Indonesians, I do not ask "is it a good thing that gay identities have emerged in Indonesia?"; I take their emergence as given. Similarly in this book I do not ask "is it a good thing that virtual worlds have emerged" or "is Second Life headed in the right direction?" While such questions are important to many persons in Second Life and beyond, in this book I take Second Life's emergence as given and work to analyze the cultural practices and beliefs taking form within it.

The idea of "virtually human" appearing in this book's subtitle can be interpreted in two ways, indexing two lines of analysis I develop throughout. First, although some insightful research has claimed that online culture heralds the arrival of the "posthuman," I show that Second Life culture is profoundly human. It is not only that virtual worlds borrow assumptions from real life; virtual worlds show us how, under our very noses, our "real" lives have been "virtual" all along. It is in being virtual that we are human: since it is human "nature" to experience life through the prism of culture, human being has always been virtual being. Culture is our "killer app": we are virtually human.

Yet it is not true that nothing is new under the unblinking light of a virtual sun. My second line of analysis is that virtual worlds do have significant consequences for social life. Drawing upon the meaning of virtual as "almost," a second interpretation of this book's title is that in virtual worlds we are not quite human—our humanity is thrown off balance, considered anew, and reconfigured through transformed possibilities for place-making, subjectivity, and community. Anthropology, "a positive and definite study of the human knowledge of the human" (Wagner 2001:xvii), can help reveal the layers of contingency within the category of the virtually human, rather than exiling such contingency into a category of the posthuman and thereby retrenching the borders of the human itself. I approach these two lines of analysis by writing an "ethnography," a text produced through fieldwork-based research, also known as ethnographic methods. Contemporary understandings of ethnographic method presume historical and comparative perspectives, and at various points I will discuss the history of virtual worlds as well as virtual worlds other than Second Life.

The online fieldsite of *Coming of Age in Second Life* might seem utterly different than Indonesia, but like my earlier work this book touches on broad issues concerning selfhood and society, and like my earlier work this book is a methodological experiment. Building upon a significant body of prior research on virtual worlds, I argue that ethnography holds great promise for illuminating culture online, but not because it is traditional or old-fashioned. Ethnography has a special role to play in studying virtual worlds because it has *anticipated* them. Virtual before the Internet existed, ethnography has always produced a kind of virtual knowledge. Borrowing a phrase from Malinowski, Clifford Geertz argued that the goal of ethnographic understanding is to achieve the "native's point of view" (Geertz 1983). The quotation from Malinowski that started this book asked you to "imagine yourself" in a new place (Malinowski 1922:4), to be virtually there. Representations of persons in virtual worlds are known as "avatars"; Malinowski's injunction to "imagine yourself" in an unfamiliar place underscores how anthropology has always been about avatarizing the self, standing virtually in the shoes (or on the shores) of another culture.

I intentionally draw upon classic anthropology to demonstrate the promise of ethnographic methods for the study of virtual worlds. This book's title is meant to recall *Coming of Age in Samoa*, the work that first established Margaret Mead's reputation (Mead 1928). At the same time, it will be obvious that I draw upon contemporary anthropological critiques of ethnographic method—not least, the vociferous debate over Mead's book. Anthropologists now recognize that the boundaries of "fieldsites" are contested and produced in part by ethnographers themselves (Gupta and Ferguson 1997). They also recognize that ethnographic research need not limit itself to a single fieldsite. Indeed there is a sense in which this study of Second Life is part of my own multisited project, an anthropology of modernity that treats gay Indonesians and Second Life residents as nodes of an emergent cultural formation that is at once transnational, national, and local, at once virtual and actual.

Many different kinds of books could be written about Second Life, each with certain audiences in mind. A challenge I face is that I wish *Coming of Age in Second Life* to be read and debated by several different groups of people. I hope the book will be useful to those with interests in anthropology, including graduate and undergraduate students. I also hope it will be read by scholars, students, and designers in fields like game studies, informatics, and science and technology studies. Another hoped-for readership includes persons who participate in virtual worlds or online games. Persons who spend time in Second Life fall into this category, including the many friends and acquaintances whose kindness, patience, and insight made this book possible. Then there are all the readers I cannot foresee who simply find the topic interesting.

It is impossible to write a book that will please all of these audiences all of the time. Some may find my writing too laden with jargon; others, too informal. Some may find my extensive use of sources distracting; others may think of literatures they would have liked to see referenced. Some may be frustrated with my sympathetic stance toward virtual worlds; others will feel I underplay their importance. Those with little experience in virtual worlds may wish I had focused on why people find virtual worlds compelling, and their potentially negative effects; others with substantial experience in virtual worlds may wish I had written a book that went into more detail about subcultures and controversies specific to Second Life. I can only hope that all parties will meet this text halfway and find in it something useful or provocative.

This book provides an ethnographic portrait of the culture of Second Life during the period of fieldwork upon which the portrait is based (June 3, 2004 to January 30, 2007).[6] Since Second Life first went online in June 2003, this book chronicles the formative years when the virtual world was "coming of age," as the book's title indicates. A problem of spatial scale appears at the outset: "Second Life" seems too big and too small.[7] Too small, because most of those who resided in Second Life during my fieldwork participated in other virtual worlds or online games, as well as blogs, forums, and other websites. The engagement ethnographic research demands makes it impossible for me to conduct ethnographic research in Thailand while conducting such research in Indonesia; similarly I could not study other virtual worlds while engaging in ethnographic research in Second Life. For this reason, comparing Second Life to other virtual worlds in detail lies beyond the scope of this book. Without good ethnographic work in place there is nothing upon which to base comparison. Obviously all virtual worlds differ and Second Life was quite distinct from, say, combat-oriented virtual worlds that existed at the same time, like World of Warcraft (Koster 2006). Yet there are common aspects to virtual worlds, just as there are features shared by all human languages even when they are mutually unintelligible.

Too big, because as was the case for many virtual worlds during the time of my fieldwork, Second Life was already so large that there were many subcultures within it. At various points I discuss subcultures in Second Life and in future writings I hope to analyze such subcultures in greater detail, but the goal of this book is to explore what might be learned from Second Life taken as a single culture. Just as it is possible to study Indonesian national culture or more localized cultures like Javanese culture, so one viable approach to Second Life is to examine its general aspects. It is typically much easier to recognize subcultures than cultures: no one during my research denied that there were subcultures in Second Life, but many questioned if there was a Second Life culture. Claims that a virtual world like Second Life is composed of nothing but subcultures mistake notions of subculture in terms of identity and style (Hebdige 1979) for anthropological notions of culture in terms of shared meanings and relations of power.

EVERYDAY SECOND LIFE.

A man spends his days as a tiny chipmunk, elf, or voluptuous woman. Another lives as a child and two other persons agree to be his virtual parents. Two "real"-life sisters living hundreds of miles apart meet every day to play games together or shop for new shoes for their avatars. The person making the shoes has quit his "real"-life job because he is making over five thousand U.S. dollars a month from the sale of virtual clothing. A group of Christians pray together at a church; nearby another group of persons engages in a virtual orgy, complete with ejaculating genitalia. Not far away a newsstand provides copies of a virtual newspaper with ten reporters on staff; it includes advertisements for a "real"-world car company, a virtual university offering classes, a fishing tournament, and a spaceflight museum with replicas of rockets and satellites.

This list of occurrences does not begin to scratch the surface of the myriad ways those who spent time in Second Life interacted with each other and the virtual world. During the time of my fieldwork, the level of "real"-world news coverage of Second Life increased dramatically, often focusing on aspects of the virtual world seen as sensational (for instance, that over US$1,000,000 of economic activity was occurring daily, or that a "real"-world musician was performing inworld). But events seen as exceptional are of limited value; they take place in the context of broader norms that at first glance may seem uninteresting, but are the true key to understanding culture. For this reason it will prove helpful to introduce Second Life not by means of some infamous incident, but through a portrait of what an uneventful afternoon might have looked like during the time of my fieldwork.[8] I do not intend this portrait to be representative of everyone's experience, just one example of what life in Second Life could be like during my fieldwork. Readers with experience in virtual worlds may find the description obvious, but I would ask such readers to consider what kinds of cultural assumptions are encapsulated within these apparently banal details of everyday Second Life.

IMAGINE YOURSELF suddenly teleported into Second Life, alone in your home. You already have a Second Life account and thus an "avatar," which we will call

FIGURE 1.2. Standing at home (image by author).

Sammy Jones. On a computer—at home, at an office, or on your laptop at a café—you start the Second Life program just as you would an email program, word processor, or web browser. After logging on with your avatar name and password, you see your avatar, who never needs to eat or sleep, standing in your home (figure 1.2). You built this house out of "primitives" (or "prims"), as objects in Second Life are known. You did so after practicing with Second Life's building tools in an area known as a "sandbox," where you can build for free but everything you build is deleted after a few hours (figure 1.3). The piece of land upon which your house sits is 1,024 square virtual meters in size; you paid a virtual real estate agent about thirty dollars for it, conducting the transaction in linden dollars or "lindens." For the right to own land you paid Linden Lab, the company that owns Second Life, $9.95 a month for a "premium account" and an additional $5 a month for the ability to own up to 1,024 square meters of land: this is known as a "land use fee" or "tier fee."

Using your mouse and keyboard you walk around your house, adorned with furniture, paintings, and rugs. You purchased some of these furnishings from stores in Second Life; others you made yourself. Deciding you are tired of the white rug in your living room, you open your "inventory," which appears on your screen as a "window" filled with folders containing items within them (figure 1.4).[9] You drag an icon named "green rug" from

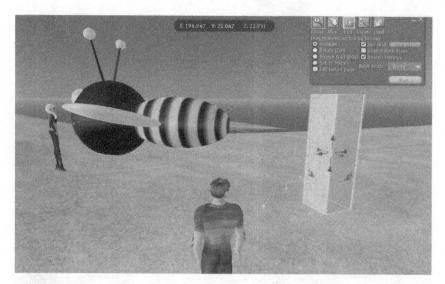

FIGURE 1.3. Building in a sandbox (image by author).

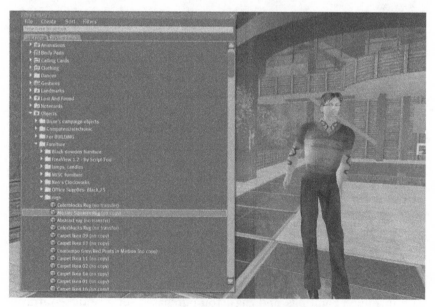

FIGURE 1.4. Perusing the "inventory" window (image by author).

FIGURE 1.5. Flying across the landscape (image by author).

your inventory window and as if by magic, it materializes in your living room. You then right-click on the white rug: a "pie menu" appears with commands arranged in a circle. You choose "take" and the white rug disappears from your home; at the same time an icon named "white rug" appears in your inventory.

Now you walk out your front door and pressing the "F" key on your keyboard, you begin to fly. Gaining altitude and speed, you see a landscape of green hills receding into the distance; as you move forward, buildings, trees, and other objects appear before you (figure 1.5). Persons in Second Life typically say objects are "rezzing" into existence, a verb that dates back to *Tron* (1982), one of the first movies to use computer-generated graphics and to represent a virtual world. The reason it takes a few seconds for objects to "rez" is that the Second Life program on your computer is a "thin client" providing only the basic interface (Kushner 2004:53): almost all of the data about the objects making up Second Life is transmitted to your computer over the Internet. In a sense, of course, the objects and the data about them are the same thing. Almost all of these objects are, like your house, not created by Linden Lab: Second Life is based upon the idea of user-created content (Ondrejka 2004a). Linden Lab maintains the basic platform for Second Life: a landscape with land, water, trees, and sky; a set of building tools; and a means to control, modify, and communicate between avatars. Nearly everything else is the result of persons or groups of people spending millions of hours every month in acts of creation. Much of this creation is for personal or informal use, but since people in Second Life can earn "real" money in the virtual world and retain intellectual property rights over anything they create, individual entrepreneurs and even corporations create objects for sale.

Continuing to fly away from your home you see three people—more precisely, three avatars—rezzing into view. You knew they would be here because you pressed "control-M" to open a window with your "world map" and noticed three green dots on the square of land your avatar was about to enter (figure 1.6). This square of land, 264 meters on a side, is known as a "sim" (short for "simulator"). Four sims are typically stored on one actual-world computer server; as your avatar enters a sim your computer receives information about the sim via the Internet. These servers retain all of the information about the sim's landscape as well as created objects or buildings, so that the virtual world persists when individuals turn their computers off.

The three avatars you now approach are being controlled by people who, like you, are currently logged onto Second Life: they could be next door to your physical location, a hundred miles away, or on another continent; there

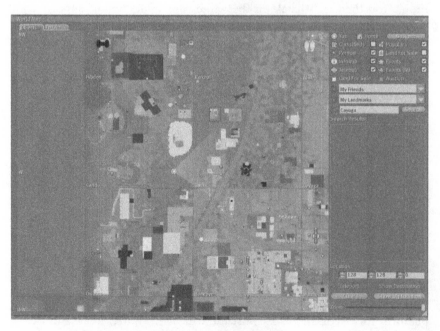

FIGURE 1.6. Looking at the world map, local area (image by author).

could even be two people controlling a single avatar together as they sit in front of a shared computer. During the time of my fieldwork it was only possible to speak audibly using third-party software and this was rarely used. However, once you are within thirty virtual meters of these three avatars they will be able to "hear" what you "say": if you type something into your chat window, the text you type will appear on their computer screens when you press the "return" key. By clicking on an avatar with your mouse you can obtain a "profile," which tells you something about the person—a short paragraph they have written about themselves, a list of their favorite places in Second Life, the groups to which they belong. All of this information refers to a "screen name"; rarely do you discover someone's "real" name. As you look through your computer screen at the back of your avatar's head and these other avatars, the persons controlling them are looking at you through their own computer screens and can click on your profile.

"How are you doing?" you type to these three persons. "Good," replies one of them, named Judy Fireside. "We are just thinking about going to the Cool Club for their 80s Dance Club Hour." You continue talking for a few minutes before deciding that you want to say something specifically to Judy Fireside, so you click on her avatar and choose "send IM" from the pie menu that appears. This opens up a window that allows you to type an "instant message" or "IM" solely to Judy. For several minutes you carry on two conversations at once—you are part of a group of four people chatting with each other, and also one of two people carrying on an instant-message conversation, perhaps commenting on what one of the other two people is saying. It is like being able to talk and whisper at the same time. You realize you want to stay in touch with Judy Fireside, so you right-click on her once again and choose "add friend" from the pie menu. This causes a message to appear on Judy's computer screen saying "Sammy Jones is offering friendship." She chooses "yes." Judy will no longer be an anonymous green dot on the world map or the "mini-map" that can be used to show your local area; you will be able to find her location and receive notification whenever she logs on or off.

Now you decide you want to go shopping for a shirt for your avatar. You say goodbye to Judy and the other two people to whom you were speaking. Opening the world map once again, you see the sim where your avatar is located and a couple others nearby. You zoom out on the map until you see Second Life in its entirety: over two thousand sims (at this point) laid out into a series of continents floating on a blue sea, known as the "mainland," and thousands of additional sims separate from the continents, known as "islands" (figure 1.7). Over ten thousand green dots cover the mainland and islands, each representing the location of a person currently logged on to

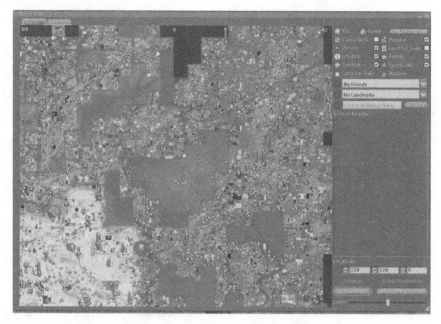

FIGURE 1.7. Looking at the world map, wider view (image by author).

Second Life. Some dots are isolated; perhaps someone is building a house, strolling through a mall, or just sitting in a forest. You see pairs of dots: two friends catching up with each other, perhaps, or a couple having sex, or a real estate agent showing a plot of land to someone. You also see clusters of as many as seventy dots: perhaps a popular dance club, a casino, even a philosophy discussion.

Where was that favorite shirt store again? You type "control-F" on your computer and a window called "Find" appears on your screen, with tabs for locating people, places, and events. Selecting the "Places" tab you type "shirt": several hundred stores selling shirts appear in the window and you recognize one as the store you had in mind. You hit the button marked "teleport" on the Find window and after a few seconds of blackness you are half a continent away with a store rezzing around you. On the wall are squares with images of shirts and prices for each: 70 lindens, 150 lindens, 95 lindens. You see a shirt you like and right-click on the square with its image, choosing "buy" from the pie menu that appears. Seventy lindens (about twenty-five cents during the period of my fieldwork) is deducted from your Second Life account, and the shirt is moved into your inventory. You open your inventory window, find the shirt, and choose the command "wear"; after a few seconds your avatar is wearing the new shirt. Then you notice that a store next to this one, designed to look like a medieval castle, is selling "textures," which can be added to the surface of prims. You have been meaning to add a deck to your house and as you stroll through this second store one of its owners, his avatar sitting on a stone staircase, asks "can I help you?" You say that you are looking for a plank texture and the owner shows you a set of wood textures on sale for 300 lindens. They look great, so you purchase the textures like you purchased your shirt a few minutes ago.

The new textures safely in your inventory, you teleport home, walk outside your house, and choose the "create" command. A box appears in front of you on the ground. You choose "edit" and turn the box into a square ten meters wide, long, and tall—normally the maximum allowable size for a single prim—then flatten it to half a meter thick. The number of prims you have to work with depends on the size of your land: you have about 450 prims available on your plot, with only 300 currently used, so there is no harm in adding a bit more to your deck. You move the square flat prim just created up against the back of your house, and then create two more prims in the shape of poles to hold up the deck. In this virtual world a deck would stay up without poles, but like most people you create structures that accord visually with the laws of physics, more or less. Now you open your inventory and select one of the recently purchased wooden plank textures, dragging it onto your newly created deck and poles.

You are moving your deck a bit to the right so that it lines up with your home's back door when the instant message window pops up on your screen. It is Judy Fireside, asking "whatcha doing?" You tell Judy to come see the new deck and she teleports over with a friend, George Walker. Before long you are all deep in conversation and George is telling you and Judy about how his "real" mother has been ill lately. "But enough about that," George says: "a friend of mine is having a wedding. I just im-ed her and she said that you and Judy can come!" You and Judy both say you would be happy to attend.

Looking in your inventory you find a tuxedo you bought a couple months ago, but have not had an opportunity to wear. You put it on your avatar as Judy and George find formal clothing for their own avatars. Judy chooses a gorgeous red and black gown, made from "flexible prims" that give the appearance of silk flowing in the Second Life breeze: it was made by a well-known designer who earns over three thousand U.S. dollars a month from her creations. Once everyone is ready, the three of you teleport to a steepled church on a virtual mountainside. Pools with fountains and schools of fish bracket the church's front door; inside there are garlands of flowers on the pews and soft piano music in the air. There are already twenty people inside the church, sitting on pews, with a best man, maid of honor, and offici-ant at the altar. You, Judy, and George take seats on a pew and send instant messages to each other so as not to disturb the solemnity of the occasion: "I've never been to this church before—it's stunning!" After a few minutes, the bride and groom prepare to walk down the aisle. They have been lovers for over a year in Second Life but have never met in the "real" world. In fact, they have not shared any information about their real-world lives—the bride might be a man, the groom a woman, either might already be married in the "real" world—but you feel genuinely happy as they exchange vows. Finally each types "I do" to the other. On your screen you see the officiant say "the bride and groom may now kiss," and each opens their inventory window to click on an icon for what is known as an "animation," a program that causes avatars to move. The avatars embrace as the audience in the pews types "yay!" "congratulations!" "I'm so happy for you!"

After the ceremony there is a party in a large club next door to the church. You click on a ball hanging from the ceiling of the club and it animates your avatar so that you dance together with the other guests, all the while chatting about the ceremony and congratulating the bride and groom. After a few songs, you glance up at the top of your computer screen and realize that you have been online for two hours; your "real" body is hungry and it is time to eat dinner. So you take your leave of the bride and groom, tell Judy and George that you will see them again soon, and quit the Second Life program as you would quit any program on your computer. Second Life disappears from your computer screen, but as you go to your kitchen to chop vegetables, you think about all those people still dancing away in a club with a bride and groom, watching a virtual sun set over a virtual sea.

TERMS OF DISCUSSION.

This composite vignette recalls a *Robinson Crusoe*-type of narrative, predicated on the use of "technical mastery" as a way to control one's surroundings (Redfield 2000:8). It describes a mere fraction of the thousands of ways people spent time in Second Life during the period of my fieldwork. Some were loners; others were members of groups with hundreds of members. Some had intense emotional and sexual relationships; others came to Second Life to sail a boat across a virtual lake, dance at a club, or play a board game, without intimacy beyond the casual acquaintance. Virtual worlds provide the opportunity for many forms of social interaction, and this can include anthropological research. Just as I can attend a wedding or build a house in Second Life, so I can interview those in Second Life about their experiences and also engage in "participant observation," following people around in their daily lives as a member of the community. To begin grappling with what is at stake in the emergence of virtual worlds, however, basic terms of discussion are sorely needed. There are important histories to virtual worlds, but many aspects of them are novel. Forging a terminology thus presents challenges, particularly because virtual worlds change so swiftly and conceptual imprecision is far from unknown (Lange 2008). For instance, notions of a "metaverse" combining virtual worlds, simulations, virtual reality technology, and lifelogging often confuse the distinctiveness of each (Cascio, Paffendorf, and Smart 2007). Keeping in mind the impossibility of perfectly representing this complex and unstable situation, I wish to set out the clearest terms possible, knowing they are open to revision.[10]

This book explores the phenomenon of *virtual worlds*, places of human culture realized by computer programs through the Internet. Another good definition for "virtual world" is "any computer-generated physical space . . . that can be experienced by many people at once" (Castronova 2005:22).[11] My definition and Castronova's both presume three fundamental elements to be present in all virtual worlds: they are (1) places, (2) inhabited by persons, and (3) enabled by online technologies.[12] In something as long as a book, synonyms are helpful to avoid repetition. For this reason I treat "virtual," "cyber," and "online" as equivalent, although others have developed vocabularies in which their meanings differ. Terms like "cybersociality" and "online culture" are thus to be taken as roughly interchangeable with "virtual world." To limit my inventory of synonyms I will not use "synthetic world" (Castronova 2005), "persistent world" (Kushner 2003), "artificial world" (Çapin et al. 1999; Schroeder 2002), "digital world" (Helmreich 1998), "mirror world" (Gelernter 1991), "possible world" (Ryan 1991; Schroeder 1996), "virtual community" (Rheingold 2000), "virtual environment" (Blascovich 2002; Schroeder 2006), or "metaverse" (Stephenson 1993). I particularly wish to avoid "synthetic" and "artificial": for some researchers these terms have value, but for my purposes they obscure how the most distinctive feature of the worlds under discussion is not that they are fabricated, but that they are virtual. The "real world" of human social life is also synthesized through human artifice.[13] Virtual worlds are self-evidently social constructions, but they are far from unique in this regard.

The term "world" appears with great frequency in the phrases above, but remains far less theorized than the words with which it is paired. "World" tends to refer to large-scale social contexts with visual and interactive components, somewhat like "environment" and "space." This differs from the more abstract notion of "community" or the more individualistic notion of "life," as in "Second Life" (not "Second World," despite the fact that most residents saw it as a virtual world). "World" is a dangerously naturalistic metaphor. It implies an entity that has come into being without human agency and that is self-contained, without boundaries: you can walk around a "world" and end up back where you started. It is for these reasons that anthropologists of globalization have found it productive to speak not of "worlds" but the "worlding" of cultural domains (e.g., Zhan 2001); it may prove useful to ask after the "virtual worlding" of human sociality online. In this regard, the philosopher Karl Popper's notion of World 3, "objective, real, and public structures" that can take the form of "social organization" or "patterns of communication," may provide one way to theorize virtual worlds (Benedikt 1991:3–4; see Popper 1979).

Many researchers speak of digital cultures or digital media. It seems "digital" came into use as a neutral synonym for terms like "electronic," "tele-," "cyber-," and even "virtual," though it is occasionally opposed to the virtual (Massumi 2002). I have difficulty identifying the analytical work "digital" is supposed to accomplish. Since these uses of "digital" imply electronic technology (not binary counting using stones or human digits, for instance), "digital" is a conceptual Klein bottle, incorporating every aspect of contemporary human life under its purview. What, nowadays, is not digital in some way? Additionally I doubt those who currently study the "digital" would recuse themselves from studying online analog technologies.

The analytic work "digital" performs appears to be one of identifying continuities. Just as one can take a social phenomenon and examine it from the perspective of gender, law, or religion (since gender, law, and religion permeate all aspects of human life, not just marriage, trials, and worship), so one can examine a social phenomenon or context from the perspective of technology (for which "digital" appears to be a placeholder). "Digital," however, is less useful for analyzing cultural logics that do *not* cross what I will term the gap between the virtual and the actual. The virtual and the actual are not reducible to each other, even in their mutual constitution (indeed, precisely because of their mutual constitution). I am aware that for many "virtual" is troubling, even dated: hopelessly linked to notions of "virtual reality" and presuming intersections of nonphysicality and computation that elide questions of materiality and political economy. However, one goal of this book's analysis is to argue for a rehabilitation and refinement of "virtual." There do exist distinct cultures in virtual worlds, even though they draw from actual-world cultures. This is why researching them "in their own terms" is now one viable methodological strategy.

As a result, the pivotal terms for my analysis are "virtual" and "actual." "Virtual" comes from the Latin *virtus*, which refers to manliness and is etymologically linked to notions of virtue, virtuosity, and virility (Fornäs et al. 2002:29; Wilbur 1997:9; see chapter 5). Notions of the virtual draw from longstanding oppositions of mind versus body, object versus essence, and structure versus agency, among others. In colloquial contemporary English, a prominent meaning of "virtual" is "almost," as when someone says "she's virtually my sister" to refer to a close friend (Lévy 2001:56). The Oxford English Dictionary phrases this meaning of "virtual" as referencing something "that is so in essence or effect, although not formally or actually."[14] Virtuality can thus be understood in terms of potentiality (Massumi 2002:30); it can be said to exist whenever there is a perceived gap between experience and "the actual." This is now the most important meaning of "virtual" with regard to virtual worlds; "virtual" connotes approaching the actual *without arriving there.* This gap between virtual and actual is critical: were it to be filled in, there would be no virtual worlds, and in a sense no actual world either. This is ultimately a reconfiguration of the binarism between nature and culture, and its boundary-marker is the distinction between "online" and "offline."

A great risk in setting forth "virtual" and "actual" as central terms is that I will be seen to be creating or reifying a rigid binarism. I set them forth in an ethnographic sense, not an ontological one. The binarism of virtual/actual is an experientially salient aspect of online culture, not just a terminological nicety (Zhai 1998). Like all binarisms, it persists in spite of attempts to deconstruct it by adding a third term or conflating the two into one. I thus ask the reader to play along with my deployment of the virtual/actual binarism, for what it reveals about the role of a distinction between virtual and actual.

Because I was originally trained as a linguist, I have learned to overcome my intellectual hostility to binarisms and appreciate their ubiquity in cognition and culture, though the importance ascribed to them varies. Yes/no, up/down, on/off—all human languages are strongly shaped by binarisms, even at the phonological level (voiced versus unvoiced consonants, for instance). The binarisms are reinterpreted and transformed, but rarely do they disappear. For instance, a range of scholars have worked to problematize the nature/culture binarism while underscoring its enduring presence in human life (e.g., Haraway 1997; Latour 2005; Ortner 1974, 1996). It is incorrect to associate virtual with culture and actual with nature. Humans make culture in virtual and actual contexts; since humans are part of nature, and the virtual is a product of human intentionality, the virtual is as "natural" as anything humans do in the actual world.

Almost as ubiquitous as the term "virtual" is the prefix "cyber," which originates in William Gibson's notion of cyberspace (Gibson 1984). This term draws upon notions of cybernetics that date to mid-twentieth-century work in computer science and engineering, above all the work of Norbert Wiener, who coined the term "cybernetics" in 1947. As indicated by the use of the Greek prefix *cyber-* ("to steer," as in the steersman of a boat), as well as the full title of Wiener's book (*Cybernetics: or Control and Communication in the Animal and the Machine*, 1948), ideas of governance and control were central to the development of cybernetics from its origins, a point often lost when the original meaning of *cyber-* is forgotten and the prefix assumed to mean "Internet-related" or simply "virtual." It now also connotes the human/ machine interface due to the term "cyborg," a combination of "cybernetic" and "organism" originally coined in 1964 and used in reference to blurrings of human and machine (Haraway 1991; Tomas 1995:33–40).[15]

The term "virtual reality" (or VR) has typically implied an environment enabled by interface technologies like data gloves and goggles.[16] It assumes that a sense of immersion "comes from devices that isolate the senses sufficiently to make a person feel transported to another place" (Heim 1998:6; see also Balsamo 1996:117, 124; Biocca, Kim, and Levy 1995; Coyne 1994; Hillis 1999; Poster 1996:189; Ropolyi 2001; Schroeder 1996; Steuer 1992; Vasseleu 1997; Woolley 1992). However, virtual reality technologies are distinct from virtual worlds: "virtual reality is primarily concerned with the mechanisms by which human beings can interact with computer simulations; it is not especially bothered by the nature of the simulations themselves" (Bartle 2004:3; see also Castronova 2005:5, 285–94; Damer 1998:298–99; Shah and Romine 1995:3). There is no reason that virtual worlds cannot employ virtual reality interfaces, but during the time of my fieldwork it was overwhelmingly the desktop computer—keyboard, mouse, and screen—by which persons interfaced with Second Life and other virtual worlds.

During my fieldwork, those in Second Life often referred to "real life," "first life," "the physical world," or "the real world."[17] Such terms are imprecise antonyms for "virtual world" because they imply that technology makes life less real: "In Net discourse, 'virtual' sometimes just denotes 'computer-based' or 'online.' This is . . . [problematic] because if it is combined with some kind of contrast with 'real' that reality becomes computer-free" (Fornäs et al. 2002:30; see also Heim 1993:60). As Annette Markham noted in her ethnographic study of a virtual world, a phrase like "in real life" often "demarcates 'those experiences that occur offline'" (Markham 1998:115). In other words, "real" often acts simply as a synonym for "offline," and does not imply a privileged ontological status: "online worlds are [not] spaces in which we simply work out offline issues and once sorted, happily leave. . . .

What happens in virtual worlds often is just as real, just as meaningful, to participants" (Taylor 2006a:19). Virtual worlds increasingly have "real" ramifications—a business, an educational course, an online partner becoming a "real" spouse. As one person in Second Life put it, "our virtual relationships are just as real as our rl [real life] ones." Such ramifications take advantage of the gap between virtual and actual. They do not blur or close that gap, for their existence depends upon the gap itself.

In short, "the virtual is opposed not to the real but to the actual. The virtual is fully real in so far as it is virtual . . . the virtual must be defined as strictly a part of the real object" (Deleuze 2004:260; see also Friedberg 2006; Lévy 1998; Massumi 2002; Virilio 1994). As a result, I do not oppose "virtual" and "real"; I refer to places of human culture not realized by computer programs through the Internet as parts of the "actual world." "Actual" is also imperfect, but I find it the best provisional term and additionally one used fairly often by those in Second Life. As discussed in the final chapter, I could speak of "actual worlds" in the plural, since human experience offline is shaped by cultural specificity, but for simplicity's sake I will refer to a singular "actual world." The limitation of "actual" is that synthesis, artifice, and fabrication are constitutive of all human sociality, from language to kinship, from agriculture to desire, from governance to ritual. They are not distinguishing features of virtual worlds but a key point of continuity between them and the actual world. The Oxford English Dictionary notes that "actual" comes etymologically from "act"; as indicated by the term "actor," it can refer to something "exhibited in deeds."[18] Virtual and actual are both the place of *homo faber*, the human as maker (Bergson 1911; Tilgher 1930).

From one perspective it could be argued that the information age has, under our noses, become the gaming age, and thus that gaming and its associated notion of play could become master metaphors for a range of human social relations (Boellstorff 2006). I now argue that the information age has become what I will term the Age of Techne. I do not mean to create a rigid timeline; at issue is not a history but a historicity, a way of thinking about change through time. It is even possible to play off this book's title and refer to "coming of Age" to the Age of Techne. Gaming must still be taken seriously; game studies is sometimes called *ludology* in reference to the Latin term *ludus*, but the topic is not *ludicrous*, whose origin in the same Latin term shows how deeply games are denigrated in the Western tradition.[19] Many virtual worlds are seen by those participating in them as games, or as having gaming as their predominant mode of sociality (Taylor 2006a:28); as a result, game studies will remain highly relevant to the analysis of many virtual worlds into the future.

Debates as to whether or not Second Life was a game were common and sometimes heated during my fieldwork. One Second Life resident offered this analysis: "Stadiums and Casinos. Venues for games? Yes. Games? No. Canvas and paint? Artistic medium? Yes. Game? No. A neighborhood bar? Social scene? Yes. Game? No . . . Don't confuse the container with the contents. SL is no more a game than a box of crayons." As this resident noted, virtual worlds are not in and of themselves games, and assuming that theories about games and play are necessary foundations to understanding virtual worlds leads to serious misinterpretations. This includes a conflation of online sociality with entertainment, obviating the consequential forms of intimacy, community, and political economy in virtual worlds. Scholars have long noted how a virtual world "is not goal-oriented; it has no beginning or end, no 'score,' and no notion of 'winning' or 'success'. . . . [Such a world] isn't really a game at all" (Curtis 1992:122).[20] As a result, "virtual worlds are not games. Even the ones written to *be* games aren't games. People can play games *in* them, sure, and they can be set up to that end, but this merely makes them venues. The Pasadena Rose Bowl is a stadium, not a game" (Bartle 2004:475).

Efforts to define what counts as a game have continued for some time (Callois 1961; De Koven 1978; Suits 1978); indeed it is the persistence of the debate itself, rather than any particular stance with regard to it, that is of the greatest import. The false analogy "game is to everyday life as virtual is to actual" has led many to conflate "virtual" with "game." There is no way to claim virtual worlds are games without trapping oneself in a definition of "game" so vague as to include most of our actual lives. For some, spending time in virtual worlds like Second Life means spending less time gaming. On those occasions during my fieldwork when persons termed Second Life a game, what they really meant was that it was a place of play, reflecting the centrality of creativity to understandings of the virtual world. For these reasons I will refer to someone logged into Second Life as a "resident" (a term used within Second Life) rather than "user," "player," or "gamer."[21]

The distinction between "games" and "play" is often unclear, since in many languages these are the same term or are derived from the same term (e.g., Indonesian *main*, German *spiel*, Dutch *spel*). In John Huizinga's *Homo Ludens: A Study of the Play-Element in Culture*, a founding text of game studies first published in Dutch in 1938, Huizinga claimed to identify three primary characteristics of play. First, "all play is a voluntary activity . . . it is free, is in fact freedom" (Huizinga 1950:7–8). Second, play is "a stepping out of 'real' life into a temporary sphere of activity with a disposition all of its own" (Huizinga 1950:8). Third, play is "'played out' within certain limits of time and place" (Huizinga 1950:8). In these second and third characteristics lie the origin of Huizinga's famous metaphor of the "magic circle" of play (Huizinga 1950:57).[22]

This has led to some confusion in the study of virtual worlds. Residents and researchers in virtual worlds are often fascinated by blurring between virtual worlds and the actual world, what T. L. Taylor terms "boundary work" or what one Second Life resident termed "bleed-through"—for instance, residents of a virtual world meeting in "real life" (Taylor 2006a) or "real life" money showing up in a virtual world (Castronova 2005). It is striking that the notion of the "magic circle" is invoked almost exclusively to indicate ways in which that circle is broken, and thus to deconstruct the virtual/actual binarism. While I share this interest in forms of interchange between the virtual and actual, what I find more significant and less debated is why we find the question of traffic between virtual worlds and the "real world" so compelling. Much research on virtual worlds is predicated on a cultural assumption that if a boundary is transgressed it is thereby blurred or weakened. However, a large body of anthropological work—on topics from gender to ethnicity to nationalism—demonstrates that crossing a boundary can *strengthen* the distinctiveness of the two domains it demarcates.

If virtual worlds are not games, then they are not video games either. Although the histories of virtual worlds and video games overlap, scholars and designers have long noted that they are not the same thing (e.g., Reid 1999:113). Many early video games from Pong onward were played in pairs or with a two-player option in which players alternated to see who could get the highest score; Gauntlet, a popular video game in the 1980s, allowed up to four simultaneous players. In chapter 2 I recount how beginning in the early 1990s, the social aspect of video gaming took on a new form with the first "massively multiple online games" (MMOGs), also known as "massively multiple online role-playing games" (MMORPGs) because so many had a fantasy or role-playing aspect to them. At the same time there emerged the first "massively multiple online worlds" (MMOWs), another synonym for virtual worlds. These terms—MMOG, MMORPG, MMOW, even MMORT (for "massively multiple online real-time strategy")—all link up to an earlier set of terms also based on the concept of multiplicity, including MUD (multi-user domain, dimension, or dungeon), MUSH (multi-user shared habitat), MUG (multi-user game), MOO (MUD Object Oriented), and MUCK (multi-user chat kingdom). None of these acronyms are commonly used in Second Life.

As massively multiple online games have become more complex, more aspects of them have become oriented toward socialization. For instance, by the early 2000s it was possible in many fantasy-themed massively multiple online games to do things like rest in a village between battles, socializing with other players. Virtual worlds and video games still cannot be reduced to each other, but many aspects of my analysis of Second Life culture will prove pertinent for those with interests in massively multiple online games.[23] In insisting that virtual worlds are distinct from video games, I argue that while the theories and methods used in game studies continue to provide extremely important insights for video games (e.g., Bogost 2007; Consalvo 2007; Wark 2007), they cannot explain virtual worlds in their entirety. Anthropology does not hold all the answers, but its theories and methods give it an important role to play in charting emergent forms of cybersociality.

THE EMERGENCE OF VIRTUAL WORLDS.

One goal of this book is substantive: to provide an ethnographic portrait of Second Life. Another is methodological: to demonstrate the potential of ethnography for studying virtual worlds. A third goal is theoretical: to contribute toward a better understanding of virtual worlds in all their constantly transforming complexity.

Second Life culture does not exist in a cyberspatial vacuum. It draws from an emerging constellation of assumptions and practices about human life—a kind of "virtual worldview" for virtual worlds. What might the set of assumptions and practices that make up Second Life culture teach us about such a virtual worldview? It is this virtual worldview that makes it possible for so many persons to "learn the ropes" of virtual worlds even as they change so quickly. For instance, while learning the intricacies of Second Life could be time-consuming, many residents told me they found it easy to participate at a basic level even if they had never entered a virtual world before. When I once asked a middle-aged woman how she was rapidly able to become skilled in Second Life despite never having played video games before, she replied "what is there to learn?" To adapt to such rapid technological change, these persons must be building upon some shared knowledge. Much is changing, but since millions of people continue to enter virtual worlds without total confusion, something must be staying the same. It is a lack of familiarity with this virtual worldview that can make virtual worlds baffling, threatening, or uninteresting to persons who did not grow up with computers as sources of pleasure and sociality as much as tools for work.

In his classic book *Imagined Communities*, Benedict Anderson showed how the invention of the newspaper made it possible, for the first time, for persons to imagine themselves as members of modern nation-states bound by "deep, horizontal comradeship" (Anderson 1983:7). Without wishing to engage in hyperbole, we may be on the verge of another massive transformation linked to technology, the creation of societies on the Internet: "for the first time, humanity has not one but many worlds in which to live" (Castronova 2005:70). This could involve new forms of culture and selfhood, ones shaped in unpredictable ways by actual-world sociality: "We do not really understand how to live in cyberspace yet" (Sterling 1992:xiii). I am not interested in questions like "is humanity going virtual" or "will we all live our lives online?"; such phrasing invites hype and casts the debate in polarizing terms. At issue is the simple fact that not so long ago, the percentage of human social life spent in virtual worlds was zero, that percentage is increasing, and social inquiry must follow this movement online. Drawing upon the work of a range of scholars of technology and society, I will develop a theory of this virtual worldview as *techne*,[24] and of the person who engages in techne not just as *homo faber* ("man the maker") or *homo ludens* ("man the player"), but above all as *homo cyber*. The human online, the virtual human. In using the term "techne," I will draw upon a philosophical distinction between knowledge (episteme) and technology or art (techne), examining how virtual selfhood is becoming predicated on the idea that people can craft their lifeworlds through intentional creativity.

During the writing of this book, I returned to Indonesia to study HIV/AIDS prevention, research that was intentionally distinct from my work in Second Life. Yet I continued to think about Second Life while doing this research; many sentences in this book, including this one, were written on a laptop in the city of Makassar on the island of Sulawesi. I found that maintaining a program of research in an actual-world context while conducting virtual anthropology was helpful in indicating what aspects of cultures in virtual worlds are truly unprecedented, and which are not. Through my ethnography of Second Life I work to pinpoint what is distinctive about virtual worlds. Not everything connected to virtual worlds is novel; it is imperative that we ascertain precisely what elements are new and in what ways they are new.[25] For instance, unlike books, newspapers, radio, and television, the existence of separate classes of people to produce and consume content does not always predominate in virtual worlds: it is much easier for "user" and "creator" to be the same person. Yet old forms of social inequality persist and new ones may appear.

While never under the illusion that I can (or should) aim for a value-free account, I have worked to avoid presenting Second Life in idyllic or pessimistic terms. Like many residents I enjoy Second Life and find this enthusiasm to be a great aid to fieldwork, just as my interests in Indonesian

culture have facilitated my research there. Some may see me as a promoter
or "fanboy" of Second Life, just as I could be seen as a promoter of gay
and lesbian Indonesians. Yet passing judgment on Second Life is not my
purpose.[26] There is a well-established history of interpreting virtual worlds
in either utopic or dystopic terms (Wertheim 1999:285), and much of what
others wrote about Second Life during my fieldwork was concerned to
evaluate its significance and suggest improvements. Particularly toward the
end of my fieldwork there was an increasing amount of press touting Second Life as revolutionary, and other press dismissing its importance and
expressing frustration over technical problems.[27] I find much of this writing helpful, but for purposes of this book seek to craft neither an apologia
for, nor an indictment of, Second Life. I am uninterested in being either
a booster or a doomsayer. My analysis, written in the language of "is" not
"ought," concerned with description not prescription, seeks to understand
emergent aspects of Second Life culture.

When presenting my research to audiences with limited experience in
virtual worlds, I have found two negative assumptions to be particularly
common. The first is that virtual worlds are hopelessly contaminated by
capitalism. Such a response is often triggered by the reality that many virtual
worlds are owned by for-profit companies, and also by the fact that some allow residents to earn actual-world money. This impression is exacerbated by
the fact that many writings on virtual worlds focus on economic issues (e.g.,
Castronova 2005; Dibbell 2006). Questions of labor, consumption, and class
are important in any discussion of virtual worlds. However, allowing such
questions to consolidate a negative impression overestimates their influence
and elides the degree to which such questions are no less important with
regard to actual-world cultures. Indonesia, for instance, is highly capitalist,
but no one has ever told me to stop studying it for that reason.

A second common negative interpretation I have encountered from
those with limited experience in virtual worlds is that they are just a form of
escapism from the actual world: "the gratifications involved in being a member of [a virtual] community aren't the same, I would suggest, as being involved in a real community. . . . We may have created the instruments of our
own enslavement—psychological and otherwise" (Berger 2002:110–11).[28]
Such naïve realists "see computer systems as alien intruders on the terrain
of unmediated experience. . . . Reality, they assert, is the physical world we
perceive with our bodily senses [and] . . . the computer is . . . a subordinate
device that can distract us from the primary world" (Heim 1998:37).

Those familiar with virtual worlds sometimes bring their own negative
assumptions, three of which I have encountered with particular frequency.

The first is that virtual worlds do not exist as such, because the things termed "virtual worlds" are too varied to be grouped together. A second assumption, mentioned earlier, is that virtual worlds are composed solely of subcultures and it is not possible to generalize at the level of a virtual world. This participates in the historical equation of culture with locality in anthropological thought, reflecting the relatively recent appreciation for how culture exists at multiple spatial scales (Brenner 2001). A third assumption, also discussed previously, is that the division between virtual and actual is unsustainable because so much of what takes place in virtual worlds draws from the actual world. This assumption obscures how referential and substantive relationships do not erase the boundary between virtual and actual; they constitute forms of social action sustaining that boundary.

These negative assumptions fail to appreciate how human experience is always culturally mediated. Several Second Life residents cited the poet W. H. Auden (1907–73) and his anthropological notion of a secondary world or second nature mediating the human: "man is a history and culture making creature, who by his own efforts has been able to change himself after his biological evolution was complete. Each of us, therefore, has acquired what we call a 'second nature,' created by the particular society and culture into which we happen to have been born" (Auden 1968:119).[29] It is true that some persons spend time in virtual worlds to be something different: women becoming men or men becoming women, adults becoming children, disabled persons walking, humans becoming animals, and so on. However, many who participate in virtual worlds do not seek to escape from their actual lives. Such negative views of virtual worlds fail to consider forms of escapism in the actual world, from rituals to amusement parks to daydreaming: the degree to which an activity is "escapist" is independent of whether it is virtual or actual. Avoiding narratives of dystopia or utopia in discussing virtual worlds is a challenge, one rooted in a history of technology which, as many have noted, has been characterized by wild optimism and wild pessimism (Balsamo 1996:132; Beniger 1986:59; Bleecker 1994:192; Graham 2002:6; Haraway 1991).

THE POSTHUMAN AND THE HUMAN.

On January 16, 2006, I—more precisely, my Second Life avatar, Tom Bukowski—was sitting at home, enjoying the view across the water channel that lies below the steep slope on which I built my house, when Dara, a recent acquaintance, stopped by to say hello. I invited her to have a seat on my front porch and we started talking (chatting via text, of course). Soon

Dara said "by the way, I read your profile and I think what you're doing is really interesting. I like intellectual activities too, not just shopping all day long." I responded by telling her about some discussion groups:

> ME: There is the Thinkers group, and also my group Digital
> Cultures—join those groups.
> DARA: From what I saw in your group meeting, I found it very
> interesting
> ME: Oh, you're already a member of Digital Cultures
> DARA: You already made me a member, don't you remember?
> DARA: Or are there a few other people running your av [avatar] too
> ME: Yes, I made you a member of Digital Cultures, I just forgot lol
> [laugh out loud]
> ME: It's just me lol, me forgetting things
> DARA: Good, hate to get to know one and a new attitude appears

This innocuous exchange reveals a social error—I had forgotten that Dara had attended a meeting of Digital Cultures, a discussion group in Second Life that I moderated during my fieldwork, and that I already had made her a member of the group. Learning from moments of failure has a long history in anthropology.[30] Yet there is something distinct to this innocuous exchange: confronted with my lapse in memory, one possible conclusion Dara draws is that "I" have not been forgetful at all. Instead, different actual-world people might be inhabiting the avatar Tom Bukowski at different times, so that what is at issue is a disjuncture between avatar and actual-world person. Dara knows that the avatar Tom Bukowski is always being controlled by a computer in some actual-world location, and that someone other than Tom Boellstorff might be sitting in front of that computer. Dara indicates that she has experienced such a situation before; she "hates to get to know" someone and then a "new attitude appears" because the person controlling a particular avatar has changed.

Throughout this book I investigate changing notions of personhood linked to the emergence of virtual worlds, with a particular interest in debates over the "posthuman." This term usually refers to ways in which "technology can enable us to overcome the limits of human form" (Nayar 2004:71; see also ibid., 11; Foster 2005:xi). My discomfort with the notion of the posthuman is partially a disciplinary effect: anthropology defines its object of study as *anthropos*, the human (Rabinow 2003). It might be possible to define "posthuman" in such a way as to make it theoretically productive, but in my view the term is misleading and based upon "implicit desires, anxieties and interests that are fuelling humanity's continuing relationship with its tools and technologies" (Graham 2002:1). I wish to "contest what the posthuman means . . . before the trains of thought it embodies have been laid down so firmly that it would take dynamite to change them" (Hayles 1999:291; see also Hayles 2005). The notion of the posthuman conflates the human with the subject of liberal humanism, and thus with disciplinary debates in the humanities. It is an overly narrow and ethnocentric definition that effaces the variability of human lifeways.

While some see virtual worlds as marking the emergence of the posthuman, through terms like *homo cyber* I argue that the forms of selfhood and sociality characterizing virtual worlds are profoundly human. But while the emergence of virtual worlds "does not necessarily mean the end of the human . . . we need to see the human as re-configured and organized differently" (Nayar 2004:21). This is one meaning of the phrase "virtually human"—in virtual worlds, we are not quite human. The relationship between the virtual and the human is not a "post" relationship where one term displaces another; it is a relationship of coconstitution. Far from it being the case that virtual worlds herald the emergence of the posthuman, in this book I argue that *it is in being virtual that we are human*. Virtual worlds reconfigure selfhood and sociality, but this is only possible because they rework the virtuality that characterizes human being in the actual world.

WHAT THIS, A BOOK, DOES.

A perfectly appropriate question to ask is: Why write a book at all? Given that my topic is a virtual world, why not a website, blog, or some other electronic form? A book will certainly be accessible to those who do not like reading long texts on a computer screen. However, my main reasons for writing a book are conceptual in nature. Just as I am interested in what happens when we use "traditional" anthropological methods to study virtual worlds, so I am interested in using the "traditional" product of those methods—the book-length ethnography. Just as the actual is reconfigured, not displaced, by the virtual, so "books are not going the way of the dinosaur but the way of the human, changing as we change" (Hayles 2002:33). Given that some readers will have had no experience with Second Life or any other virtual world, the book form offers me the opportunity to describe some everyday experiences of Second Life. Even with something as long as a book, I am forced to make difficult decisions as to what to include. I could write a whole book about any number of topics in Second Life, from gender, race, and love to economics and governance. However, the book form does permit me to focus on Second Life culture as a whole: as Malinowski noted, "an Ethnographer who sets out to study only religion, or only technology, or only social organization cuts out an artificial field for inquiry, and he will be seriously handicapped in his work" (Malinowski 1922:11).

There is a parallel between my methods and their product, reflecting the particular if often unacknowledged effects of the book form: "Any printed book is, as a matter of fact, both the product of one complex set of social and technological processes and also the starting point for another" (Johns 1998:3). In participant observation, the researcher cannot be everywhere at once—unlike a survey, it is not possible to gather data from thousands of people in multiple locations. Similarly ethnographies cannot be everywhere at once; their claims are specific to the contexts in which they are written. I find these "limitations" to force a helpful structure upon my analysis. Without the benefit of hyperlinks, and without the ability to update the text once published, the book form forces me to present my argument in a linear order and make it specific to the period of time during which the research was conducted.

As a result I write about Second Life in the past tense; this book explores a period when Second Life was "coming of age." I see it as a strength that this text will be dated by the time it appears in print, over a year after the research upon which it is based came to an end: this compels me to look beyond the controversies and celebrities of the day that take up so much attention in writing on virtual worlds. With its limited ability to reproduce graphics, the book form allows me to craft a conceptual narrative; it compels me to step back from the visuality that is central to the experience of many virtual worlds. Since I cannot say everything at once in a book, I am forced to put off some of the most important topics until later chapters, so that I can first address preliminary issues. Given that virtual anthropology remains a new enterprise, I am forced to engage in a good deal of conceptual ground-clearing so as to set the stage for my discussions about Second Life. I introduce terms and concepts in earlier chapters that I use in later chapters, assuming the reader is aware of them. These chapters are not designed to be read in any order: they constitute a cumulative argument.

In their titles and headings, this book's chapters evoke classic ethnographies such as Mead's *Coming of Age in Samoa*, Evans-Pritchard's *The Nuer* (1940) or Malinowski's *Argonauts of the Pacific* (from which this introductory chapter's title is taken). Chapter 2, "History," tells five different histories relevant to this study. It also opens a theoretical discussion concerning the concept of techne. Chapter 3, "Method," explores how I conducted my research, as well as broader questions concerning ethnography in virtual worlds. It continues the argument, introduced in this chapter, that ethnography may be particularly well-suited for the study of virtual worlds because from its beginnings it has worked to place the reader "virtually" in the culture of another.

Chapters 1 through 3 constitute Part 1 of this book, "Setting the Virtual Stage"; they provide a theoretical and methodological agenda for the anthropological study of virtual worlds. With this foundation in mind, chapter 4, "Place and Time," opens Part 2, "Culture in a Virtual World," by moving into a more detailed analysis of Second Life itself. My research has convinced me that the pivotal issue with regard to virtual worlds is their character as social *worlds*. It is for this reason that I begin by exploring place and time. Chapter 5 looks specifically at personhood, including gender, race, and embodiment. Chapter 6 explores the friendships and relationships that for many residents are the most significant aspect of Second Life. Chapter 7 examines community in Second Life, as well as "griefing" or antisocial behavior.

Part 3, "The Age of Techne," opens with chapter 8, which examines questions of economics, politics, governance, and inequality. Economic issues are often at the forefront of popular and academic discussions of virtual worlds (e.g., Castronova 2005), not least because they raise fundamental questions about referential relationships between the actual and the virtual. These topics were particularly common in press coverage about Second Life during my fieldwork because it was possible to earn "real" money inworld. By holding off on a discussion of economics until this chapter, I do not mean to ignore its importance—rather, the opposite. By waiting until this point, I can draw upon earlier chapters to investigate how what I term "creationist capitalism" shapes Second Life's culture. In chapter 9, I ask what *Coming of Age in Second Life* tells us about virtual worlds, and consider what place "the virtual" might hold in human existence into the future.

Chapter 2

HISTORY

Prehistories of the virtual—Histories of virtual technology—A personal virtual history—Histories of virtual worlds—Histories of cybersociality research—Techne.

PREHISTORIES OF THE VIRTUAL.

Too often, virtual worlds are described in terms of breathless futurism and capitalist hype. Above all they seem *new*, and this apparent newness is central to their being interpreted as harbingers of a coming utopia of unforeseen possibilities, intimations of a looming dystopia of alienation, or trinkets of a passing fad. Yet the fact that millions of persons now regularly enter virtual worlds, adapting to them with varying degrees of ease, indicates that something is staying the same; something is acting as a cultural ground upon which these brave new virtual worlds are figured. Because virtual worlds appear so novel and in such a constant state of change and expansion, understanding their history can be difficult. However, virtual worlds did not "spring, like Athena from the forehead of Zeus, full-blown from the mind of William Gibson.... [They have encoded within them] a complex history of technological innovations, conceptual developments, and metaphorical linkages" (Hayles 1996b:11).

Throughout human history, technologies—from the wheel to the book and beyond—have shaped forms of selfhood and community. Indeed the distinction between society and technology is misleading. Technology, like language, gender, religion, or any other domain, always comes to be through particular cultural and historical circumstances—as neatly summarized by the well-known quotation from the computer scientist Alan Kay that "technology is anything that wasn't around when you were born."[1] This chapter recounts the history of Second Life and virtual worlds more generally, but there are many ways to tell that history. Rather than attempt to provide a definitive chronology, I present several different histories: each sheds light on the others, resulting in a multifaceted (but still partial) background to the emergence of virtual worlds.

A first way to tell the history of virtual worlds is to claim that humans have always been virtual: "virtuality . . . has followed human culture from its very beginning. Symbols open up imaginary worlds that tend to be virtual worlds by including traits that imitate real social worlds" (Fornäs et al. 2002:30). Indeed, some have seen as the first virtual reality spaces the "subterranean cyberspaces" created by prehistoric cave paintings (Rheingold 1991:379–80; see also Heim 1995:69). In such an interpretation "Virtual reality is older than sin. It is the hallucination of heaven, the peyote vision, the dionysiac stupor. It is the play, the novel, the opera, any system devised for losing ourselves in another world" (Schwartz 1996:362). Dreams, rituals, imagination, even language itself (as claimed by Nietzsche; see Poster 1998:188–89) could all be considered virtual. The idea of a "memory palace" as a mnemonic device is interesting in this regard. One imagines, say, a house, and then "places" in particular "rooms" of the house items to recall. Later, imagining oneself walking through the house can help in "re-collecting" what one wished to remember (Neva 2005, Spence 1984; Woolley 1992:138–40; Virilio 1994:3). Such "memory palaces," associated with cultures without writing, could be seen as the first virtual worlds. The development of writing can also be seen as the technology making virtual worlds possible (McLuhan 1962). Writing allows ideas, stories, and beliefs to persist over time and move to places distant from their point of utterance, and computer programs are forms of writing. Like virtual worlds today, in earlier times writing, as a form of techne or human craft, was seen as threatening: "essentially the same objections commonly urged today against computers were urged by Plato . . . against writing. Writing, Plato has Socrates say . . . is inhuman, pretending to establish outside the mind what in reality can be only in the mind. It is a thing, a manufactured product" (Ong 1982:79).

Another early elaboration of the idea of a virtual world in the Western tradition also comes from Plato. Book 7 of *The Republic* opens with the "allegory of the cave," which several researchers identify one of the oldest and most significant notions of a virtual world in the Western tradition (Hayles 1996b:34; Heim 1991:64, 1995:69; Hillis 1999:39; Ropolyi 2001:172; see also Wark 2007):

> Behold! Human beings living in an underground den, which has a mouth open toward the light and reaching all along the den; here they have been from their childhood, and have their legs and necks chained so that they cannot move, and can only see before them. . . . Above

and behind them a fire is blazing at a distance, and between the fire and the prisoners there is a raised way; and you will see, if you look, a low wall built along the way, like the screen which marionette-players have in front of them, over which they show the puppets. . . . They see only their own shadows, or the shadows of one another, which the fire throws on the opposite wall of the cave. (Plato 1991:253–54)

This allegory implies that the actual world is but a shadow of the world of ideas; for instance, any triangle in the world is an imperfect instantiation of the idea of "triangle." What often escapes commentary (but see Graham 2002:189) is that in Plato's story it is *the physical world* that is "virtual." Between Plato's time and our own, a reversal has taken place with regard to dominant Western understandings of what is real; we now presume that nonphysical worlds are ontologically subsequent to physical ones. One intriguing possibility is that with the emergence of new technosocial forms like virtual worlds, Neo-Platonist notions of the virtual might reappear, as in Bruce Sterling's notion of "spimes," "manufactured objects whose informational support is so overwhelmingly extensive and rich that they are regarded as material instantiations of an immaterial system" (Sterling 2005:11).

While a detailed charting of these transformations in understandings of virtual and actual is beyond the scope of this book, a key development is the shift from a metaphysical notion of the world organized as a "Great Chain of Being"—with God at the top in an unbroken chain of causality from angels and humanity down to animals, plants, and inanimate objects (Lovejoy 1936)—to an empiricist mindset that valorizes data available to the senses and presupposes a fundamental break between the physical and spiritual. This shift can be linked to a range of thinkers, from the mind/body dualism associated with René Descartes (1596–1650) to Enlightenment-era doctrines of scientific knowledge (like the notion of positivism, developed by Auguste Comte [1798–1857]). Even before this shift, the notion of "the virtual" presumed a gap between virtual and actual—for instance, as articulated through the work of the medieval logician John Duns Scotus, who used the term "to bridge the gap between formally unified reality (as defined by our conceptual expectations) and our messily diverse experiences" (Heim 1993:132). In this tradition, "virtual" referred to "the physical qualities (or virtues) that things have, and to the effects of these qualities, like the virtual heat of wine or of sunshine. It then came to describe the state of being effective or potent. Not until the seventeenth century was the term first used for the essence or effect of qualities by themselves" (Strathern 2002:305).

This prehistory of the virtual, like all the histories I relate in this chapter, reflects how the Western tradition has dominated the contexts from which Second Life and other virtual worlds have arisen, not to mention computing more generally (Helmreich 1998, 2004). This tradition would "distinguish Culture itself, as intrinsically artificial, from Nature, the source of all that was natural. Cultures, in this European view, were artificial creations natural to the human condition" (Strathern 1992:48). Despite this domination, non-Westerners have reflected on similar ideas for centuries. For instance, "the Chinese text of oracular wisdom, the I Ching" can be seen as evoking a kind of virtual world (Aarseth 1997:9). The eighteenth-century novel *The Story of the Stone, or the Dream of the Red Chamber* (Xueqin 1973), considered to be one of the greatest works of Chinese literature, is fundamentally concerned with the nature of reality. For instance, the inscription to the gateway of the "land of illusion" in chapter 1 of the novel reads "Truth becomes fiction when the fiction's true; real becomes not-real where the unreal's real" (Xueqin 1973:55). The narrative pivots around the relationship between ideal and actual, and a place termed the Garden of Total Vision (Levy 1999:108).[2] With a narrative predicated upon the incarnation (or avatarization) of a stone as a human boy, It draws upon both Buddhist and Daoist notions of being and nonbeing (Yu 1997; Zhai 1998:84). This in turn links up to Hindu notions of reality and unreality, reflected in terms used for the Internet in many parts of Asia (like *dunia maya* in Indonesian), and rediscovered in the contemporary notion of the "avatar."

During my fieldwork, notions of virtual worlds that I encountered in Second Life and elsewhere appeared to draw primarily from Western traditions. However, cybercultures could already be found worldwide, creatively reworking ostensibly Western notions of the virtual (e.g., Chee 2006; Gottlieb and McLelland 2003; Ito, Okabe, and Matsuda 2005). This recalls dynamics of cultural transformation under conditions of inequality I encountered during my research in Indonesia. Gay Indonesians acknowledge that their concept "gay" originates in the West, but feel it has become reterritorialized, so that *gay* is now an Indonesian-language term, not just an English one, taking on new meanings in its new context (Boellstorff 2005, 2007).

HISTORIES OF VIRTUAL TECHNOLOGY.

The prehistories recounted above define "virtual" broadly. A second history of virtual worlds would begin with the replacement of the camera obscura (a device where light passing through a small aperture creates an image on a darkened wall) by devices like the stereoscope, which were "based on a radical abstraction and reconstruction of optical experience" (Crary 1990:9). It would also include the invention of the printing press in the sixteenth century and the subsequent emergence of print media and extended narrative forms like the novel, of which *Robinson Crusoe* is an important early example, cited by von Neumann and Morgenstern in their theory of games (von Neumann and Morgenstern 1944:9–15). The growth of the postal system in the nineteenth century (postage stamps were first used in the 1840s) and the associated rise of "pen pals" could also be seen as a form of virtual world still relevant today (Ahearn 2001; Constable 2003). These print technologies shaped new forms of human sociality: "all media have always offered entrances to imagined spaces or 'virtual realities,' opening up symbolic worlds for transgressive experiences" (Fornäs et al. 2002:30). As noted in chapter 1, there is strong evidence that the "imagined community" of the modern nation-state would not have been possible before the rise of "print capitalism" (Anderson 1983).

Above all, this second history of virtual worlds would focus upon the rise of electronic mass media in the late nineteenth century, particularly communication technologies like movies as well as the telephone, telegraph, and television (Marvin 1988; Mrázek 1997; Stein 1999). The "tele-" prefix in these latter terms refers to distance, but unlike the telescope these nineteenth- and twentieth-century technologies link two places by creating a third, virtual place, one seen by participants to have social consequences. A phone conversation, for instance, is a unique event taking place "within" telephone technology. With the rise of electronic mass media, the time delay involved in postal correspondence or print media could disappear; in comparison to static technologies like photographs, movies and audio recordings "were able to store . . . time" (Kittler 1999:3). The telephone probably represents the first virtual world in the contemporary sense of the term: "cyberspace is the 'place' where a telephone conversation appears to occur. Not inside your actual phone, the plastic device on your desk. Not inside the other person's phone, in some other city. *The place between* the phones" (Sterling 1992:xi; see Ronell 1989).[3] Movies and television inaugurated a new emphasis on visuality: "since the early nineteenth century, fabricated visual spaces (such as those deriving from optical techniques) have slowly managed to substitute for and displace corporeal space-worlds" (Holmes 1997:10). Television can be seen as having provided a "collective parallel world" for millions of persons around the world since the 1950s, a kind of rudimentary cyberspace (Wertheim 1999:243). Scattered attempts to develop more immersive "virtual reality" occurred as well: "In the mid-1950s, the movie industry went through a period of experimentation that introduced Cinerama and Cinema-scope. In 1956, Morton Heilig invented an arcade-style attraction called Sensorama . . . You sit on a seat, grasp motorcycle handlebars, and hold your head up to two Stereo-mounted lenses. . . . Wind blows in your face at a velocity corresponding to your movement in the scene" (Krueger 1991:66; see also Rheingold 1991:50).

Many writers on virtual worlds have emphasized how "through such seminal ideas as information, feedback loops, human-machine interfaces, and circular causality, cybernetics provided the terminology and conceptual framework" from which notions of virtual worlds were, in part, developed (Hayles 1996b:34; see also Hayles 1999; Mindell 2002; Morse 1998; Tomas 1995:23–33). In the previous chapter I mentioned that the term "cybernetics" was invented in 1947 by the MIT mathematician Norbert Wiener and has served as a theoretical resource for conceptualizing virtuality ever since. Work on cybernetics reflected a kind of minor tradition throughout the second half of the twentieth century in which technology was viewed as something that could allow humans to manipulate their environments for the greater good (Lévy 1997; Mehrabian 1976). Many anthropologists became interested in cybernetics during the middle of the twentieth century, particularly Margaret Mead and Gregory Bateson. Bateson's interest in cybernetics linked up to an interest in "play" as an "instance of signals standing for other events," so that "the evolution of play may have been an important step in the evolution of communication" (Bateson 1972:154; Mead 1968).

Throughout the last century, science fiction and fantasy literature have been fundamental to imaginings of virtual worlds. Authors like Isaac Asimov, Ray Bradbury, Arthur C. Clarke, and Robert A. Heinlein have had a significant impact, as have utopian narratives like those of the original *Star Trek* television series. Most crucial, however, have been fantasy works like C. S. Lewis's *Narnia* series of novels (first published in 1950) as well as J.R.R. Tolkien's *Lord of the Rings* (first published in 1954). This trilogy has been "the single most important influence on virtual worlds from fiction. . . . [C]reating a fully realized, make-believe world was shown to be actually possible" (Bartle 2004:61). Prefiguring the phrase "Second Life," W. H. Auden referred to literature as "Secondary Worlds" and spoke of a desire "present in every human being" to "make new secondary worlds of our own or, if we cannot make them ourselves, to share in the secondary worlds of those who can" (Auden 1968:49). While the notion of a "second nature" created through a "set of socially imposed laws" extends at least back to Hegel (N. Smith 1996:49; see also Helmreich 2004:276), Auden credited the notion of "secondary world" to Tolkien's essay "On Fairy Stories" (Auden 1968:49). In that essay, Tolkien described how the author of a fairy tale "makes a Secondary World which your mind can enter. Inside it, what he relates is 'true': it accords with the laws of that world. You therefore believe it, while you are, as it were, inside" (Tolkien 1966:37). *The Lord of the Rings* was a major inspiration for the Dungeons and Dragons role-playing game, first released in 1974, which was crucial to the development of video games and virtual worlds: "It's almost impossible to overstate the role of Dungeons & Dragons. . . . Scratch almost any game developer who worked from the late 1970s until today and you're likely to find a vein of role-playing experience" (King and Borland 2003:4; see also Mona 2007; Reid 1999:108). The GURPS or "Generic Universal Role Playing System," created in 1986, allowed for creating role-playing games around a range of scenarios, permitting the rise of many different kinds of role-playing games that are ancestors of virtual worlds (Rheingold 2000:xv; Sterling 1992:108).

Beginning in the 1980s a growing body of "cyberpunk" literature and film addressed the question of virtual worlds, drawing upon a tradition of pessimistic and antimodern narratives of technology dating back at least to *Frankenstein* (Shelley 2007 [1818]; see also Benjamin 1955; Ellul 1964; Giedion 1948; Habermas 1970b; Marcuse 1964; Veblen 1921). The best-known example of cyberpunk literature is William Gibson's *Neuromancer*, in which the term "cyberspace" was first coined (Gibson 1984:12), but an important predecessor was the 1981 novella "True Names," in which Vernor Vinge foresaw many aspects of virtual worlds discussed in this book, including griefing, lag, and the question of actual-world disabilities (Vinge 2001 [1981]). Neal Stephenson's novel *Snow Crash* provided the term "metaverse," a popular synonym for "virtual world." Like the work of Gibson, Vinge, Pat Cadigan, Philip K. Dick, Bruce Sterling, and others, Stephenson told a powerfully prescient story of virtual worlds, addressing issues like the workings of "avatars" and questions of inequality (Stephenson 1993).[4]

Particularly since the 1990s, a number of movies informed by cyberpunk have also explored questions of virtual worlds. For instance, *The Matrix* (1999) and its sequels presented a virtual world whose purpose was to keep humanity in a kind of stasis, completely disengaged from the actual world, while *The Truman Show* (1998) depicted someone trapped inside a physical "virtual" world: a small town encased within a giant dome.[5] While characterized by a negative tone, this body of work has worked to "complicate the utopian/dystopian dialectic structuring much science fiction and most commentaries on new technologies, by defining technology as neither an external threat nor a set of tools under our control," but as intimate to human being (Foster 2005:xii). An interest in the human has been a constant theme of this literature: "cyberspace exists, insofar as it can be said to exist, by virtue of human agency" (Gibson 1988:129).

A PERSONAL VIRTUAL HISTORY.

I have just told two possible histories of virtual worlds—one reaching back to antiquity, the other to the mid-nineteenth century. Each represents a valid approach for asking how virtual worlds have come into being and what they can tell us about the human condition. Before turning to the specific history of virtual worlds themselves, it is appropriate to bring my own personal history into the narrative. An important aspect of ethnographic method involves situating the researcher—not as a form of confessional or to claim a privileged intimacy with those one studies, but as one technique for weaving accountability into the analysis.

Born in 1969—the same year that ARPANET (Advance Research Projects Agency Network), the precursor to the Internet, first went online—I am a member of the first generation of persons in the United States for whom video games were a part of everyday life. I remember when a babysitter first brought over Pong in the mid-1970s and plugged it into our television set; my Intellivision home video game, first released in 1980 (Herman 2001:45), was a cherished possession of my early teenage years. During those years most of my allowance was spent in the form of quarters into video games at the local arcade in Lincoln, Nebraska, where I grew up. The names of those games are etched into the collective memory of many of my generation: Pac-Man, Space Invaders, Q-Bert, Joust, Defender, Gauntlet, Galaga, Dig-Dug. This familiarity with video games was part and parcel of a general familiarity with computers that can be as difficult for older generations to understand as it can be difficult for younger generations to appreciate.

I remember when, in the early 1980s, I spent a day at my father's office. At that time he worked in the research wing of an oil company, and his office had a green cathode-ray terminal hooked up to a large mainframe computer. On that day, my father showed me a text-based game called Adventure that someone at the company had installed on the mainframe (figure 2.2a and b). I remember my fascination at the idea of moving in a seemingly vast virtual place, quite unlike any video game I had played.

Since my parents bought me an Intellivision rather than an Atari, the second game that shaped my interest in virtual worlds was not the graphical version of Adventure, but Utopia, which I began playing in high school

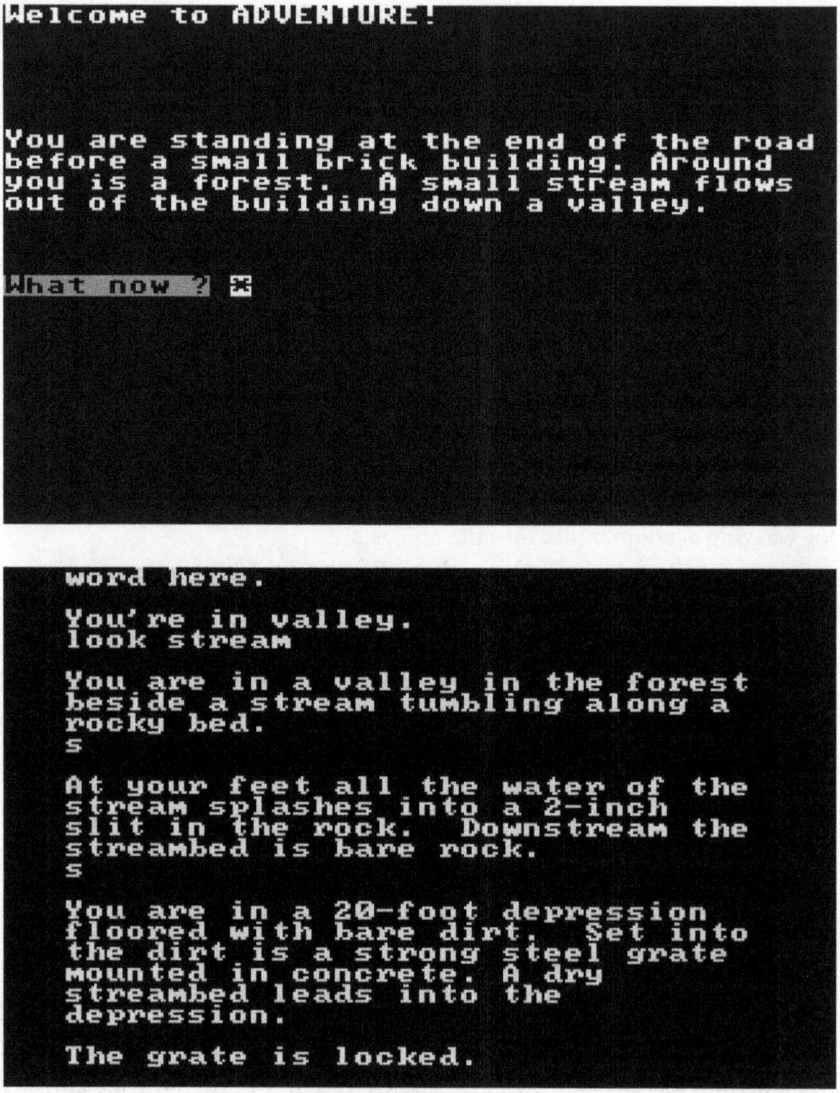

```
Welcome to ADVENTURE!


You are standing at the end of the road
before a small brick building. Around
you is a forest.   A small stream flows
out of the building down a valley.


What now ?  ▨
```

```
word here.
You're in valley.
look stream

You are in a valley in the forest
beside a stream tumbling along a
rocky bed.
s

At your feet all the water of  the
stream splashes into a 2-inch
slit in the rock.   Downstream the
streambed is bare rock.
s

You are in a 20-foot depression
floored with bare dirt.   Set into
the dirt is a strong steel grate
mounted in concrete. A dry
streambed leads into the
depression.

The grate is locked.
```

FIGURES 2.1A AND 2.1B. Screenshots of *Adventure* (http://www.gb64.com/oldsite/rare/
Colossal_Cave_Adventure.gif, accessed December 27, 2005; http://retrograde.trustno1
.org/pics/MSADV2.GIF, accessed December 27, 2005).

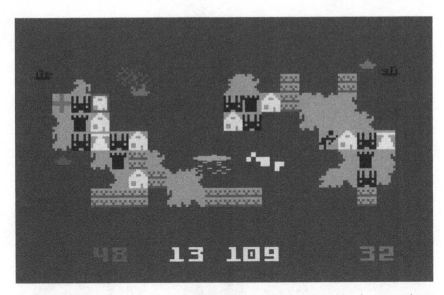

FIGURE 2.2. Screenshot of *Utopia* (http://upload.wikimedia.org/wikipedia/en/7/7d/ Utopia_%28Intellivision%29.png, accessed December 27, 2005).

(figure 2.2). In Utopia—which could be played by two players or one player versus the computer—a player controlled one of two continents set in a blue sea, working to accumulate points by growing crops and fishing while avoiding problems caused by violent weather, pirates, overpopulation, and rebellion. By this time I had also read J.R.R. Tolkien's *The Lord of the Rings* at least fifteen times, the single-volume special edition my mother gave to me one Christmas a cherished possession.

In college I remember my fascination at encountering Cosmic Osmo, a whimsical point-and-click world for the MacIntosh. The creators of Cosmic Osmo would go on to develop the Myst series of games, which pioneered forms of graphical realism and immersion taken up by many virtual worlds.[6] I was beginning graduate school when I discovered SimEarth, which had been released a few years earlier (in 1990; figure 2.3). Then in the late 1990s I started playing SimCity 2000 (figure 2.4). SimEarth and SimCity were in a certain sense games, but above all they were simulations. The pleasure in engagement was obtained not from gaining points or defeating an opponent, but watching life forms evolve, or a city grow as its highway system improved. These simulations proved a helpful distraction as I wrote my dissertation on sexuality in Indonesia.

In 2004, I finished the manuscript for my first book and felt a sense of closure in regard to my anthropological work to date. When, as is typical

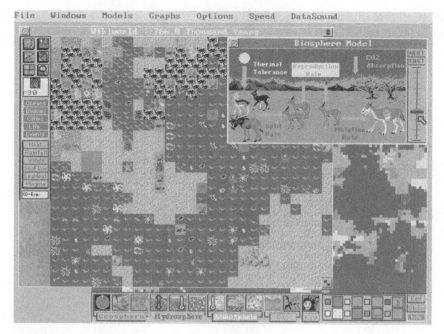

FIGURE 2.3. Screenshot of *SimEarth* (http://upload.wikimedia.org/wikipedia/en/3/38/ SimEarth_IBM_PC.png, accessed December 27, 2005).

at this stage, the question "what should I research next?" arose, I came to the situation with a history of personal involvement in technologies linked to the history of virtual worlds. Since I had played SimEarth and SimCity, I briefly explored The Sims Online (discussed below) before hearing about Second Life. The rest, we can say, is the history of this book.

HISTORIES OF VIRTUAL WORLDS.

The three narratives thus far provide differing perspectives on the history of virtual worlds, but a more direct history begins in the mid-twentieth century. There are two primary and intertwined "streams" to this contemporary history of virtual worlds: the phenomenon of virtual reality and the rise of video games.

The first emergence of a virtual world along the lines of Second Life most likely occurred in 1970 in the context of a project by Myron Krueger, who was also probably the person to coin the term "artificial reality" (Woolley 1992:6). One day, Krueger and a colleague—working in two different buildings on the same university campus—were each looking at an image of a waveform at their computer displays. The waveform in question was

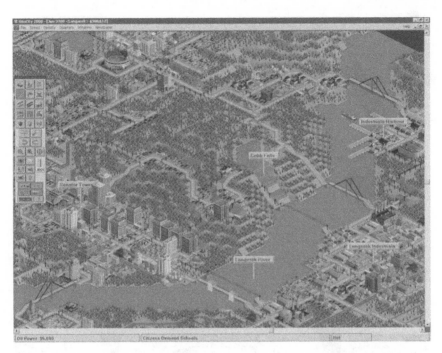

FIGURE 2.4. Screenshot of *SimCity 2000* (http://upload.wikimedia.org/wikipedia/en/b/bc/SimCity2000_Windows_In-Game_Screenshot.png, accessed December 27, 2005).

part of a computer installation called Metaplay that projected the image of a person on a wall coupled with computer graphics (so that, for instance, a person sitting on an empty floor might appear to be sitting in a computer-generated bathtub; Krueger 1983:23). Krueger and his colleague used a telephone to discuss the waveform:

> However, after a few minutes of frustrating discussion, we realized that we had a far more powerful means of communication available. Using the two-way video link described in Metaplay, we turned the [cameras on ourselves seated at our respective computers; figure 2.5]. . . . As we did this, we used our hands to point to various features on the composite display. It was exactly as if we were sitting together at a table with a piece of paper between us. After a while, I realized that I was seeing more than an illusion. As I moved my hand to point to the data my friend had just sent, the image of my hand briefly overlapped the image of his. He moved his hand. . . . I was struck with the thought that he was uncomfortable about the image of my hand touching the image of his. . . . The inescapable conclusion was that the same etiquette of personal space

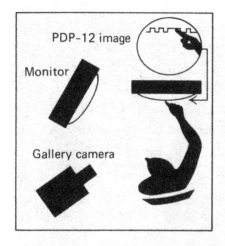
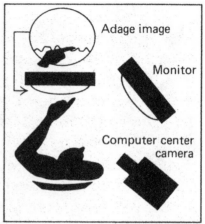
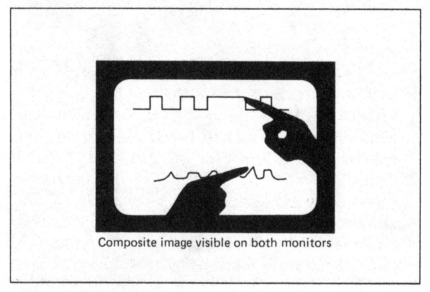

FIGURE 2.5. The origins of VIDEOPLACE (Krueger 1983:126).

and avoidance of touching that exists in the real world was operating at that moment in this purely visual experience. (Krueger 1983:125–27)

From this serendipitous event Krueger developed Videoplace, which could be seen as the first virtual world (figure 2.6). In an updated edition of *Artificial Reality* published in 1991 (eight years after the first edition), Krueger extended his analysis in two telling ways. First, he included an image (figure

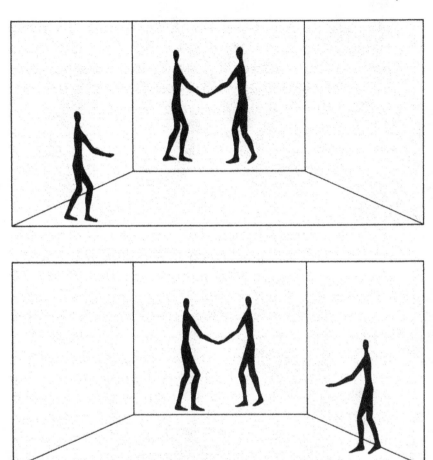

FIGURE 2.6. An early virtual handshake, from VIDEOPLACE (Krueger 1983:128).

2.7) demonstrating how virtual worlds differ from telecommunications (or mass media more generally): "whereas we usually think of telecommunication as being between two points . . . [t]wo-way telecommunication between two places creates a third place consisting of the information that is available to both communicating parties simultaneously" (Krueger 1991:37). Second, Krueger was now able to speculate that the dyadic virtual worlds he had created could become what would, a few years later, be termed "massively multiplayer" (figure 2.8). This notion of a what Krueger termed a "megaenvironment" in 1991 (but had not entered his thinking in 1983) prefigures virtual worlds like Second Life to a striking degree, albeit underestimating its size by several orders of magnitude:

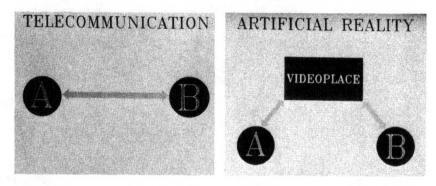

FIGURE 2.7. The idea of an "artificial reality" or virtual world (Krueger 1991:37).

FIGURE 2.8. The "megaenvironment" (Krueger 1991:63).

Each participant would enter a large and complex graphic world from a different physical location. Each would see only a small portion of that world, including her own image and those of other participants who are also in that part of the graphic world. The participant could interact with the others or could leave the current location and travel to a different part of the graphic world. Along the way, she would encounter other participants from other real locations. Such a megaenvironment could include hundreds of participants. (Krueger 1991:62)

Like many early incarnations of virtual worlds, Videoplace often focused on education (see also Seymour Papert's notion of "microworlds" [Papert 1980]). It contained several elements that distinguished it from other technologies like the television, telegraph, telephone, newspaper, and film, as well as correspondence by mail. It involved the simultaneous presence of multiple people in what they experienced as a *place* distinct from the actual world. People interacted within the virtual world and also with the virtual world itself. The world persisted even as individuals entered and left it. This characteristic of persistence has been fundamental to virtual worlds ever since. A conference call ends when everyone hangs up, and a virtual world like Second Life can go permanently offline, but while they exist as virtual worlds they persist beyond the logging off of any single resident. Persistence can be temporally circumscribed; it is not the same thing as eternal existence.

While the work of people like Myron Krueger is absolutely crucial to the history I am now telling, virtual worlds originate above all from video games (Bartle 2004:2). The first video game (which involved firing missiles at a target) was created in 1947; in 1958 Willy Higinbotham, a scientist at the Brookhaven National Laboratory, invented an interactive tennis game on a programmable oscilloscope (Kent 2001:18; Poole 2000:29–30). However, the first video game to leave an individual lab and achieve wide influence was Spacewar, created by a group of students at MIT in 1961–62.[7] The first home video game console, the Magnavox Odyssey, was released in May 1972 and was not very successful, among other reasons because company advertising implied it would only play on Magnavox televisions (Herman 2001:12; Kent 2001:24–26). That November the recently incorporated Atari released what became the first popular video game, Pong (Kent 2001): since this was primarily a two-player game, the simple representation of a tennis court and paddles could be seen as an early virtual world. Space Invaders, released in 1978 (Poole 2000:34), was the first video game to have computer-controlled entities (aliens descending in lockstep from the sky);

with its presentation of an earth under attack from space, it also presumed a kind of virtual world.

Later video games gave an even stronger sense of presence in a virtual world, particularly when the world in question scrolled across the screen. One of the earliest instances of this was Defender, released in 1980 (Herman 2001:51), and one of the most popular was Super Mario Bros., released in 1985, which not only scrolled left/right and up/down, but contained secret passages that added to a sense of presence (Herman 2001:111). Doom, released in 1993, is "widely recognized for its pioneer use of immersive 3D graphics, networked multiplayer gaming, and the support for players to create custom expansions,"[8] and played a major role in the development of virtual worlds (Kushner 2003). Video games employing first-person perspective date back to the 1970s (in particular, Mazewar), but it was with Doom and its successors that the kind of self-centric visuality so fundamental to contemporary virtual worlds was broadly developed and implemented.[9] Even when these video games were primarily single-player, the increasingly graphically complex and interactive character of the worlds they created (with, for instance, trees that shook when you ran into them) provided concepts and programming architecture for virtual worlds like Second Life.[10]

Throughout this history of video games, there have existed programs that were labeled games at the time but can be seen as virtual worlds in retrospect. This is because the "games" in question did not have scoring (or deemphasized it), and often did not involve player death—a key component of most video games, where after one's lives were used up, "game over" would appear on the screen. A "game" known as Hunt the Wumpus is another contender for first virtual world, dating from 1972 (Herz 1997:9–10; Koster 2003:439).[11] Another early virtual world was the "game" known as Hamurabi or Kingdom, "fifty lines of BASIC code that crudely simulated a feudal domain" (Herz 1997:9) and which first appeared in 1979.[12] However, the first virtual world to be entered by a substantial number of persons was Adventure (its original full name was Colossal Cave Adventure), the first version of which dated from 1976 (Koster 2003:442; Lastowka and Hunter 2006:18). An "early descendant" of Adventure with a nearly identical interface, Zork, was created in 1977 and also become well-known.[13] Adventure is legendary in the history of virtual worlds: "Adventure is a virtual world in a conceptual way: the game is played in an imaginary underground world of caves and chambers, and players proceed through that world . . . typing commands such as 'go north' and 'pick up sword.' The physical space is not displayed but described; the only visual scenes are in the player's mind's eye" (Rheingold 1991:23).[14]

A graphical version of Adventure, created by Warren Robinett and released in 1978, was the first "game" to employ many of the conventions used
for representing place in virtual worlds to this day (Robinett 2003). It has
been influential in the development of virtual worlds more generally. For
instance, it is the only virtual world mentioned in the 1981 novella "True
Names," discussed earlier in this chapter (Vinge 2001 [1981]:251, 272), and
its principles were taken up by the Myst series of "games," in which one explored a rich graphical world solving puzzles. Utopia, a "groundbreaking
simulation" regarded by some as the first graphical virtual world, was released in 1982 for Intellivision (as noted earlier, I played Utopia as a teen-
ager).[15] Unlike Adventure, Utopia (and also Hamurabi) were to some degree
simulations, since they tried to replicate actual-world events (e.g., rain and
schools of fish in the case of Utopia) and had chains of causality (in Utopia,
if you failed to notice that certain areas receive little rain and planted crops
there, the crops would die and your populace would go hungry, then rebel).

Until this point, the idea of simulation in video games typically referred
to things like flight or other combat simulators, so that, for instance, "game
historians generally agree that Battlezone, a 1980 Atari arcade game described as a 'hyperrealistic tank combat simulator' was probably the first
game depicted from a first-person perspective" (McMahan 2003:70; see
also Kent 2001:148–49). In other words, what was "simulated" in these
simulators was sensory perception and often interface (a joystick similar
to the joysticks used to fly actual-world airplanes, or a periscope similar to
an actual-world tank's periscope). The simulation was less concerned with
the actual world the simulation evoked: for instance, Battlezone used vector
graphics to indicate hills in the distance, but no care was taken to create a
sun that would rise and set beyond those hills.

Another significant development in the history of virtual worlds was
the rise of the "Sim" games, including SimCity (released in 1989), SimEarth
(released in 1990), SimLife (released in 1992), SimFarm (released in 1993),
and SimAnt (released in 1991).[16] One thing these simulations shared with
their predecessors—all the way back to Adventure—is that they were not
persistent. They were self-contained on whatever computer was being used
at the time; when that computer was shut off, the simulation disappeared
as well. For this reason, these worlds were also fundamentally single-player:
persons could take turns operating the computer being used, but for the
most part people participated in these worlds one at a time.

As these simulations became more complex, some Internet-based communities took on features of virtual worlds. The Internet began in the late
1960s as ARPANET, a project developed by the United States Department

of Defense (Abbate 1999; Hafner and Lyon 1996); the Internet was created
as a civilian analogue in 1983 (Fornäs et al. 2002:18). As Internet use began
to spread beyond military and academic environments, the first public bulletin board system was created in 1978 (Sterling 1992:65). Usenet, one of
the longest-lasting systems allowing persons to exchange messages online,
came into being in 1979 (M. Smith 1999), and the first Internet Relay Chat
system began in 1988 (Campbell 2004:29). Several BBS or IRC systems became fairly well-known; for instance, the WELL (Whole Earth 'Lectronic
Link), connected to the *Whole Earth Catalog* and whose users were primarily located in the San Francisco Bay Area (Sterling 1992:225; see Hafner
1997; Turner 2006:141–74). These email and discussion lists (known by a
range of names, including listservs, Internet Relay Chat [IRC], and bulletin
board systems [BBS]) can be seen as virtual worlds, albeit primarily asynchronic (participants exchanged postings but did not interact at the same
time; Kollock and Smith 1999:5).

   These forms of online communication soon gave birth to formats where
multiple persons could interact online at once. In 1978–79, Roy Trubshaw and
Richard Bartle programmed MUD (later known as MUD1), the first "multi-
user dungeon" (Bartle 2004:4; see also Cherny 1999:5; Curtis 1992:122; Lastowka and Hunter 2006:19–20; Reid 1999:107; Sundén 2003:20–21).[17] MUDs
quickly became popular, with multiple versions of any particular MUD appearing on separate computer networks. A study of online traffic in 1993
"showed that just over 10% of the hits belonged to MUDs; in other words,
before the advent of the World Wide Web (WWW) MUDs constituted some
10% of the Internet" (Bartle 2004:12).[18] It was with MUDs that the idea of
virtual worlds began to circulate more widely. One Second Life resident recalled how "though I never played much of them, I was fascinated by the idea
of people creating the world around them, and this was before I heard about
SL. I can remember wondering when a 'graphical MUD' will come out."

   Many of these MUDs were based on fantasy combat scenarios (for instance, slaying dragons), and were therefore seen as games to some extent.
However, MUDs in which combat was deemphasized or absent appeared
quite early on. TinyMUD, designed by Jim Aspnes in 1989, is often considered the first "social" virtual world (Shah and Romine 1995:2; see also
Aarseth 1997:13; Bartle 2004:9; Bruckman 1996:319; Cherny 1999:6; Koster
2003:451; Reid 1999:126). A series of social MUDs based on TinyMUD
soon appeared, such as TinyMUSH and TinyMUCK (which incorporated
an inworld programming language, "Multi User Forth" or MUF, presaging
Second Life's inworld Linden Scripting Language). Other social MUDs not
directly based upon TinyMUD have included UberMud, UnterMud, and

above all LambdaMOO, created by Steven White and Pavel Curtis in 1990, which became the best-known MUD (Carlstrom 1992; Cherny 1999:6; Dibbell 1998; Koster 2003:452–55; Mnookin 2001; Nakamura 2002; Rosenberg 1992; Shah and Romine 1995:236–37; Sundén 2003:21; Turkle 1995).

Whether "combat" or "social" in nature, all of these MUDs were "entirely textual" virtual worlds (Curtis 1992:121); that is, they did not incorporate graphics, and thus "the typical MUD user interface is most reminiscent of old computer games like Adventure and Zork" (Curtis 1992:122). However, advances in Internet and graphics technology raised the possibility that graphical versions of MUDs could be created. Still often labeled "massively multiplayer online role-playing games" (MMORPGs) or "massively multiplayer online worlds" (MMOWs), these graphical virtual worlds were distinct in that they were "the first persistent (twenty-four hours a day, seven days a week) [virtual] worlds, and the first instance of individualized mediated experiences within a mass audience (each player's experience is unique despite the large number of simultaneous participants)" (Wolf and Perron 2003:11). Habitat, a two-dimensional simulation of Tokyo designed for use on the Commodore 64 personal computer, was released in 1985 and is generally known as the "the very first networked virtual world in which there were people represented as avatars and who were able to communicate and form a 'virtual community'" (Damer 1998:522; see also Castronova 2005:55; Koster 2003:448; Lastowka and Hunter 2006:21–22; Stone 1995:120); another early graphical virtual world (dating from 1996) was The Palace (Damer 1998; Nakamura 2002). AlphaWorld (first released in 1995 and later renamed Active Worlds) was, along with Worlds Chat, probably the first three-dimensional virtual world (Damer 1998:17–52; 97–160; Koster 2003:458; Taylor 2006a:25).[19] With the emergence of these graphical virtual worlds, the distinction between "virtual reality" and "virtual world" became clear:

> The essential lesson that we have abstracted from our experiences with Habitat is that a cyberspace is defined more by the interactions among the actors within it than by the technology with which it is implemented. While we find much of the work presently being done on elaborate interface technologies—DataGloves, head-mounted displays, special-purpose rendering engines, and so on—both exciting and promising, the almost mystical euphoria that currently seems to surround all this hardware is, in our opinion, both excessive and somewhat misplaced. (Morningstar and Farmer 1991:274)

Particularly at the outset, many of these "visually immersive" virtual worlds were oriented toward combat. The first to gain a large number of residents was probably Ultima Online, which was "a frontrunner on issues still under heavy debate. It was one of the first [virtual worlds] to confront mass player protest, not to mention the sale of virtual items for real world currency" (Taylor 2006a:26; see also Castronova 2005:55–56). Ultima Online was followed by a series of combat-oriented virtual worlds in the late 1990s and early 2000s, including EverQuest, Lineage, and Lineage II. Many of these prohibited players from killing each other or limited such combat to "player versus player" (PvP) servers in contrast to "player versus environment" (PvE) servers. In the latter case, residents had to work together to kill animated monsters, creating "social interactions" that residents often identified "as the primary reason for spending so many hours online" (King and Borland 2003:222). As with MUDs before them, graphical virtual worlds emphasizing noncombat sociality became increasingly salient. One of the first such worlds with a large base of residents was The Sims Online (often abbreviated "TSO"), which went online in December 2002.[20] Other virtual worlds like Active Worlds, There, Project Entropia, and A Tale In the Desert also coexisted with Second Life during the time of my fieldwork, and some Second Life residents participated in these virtual worlds as well; additionally they often participated in more combat-oriented virtual worlds like World of Warcraft, Lineage II, and City of Heroes.

During the time of my research, the history of Second Life was best documented on the "SL History Wiki."[21] According to this history, Linden Lab began as a company interested in designing haptic virtual reality technologies (those involving touch). By the summer of 2001, Linden Lab engineers had created a virtual world (originally to work with haptic hardware) with a terrain and water, and also avatars (which at this point were eyeballs, not whole bodies). At the 2006 Second Life Community Convention, Philip Rosedale, the Founder and Chief Executive Officer of Linden Lab, recalled a company board meeting in 2001 where the virtual world was being demonstrated and a group of engineers started playing with the virtual world, making objects that looked like a simple city and even a snowman. Incidents like this led Rosedale and others to conclude that the virtual *world* aspect of their technology was more important than its (haptic) virtual *reality* component, and so further developed the virtual world, which first went online in March 2002 under the name Linden World. Second Life went public as a full-fledged virtual world in June 2003 (version 1.0), and the software (free to download) has been constantly updated since that time. I began my research in Second Life in June 2004 with version 1.4, about one year after it first went online, and ended primary research for this book in January 2007 with version 1.13.

Histories of cybersociality research.

Alongside this history of contemporary virtual worlds it is possible to trace a history of research and commentary about them. This has included forms of science fiction writing and journalism; with the rise of blogs and Web sites, the amount of such writing has grown exponentially and has been joined by photography and machinima ("machine cinema," or movies made within a virtual world). Throughout this book I draw upon this insightful body of work, including a nascent literature concerning Second Life itself. Some of this work was produced in universities but much of it originated outside the academy, often from the field of game design.

Since my focus is on ethnography as a means for exploring culture in virtual worlds, in this section I focus on the history of ethnographic research, which at the time of my fieldwork was a relatively recent development: "[S]ocial research into [virtual worlds] to date can crudely be characterized as consisting of two phases. The first phase corresponds to the use of psychological approaches depending on experimental methods. . . . [The second] corresponds to the. . . . claiming of the Internet as a cultural context. Participant observation and explicitly ethnographic approaches have increasingly claimed online contexts as field sites in their own right" (Hine 2005:7).[22] Since at least the 1970s, some researchers concerned with emerging forms of "computer-mediated communication" have speculated how such forms of networked sociality could lead to "electronic tribes" (Hiltz and Turoff 1978:482–84). As Hine notes, little of this early research was ethnographic, but it did touch upon questions of governance, community, and identity that have proven to be enduring themes in the study of cybersociality.

The first ethnographies of virtual worlds were probably Michael Rosenberg's 1992 ethnography of WolfMOO and John Masterson's 1994 ethnography of Ancient Anguish (Bartle 2004:491; see Masterson 1994; Rosenberg 1992). Many further ethnographically informed studies of text-based virtual worlds have appeared since that time, including studies of BlueSky (Kendall 2002), Cybersphere (Schaap 2002), DhalgrenMOO (McRae 1997); ElseMOO (Cherny 1999); LambdaMOO (Carlstrom 1992; Curtis 1992; Dibbell 1998; Mnookin 2001; Nakamura 2002; Rosenberg 1992; Turkle 1995), WaterMOO (Sundén 2003), and the Whole Earth 'Lectronic Link or WELL (Rheingold 2000). Much of this research has focused on specific topics, like community (Baym 2000; Blascovich 2002; Bogost 2004; Ducheneaut, Moore, and Nickell 2004; Fernback 1999; Hudson-Smith 2002; Markham 1998; Reid 1999; Kollock and Smith 1999; Wellman and Gulia 1999), economics and politics (Castronova 2005; Dibbell 2006; Nayar 2004), embodiment (Biocca

1997; Çapin et al. 1999; Ito 1997; Stone 1991; Sundén 2003; Taylor 2002; Vasseleu 1997), gender, sexuality, and romance (Ben-Ze'ev 2004; Bruckman 1996; Campbell 2004; Kendall 2002; McRae 1997; Schaap 2002; Sveningsson 2002; Wakeford 2000), identity (Bromberg 1996; Donath 1999; Rheingold 2000), language (Cherny 1999), law (Golub 2004; Herman, Coombe, and Kaye 2006; Mnookin 2001), race (Kolko, Nakamura, and Rodman 2000; Nakamura 2002), and religion (Schroeder, Heather, and Lee 1998).

By the time of my fieldwork there were also a growing number of studies of graphical virtual worlds informed by ethnographic methods, including research on Star Wars Galaxies (Ducheneaut, Moore, and Nickell 2004; Jenkins 2006; Thomas 2005), The Palace (Guimarães 2005), Active Worlds (Hudson-Smith 2002), Habitat (Morningstar and Farmer 1991; Stone 1995), EverQuest (Fornäs et al. 2002; Castronova 2005; Jakobsson and Taylor 2003; Taylor 2006a), and World of Warcraft (Nardi and Harris 2006). Some works had examined multiple virtual worlds (e.g., Fornäs et al. 2002; Juul 2005).

An increasing body of work during the time of my research asked methodological questions about how to engage in ethnography online (Hakken 1999; Hine 2000, 2005; Jacobson 1999; Q. Jones 1997; Jones 1999; Markham 1998; Miller and Slater 2000; Paccagnella 1997; Reed 2005; Ruhleder 2000; Schroeder 2002). This research linked up to innovative works written by designers of virtual worlds (Bartle 2004; Damer 1998; Mulligan and Patrovsky 2003; Ondrejka 2004a, 2006a; Pearce 1997; Salen and Zimmerman 2004; Wardrip-Fruin and Harrigan 2004). Such methodological debates are of vital importance.

TECHNE.

All these histories of virtual worlds imply histories of the human ability to fashion and live in them. To discuss cave paintings is to ask after the ability of humans to imagine and paint what they imagine on a cave wall. To discuss the early virtual world "Adventure" is to ask after the ability of humans to imagine places and then program them into a computer. Virtual worlds like Second Life are strikingly new social forms, having come into being only in the late 1990s and early 2000s. As noted earlier, since millions of human beings can enter and reside in such virtual worlds, it is clear that concepts and practices from the actual world are being brought into them. A primary claim in this book is that the fundamental thing brought in is techne. As a result there is one more history to tell, the history of techne itself. This is a more theoretical history that some readers may find less compelling than the other histories I have related. However, it is only through such conceptual work that research can illuminate the implicit cultural logics of the virtual that too often are out-shone by sensational but fleeting controversies and novelties online.

Both "technology" and "technique" are derived from the Greek root τέχνη (which I render as "techne"), and terms based upon this Greek root can now be found in most languages worldwide (for instance, Indonesian *teknologi*). Techne refers to art or craft, to human action that engages with the world and thereby results in a different world. Techne is not just knowl-edge about the world, what Greek thought termed *episteme*; it is intentional action that *constitutes a gap* between the world as it was before the action, and the new world it calls into being. The philosopher Bernard Stiegler noted how Aristotle defined techne as concerned with "bringing something into being" (1998:9). For Aristotle, "the goal of techne" was thus "to create what nature found impossible to accomplish" (Guattari 1995:33, cited in Doel and Clarke 1999:268). It is in this sense that technology can be de-fined as "any intentional extension of a natural process. . . . Respiration is a wholly natural life function, for example, and is therefore not a technology; the human ability to breathe under water, by contrast, implies some techno-logical extension" (Beniger 1986:9; see also Spengler 1932).

Just as one of the earliest known evocations of a virtual world dates to Greek thought—Plato's allegory of the cave—so techne has a Greek myth of its own, the story of the brothers Prometheus (whose name means "fore-sight") and Epimetheus (whose name means "hindsight"). Prometheus and Epimetheus created clay figures that had life breathed into them by the god-dess Athena: Prometheus's figures became humans and Epimetheus's fig-ures became animals. Epimetheus was charged with giving a positive trait to these creatures: some were given the ability to fly, others to swim, some sharp claws, and so on. When it was time to give a positive trait to humans, Epimetheus found he had none left: humans were destined to be hairless and weak, without powerful eyesight, hearing, or smell, unable to fly or move with speed upon the ground. Due to an earlier dispute, Zeus had even denied humans the secret of fire, but Prometheus, "being at a loss to provide any means of salvation for man, stole from Hephaestus and Athena the gift of skill in the arts [techne], together with fire . . . and bestowed it on man" (Stiegler 1998:187), bringing the origins of civilization as well.[23]

In the story of the Garden of Eden, knowledge about the actual world founds the human journey, a bite from the apple symbolized in the Apple Inc. logo (Halberstam 1991). In the Greek origin myth, the gift making hu-mans uniquely human is not a bite from an apple but a spark from a flame. It is not knowledge about good and evil in the actual world, episteme, but *the ability to craft gaps*, techne—the flame and the ability to use it, which together can turn raw food into cooked, forge pottery and machines, and cast the shadows on Plato's cave. Contemporary scholars of virtual worlds have thus been able to see Prometheus as giving humans the "first power-up. . . . Whether our digital fire is turned to destructive or creative purposes is still up to us" (Poole 2000:216, 240). As their names indicate, knowledge (associated with Epimetheus) is oriented toward the past, while the gift of Prometheus, techne, implies a future orientation. It is linked to a world that can be changed by human craft, and "tends not only to create a new human environment, but also to modify man's very essence" (Ellul 1964:325). This is a "technological reason" concerned with "the constitution of ethical subjects" and "practices of living" (Collier and Lakoff 2005:25). I intend the term *homo cyber*, the virtual human, to reference both the forms of human social life emerging online, and the way that human being has always been constituted through techne. As noted earlier and as this discussion of Greek history indicates, I am acutely aware of the Western origins of "virtual" and "techne." However, rendering this "Western origin" as a "Western bias" would ignore the reality of Western domination, oversimplifying the complex and contingent ways in which these concepts have been transformed worldwide.

The Greek origins of "techne" have been a source of fascination to a range of thinkers interested in questions of technology and the human, dating back at least to Mary Shelley's *Frankenstein*, subtitled "the modern Prometheus" (Shelley 2007 [1818]). In his essay "The Question Concerning Technology," Heidegger noted that "from earliest times until Plato the word *techne* is linked with the word *episteme*," but differ in that techne "reveals whatever does not bring itself forth and does not yet lie here before us. . . . Whoever builds a house or a ship or forges a sacrificial chalice reveals what is to be brought forth" (Heidegger 1977:13). The individualist struggles of Robinson Crusoe for survival can be seen as a search for "the means to reestablish technical mastery" over life (Redfield 2000:6); that is, for the primacy of techne over episteme. Stiegler defined techne as a "way of revealing" that "brings into being what is not" (1998:9).[24] Lyotard asked if the answer to the question "what shall we call human in humans?" (1991:3) might lie in the capacity of persons "to acquire a 'second' nature which, thanks to language, makes them fit to share in communal life, adult consciousness and reason" (3). It was in regard to this "second nature"—recalling Second Life, Auden, and the premises of cultural anthropology—that Lyotard contended that "technology wasn't invented by us humans. Rather the other way around" (12). Noting that the term "*techne* is the abstract from *tikto* which means to engender, to generate (*tekontes*, the genitors, *teknon*, the offspring)" (52), Lyotard concluded that "'life,' as they say, is already technique" (52), allowing us to ask how Second "Life" might itself represent a form of technique.

The French philosopher Michel Foucault (1926–84) is well-known for his writings on sexuality, but less noted is that his last major works turned from macrological questions of institutional power to the history of micro-practices by which persons come to inhabit subject positions. Foucault explored how in ancient Greek thought, rules for self-conduct were designed to be modified for personal circumstances. "[E]verything was a matter of adjustment, circumstance, and personal position," and as a result "there was no need of anything resembling a text that would have the force of law, but rather, of a *techne* or 'practice'. . . . [I]n this form of morality, the individual did not make himself into an ethical subject by universalizing the principles that informed his action; on the contrary, he did so by means of an attitude and a quest that individualized his action, modulated it, and perhaps even gave him a special brilliance by virtue of the rational and deliberate structure his action manifested" (Foucault 1985:62).

Techne is above all intentional and *creative*. Foucault was particularly interested in how techne worked as an "art of existence" (1986:43): "This *techne* created the possibility of forming oneself as a subject in control of his conduct; that is, the possibility of making oneself like the doctor treating sickness, the pilot steering between the rocks, or the statesman governing the city—a skillful and prudent guide of himself, one who had a sense of the right time and the right measure" (Foucault 1985:138–39).

An emphasis on craft, often phrased in terms of technology, has been a constant theme in understandings of virtual worlds, even nonelectronic forms of virtuality like fiction and dance (Langer 1953). J.R.R. Tolkien, whose works played such an important role in the history of virtual worlds, emphasized that "a special skill, a kind of elvish craft . . . produces a Secondary World into which both designer and spectator can enter" (1966:49, 52). In more reflective contexts, Second Life residents would sometimes say things like: "It's innate in our minds, embracing external tools to extend our minds. Our minds don't stop at the skull, to put it one way. How many of you have ever said 'I can't think this through; I need to write it down to organize my thoughts?' Writing, written language: those are technologies, and we use them to really extend our 'self' and our mind's functioning."

"Techne" names the bootstrapping ability of humans to craft themselves. Animated by a pragmatics more than a semantics, it is the articulating concept linking humans and virtual worlds, reflecting the importance of the "technological imagination" to culture (Balsamo forthcoming). I was fascinated by how notions of a "workaround" or "patch" were employed in Second Life (and in computing more generally), cropping up in everything from updates to the platform to everyday conversations about building a house. A "solution" represents correct knowledge, but what validates a "workaround" or "patch" is that through craft, a problem is bypassed without necessarily being removed or even fully "known." Techne can obviate episteme.

In this discussion and throughout this book, I might be seen to be trying to have it both ways; I claim that notions of the virtual and of techne are in one sense as old as humanity, and in another sense I claim that something very new is happening in virtual worlds. This is intentional. It is crucial to keep in mind the history shaping the present moment, while also identifying how that present moment is not reducible to its history. What makes virtual worlds different from all hitherto existing forms of virtuality is that *techne can take place inside them*, rather than solely in the actual world to produce them: "where most tools produce effects on a wider world of which they are only a part, the computer contains its own [virtual] worlds in miniature" (Edwards 1990:109). Techne makes wood and ideas into a newspaper, but techne not only makes silicon and ideas into a virtual world; techne can take place within that created world itself. In virtual worlds, techne *produces a gap between actual and virtual in the realm of the virtual*. Swallowing their own ontological tails, virtual worlds for the first time allow techne to become recursive, providing humans with radically new ways to understand their lives as beings of culture as well as physical embodiment.

In his discussion of "recursive publics," Christopher Kelty noted that participants share a "profound concern for the technical legal conditions of possibility for their own association," and "the Internet is the condition of their association" (2005:185). Speaking of such technological conditions of possibility is not technological determinism, because it is open to contingency. Drive-in movie theaters could not have come into existence without the automobile, but were not an inevitable consequence of the automobile's invention. Many aspects of virtual worlds are not new, but some are. Those new things have virtual worlds as their condition of possibility, but not in a determinist sense.

I use the phrase "the Age of Techne" in a tongue-in-cheek manner, to flag a cultural moment when techne becomes recursive, an end as well as a means, a moment for which virtual worlds are the condition of possibility. Roughly equivalent to "the virtual age" or "the age of digital machines" (Stone 1995; Poster 2006), and recalling the "age of mechanical reproduction" (Benjamin 1955), this is not a strict periodization. I do not claim that we now live in a disenchanted world (in Weber's sense), for which virtual worlds and other technologies provide new opportunities for an age of reenchantment. The provisional phrase "Age of Techne" flags my hypothesis that to the degree any common denominator exists between emerging forms of culture in virtual worlds, it is this new salience for techne as the intentional crafting of world, self, and society.

In the following chapter I turn to the methodological implications of my argument thus far. Throughout its history, the goal of anthropology—and ethnography more generally—has been to learn about other cultures: ethnographic inquiry has sought to produce forms of knowledge, forms of episteme. It thus tends to understand culture in terms of knowledge, so that an "anthropological space" created by new technologies is presumed to be a "knowledge space" (Lévy 1997:5). However, what would ethnography look like if it worked to produce not episteme, but techne? How would this redefine culture and raise reflexive, indeed post-reflexive, questions for ethnography itself? What if in this book I seek not just to describe techne, but to enact it at a methodological level—so that the book's effect is not just to produce knowledge, but to craft a toolkit for the virtual?

Chapter 3

METHOD

Virtual worlds in their own terms—Anthropology
and ethnography—Participant observation—Interviews,
focus groups, and beyond the platform—Ethics—Claims
and reflexivity.

VIRTUAL WORLDS IN THEIR OWN TERMS.

On August 31, 1925, Margaret Mead arrived on the shores of Samoa "to in-vestigate the particular problem" of whether youth always experience grow-ing into adulthood in terms of stress and conflict (Mead 1928:9).[1] Opening by describing a Samoan dawn that "begins to fall among the soft brown roofs" while "the slender palm trees stand out against a colorless, gleaming sea" (Mead 1928:14), *Coming of Age in Samoa*—the book that resulted from her research—was an immediate international sensation. Translated into fifteen languages, it launched Mead's lifelong career as the foremost popu-larizer of cultural anthropology.

Five years after her death in 1978, the anthropologist Derek Freeman published *Margaret Mead and Samoa: The Making and Unmaking of an An-thropological Myth* (Freeman 1983). Despite having never produced a book on his own research in Samoa, Freeman "generated unprecedented con-troversy over Margaret Mead's fieldwork" (Brady 1983:908). His primary claim was that Mead had allowed herself to be misled by her young Samoan interlocutors, taking at face value their tales of adolescent sexual freedom. These charges have not weathered the test of time. Many anthropologists who conducted subsequent fieldwork in Samoa concluded that despite shortcomings in her work, Mead accurately captured many aspects of Sa-moan culture (e.g., Holmes 1987; Mageo 1998; Orans 1996). Others noted how Freeman omitted scholarship supporting Mead's conclusions (Holmes 1987; Shankman 1996; see also Feinberg 1988; Nardi 1984; Weiner 1983).

In titling this book *Coming of Age in Second Life*, I evoke both the path-breaking spirit of Mead's first book and the late twentieth-century debate it engendered over methods. After all, Freeman's accusation against Mead was that she made things up, and what are virtual worlds if not made up?

When I decided to conduct research in Second Life, I did not begin with any specific topic in mind—economics, for instance, or sexuality, or governance. Instead, my founding question was methodological: What can ethnography tell us about virtual worlds?

It may seem preposterous to contend one can study virtual worlds "in their own terms," but condensed in this key phrase is my foundational methodological conceit, which like all such conceits is also a theoretical claim. For the research upon which this book is based I conducted my research entirely *within* Second Life, as the avatar Tom Bukowski. I made no attempt to visit the offices of Linden Lab, the San Francisco-based company that owns and manages Second Life, or to meet Linden Lab staff, though I would sometimes interact with them at conferences, or within Second Life. I also made no attempt to meet Second Life residents in the actual world or learn their actual-world identities, though both happened on occasion. I took their activities and words as legitimate data about culture in a virtual world. For instance, if during my research I was talking to a woman, I was not concerned to determine if she was "really" a man in the actual world, or even if two different people were taking turns controlling "her." Most Second Life residents meeting this woman would not know the answers to such questions, so for my ethnographic purposes it was important that I not know either. Research on online communities that includes meeting residents in the actual world is perfectly legitimate, but addresses a different set of questions (e.g., Orgad 2005; Ruhleder 2000; Wakeford 1999).

To demand that ethnographic research always incorporate meeting residents in the actual world for "context" presumes that virtual worlds are not themselves contexts; it renders ethnographically inaccessible the fact that most residents of virtual worlds do not meet their fellow residents offline. If one wants to study collective meaning and virtual worlds as collectivities exist purely online, then studying them in their own terms is the appropriate methodology, one that goes against the grain of many assumptions concerning how virtual worlds work. Why is the punchline of so many studies of online culture the identification of continuity with the offline? Why does it feel like a discovery that the online bleeds through to the offline, and vice versa?

My decision to conduct research wholly within Second Life had enormous implications, putting into practice my assertion that virtual worlds are legitimate sites of culture. Many writings on virtual worlds emphasize the permeability between the virtual and actual—for instance, by highlighting the actual-world consequences of virtual commerce. In his study of gay male identity, John Campbell claimed that "online and offline experiences blend into a single, albeit multifaceted, narrative of life" (Campbell 2004:100). Yet

Campbell's own ethnographic data suggest many ways in which online and offline personas do not match up; for instance, an older gay man might claim to be younger, or "gay men" might not be gay (or even men) in the actual world. In *The Internet: An Ethnographic Approach*, Daniel Miller and Don Slater contended that their "ethnography of the Internet in Trinidad, or of Trinidad on the Internet" demonstrates "how Internet technologies are being understood and assimilated somewhere in particular (though a very complex 'somewhere,' because Trinidad stretches diasporically over much of the world)" (Miller and Slater 2000:1). This assumes that online cultures are ultimately predicated upon actual-world cultures, an assumption sometimes methodologically operationalized by efforts to meet residents of virtual worlds in the actual world, although researchers have long noted the difficulty of ascertaining actual-world identities (Curtis 1992:125). Some researchers have gone so far as to criticize treating any virtual world as "a completely separate, isolated social world" (Kendall 2002:9; see also Wittel 2001:62), or to claim that "one current limitation of the study of [virtual worlds] is that we know little about how online behaviors affect users' behavior offline" (Schroeder 2002:10). Such assumptions are often linked to the belief that "the number-one challenge is generalizability to the real world" (Giles 2007:20). This view presumes that research on virtual worlds must have the ultimate goal of addressing the actual world, which is taken to be the only "real" social world. It is a view predicated on skepticism toward the idea of conducting ethnography in virtual worlds in their own terms: Is there enough detail in them? What about the fact that you can't know who the people are offline?

One risk I run in saying that it is possible to study virtual worlds in their own terms is that like classical ethnographers, I could be seen to be leaving to one side the cross-cutting histories that condition the lives of these worlds and those who participate in them. My response is that since people find virtual worlds meaningful sites for social action, cultures in virtual worlds exist whether we like it or not; our task as ethnographers is to study them. To take virtual worlds in their own terms is not to claim, as some Artificial Life researchers have done, that their computational worlds are totally self-contained (see Helmreich 2004:285). Assuming that the significance of virtual worlds hinges on continuity with the actual world oversimplifies the referential relationships between actual and virtual, obscuring many of their most crucial consequences for culture and the human. It is a commonplace of technology studies that "technologies are developed and used within a particular social, economic, and political context" (Chee 2006:226; see also Franklin 1992:15–17). But with the emergence of virtual worlds, the virtual world itself becomes a particular social, economic, and political context.

Perspectives doubting the possibility of studying virtual worlds in their own terms miss how as virtual worlds grow in size, ethnographic research in them becomes more partial and situated, much like ethnographic research in the actual world. For instance, when Lynn Cherny conducted ethnographic research in ElseMOO in 1994, there were about 100 persons participating in the world, with around 20 online at any one time (Cherny 1999:39–40). In contrast, by the time I submitted the final manuscript for this book in November 2007, there were over ten million registered Second Life accounts, with over 1.5 million people logging on per month and sometimes over 50,000 persons inworld at once. While a few of these residents had met in the actual world before entering Second Life, or met in Second Life and then sought each other out in the actual world, it was no longer possible for the vast majority to do so, or even verify the identities of those they met online.

Because virtual worlds are quite new, it is to be expected that as persons have built and entered them they have imported and reconfigured everyday aspects of the actual world, from gravity and sunlight to embodiment and language. As Auden noted even for the case of literature, "a secondary world must draw its building materials from the primary world, but it can only take such material as its creator is capable of imaginatively recombining and transforming" (Auden 1968:94). Yet despite the fact that "discussions of these technologies [tend to treat] them as enhancements for already formed individuals to deploy to their advantage or disadvantage" (Poster 1996:184), virtual worlds are not just recreations or simulations of actual-world selfhoods and communities. Selfhood, community, even notions of human nature are being remade in them.

Actual-world sociality cannot explain virtual-world sociality. The sociality of virtual worlds develops on its own terms; it references the actual world but is not simply derivative of it. Events and identities in such worlds may reference ideas from the actual world (from landscape to gender) and may index actual-world issues (from economics to political campaigns), but this referencing and indexing takes place within the virtual world. The way persons from Korea participate in Second Life might differ from the way persons from Sweden do. But if Koreans and Swedes really do participate in Second Life differently, that difference will show up within Second Life itself; it will be amenable to ethnographic investigation inworld. This is a crucial difference between ethnography and methodologies that seek an outsider perspective on culture. A political rally for John Edwards in Second Life in 2007 may have referenced an actual-world campaign, but even if video from an actual-world meeting was streamed into the rally, the rally itself took place in the virtual world.

Studying a virtual world in its own terms does not mean ignoring the myriad ways that ideas from the actual world impinge upon it; it means examining those interchanges as they manifest in the virtual world, for that is how residents experience them when they are inworld. Exploring these connections does not entail that every research project on virtual worlds must have an actual-world component. Second Life has trees, which reference trees in the actual world, but if I were to study trees in Second Life it would not always be necessary that I take bark samples from actual-world trees. When the American Cancer Society held a fundraiser in Second Life, I studied how that showed up in Second Life, without any methodological need to go to the headquarters of the American Cancer Society in Atlanta, Georgia (just as very few Second Life residents who participated in that fundraiser traveled to Atlanta).

I am fortunate that this book represented a second project alongside my research in Indonesia: this helped me see how many of the issues raised about ethnography in virtual worlds are common to ethnographic research anywhere. As a result, I will sometimes draw out parallels between my ethnographic work in Second Life and in Indonesia. I do this to illustrate as clearly as possible that not every challenge of researching online culture is unique to that online context. For instance, much of my research in Indonesia concerns gay Indonesians. Both I and these Indonesians are quite clear that the term "gay" comes from outside Indonesia, but when conducting ethnography in Indonesia I do not spend time in San Francisco; I study the term "gay" as it shows up in Indonesia itself. It is not true that every study of, say, Puerto Ricans in New York City is flawed if the researcher does not conduct research in Puerto Rico as well. Treating Second Life as a culture need not imply that it is mistakenly set apart; all ethnographic research has a limited scope, and speaking of the inhabitants of "Indonesia" or "New York City" does not mean one is failing to take forms of interconnection into account.

The goal of *Coming of Age in Second Life* is to demonstrate the existence of a relatively enduring cultural logic shared in some way by those who participate in Second Life, though their stances toward this cultural logic differ. There are many fascinating and distinct subcultures in Second Life, some of which I address in this book and others that I hope to address in future publications. But Second Life is more than the sum of its subcultures, and in this book my primary goal is to explore overarching cultural norms. The idea that culture is like a language has led many astray in the history of social thought.[2] However, one way in which the metaphor (or exemplification) is illuminating is that members of a culture share many things—assumptions, practices, forms of social relations—as speakers of a language share grammar and vocabulary, even when they use that language to disagree. It is these shared elements that make it possible to speak of "English" or "Indonesian," even as we recognize dialects, multilingualism, and fuzzy boundaries between languages. Similarly persons participate in Second Life in many ways, and there are fundamental disagreements over what Second Life is and should be, but these variations and disagreements are only intelligible because articulated against a set of grounding assumptions.

As an anthropologist I examine mundane social interaction in order to identify as many of these grounding assumptions as possible, assumptions whose taken-for-grantedness means they are not always the topic of explicit commentary. I work to show how these assumptions articulate with each other, the histories from which they draw their coherence, and the differing ways those in Second Life follow, transform, and resist them. I do not claim to know how everyone in Second Life thinks and feels (just as I do not claim to know how every Indonesian thinks and feels), only to provide some partial insight into Second Life culture. The ethnography of virtual worlds should not take the methodological form of "culture at a distance"—as when Ruth Benedict, in *The Chrysanthemum and the Sword*, studied Japanese culture during World War II without setting foot in Japan (Benedict 1946). The social sciences and humanities have only begun to acknowledge the speed with which virtual worlds are becoming taken for granted among all age groups and actual-world geographies. What promise do "traditional" anthropological methods hold for studying virtual worlds, which might appear so radically new as to render such methods irrelevant?

ANTHROPOLOGY AND ETHNOGRAPHY.

The task of this chapter is to explain how I gathered my data, and along the way to raise general points about methodologies for virtual anthropology (or "the ethnography of virtual worlds"). I prefer "virtual anthropology" to "virtual ethnography" because "to qualify the term *ethnography* with the term *virtual* is to suggest that online research remains less real (and ultimately less valuable) than research conducted offline" (Campbell 2004:52). Anthropologists typically do not speak of "legal ethnography," "medical ethnography," and so on: they speak of "legal *anthropology*," "medical *anthropology*," and now virtual *anthropology* as subdisciplines for which an unqualified "ethnography" is the modality.

"Ethnography" is the method anthropologists and others use to study "culture," one of the discipline's originary concepts. In his famous 1871 definition Edward B. Tylor, a founding figure in anthropology, termed culture "that complex whole which includes knowledge, belief, art, morals, law, custom, and any other capabilities and habits acquired by man as a member of society" (Tylor 1871:1). More compelling definitions of culture have appeared since that time, but this early characterization provides a helpful starting point. Tylor refers to a "complex whole"—and what is a virtual world if not a complex whole, however networked?—defined in terms of "capabilities and habits" rather than knowledge and belief; that is, by techne rather than episteme. Since approximately the 1980s, many in anthropology and elsewhere have critiqued the culture concept for eliding issues of difference, inequality, and materiality. Such critiques extend back to the early decades of anthropology, for instance, in British social anthropology, which tended to see "culture" as a German, romantic concept that obfuscated social dynamics (Radcliffe-Brown 1952 [1940]). Most contemporary ethnographers now use the concept in a more refined manner, harking back to Geertz's formulation that as humans we are "incomplete or unfinished animals who complete or finish ourselves through culture—and not through culture in general but through highly particular forms of it" (Geertz 1973a:49). I speak of "culture in virtual worlds" rather than "virtual culture" to underscore how cultures in virtual worlds are simply new, "highly particular" forms of culture.

How to conduct research in virtual worlds has long been a source of consternation. Some of the most significant analyses of virtual worlds have been produced by writers of fiction, and also by persons whose blogs and websites insightfully explore various aspects of cybersociality. Scholars and practitioners from a range of fields including media studies, computer science, informatics, psychology, sociology, literary studies, and cultural studies have also made significant contributions. Yet since the emergence of a scholarly literature on virtual worlds in the early 1990s, many have wondered about the role of a "postorganic anthropology" in understanding them (Tomas 1991:33). Where are the anthropologists? Anthropologists have shed their discipline's Malinowskian associations with the study of "primitive" and "isolated" societies. However, despite the growing enthusiasm for ethnography in virtual worlds, anthropologists—supposedly the experts in ethnographic methods—have been latecomers to the conversation. While a few anthropologists have been involved in online research, in general the discipline has been slow to recognize the foundationally cultural character of virtual worlds, and thus the promise of ethnographic methods for studying them.

Although now commonly identified as useful (e.g., Fornäs et al. 2002:4), some online researchers employ the term "ethnography" in unclear ways. Judith Donath, for instance, identifies it as "an interpretation of closely examined social discourse," but in equating ethnography with interpretation she is silent on what methods are to be used, as well as what constitutes close examination (Donath 1999:31). Most research published before my own investigated text-based formats, including IRC and MUDs, or graphical virtual worlds with a combat emphasis, like Everquest or World of Warcraft. It is possible to research these important virtual worlds ethnographically (e.g., Nardi and Harris 2006), but in terms of methodological experimentation they have limitations. Frank Schaap noted with reference to his research in the role-playing Cybersphere MOO that "I felt I couldn't play an anthropologist as a character, because I didn't know how to fit an Anthropologist or a Researcher into the theme of the world" (2002:29). Researchers in text-based virtual worlds often made assumptions about visuality and embodiment that are simply not applicable to graphical contexts where three-dimensional visualization is fundamental to sociality. Only in the context of text-based virtual worlds could one claim that "by definition online ethnography describes places that are not spaces. Disembodied persons people these places" (Rutter and Smith 2005:84). The idea that online observation and interviewing "might be as legitimate for ethnography as is face-to-face-interaction" (Fornäs et al. 2002:38) assumes that what takes place via the Internet is not "face-to-face." While language is certainly important to the ethnography of virtual worlds, such ethnography is not "language-centered," as in the case of research on online archives (Fabian 2002).

Many analyses of online culture have used symbolic or semiotic frameworks that define culture in terms of knowledge of schemas, cognitive maps, and meaning (e.g., Salen and Zimmerman 2004). Such definitions reflect the mid-twentieth-century "cognitive" anthropological belief that "a society's culture consists of whatever it is one has to know or believe in order to operate in a manner acceptable to its members" (Goodenough 1964:36). Such a view of culture in terms of episteme rather than techne may be attractive to some with backgrounds in game studies because it is congruent with an understanding of social relations in terms of rules. Rules are often identified as the foundational characteristic of anything to be termed a game (De Koven 1978:45; von Neumann and Morgenstern 1944:49); game design, programming, and even playing a game can be seen as crafting, coding, or implementing rules. This has led some researchers to speculate on the possibility that virtual worlds could be manipulated by researchers, providing "the opportunity to see large-scale social outcomes from a truly probabilistic, experimental perspective as in a petri dish" (Castronova 2006:183). None-theless viewing culture in terms of rules—rather than in terms of Tylor's more prescient emphasis on capability and habit—has serious limitations. Geertz observed how viewing culture in terms of rules confuses a derived representation with lived social experience; it is like confusing the score of a Beethoven quartet "with the skills and knowledge needed to play it, with the understanding of it possessed by its performers and auditors" (Geertz 1983:11). As Malinowski noted at the outset of the anthropological enter-prise, "the Ethnographer has in the field . . . the duty before him of drawing up all the rules and regularities. . . . But these things, though crystallized and set, are nowhere explicitly *formulated*" (Malinowski 1922:11).

This impoverished model of culture in terms of knowing rules has methodological implications. It implies that learning a culture is like learn-ing the rules of a game. Since players cannot play a game unless they know they are playing a game and know the rules of that game, it further suggests that people can describe their culture when asked, implying one can learn how a culture works through elicitation methods. By "elicitation methods" I mean methods like interviews or surveys that involve asking questions and receiving answers. In contrast, participant observation is the central meth-odology for ethnography because it does not require that aspects of culture be available for conscious reflection. It allows the researcher to become in-volved in crafting events as they occur; participant observation is itself a form of techne. Elicitation methods assume people are able to articulate the various aspects of the cultures that shape their thinking. Yet even a simple example from language shows how this assumption limits our methodolog-ical reach. To try to understand virtual worlds based on elicitation methods is like trying to construct a grammar of English by asking speakers to de-scribe how English works. Few English speakers would be able to explain, for instance, that the first "n" in "inconceivable" becomes "m" in words like "impossible" because the following sound ("p," in this case) is a bilabial plo-sive (that is, made with the lips) and as a result the "n" sound shifts to a bilabial articulation as well. Yet any English speaker "knows" this phono-logical rule even if they cannot describe it. Like language, many aspects of culture are only imperfectly available for conscious reflection. They take the form of "common sense": in culture "what is essential goes without saying because it comes without saying" (Bourdieu 1977:167). Research on virtual worlds can make effective use of elicitation methods, but must also move beyond them to develop methods based upon techne, not just episteme.

Some aspects of Malinowski's legacy help explain why anthropologists and nonanthropologists alike have been slow to acknowledge the usefulness of ethnography for studying virtual worlds. Matti Bunzl has argued that Franz Boas (1858–1942), a founding figure in United States anthropology, might prove a better historical model. Bunzl notes that "in a Malinowskian framework, the production of anthropological knowledge was a function of mere observation, as long as it occurred across—and, thereby, reproduced—a cultural chasm between ethnographic Self and native Other" (Bunzl 2004:438). This supposed cultural chasm has led many to mistakenly conclude that ethnography will not be objective if researchers are similar to (or personally involved with) those they study, with the result that persons conducting ethnographic research in communities to which they somehow belong may see themselves as "virtual anthropologists" (Weston 1997). In contrast, "in Boas's fieldwork, a constitutive epistemological separation between ethnographer and native was absent" (Bunzl 2004:438). Thus, "Boasian anthropology did not produce 'native' anthropology as the *virtual* Other of 'real' anthropology" (Bunzl 2004:439, emphasis added). Franz Boas was Margaret Mead's teacher at Columbia and wrote the foreword to *Coming of Age in Samoa*. Like Mead, in this book I draw upon a Boasian framework that seeks equality and complicity rather than hierarchy and distance. To some, ethnographic research (including this book) may seem "anecdotal," but such an interpretation fails to recognize how ethnographic research connects seemingly isolated incidents of cultural interchange (Malaby 2006c). This is what Boas identified as a "cosmological" approach to knowledge, which "considers every phenomenon as worthy of being studied for its own sake. Its mere existence entitles it to a full share of our attention; and the knowledge of its existence and evolution in space and time fully satisfies the student" (Boas 1887:642). By holding at bay the scientistic rush to comparison and generalization (often before the phenomena at hand are properly identified and understood), ethnographic analysis "can be crucial . . . for imagining the kinds of communities that human groups can create with the help of emerging technologies" (Escobar 1994; see also Jacobson 1996).

As discussed further below, the open-endedness of Second Life meant that I was able to subordinate interviews and surveys to participant observation, the centerpiece of any truly ethnographic approach. Not only did I create the avatar Tom Bukowski; I shopped for clothes for my avatar in the same stores as any Second Life resident. I bought land with the help of a real estate agent and learned how to use Second Life's building tools.[3] I then created a home and office for my research named "Ethnographia," purchasing items like textures, furniture, and artwork. I learned games created and played inside Second Life, like "Tringo" (a combination of Tetris and Bingo) and "primtionary" (a variant of Pictionary). I wandered across the Second

Life landscape, flying, teleporting, or floating along in my hot air balloon, stopping to investigate events, buildings, or people I happened to encounter. I also used the "events" list and notices in Second Life publications to learn of interesting places to visit. In turn, many people stumbled upon my house, either during leisurely explorations of their own or to attend an event I was hosting. I joined many Second Life groups and participated in a range of activities, from impromptu relationship counseling to larger-scale events like a community fair. While I did not seek notoriety, on one occasion my activities garnered brief actual-world press—namely, my experiment of having a friend who was running for city council in my actual-world hometown of Long Beach, California acquire an avatar and hold a campaign event, the first case of an actual-world political candidate appearing in Second Life.

All this experience did not give me a totalizing understanding of Second Life. Ethnographic knowledge is situated and partial; just as most Indonesians have spent more time in Indonesia than I and know many things about Indonesia that I do not know, so many Second Life residents spent more time inworld than I, and every resident had some kind of knowledge about the virtual world that I lacked. One of the many things I did gain from my research was a network of acquaintances and friends, all of whom knew of my research, since my "profile" mentioned that I was an anthropologist. I was struck by how the idea of someone conducting ethnography made sense to residents. My interest tended to be slotted into the kind of reflexivity and curiosity that was common in Second Life, showing up in everything from blogs to the large number of journalists and educators active inworld. Residents often commented upon my seeming comfort with Second Life, particularly my skills at building (an unexpected benefit of my growing up as a video gamer). One resident noted "you seem so comfy in here—like you study it yet still live it." I also encountered residents already familiar with anthropology, as in the following exchange:

> URMA: Do you conduct field research . . . participant observation?
> ME: Yeah, participant observation, but also interviews and focus groups
> URMA: Its an interesting topic, Virtual Lives. And its not like you have to go some exotic land. I mean . . . it's a far-off place, but it's not like you're studying the culture of the River Valley Dani [in Papua New Guinea, an Indonesian province] or anything lol

I found remarkable the degree to which the challenges and joys of my research in Second Life resembled the challenges and joys of my research in Indonesia. Claims of a methodological chasm between virtual and actual are overstated. For example, Jennifer Sundén's question "How then to start writing a culture that is already written?" is provocative (Sundén 2003:18), but the phrasing elides how actual-world cultures are also "written" in that they are the product of human artifice. I thus disagree with any claim that with regard to virtual worlds "there is no incontrovertible basis on which to decide whether an approach is or is not ethnographic" (Hine 2005:8). I would turn to Marilyn Strathern's thesis that "the nature of ethnography entailed in anthropology's version of fieldwork" involves "the deliberate attempt to generate more data than the investigator is aware of at the time of collection . . . Rather than devising research protocols that will purify the data in advance of analysis, the anthropologist embarks on a participatory exercise which yields materials for which analytical protocols are often devised after the fact" (Strathern 2004:5–6). Mead herself summed up this vision of the ethnographic project as an "open-mindedness with which one must look and listen, record in astonishment and wonder, that which one would not have been able to guess" (Mead 1950:xxvi).

PARTICIPANT OBSERVATION.

In line with its status as ethnography's signature method, this book is built around an analysis of social interaction gathered through participant observation. Some disciplines focus on the conscious products of culture: texts, dances, codes of law. Anthropologists examine these too, but prioritize the everyday contexts in which people live. A Second Life resident once commented on my participant observation methodology by noting that: "you're mixing up two agendas in Second Life. The research and presumably, just fun and games too. Don't you find that one affects your perceptions of the other?" My chat log reveals that I answered by saying "it's what anthropologists call 'participant observation,' and it does shatter the illusion, but anthropologists tend to believe that methods like surveys give the illusion of objectivity." I also noted that when conducting participant observation research in Indonesia, I also have "fun and games," spending time with friends or going to a movie.

There is no illusion of detached objectivity to shatter in participant observation because it is not a methodology that views the researcher as a contaminant. It constantly confronts the differing forms of power and hierarchy produced through fieldwork, not all of which privilege the researcher. The term "participant observation" is intentionally oxymoronic; you cannot fully participate and fully observe at the same time, but it is in this paradox that ethnographers conduct their best work. Unlike elicitation methods, participant observation implies a form of ethical yet critical engagement between researcher and researched, even when the researcher is clearly not a member of the community being studied. It is "a method of being at risk in the face of the practices and discourses into which one inquires . . . [a] serious nonidentity that challenges previous stabilities, convictions, or ways of being . . . a mode of practical and theoretical attention, a way of remaining mindful and accountable" (Haraway 1997:190–91). It has long been identified as a method based on vulnerability, even failure, on learning from mistakes: "over and over again, I committed breaches of etiquette, which the natives, familiar enough with me, were not slow in pointing out" (Malinowski 1922:8).

A common tactic in writing on virtual worlds is to emphasize the sensational: men participating as women; nonnormative sex practices like sadomasochism; persons earning large sums of actual-world money through online enterprises. Looking to the unusual to tell us about culture, however, is of limited use. If in the actual world we were to do nothing but read the headlines of our newspapers, magazines, and television reports, we would not have an accurate understanding of everyday life. Similarly extraordinary events in Second Life are fascinating, but paint a misleading picture of its culture. Ethnographers are not oblivious to the newsworthy or the extraordinary, but find that culture is lived out in the mundane and the ordinary. The goal is to find methods attuned to the banal dimensions of human life, what Pierre Bourdieu termed the "habitus": "a subjective but not individual system of internalized structures, schemes of perception, conception, and action" (Bourdieu 1977:86).

To illustrate how participant observation works to discover culture through nonelicited, everyday interaction, consider the following scene, taken with only minor modifications directly from my fieldnotes. On the day in question it was 9:16 p.m. local time when, having logged onto Second Life a few minutes earlier, I took up my friend Kimmy's invitation to come see her new house. I teleported to her location and found myself in the kitchen of a standard-looking two-story house standing on a small island; similar islands dotted the landscape nearby, fitted out with other homes. Kimmy was hanging out with her friend BettyAnne, and the three of us moved to Kimmy's new living room to talk, watching palm trees sway outside the window. Fifteen minutes later, my chat log recorded that we were discussing going to play a game of golf when an unknown person, "Laura," teleported into the kitchen:

> ME: Hello Laura!
> KIMMY: Hi Laura . . . can I help you?

LAURA: Hi, I'm new. Just arrived.

KIMMY: Ahh, she's a noob [newbie]

LAURA: Is it possible to change my clothes now?

ME: Yes, right click on yourself and choose "appearance"

KIMMY: Here are some clothes. If you go to inventory at the bottom right, they should be in your clothing folder

LAURA: ty [thank you]

KIMMY: If you right click the clothing and pick "wear," you should be able to wear it

LAURA: How about my hair? It's a mess.

KIMMY: Hmm. I wish I had some prim hair to give you, but I can't transfer any of it. You'll have to go into "appearance" and play with the sliders.

KIMMY: I can give you some landmarks for some great clothing stores though

KIMMY: I got my hair at that place I just gave you a landmark for

LAURA: I'd love some

KIMMY: Check the upper right hand corner. How much money do you have?

LAURA: Zero so far. how can I earn some?

KIMMY: Ah. do you have a freebie account?

LAURA: Yeah, I didn't know which one to choose

ME: The easiest way to "earn" money is to convert dollars into linden dollars using a credit card

KIMMY: Alright, if you had a pay account they would give you money every Tuesday

LAURA: Ty. I will look into it

ME: You can also earn money in a zillion ways but they aren't always easy lol—selling things, stuff like that

KIMMY: The only way you can earn money other than that is dancing at a club, being a stripper or an escort lol . . . or find some other job that has a boss that pays you to do a service of some sort.

LAURA: I might go for a look around. Nice talking to you.

KIMMY: Nice to meet you, Laura, keep in touch

LAURA: Alright Kimmy and BettyAnne and Tom, bye :)

[Laura's avatar disappears]

BETTYANNE: Aww, she looks just like I did

KIMMY: lol

KIMMY: We're all born like that

This innocuous scene began when Laura teleported into Kimmy's house as Kimmy, BettyAnne, and myself were talking. Laura probably saw green dots on the world map indicating that three persons were at this location, and came to investigate. We saw her wandering around in the kitchen, looking lost, but she could have been someone bent on "griefing" (harassing or mistreating others, see chapter 7) so we were cautious. Kimmy, BettyAnne, and I clicked on "Laura" to obtain her profile, which informed us that the avatar had been created that very day, meaning she could be an additional avatar (or "alt") of a longtime resident, or the primary avatar of someone entering Second Life for the first time.

It quickly became clear that the latter was the case; Laura was, as Kimmy put it, a "noob" or "newbie" (or doing a convincing job of appearing to be a newbie). When Laura asked how to change her clothes, Kimmy, who had some free-to-copy women's clothes in her inventory, gave some to Laura and explained how to access them. Such generosity was common in Second Life during my fieldwork. Laura's appearance changed as she put on the clothes Kimmy had given her: a pair of faded jeans, a tank top showing off her virtual shoulders. Laura then asked about hair and Kimmy said she wished she had "prim hair" to give her, but "can't transfer" it. "Prim hair" was hair constructed from prims, the objects used to make everything from vehicles to buildings, and was typically better-looking than the default hair that came with one's avatar. However, all of the prim hair Kimmy had was "no transfer"—copies of it could not be given away. This was because prim hair was a relatively valuable commodity and those who sold it usually made their creations "no transfer." Although Kimmy could not give Laura any of the prim hair she had previously purchased, she could give Laura "landmarks" that contained information about the location of stores that sold prim hair.

It was through this commodity that the conversation turned to economic matters. Kimmy told Laura to check the upper-right hand corner of her screen and see how much money she had. Laura replied "zero," which refers to Linden dollars (one U.S. dollar was trading for about 280 Linden dollars at the time). Laura asked "how can I earn some [money]." Kimmy did not answer directly but inquired after what kind of account Laura had. At this point in Second Life's existence there were three levels of membership: a free account with no verification of payment method (like the successful use of a credit card), a free account where a payment method had been verified, which implied the person's actual-world identity was known to Linden Lab; and a "premium" account that cost $9.95 a month (six dollars a month if paid yearly). This premium account, which Kimmy termed a "pay account," paid back about $1.50 in Linden dollars each week at the time, and also allowed one to own land. I mentioned to Laura that she could sell things in Second Life and Kimmy added that she could also make money for service work, including being a stripper or escort. Having received advice and free clothing, Laura thanked Kimmy, BettyAnne, and myself for our help and teleported away to explore some other part of Second Life. After Laura left, BettyAnne said "aww, she looks just like I did," referring to the unadorned and generic look of Laura's brand-new avatar. "We're all born like that," Kimmy replied.

This unassuming excerpt from my thousands of pages of fieldnotes reveals how ethnographic methods draw upon participant observation to find social meanings as they are implicitly forged and sustained in everyday interaction. From this excerpt we gain insight into a range of cultural domains, from gender (discussions about clothing, hair, and work as a stripper involved female-gendered avatars, though the persons involved might be male or transgendered in the actual world), to economics, to ideas about an avatar life course (in which people are "born" as "newbies" and then mature), to language (such as the use of "lol" for "laugh out loud," or the use of emoticons like ":)" for a smiley face). Crucially through such participant observation data we can see links between these cultural domains: rather than an interview or survey that asks about gender, then about economics, and so on, through participant observation we can see which cultural domains crop up together and how they are interconnected. Participant observation demonstrates the historically specific character of "common sense," revealing it to be not "human nature" but culture, one valid yet particular way of living a human life.

When conducting ethnography in virtual worlds, the ability to do things like save chat logs and record audio or video is a great boon in comparison to actual-world environments where audio recording can be disruptive and one is often forced to rely on memory or hastily handwritten notes. However, the ease of obtaining data in virtual worlds can also be a curse, because those very processes of memory and handwriting force ethnographers to focus on what seem to be the most consequential incidents encountered during participant observation. Ethnographers of virtual worlds often face the challenge of filtering through large amounts of data. My own data set constituted over ten thousand pages of fieldnotes from participant observation, interviewing, and focus groups, plus approximately ten thousand additional pages of blogs, newsletters, and other websites.

INTERVIEWS, FOCUS GROUPS, AND BEYOND THE PLATFORM.

Research is most effective when each component method is keyed to a specific set of questions. Participant observation is useful for gaining a conceptual handle on cultural assumptions that may not be overtly discussed. In comparison to the more isolated contexts of surveys and interviews, it is useful for seeing what kinds of practices and beliefs emerge as members of a particular culture interact with each other. Participant observation can illuminate debates and issues of which the researcher was unaware prior to the research, and so could not have thought to include on a list of interview questions or a survey form. For these reasons, participant observation must be the fundamental method of any full-fledged ethnography. However, anthropologists have always used many methods in addition to participant observation (Ortner 2006:81). In my earlier fieldwork in Indonesia I complemented participant observation with interviews, archival research, the analysis of texts, and focus groups. I found all of these ancillary methods helpful for my research in Second Life as well.

I conducted about thirty formal interviews and thirty informal interviews during my fieldwork. By "formal interview" I mean an interview where I explicitly asked a resident "may I interview you about your experiences in Second Life" and the resident consented. I used a consent form for these interviews, as I did in Indonesia (see figure 3.1). The form was reviewed and approved by the Institutional Review Board at my university (as was my research overall); it would be signed by the resident typing "I agree to participate in your study." As in most ethnographic projects I selected interviewees through a procedure where those already interviewed would recommend acquaintances, or I would discover such persons through my own participant observation. Such a "snowball sampling" method is inappropriate for statistical research, but is a desirable approach for ethnographers, who typically acknowledge their partiality and seek to trace social networks rather than artificially isolate members of a culture through randomization.

Interviews can be highly effective when placed in the context of participant observation. Culture can be implicit and even subconscious, but much of it is part of everyday awareness; members of a culture can sometimes be its most eloquent interpreters. In the case of my research, interviews allowed residents to reflect upon their virtual lives and discuss what they saw as significant or interesting aspects of Second Life. Their insights then fed back into my participant observation, in that I learned about new topics or social groups to investigate. While there is a clear hierarchy in any interview context, Second Life residents typically found being interviewed to be a re-

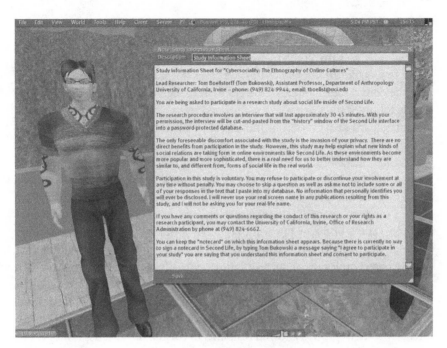

FIGURE 3.1. The consent form used for interviews inside of Second Life (image by author).

warding experience. They appreciated the chance to talk though issues they had often been pondering for some time; interviews were often two-way affairs, with the "interviewee" asking questions to which I would respond. I did not have any problem getting people to agree to an interview. I faced having a list of people wishing to be interviewed; after being interviewed, many residents asked to be interviewed again, or became friends with whom I would socialize on a regular basis. I purposely worked to interview a spectrum of residents, including residents I met in shopping malls, clubs, and other informal contexts, even persons who randomly happened to fly past my house. On a few occasions I conducted group interviews with up to four residents at once. Sometimes this was because a friend of a resident dropped in while the resident was being interviewed and wished to join in. In other cases I interviewed couples in an intimate relationship, or even three people in a polyamorous relationship, as well as persons who were kin in the actual world (a husband and wife, or siblings, or a parent and child).

In addition to these formal interviews, I conducted about the same number of informal interviews that grew out of participant observation. For instance, it often happened that I would be participating in some activity with three or four residents and fall into a conversation about our experiences in Second Life. Then over a period of time, all of the residents would log off save one, and my conversation with that one remaining resident would began to feel like an interview. In such cases it was usually not appropriate to stop the conversation and ask the resident to sign a consent form; instead, I simply followed the normal ethical procedures I would follow when conducing participant observation in Indonesia (see below).

During my research in Indonesia I held a series of focus groups, but found them unhelpful given the amount of work it took to organize them. In Second Life the logistical barriers to convening a group of people were less significant, but despite this fact focus groups were not a core methodology. I created my own group, "Digital Cultures," and held about forty meetings of the group at my home or the homes of other group members throughout my research. These focus groups were organized around a "blurb," or topic that I wrote based on issues of current interest identified through my participant observation work and suggestions by Second Life residents (figure 3.2). The meetings lasted an hour and drew up to forty residents (the maximum number of avatars that most sims could contain during my fieldwork). Unlike interviews, focus groups allowed residents to collectively discuss issues about Second Life. Side conversations and digressions provided their own data, revealing connections residents were drawing between different domains of

FIGURE 3.2. A focus group at my home in Second Life, Ethnographia (image by author).

Second Life culture. Because focus groups were advertised on the Second Life "events" database, they tended to draw residents with an interest in intellectual debate. This makes the over 1,000 pages of chat text I gathered from focus groups more specific than that I gathered from participant observation or even interviews, but "specific" does not mean "biased." The persons who participated in focus groups participated in a wide range of activities and were far from homogenous in their understandings of Second Life culture.

While there were residents whose experience was limited to the virtual world itself, often known as "the grid,"[4] for many residents websites, blogs, and even full-fledged periodicals (with staff and advertising) were important, and so I drew upon these as well. Through these media residents offered analysis and commentary on many aspects of the virtual world. As an individual researcher, I could not familiarize myself with every subculture or region of Second Life (just I have not been to many parts of Indonesia). Resident-produced media provided valuable information about parts of Second Life I did not personally research on an intensive basis.[5]

ETHICS.

Any form of inquiry raises the question of power relationships between the researcher and those studied. The details vary depending upon the personal history of the investigator, the status of the communities examined, and the methodology used, but concerns regarding ethics persist. For some time, anthropologists have examined the implications of the fact that their discipline, like all social scientific and humanistic disciplines, was first formalized in nineteenth-century contexts of colonial encounter (Asad 1973). Questions of power, complicity, and accountability remain part of any ethnographic project—not uncomfortable realities to be broached then set aside, but important sources of insight and collaboration. Such issues are widely seen as pressing with regard to virtual worlds: "online research is marked as a special category in which the institutionalized understandings of the ethics of research must be re-examined" (Hine 2005:5; see also Kendall 2002:241–43). My research was thus not just an experiment in methodology, but an experiment in the ethics of virtual anthropology.

During my research I worked to avoid being identified with any particular subset of residents, although I could only join a limited number of groups and spent more time with some residents than others. My avatar took on different fashions, genders, and even species during my research, but my default embodiment was both white and male, in line with my actual-world embodiment, and I was also openly gay. When debates or conflict broke out in my presence, I did not feign neutrality (I would, for instance, file an "Abuse Report" if I saw someone mistreating another resident), and gave my own opinions in informal conversations, interviews, and focus groups. However, I did work to interact with residents whose political and personal views might not reflect my own.

There is often a misunderstanding of "cultural relativism" that portrays anthropologists as believing there is no way to judge cultures or decide between right and wrong: as if in culture X they believe in killing every third-born child, then we would have no right to say that should not happen. In fact, anthropologists make prescriptive judgments all the time and even work to change cultures, as in the case of my HIV prevention work in Indonesia. Anthropologists know that claims like "in culture X they believe in killing every third-born child" mistakenly assume that cultures are homogenous, without dissent or debate, and do not change over time. The point is not to avoid prescription but to keep description and prescription distinct. For instance, if there were a culture in which some members believed in killing every third-born child, there would be utility in working to understand the cultural logics by which this made sense, without thereby condoning the practice.

In addition to a primary account (like my Tom Bukowski avatar), many Second Life residents also had one or more alternative avatars or "alts"— entirely different avatars with different screen names. The two accounts were indistinguishable from avatars held by two separate persons. I briefly tried experimenting with an alt, but soon decided it was ethically and methodologically inadequate for ethnographic research. I never hid the fact that I was conducting research, going so far as to include this information in my profile. Any resident could read this profile and see that Tom Bukowski was an anthropologist. With an alt, such information would not be available unless I listed it on the alt's profile as well, negating the purpose of an alt in the first place. It might seem that alts could allow an anthropologist to observe an undisturbed culture in action, where people spoke freely without realizing there was a researcher in their midst. What this perspective misses is that ethnography is predicated on *participant* observation, not abstracted observation. Conducting research with an alt would not allow the tension between participating and observing to produce the kinds of complicity and failure that are necessary for ethnographic knowledge.[6]

Aside from the issue of alts, ethical questions can arise due to the possibility that persons could be sitting with the researcher in the actual world. Seeing only the researcher's avatar, residents of the virtual world would not know that additional people were watching the computer screen. I became aware of this issue when, on a handful of occasions, I had such actual-world onlookers. In one case, a colleague sat with me in my actual-world office while I was online with Kiancha, a Second Life acquaintance:

ME: Hey Kiancha, can't talk long but I have a friend here in my office interested in sl, say hello!

KIANCHA: I'd love to meet your friend.

ME: My friend is really impressed—hasn't been in a virtual world before

KIANCHA: Hello, friend of Tom. Where are you?

ME: She's here with me in California, lol

KIANCHA: Ha, she doesn't have an avatar yet, eh?

ME: No, not yet, but who knows?

KIANCHA: Tom is really super at adding content to this game, friend.

Note how in this exchange, Kiancha tried to reach beyond the screen and address my friend, asking "where are you?" Since my friend did not have an avatar, I was forced to respond on her behalf. The friend could have typed a response on my computer's keyboard, but the response would have come from my avatar, only adding to the confusion. Despite these barriers, Kiancha still moved between addressing me ("she doesn't have an avatar yet, eh?") and the virtually absent friend ("Tom is really super at adding content," a reference to my discussion groups).

On three occasions I gave conference presentations where I had twenty or thirty people looking over my virtual shoulder in this way. These experiences were even more disconcerting; unlike the example with Kiancha above, there was no way for a Second Life resident to respond to a multitude of virtually disembodied persons. Since they did not have avatars, participants in these conferences also found it hard to relate to me as an avatarized self (Tom Bukowski), and in two instances asked me to exit Second Life in order to address them in the actual world. After these experiences I decided to forbid actual-world persons to observe me online without having avatars of their own, so that they could participate in the virtual world like any other resident.

It is ethically preferable to use a consent form for interviews or any elicitation method; this is because unlike participant observation, elicitation methods create a social situation that would not exist otherwise. For my Second Life research, I had residents sign this consent form using only their screen names. I did this because another aspect to my ethical and methodological practice was that I did not try to verify any aspect of residents' actual-world lives. Residents did not typically offer such information or find it relevant. On those occasions where a resident would provide such information (for instance, that they were disabled, living in Germany, or a forty-eight-year-old housewife with two children), I did not try to confirm these statements. What was important were the contexts in which such information came up and what such information was supposed to accomplish: for instance, did other residents interpret it as a sign of trust or intimacy?

This question of the actual-world lives of residents of virtual worlds extends to the most fundamental questions of selfhood, with important methodological consequences. One could imagine a situation where an actual-world person "Sam" had two avatars, "Jenny" and "Rick," and invested the time so that each avatar had its own social network. One could then imagine an ethnographer like myself interviewing Jenny and Rick on different days without realizing that I was interviewing "Sam" twice. I do not think such a thing happened during my research, but the methodological and theoretical point is that in an important sense it would not matter: Jenny and Rick would be distinct social actors in Second Life, and this would be sufficient warrant to interview each of them. The reverse situation could also take place, for example where "George" and "Donna," a married couple in the actual world, take turns controlling the single avatar "Jenny" in Second Life. I might then interact with Jenny on two different days without realizing that on the first day I was "actually" talking to George, and on the second day "actually" talking to Donna. Since Jenny would be a single social actor and other residents might well know nothing of George and Donna, it would be appropriate to treat my ethnographic data about "Jenny" as coming from a single person.

In my research (as in any ethnographic project), questions of ethics extend from research to writing: it is in its published form that my research has the greatest potential to have positive or negative effects upon Second Life's residents.[7] The most fundamental ethical decision—one I made with regard to my Indonesia research as well—was to maintain confidentiality with regard to resident identities, to protect privacy with regard to their virtual and actual lives. Even when residents said I could name them, I have employed pseudonyms so as not to inadvertently identify their friends. This devotion to confidentiality may seem quaint, since in the context of the Internet there appears to be little remaining expectation of privacy. Typically residents knew that anything they said could be recorded by Linden Lab, by residents nearby, or by a scripted object hidden on a piece of land, and that such recorded information could then be disseminated via a blog or other form of website. Nonetheless attempts to respect privacy were common in Second Life during the time of my research; for instance, residents normally asked permission to quote other residents if writing something for public consumption.

A twist to this principle is that I have also used pseudonyms for the virtual-world identities or "screen names" of Second Life residents.[8] As discussed later, the screen name is the one unchangeable aspect of a Second Life account (as in many virtual worlds), and significant meaning is attached to it. I have also changed details about residents' virtual-world lives that could be used to identify them. I have paraphrased quotations from my residents to make them difficult to identify using a search engine. In some cases I combine quotations from more than one person, or change details of a location or incident, so that the original event cannot be discerned from the narrative. Some may think they can determine the identities of those I discuss in this book, but it will be impossible to know for sure.

The importance of using confidentiality to protect privacy was illustrated by a controversy that broke out in Second Life in October 2004. A professor was teaching a freshman English course focusing on how technology affects communication. Students in the course were given an assignment to spend time in Second Life and write about their experiences. Unfortunately some of these students began posting derisive online commentaries, complete with chat excerpts that included the screen names of Second Life residents. Several discussions were held in Second Life to defuse the controversy, which could have been avoided had the students been trained in ethnographic methods. There are also theoretical reasons for maintaining confidentiality. Confidentiality deemphasizes individual personalities, allowing for a focus on broader cultural logics. In virtual worlds there is often a tendency to emphasize controversies and celebrities; ethnography's real promise lies in showing how banal, unassuming aspects of everyday life have profound consequences for how we think and act.

CLAIMS AND REFLEXIVITY.

Like all ethnographies, this book is a form of situated knowledge (Haraway 1988), one story of Second Life during a particular period of time. As one person in Second Life put it in a note to those new to the virtual world, "the fundamental rule of Second Life is that everything changes constantly": a different person emphasized "leave Second Life for a week and it's like you've left the country for a decade." I began conducting fieldwork in Indonesia in 1992; since that time Indonesia has witnessed many social and political changes and its population grew from 190 million to about 225 million. In comparison, by the time I completed the manuscript for this book the number of registered accounts grew from 5,000 to over ten million, a 2,000-fold increase.

The purpose of any method is that it allows one to make claims. Statistical methods make claims based on the premise that the community studied has been sampled at random: a researcher might claim that one-third of Californians wish they ate more fruit, with a particular margin of error. Leaving aside all the ways we could debate the meaningfulness of such a claim, and acknowledging the power of quantitative methods to answer certain kinds of questions (e.g., Ducheneaut et al. 2006), it is clear that ethnographic claims work differently. For instance, during my Indonesia research I interviewed and conducted participant observation research with approximately as many persons as I did during my research in Second Life, but Indonesia is a populous nation spread over more than three thousand inhabited islands. In my book *The Gay Archipelago*, which focused on gay and lesbian Indonesians, I emphasized that by saying gay men and lesbian women were found *throughout* Indonesia I was not saying they were found *everywhere* in Indonesia (Boellstorff 2005:23); I also emphasized that I was not claiming I knew how every gay and lesbian Indonesian thought, only some insight into cultural assumptions shared by many such Indonesians. After spending a year with a group of ten or twenty Spaniards, most researchers would gain some fluency in the Spanish language. The language skills acquired could be used to converse with hundreds of millions of people worldwide, though one would not learn every vocabulary item or regional dialect. In an analogous manner, ethnography provides insight beyond the sample of persons with whom the ethnographer directly interacts. The mode of explication in ethnography is rarely the categorical claim or positivist law: "Everyone does X." Instead, ethnographers look for tendencies, habits, assumptions, things that are usually true: "In X society, women are usually ranked over children"; "In Y society, persons typically marry before they are thirty." In other words, ethnography seeks to know what is *virtually* true. Once again, ethnography comes to the virtual with the "virtual" already in hand.

While quantitative researchers use devices like margins of error and sample size to vouch for their claims, ethnographers rely on what James Clifford identified as "ethnographic authority" (Clifford 1983)—a researcher's claim that "I was there" and so can represent, even partially, the culture in question. In ethnographic writing, vignettes, italicized foreign terms, and long quotations often serve the problematic function of attempting to render the researcher transparent, so that the "real voices" of those studied can be "heard." In this regard it is instructive to note how some virtual-world researchers provide extensive excepts from chat logs. Typographical errors are often retained to give these excerpts a "naturalistic" feel; some researchers go so far as to place such excerpts in a Courier or Arial font that metaphorically stands in for a computer screen by working to "recall and reproduce the hyperbolic regularity of Machine Age typewriting" (Bukatman 1994:80; see, e.g., Baty 1999; Campbell 2004; Dibbell 2006; Kendall 2002; Kivits 2005; Markham 1998; Rheingold 2000; Schaap 2002). Such excerpts often appear as follows:

```
You are logged into ExampleMOO. You are in a
   small room with Sam and Joe.
Sam: hello there :)
Joe: how r u? whats going on?
You: Im fine!
```

These graphical and narrative devices lie squarely in the tradition of establishing ethnographic authority by having one's materials take on the appearance of "raw data." Such devices appear egalitarian but in fact create more hierarchy, because they imply that to disagree with a researcher's conclusions is to insinuate that the "voices" of those studied are themselves wrong. Must ethnographic authority depend upon a claim that the reader has access to the unmediated voices of those being studied? Or can ethnography work to illuminate culture through the imbrication of data and analysis, a rhetorical analogue to the paradox of "participant observation?"

Excerpts from fieldnotes are nothing new to anthropology, and I will provide such excerpts throughout this book, but I do not try to give them the appearance of raw data. I use the same fonts that I use elsewhere. Given the speed at which people typed and the large number of residents for whom English was not a first language, there was a high tolerance for typographical errors when chatting in Second Life. I have edited out most typographical errors for the sake of readability; this recalls how I translated excerpts from my Indonesia fieldwork into colloquial English. The only "naturalistic" elements I retain are a few emoticons (like :) for a smiley face) and common slang terms or contractions like "im" for "instant message" (such terms are referenced in the glossary).

An interesting aspect of doing research in virtual worlds is that no one is a true "native." Some residents began participating in Second Life earlier than others, but no one was born there. It has been a commonplace that anthropologists are never truly members of the cultures they study. Even for those who are in some way members of the societies in which they conduct research, the fact of being a researcher alters their relationship to the field-site. My self-identification as a researcher was meant to replicate this sense of distinction. Yet given that I entered Second Life when it had only 5,000 registered accounts, by the time my research ended I was approximately in the top 0.1 percent of oldest avatars. We were all members of an emergent cultural location for which not only dated terms like "native," but also their contemporary stand-ins, like "indigenous," were inapplicable.

PART II: CULTURE IN A VIRTUAL WORLD

Chapter 4

PLACE AND TIME

Visuality and land—Builds and objects—Lag—Afk—
Immersion—Presence.

VISUALITY AND LAND.

One evening in Second Life I received an instant message from an acquaintance, Samuel: "would you like to teleport real quick to see how blight is driving people crazy? There's another big sign demo out here in Greenacre." I accepted Samuel's teleport offer and after several moments of blackness was alongside him and five other people, floating in the air near two structures in the eastern part of the Greenacre sim. Below us was "Zazzy's," a black building with brightly colored windows, their neon reds, blues, yellows, and greens in a constantly changing pattern. Through the windows one could see a range of items for sale. "I'm sick about this," Samuel said. "This glowing monstrosity was just built on this land."

Looking past the new store with its neon windows I saw a second building, a streamlined metal-and-wood structure with modern furniture and a large deck facing the Second Life ocean. This was Joanie's, a popular dance club. Zazzy's new store was adjacent to Joanie's, and on her side of the border a series of signs had been put up to block Zazzy's store from view (figure 4.1). Authored by a group calling itself "Polite Neighbors," the signs read:

> If you support Joanie's, do not buy from this store!!! Stores of this nature belong in commercial areas. For someone to take the atmosphere of one of the most Romantic Venues in all of Second Life and trash it with flashing Nightclub lights is rude and uncalled for . . .

As we surveyed the scene we suddenly noticed Zazzy floating near his store, complaining about the protest signs: "if they think that by being mean they will get me to go they are wrong." Samuel moved toward Zazzy and began speaking to him:

SAMUEL: You have no idea how much effort people have put into making this area nice. Your store here comes as a horrible shock. People here hate blight like this.

FIGURE 4.1. The protest at Zazzy's store (image by author).

SAMUEL: They need to have neighbors who are considerate. You just barged in here with this flashing monster, ruining the view, they don't like this flashing crap, it's really hard on the eyes.

SAMUEL: We all have to live here on this sim. This is a neighborhood. Try to understand what they are going through.

SAMUEL: I know these people, they spent months building up their club from scratch. Your store ruins the whole look of this area.

SAMUEL: It is causing a heart attack, it's huge and flashing and obnoxious. I'm having an epileptic fit here dude

SAMUEL: Try to understand that all the work you put in your store, Joanie did the same on her club. Whatever you can do to make Joanie's view less a shock please try.

SAMUEL: This is a neighborhood. Try to understand: this club is this woman's LIFE

SAMUEL: It's her SECOND LIFE

SAMUEL: She has spent MONTHS working on it, 24/7, getting in customers.

SAMUEL: It's the highlight of this whole sim and the area

ZAZZY: This store is my life too

SAMUEL: Yeah but she was here first dude, Joanie moved here when the sim was new and now it's like threatened for her. Zazzy, why did you build out to the property line? when you do that, it ALWAYS makes people mad. It's that feeling you are crowding her that is getting to her.

SAMUEL: We care about this neighborhood Zazzy. We live here.

To those unfamiliar with virtual worlds all this might seem nonsensical, even trivial. After all, the incident took place within Second Life, which at the end of the day is a body of binary digital information: ones and zeros rendered on a computer screen. What such an interpretation would miss is how placemaking is absolutely foundational to virtual worlds. The conflict over Zazzy's store exemplifies some of the most basic cultural assumptions shared by Second Life residents during the time of my fieldwork, assumptions common in many other virtual worlds as well. Many studies of virtual worlds have focused on identity (particularly gender), economics, or language (e.g., Castronova 2005; Cherny 1999; Schaap 2002). These are important issues I address later in this book, but prioritizing them obscures how place, above all else, makes virtual worlds what they are: "they may simulate abstractions of reality; they may be operated as a service; creating them may be an art; people may visit them to play games. Ultimately, though, they're just a set of locations. Places" (Bartle 2004:475; see also Fernback 1999; Gelernter 1991:23; Graham 2002:4; Poster 1996:188–89). Even the term "resident" underscores how "a sense of place" is fundamental to Second Life (Ondrejka 2004c:3; see Turner and Turner 2006).[1]

A few commentaries have assumed on philosophical grounds that "the virtual, as such, is inaccessible to the senses" (Massumi 2002:133), so that "place" and "virtual" cannot coexist: "there is no 'place' in the virtual beyond the metaphor" (Rutter and Smith 2005:85). This belief that placemaking is antithetical to the virtual has a fairly long history in studies of mass media (e.g., Meyrowitz 1985). Other philosophical and empirical work, however, has shown the salience of place and sensory experience online, including in virtual worlds (Hillis 1999:73, 88; S. Jones 1997; Markham 1998:40; Morse 1998:181; Poster 1996:186; Reed 2005:230). That virtual worlds are places means they can be fieldsites; it makes an ethnographic approach conceivable. Virtual worlds are not the latest example of globalization making place irrelevant; globalization makes place relevant in new ways, and what makes virtual worlds so revolutionary is that they are new kinds of places. What some have described as "a shift from the 2D web to the 3D web" is really the shift from network to place, or, more accurately, the addition of online places, since networks will continue to exist.

My starting point for discussing place is the central role of vision in Second Life during the period of my fieldwork. This is part and parcel of how "with the shift to graphical virtual worlds . . . the connection between identity and knowing . . . is problematized and complicated by the visual" (Thomas 2005:1; see also Virilio 1994; Weheliye 2002). Consider the relationships of place and vision in the conflict over Zazzy's store. What had to be presupposed by all parties for this conflict to exist? We all shared an understanding of a virtual world with land that could be bought and sold and built upon, proximity, area, residency, buildings, a community in the vicinity of a building, indeed a neighborhood, a neighborhood in which people live, into which they put effort so that it looks nice. And also: a view, a view that can be ruined by blight, that can be trashed by flashing lights or a glowing monstrosity built out to the property line, by buildings that can shock and make people feel crowded, driven crazy, and threatened.

The simultaneous presence of more than one person has been key to cultural understandings of virtual worlds. This is why nongraphical virtual worlds like MUDs could be understood as places; even the "place" where a telephone conversation seems to occur can be seen as a virtual world (Sterling 1992:xi; see chapter 2). A broad cultural shift during the time of my fieldwork was that the notion of "virtual world" increasingly presupposed three-dimensional visuality: a defining characteristic of a virtual world (versus a blog or website) was that it was a place in which you could look around.[2] Consider the emphasis on vision in the following definition: "a user can log into [a virtual world] from any computer on the Earth. . . . The screen turns into a window through which an alternative Earth . . . can be seen. . . . The window by which your computer is depicting the world is, in fact, the surface of somebody's eye, and that somebody is *you*" (Castronova 2005:6, emphasis in original). An emphasis on visuality as precondition for knowledge and agency predates the emergence of virtual worlds: "the roots of yearning for a virtual world are partly anchored by an ongoing Western belief in the eye as the most noble organ, and in vision as a sensual metaphor for extending understanding" (Hillis 1999:37). Even the notion of nation-states as "imagined" communities (Anderson 1983) refers etymologically to the notion of an "image."

In the dominant Western tradition, vision and place are linked through the idea of the landscape, which "represents a way of seeing—a way in which some Europeans have represented to themselves and to others the world about them and their relationship with it, and through which they have

commented on social relations" (Cosgrove 1998:1). When one resident defined Second Life as a "landscape engineered by its residents," his notions
of landscape, residency, and engineering thus reflected a pivotal aspect of
virtual worlds. The clash over Zazzy's new store was not that it encroached
on any building but that it damaged a landscape. This is intelligible because
it links up to an actual-world history within which "in landscape we are
offered an important element of personal control over the external world"
(Cosgrove 1998:18). A perceived loss of control over landscape can thus
have consequences for a sense of efficacy, since landscapes ascribe power
"to the unitary viewer who can also be understood to depend on his or
her eyes for a 'point of view' . . . [and] naturalize a distinction between the
self and a living world" (Hillis 1999:86). Second Life residents were aware
of this when they told me how the presence of an "ugly" building could
compel neighbors to move, "just go inside and never look outside," or turn
down the "draw distance" on the Second Life program so that everything
beyond sixty-four virtual meters would be lost in a grey mist. One resident
noted "the problem is seldom what one has on one's land, but what is in
one's view." Another complained that "just taking my new home in Lake-
land as an example: I have this wonderful oasis there. And now on one side
there is a sex club, and on the other end a slave dungeon."

Since there was little official zoning in Second Life, much of its landscape consisted of small plots of land (512 to 2,048 square meters) with
homes or stores on them, a quite chaotic jumble of styles and scales of
building. In response to this, a number of experiments to create zoning
agreements between residents took place during the time of my fieldwork.
Zoning guidelines often included prohibitions on billboards, spinning signs
in the air, and building out to the property line, as well as limits on building
height. These guidelines worked to protect the visual field, yet often resulted
in what was disparaged as "endless suburban sprawl."

In *Techniques of the Observer: On Vision and Modernity in the Nineteenth Century*, Jonathan Crary tracked how "a reorganization of the observer occurs in the nineteenth century . . . visual experience . . . is given an
unprecedented mobility and exchangeability, abstracted from any founding
site or referent" (Crary 1990:14). As the title "techniques of the observer"
indicates, Crary focused on questions of technique and observation, noting
how vision became valorized over sound (see also Friedberg 2006; Sterne
2003). He pointed out the polysemy of "observer," which refers not just to
seeing but to "observing rules, codes, regulations, and practices. Though
obviously one who sees, an observer is more importantly one who sees
within a prescribed set of possibilities, one who is embedded in a system

of conventions and limitations" (Crary 1990:5; see also Crary 1999). While never mentioning anthropology, Crary here linked observation to the Malinowskian tradition within which "participant *observation*" would, by the mid-twentieth century, become the dominant mode of ethnographic investigation. To, in Crary's words, be "embedded in a system of conventions and limitations" is to be within a culture. Crary's interest in technique linked these methodological issues to questions of techne. In this regard it is striking that Crary opened *Techniques of the Observer* by noting that the book: "was written in the midst of a transformation in the nature of visuality probably more profound than the break that separates medieval imagery from Renaissance perspective. The rapid development [today] . . . of a vast array of computer graphics techniques is part of a sweeping reconfiguration of relations between an observing subject and modes of representation" (Crary 1990:1).[3] The notions of place and landscape that shaped the most fundamental principles of Second Life's culture—and reflected an American sense of landscape in terms of undiscovered frontier (Healy 1997)—were part of this "sweeping reconfiguration of relations between an observing subject and modes of representation." This reconfiguration is one aspect of what I term the Age of Techne.[4]

During my fieldwork Second Life appeared as a series of square "sims" (simulators) 256 meters on a side, linked into a "mainland" of several continents, surrounded by thousands of single-sim islands. Some of these islands touched each other, forming medium-sized landmasses. Linden Lab terraformed new land, providing rivers, bays, rolling hills, even mountain regions with a snowy theme.[5] However, the most popular land often had a low-lying, beachfront feel to it. Land was continually added as new residents joined Second Life; as there is no way to increase the amount of land on the planet earth, such a capability represents a distinguishing feature of virtual worlds and complicates the scarcity presupposed by actual-world theories of property. By August 2006 over half of Second Life was islands, leading to concerns over the "future of the mainland."[6]

A fundamental assumption of Second Life was that land was owned. Linden Lab divided the land into parcels that were sold "at auction"—that is, to the highest bidder within a set period of time. Land could be resold at will for any price, and could also be subdivided or joined to other contiguous parcels of land. Through the work of savvy land owners and people working as real estate agents, parcels could sell for hundreds of U.S. dollars or more. While virtual, Second Life "real" estate was quite "real" in economic terms.

How could virtual land gain differential value, since it was all online? Given the importance of landscape, it is to be expected that surroundings played a role: someone wishing to build a home might have avoided land near Zazzy's store, for instance, and a waterfront was a plus. Linden Lab created differential land value by labeling all sims "PG" or "M" ("parental guidance" or "mature," terminology taken from the motion picture ratings system).[7] Linden Lab also created differential value by adding "telehubs" in the version 1.1.0 (October 2003) upgrade to the Second Life platform.[8] Under this encoded relationship between place and time, if attempting to teleport to a particular location a resident would appear at the nearest tele-hub, a location outfitted with a building that usually looked like a bus stop or kiosk. After rezzing at the telehub, a resident would have to fly to their destination.[9] Land near telehubs became valuable, particularly desirable for commercial venues like stores or clubs, since residents had to cross such land en route to other locations. Some residents liked the telehub system because it forced persons to fly over large swaths of the Second Life landscape, where they would encounter buildings of which they might otherwise be unaware. Other residents found the teleport system cumbersome. The fact that objects had to "rez" (see chapter 1) meant that flying away from a tele-hub often resulted in bumping into buildings that were not yet visible because the data of which they were composed had not entirely downloaded. Due to these issues, the December 2005 (version 1.8) upgrade to the Second Life program eliminated telehubs and allowed "point-to-point" teleporting anywhere in Second Life.[10] While they existed, telehubs recreated a feature of actual-world physicality that is not obligatory in a virtual world—the idea that it takes time to traverse distance (Williams 1996:295).

The Second Life platform allowed landowners to limit access to a select group of residents, or to ban particular residents from entering their land. In either case, when approaching land so designated the resident in question would encounter "ban lines" floating in the air, composed of red text reading "no entry." During my fieldwork many landowners did not use ban lines; they permitted full access, protecting their properties by using a default setting that prevented visitors from altering anything built on their land. One reason for permitting access was that the amount of time avatars spent on a given parcel of land was calculated by Linden Lab into a figure known as "dwell" or "traffic."[11] For much of my fieldwork Linden Lab provided cash incentives for parcels with "high traffic" (that is, a high number of visits by avatars); even after this was phased out, traffic provided one of the few quantitative measures for the social status of a property. In addition to low traffic scores, ban lines were disparaged for making it difficult to fly across the terrain and for their effect on the visual field: "ban lines are eyesores," as one resident put it.

In place of ban lines, residents seeking privacy were more likely to use "sky builds." A Second Life landowner had rights over the "air" above their land. Since avatars could fly and teleport, and since virtual objects could ignore gravity and stay suspended aboveground, residents could create a room (even an entire home and yard) hundreds of meters in the air, invisible to casual passers-by at ground level.[12] I recall being introduced to the "skybox" of my friend Rhed. After some fumbling around to find a "teleporter," hidden in a potted plant in her ground-level home, I found myself transported to the edge of a small pond. Rhed and I were now hundreds of meters in the air in a large box, on the inside of which Rhed had placed images depicting a countryside receding into the distance. This was a virtual virtual landscape. When I complimented Rhed on the idyllic images, she noted that:

> RHED: The scenery on the walls . . . is actual scenery here in sl
> ME: Oh wow, you're right
> RHED: It took a while to get all the edges to line up so that it flowed smoothly. I wanted to go for that outdoorsy feel. Sometimes people pop up here who heard about it from someone else. I thought about hiding it better, but it's nice to see people enjoy this place. When my partner and I come up here and need privacy, I just pick up the teleporter, lol

It was only when reviewing my fieldnotes from this day that I was struck by Rhed's emphasis that the images in her skybox represented, in her thinking, "actual" (not virtual) scenery of Second Life and an "outdoorsy" feel. The referentiality here is complex: Rhed knew that her skybox, outfitted with images of Second Life at ground level, simulated an already virtual landscape, yet this doubly virtual visual field could represent an emotional landscape of pastoral bliss. Sky builds constituted an attempt to forge privacy by removing a structure from the landscape (rather than highlighting its exclusivity with ban lines). Yet sky builds could be incorporated into a social landscape in which both free access to land and "free" sight lines across a landscape virtually embodied an aesthetic of openness and community.

BUILDS AND OBJECTS.

As Linden Lab proclaimed in its advertising during the period of my fieldwork, Second Life was "imagined, created, and owned by its residents." Ownership was more complicated than suggested by this slogan (and in late 2007 the word "owned" was quietly dropped from it). Yet it was true that less than one percent of things found in Second Life during my fieldwork were created by Linden Lab: it was a resident-built environment organized around the creating and selling of objects. Through building, Second Life was constituted as a commodity economy, with consequences for under-standings of selfhood and society. But this virtual world was not simply a reification of neoliberal thought or a showcase for runaway consumerism; it was also a place for forms of barter, donation, and communal owner-ship. Building was a common activity for many residents, a source of great pleasure and meaning. While often solitary, building could also be a form of socializing: residents would say things like "I found that my building has let me come into contact with many people," or "I started in Second Life by building, and then I stumbled upon friendships."

"Building" occurred when residents used the built-in capabilities of the Second Life program to create "primitives," or "prims" for short. They did this without exiting Second Life; other residents could watch as someone created content, and groups could build collaboratively (figure 4.2). Prims began as a wooden box one-half meter on a side; once "rezzed" their creator could change their size (up to ten meters on a side), transform them into

FIGURE 4.2. The ability to build in "real time" inworld (image by author).

other shapes like a pyramid or sphere, rotate them, or make them hollow.[13] They could be linked together to create large and complicated structures consisting of hundreds or even thousands of prims. Residents could also place "textures" on a prim to change its appearance, like the images inside Rhed's skybox. Textures were aesthetically important; additionally, a good texture (say, a brick pattern) could make an object appear to be composed of more prims than was the case, reducing download time. Textures exemplified the implicit visual economy of surfaces in Second Life: meaning was located primarily on the surface of objects. Prims could also have "scripts," or computer programs, placed inside them, written in a programming language internal to Second Life, LSL (Linden Scripting Language).[14] Scripts could do everything from make a texture rotate (so that, for instance, a water texture would appear to flow across a prim's surface), produce glowing particles, or offer an avatar a "notecard" containing text and images, to truly complex behaviors like acting as a blackjack dealer or managing a series of rental properties.

When linked to a plot of land, things created from prims were often known as "builds": buildings were builds, but so were waterfalls, parks, forests, and plazas. When prims were not linked to a particular piece of land or were simply smaller, they were typically known as "objects": this referred to items like vehicles and clothing, but could also include sofas or paintings, even partially functional laptop computers and musical instruments. The distinction between builds and objects was heuristic, and either "build" or "object" could be used as an overarching term. Whether composed of one prim or hundreds, when placed on a piece of land objects persisted in Second Life even when their creator was offline, since the data was held on servers, not the creator's personal computer. An object of any size (or a copy of the object) could also be placed in an avatar's "inventory": this was like taking information about an object, with the proviso that in question was a virtual object already composed solely of information. An object in an avatar's inventory was thus a virtual virtual object. When dragged out of an avatar's inventory onto the ground, the object rezzed into virtual existence, and any avatar could then see and interact with it.

Prims were linked to property in that one was allocated 117 prims for each 512 square meters of land one owned. This scarcity function was one means by which Linden Lab worked to ensure that the Second Life landscape rezzed as quickly as possible as one moved across it: a large number of prims in one area would take a correspondingly longer amount of time to download. This scarcity function also shaped land value; a major reason residents wished to acquire additional land was to have their prim allocation increased.[15] It was common to encounter situations like the one I experienced one day when teleporting to the home of Mick. I was startled to find him standing in the middle of an empty living room:

ME: Am I still rezzing or is your furniture missing?
MICK: My furniture is missing. I needed the prims temporarily [to build something else]

Manufacturers of objects like furniture often advertised their products as "low prim": a resident with a small piece of land permitting, say, only 200 prims might balk at a chair composed of 50 prims, since to rez it would consume one-fourth of one's prim allotment. There were a few exceptions to this linkage of prims to parcels of land. Vehicles created from prims could move across the Second Life landscape. Prims attached to an avatar did not count toward the total prims allocated to a parcel. Residents could thus link together small prims to create hair, jewelry, glasses, weapons, shoes, and other items.[16]

Because objects could have permanence only on property, residents without property were largely excluded from building, an important dimension of Second Life sociality. Such residents often termed themselves "homeless." Some residents were homeless because they did not like building or saw no benefit in owning property; others were homeless because they could not afford to own virtual land. During the time of my fieldwork, those without property had limited possibilities for building. If they belonged to a group that owned land in common, they might be able to build on that land. Otherwise, residents without land could build only in "sandboxes," sims set aside by Linden Lab in which anyone could build but within which all builds were deleted after a short period of time (typically, every twelve hours). Sandboxes were significant locations for social interaction; they acted as a commons where persons without shared interests or social networks could interact as they learned how to use the building function of the Second Life program or experiment with a new idea. This emergent social character of sandboxes is one reason why during my fieldwork, a number of landowners marked off portions of their land as small "sandboxes" by changing a setting so that any avatar could build there; this attracted residents to the land, increasing its popularity and "traffic."

Fundamental to Second Life culture during my fieldwork was that textures, scripts, prims, and even entire builds could be sold; Second Life was a commodity economy. Drawing upon the work of anthropologist Marilyn Strathern, Alain Pottage has argued that "in a commodity economy, both persons and things are objectified as things. . . . The agency of persons is therefore understood in terms of an idiom of labor, or productivity, so that personal relations are reified in the composition of things" (Pottage

2001:114).[17] This is an aspect of what in chapter 8 I term "creationist capital-ism"; it is a social order constituting relationships between persons through what are held to be prior acts of individual creativity—in the case of Second Life, through building. Yet Second Life was not simply a testament to crass capitalism. The price of any object in Second Life could be set to zero; that is, infinite copies of an object could be given away. Thousands of such free objects circulated through the virtual world, objectified analogues to the acts of altruism I examine in chapter 7.

It may be that despite Second Life's corporate underpinnings and wide-spread consumerism, a gift economy played an important role. Pottage notes how "gift exchange stages a relation between persons. . . . Persons constitute themselves as such, *actualizing* the *virtual* relations from which they are com-posed, by anticipating the effect on their counterpart in the exchange relation" (Pottage 2001:114, emphasis added). Through gift exchange—even when no gift is immediately expected in return—virtual relations become "actual," a form of self-constitution that in the Age of Techne is possible entirely within a virtual world. Given my interest in methodology, I am intrigued by how Pottage links this distinction between commodity and gift economies to eth-nographic representation: "The 'reflexive position of seeing oneself through others' that is so characteristic of a commodity economy has an 'anthropo-logical companion: concern about the representation of others' (Strathern 1999:252). . . . The reference to gift exchange opens a different horizon . . . an exchange of perspectives . . . in which the interaction itself 'creates' what is observed by supplying its context. . . . In this mode, ethnography itself might be presented as a mode of (gift) exchange" (Pottage 2001:115).

This invocation of gift exchange underscores the social meaningful-ness of objects. For instance, the psychologist D. W. Winnicott's notion of "transitional objects" identified objects like a child's teddy bear or blanket that "belong at once to them and to the outside world" (Rudnytsky 1993: xii), working to create a "potential space between the individual and the environment" that is "the place where cultural experience is located" (Win-nicott 1993:8). In Second Life, itself a space of potentiality, all objects were transitional objects. They instantiated experientially real places; like objects in the actual world, they could participate in forms of social action and take their worlds "as present or given" (B. Smith 1996:195; see also Latour 2005:70–72).

In virtual worlds like Second Life, transitional objects could be inhab-ited and embodied in new ways. For instance, for many Second Life resi-dents the analogue to the child's teddy bear or blanket was the home, which acted as a personal virtual place. One resident described how when entering

Second Life "I log in and walk around my house. I love being here." Another noted how "having a place that I can go to when I want is a security for me . . . a refuge even." A third resident, recovering from a serious injury in the actual world, spoke of his Second Life home by saying "I built this place to relax. It's my place, it's mine."

Builds and objects demonstrate the need for a theoretical framework that acknowledges the truly novel implications of virtual worlds without predicating their significance on their being different from the actual world—a theoretical framework I have elsewhere termed an anthropology of similitude (Boellstorff 2005). As late as the 1990s, scholars could conclude "there seems to be a widespread acceptance of Heidegger's claim that the authenticity of dwelling and of rootedness is being destroyed by the modern spread of technology" (Harvey 1993:12). However, residents of Second Life found technology a precondition for virtual dwelling and rootedness; while online they inhabited virtual but authentic places. Building could act as a craft—a form of techne—by which the virtual became real.

Lag.

During the conversation at Zazzy's store, Samuel noted that "Joanie's is one of those nice clubs that is low-lag, and now it's lagged by this stupid store. This is just awful." By "lag" Samuel meant that many of the prims making up Zazzy's new store had scripts inside them (for instance, to make the windows change color). The processing power needed to run the scripts was seen to slow down the Second Life program, so that patrons of Joanie's might find themselves dancing out of sync with the music, or might not hear the music altogether. By saying Joanie's club was "low-lag," Samuel implied that Joanie avoided unnecessary scripted prims (for example, she might have chosen a still pool over a fountain requiring scripts to create the effect of moving water), and that Zazzy had not been so conscientious.

Many forms of computer-mediated communication are asynchronic in that people need not be online at once; email is a well-known example. Even in virtual worlds, forms of asynchronic sociality are important to resident experience (Bogost 2004). For instance, Second Life residents often built collaboratively: one person might work constructing a building, then log off; several hours later, another person would log on and add to the building. Despite such asynchronic sociality, a key factor making virtual worlds seem like "worlds" at all was that sociality in them was primarily synchronic (e.g., Fornäs et al. 2002:17). The vast majority of social interaction in Second Life took place between residents who were "inworld" at the same time.

The virtuality of online worlds inheres in their status as places, but it is with regard to time, particularly synchronic sociality, that the actual world intrudes most fundamentally into online culture. As Sherry Turkle noted with reference to playing video games, "in reality there is so much time. Doing some things precludes others" (Turkle 1984:83). One Second Life resident echoed this observation by saying that "you can have a dozen different avatars, but it still doesn't buy you time. There's still only one person at the keyboard." While in many cultures time is experienced as a continuous movement, in all virtual worlds during the period of my fieldwork cybersociality was bracketed by "logging on" and "logging off." This distinction between online and offline may be the most consequential boundary-marker between the actual and the virtual. Between logging on and logging off was the "session," the period of time during which, in Turkle's terms, the virtual precludes the actual. If sitting in a room in Second Life talking to three other people, it could be that in the actual world my conversation partners were located in Brazil, Japan, and Greece. However, for the sociality to be synchronic, all four of us had to be inworld *at the same time*.

One of the most common topics of incidental discussion during my fieldwork was "lag," a sense of disjuncture between actual-world time and virtual-world time. For instance, one day I was participating in a trivia game when one resident shouted out an answer. Then another resident complained "The lag ate me! I was going to say that!" In other words, in the actual world this person knew the answer to the trivia question, but her avatar was unable to express her thoughts in the virtual world because of lag. Almost every period of time I spent in Second Life was marked by lag being mentioned in some offhand manner—textures taking a long time to rez, avatars temporarily without clothing or jewelry, jerky bodies strolling down an urban street. As one resident put it, "small talk about lag is like talking about the weather in rl." The phenomenon of lag may seem utterly boring compared to the sensational topics that dominate the literature on virtual worlds—gender swapping, cybersex, virtual sweatshops. Often, however, ethnographic research discovers its greatest insights in the most innocuous, tacit dimensions of social life. As time out of virtual joint, lag provides a socially salient means to ethnographically explore the coconstitutive status of temporality and place. Lag reveals how a problem with notions like "time/space compression" (Harvey 1989; see also Fornäs et al. 2002:9) is that time resists compression in a way that place does not; the "death of distance" (Cairncross 2001) does not correspond to a death of time. It is not always the case that "Internet time" accelerates our experience of time (Gleick 2000); it can lead to the form of deceleration experienced in virtual worlds as lag. Globalizing forces can lead

to forms of "temporal integration" requiring, for instance, computer techni-
cians on different parts of the globe to labor at the same time, producing
a temporal inequality where some workers have their sleep schedules disrupted and others do not (Aneesh 2006:84–99). This robustness of time in
relation to space is central to the constitution of virtual worlds.

Scholars of cybersociality have discussed lag since the days of MUDs
(e.g., Carlstrom 1992; Shah and Romine 1995:27), noting how lag reveals
"the extent to which time delays in communication disrupted the feeling
of shared space" (Kendall 2002:7). In the context of Second Life, lag originated in the truly immense amount of information represented by its land,
the objects on that land, and the avatars inhabiting that land. By early 2007
there was by one estimate about one petabyte (a million gigabytes) of data in
Second Life. At that point, were all of the books in the Library of Congress
digitized (about 30 million volumes), it would have been equivalent to only
about 2 percent of the data stored inside Second Life.[18] The subset of this
data located in the proximity of any avatar had to be continually rezzed into
existence as that avatar moved about the world. During the period of my
fieldwork the Second Life program favored rezzing the landscape first, then
avatars, followed by prims (builds and objects). As a result, while lag could
occasionally take the form of a delay in the appearance of text chat or in a
sound being heard, it most often manifested itself as a longer-than-normal
amount of time for builds and objects to rez: an incomplete landscape, a
failure of the visuality so important to virtual worlds. Technically this was a
decline in the FPS or "frames per second" rate at which the visual field was
updated. Residents could only know the exact FPS if they opened a special
window called the "Statistics Bar." According to residents who looked at this
information (and based on my own experience), the best possible FPS one
could get in Second Life during the period of my fieldwork was around 22;
15 to 20 was considered good, below 10 less so, and anything below about
5 FPS would be experienced as lag. Many residents never bothered opening
the Statistics Bar: lag was primarily experienced rather than quantified. The
point at which a low FPS became interpreted as lag varied: some residents
experienced even as slight delay as lag, while others, particularly those with
substandard Internet connections or older computers, were more accus-
tomed to delayed rezzing and would not term it "lag" until the delay became quite pronounced.

Lag existed because Second Life, like all "massively multiple" virtual
worlds during my fieldwork, was based on a "client-server" architecture,
where most of the virtual world was housed on servers rather than the
personal computers of residents (Castronova 2005:82). Were the virtual

world stored on individual computers it would not be persistent; parts of the world would disappear as residents shut down their computers. Client-server architecture avoids this problem but requires that the virtual world be accessed through the Internet—and it is this fact that made lag such an issue.[19] "Sim load" lag, the primary form of lag in Second Life during my research, referred to the processing power needed for any sim and thus the server supporting it. For instance, as more residents entered a sim it would take more time for information about objects in the sim to be streamed to those residents' actual-world computers. As the number of residents in a sim increased, lag would become noticeable. In other words, lag increased in proportion to synchronic sociality. When I once heard someone new to Second Life ask "are some parts of SL laggier than others?" a more experienced resident replied "most definitely; look for something relatively quiet." Any large event—a dance at a club, a live music performance, a class on "how to build," an inworld "town hall" meeting with Linden Lab staff—would experience lag, even when residents asked each other to remove objects attached to their avatars like shoes and jewelry (particularly "bling," jewelry with embedded scripts that emitted particles). As in the example of Zazzy's store, lag could also be caused by scripts, since they had to be downloaded and then executed inworld. For this reason it was common to hear things like a club manager announcing: "whoever's firing that damn gun cut it out—those things lag sims down."[20]

Lag was relative, not absolute; while most forms of lag slowed everyone down equally in one virtual locale, all lag was relative to the actual world. The continents and islands making up Second Life did not need to be located in relation to Europe, North America, or Japan: there was no expectation that the Second Life map should correlate with any actual-world geography. In contrast, the default time for the clock constantly present in the upper-right hand corner of the Second Life program was "Second Life Time," but this was identical to Pacific Standard Time, the time zone in which Linden Lab's offices were located. The clock could be changed to any time zone, but had to correspond to some actual-world time. Once while dancing at a club, I noticed the following exchange:

PERSON A: Is anyone in Northern California by any chance?
PERSON B: <~~ Nor Cal
PERSON A: How's the weather? I have to pack for Thurs-Sun.
PERSON B: Hottest July on record here.
PERSON C: I WISH this was California, because then it wouldn't be 1:00am

In this example "California" first indexed an actual-world location with nice weather but shifted to indexing a time zone, and it was temporality that made it attractive in relation to Second Life. It was not necessary to hold events in two distinct geographical parts of Second Life for residents whose actual-world locations were in the United States versus Europe.[21] In contrast, "European time" events were common from the beginning of my fieldwork: a club might hold a dance at 8pm Pacific Standard Time, and another at 1pm Pacific Standard Time so that Europeans could attend during their evening. While residents from across the actual world could be found in Second Life, the predominance of North Americans in its early years meant that residents from Europe, Asia, and elsewhere sometimes complained of getting "left out" because important events would be scheduled in the middle of their nighttime. One resident spoke of being "always jet-lagged from living evenings on Pacific Standard Time," which has become the new Greenwich Mean Time for many virtual worlds.[22]

This temporal inequality was distinct from lag, but both reflected how time resisted virtualization in a way that place did not. It is therefore incorrect to assume that "everything in the new computer world is temporary and fleeting. . . . Time is now a resource, not a reference point" (Rifkin 1987:155). Virtual worlds create a gap between virtual and actual not just in terms of place, but in terms of time as well. But where the gap with regard to space is typically intended and desired, the gap with regard to time is not. The gap with regard to space constitutes the binarism between virtual and actual; the gap with regard to time threatens it. Even when place becomes virtual, time remains actual. In a sense, techne produces an "intratemporality" that links actual and virtual with regard to time (Stiegler 1998:4). This touches on longstanding questions of time in human sociality. In *Being and Time* (Heidegger 1962), Martin Heidegger worked to show how "different ways of being . . . are all related to human being and ultimately to temporality" (Dreyfus 1991:1). To simplify one aspect of a complex philosophical argument, Heidegger distinguished between the "thrownness" of everyday life and what he termed "breakdown." One of his favorite examples of this was that of a man hammering a nail: in the activity of doing so, the man is not aware of the hammer as such, only of the activity of hammering. It is only when, for instance, the handle of the hammer cracks that a moment of breakdown ensues and the hammer as an object enters conscious perception. This breakdown "necessitates a shift into a mode in which what was previously transparent becomes explicitly manifest. Deprived of access to what we normally count on, we act deliberately, paying attention to what we are doing" (Dreyfus 1991:72).

Lag is nothing less than an interruption in the thrownness of temporality, a breakdown of time made possible by the gap between virtual and actual. In this sense, lag is an annoyance but is also a kind of gift from virtual worlds; it represents a moment of breakdown demonstrating the cultural construction of time. Lag is not like waiting for a bus to arrive or an email to download; it is experienced not as a delay *in* time, but a delay *of* time, a breakdown in the thrownness of time. Concerns with lag may reflect ways in which virtual worlds contribute to a "synchronic society" that "sets high value on the human engagement with time" (Sterling 2005:53). During my fieldwork, Linden Lab updated the Second Life program approximately once a week, and residents expected that the technology used to create and sustain Second Life would continue to advance. Yet everyone knew that no possible future technology would allow one person in Chicago at 1:00 p.m. to be in any virtual world simultaneously with another person in New York at 5:00 p.m. (where the time-zone difference between those cities is one hour). When one Second Life resident—living in the United States while her boyfriend lived in Europe—said "we have time issues," she was referring to this problem of simultaneity, the resistance of time to virtualization. She did not have "place issues" because Second Life created a virtual place she could share with her boyfriend. When exchanging email with her boyfriend, these "time issues" did not exist: but in virtual worlds, shared *virtual* place assumes shared *actual* time.

AFK.

One day in Second Life, I was dancing at a club with my friend Denny when we saw a mutual acquaintance, Jeff, at the other end of the room. We walked over and said "hello"; Jeff did not reply, but there was no apparent lag in the club. Neither of us took offense; Denny typed "looks like he's afk" and we continued to dance. About five minutes later Jeff suddenly turned to face us: "I'm back, was afk on phone." "No problem, wb [welcome back]," Denny replied.

This was an incident of "afk" or "away from keyboard." (A related term is "brb" or "be right back.") This state of affairs, where a person leaves their computer without logging off, so that their avatar remains, was commonplace in Second Life and other virtual worlds during my fieldwork. In many actual-world cultures, to have someone stare at you blankly for two minutes when you approach them would be interpreted as rudeness or intoxication. In Second Life, afk occurred so often—yet was so rarely the topic of explicit discussion—that like lag, it might appear to be no more than a distraction.

No one came to Second Life so that they could go afk. Yet this apparently peripheral phenomenon strikes at the center of questions of selfhood and sociality in virtual worlds. Afk and lag are both apparently banal aspects of cybersociality with important theoretical implications for questions of place and time.

Like all aspects of virtual worlds, afk has a history. It is not really possible to be afk from a newspaper or other print media: afk presupposes synchronic virtual sociality. A busy signal is not really afk, but just as telephone conversations can be seen as the first form of cyberspace (Sterling 1992:xi), so the dawn of afk was probably some unrecorded, mundane incident at the beginning of the telephone era where someone in the middle of a conversation set their receiver down on a table without hanging it up to answer the door or pour tea from a kettle in the next room. Although "afk" is a contraction of "away from keyboard," what afk really means is "away from virtual world, but with virtual self still present." Before it even had a name, observers noticed the phenomenon of afk in early text-based virtual worlds: "it is often the case that MUD players are connected but idle, perhaps because they have stepped away from their terminal for a while. Thus, it often happens that one receives no response to an utterance in a MUD simply because the other party wasn't really present to see it" (Curtis 1992:133).

During my fieldwork Second Life was accessed through a computer program available as a free download from Linden Lab. Once the program was activated, you could access Second Life from your computer after entering the name and password of an avatar. As long as the program was running, your avatar existed in Second Life and could be seen (or bumped into) by anyone in the avatar's proximity. If you selected "quit" and shut down the Second Life program, your avatar disappeared from Second Life until the next time you logged on (though any objects or buildings you created would persist). However, if you got up from your chair in the actual world without shutting down the Second Life program, stepping away for a few minutes to use the bathroom or send your child off to school, your avatar did not disappear from Second Life. It remained there, standing and looking around, sitting on a sofa, or dancing at a club thanks to an automated animation. After about three minutes the avatar's head would bow down and the word "away" appear over it;[23] after about fifteen minutes the program would shut down of its own accord, but sometimes the program failed to do so, or residents would install a program to click the mouse button every few minutes, fooling the program into thinking they were present.

There were many reasons for going afk, which could last from less than a minute to hours. Some had to do with actual-world embodiment: a need to eat or sleep. Often Second Life residents went afk for domestic reasons: to fix dinner for their families, dust the furniture, or spend time with an actual-world spouse. Persons entering Second Life while at the office would go afk to attend a meeting or use the office computer for work-related activities (compare Kendall 2002:23–29). Those who worked at home could also alternate between Second Life and other programs on their computers. Residents spoke of going afk to check their email, surf the web (including looking at Second Life-related websites or blogs), or use Photoshop to design clothing to sell in Second Life. Multitasking in and out of virtual worlds in this way dates back to the earlier days of MUDs (e.g., Turkle 1995:184), revealing how "windows have become a powerful metaphor for thinking about the self as a multiple, distributed system" (Turkle 1995:14). Uses of "afk" for this kind of multitasking underscore how "away from keyboard" often did not literally mean being away from the keyboard; rather, it meant being away from virtual sociality.

I have emphasized that during the time of my fieldwork one of the most fundamental distinctions in Second Life culture was being online (or "in-world") versus offline. There were many websites associated with Second Life, but residents clearly understood the difference between such sites and the Second Life program itself, which was either on or off. In the phrase "away from keyboard," the term "keyboard" stood in metonymically for the personal computer as a whole. It referenced the presence of a person in front of their computer, and by implication their presence in a virtual world. Afk revealed the complexities of presence, but multiple redeployments of the virtual/actual binarism were occurring, not the erasure or transcendence of that binarism. While the logged-off resident was not present even in a virtual sense, the afk resident was actually absent but virtually present—we could even say "virtually virtually present." This explains why it was that during my fieldwork, many residents used the notion of afk metaphorically within Second Life itself. For instance, if someone was online and received an im (instant message) demanding an involved response (a renter having trouble with their property, a partner in need of comfort, etc.), it was common to say "I'm going afk" with the understanding that the person was not actually stepping away from their keyboard or even minimizing the Second Life program, but would be focused on instant messaging privately to another person and thus would not be responding to chat in their avatar's vicinity. As one resident observed, afk could just mean "temporarily distracted" and "cannot be taken literally anymore." In fact, there was a continuum with afk at one pole and a focus on one's avatar's immediate environment on the other: this is why one encountered phrases like "sorry, had to go afk-ish." One's avatar was present at any point on this continuum; what varied was the presence of one's actual-world self in the virtual context. This is why one resident noted that there was a need to define afk with care, because "I'm always watching chat unless I say otherwise, but that doesn't mean I'm always responsive."

Confusion could even arise as to whether a particular invocation of afk was meant to index the virtual or actual world. I recall when I was once sitting with Trishie, a resident living in Second Life as a child. We were in her playhouse when I noticed some plates with sandwiches sitting on top of a toy table:

> TRISHIE: Mommie left us lunch.
> ME: Yum!
> TRISHIE: Yes, it's good
> TRISHIE: Brb, gotta check my meatloaf.
> ME: Ok

In this interaction, Trishie and I were talking about virtual food in her playhouse when she suddenly said she had to go afk and would "be right back" (brb) because she had to check an actual-world meatloaf in an actual-world oven.[24] Trishie had told me earlier that in the actual world she was a mother with two children; she was preparing food for her actual-world children while her virtual-world parents had left food for her in Second Life.

Regardless of the degree to which someone went afk, unless they logged off of Second Life (or the program logged them off automatically), at some point the person would return. Residents typically said they were "back"; "welcome back" or "wb" was thus a common response to someone who had been afk. This notion of "back" implied that the person and avatar, separated temporarily due to being afk, were reunited: it signaled that the actual was once again present in the virtual. There was often a moment of readjustment after being afk, marked by activating the "history" window and reading the chat it had recorded. Since during the time of my research text-based chat was the primary means of communication, it was possible for persons who had been afk to catch up on a conversation from which they had been actually absent but virtually present, as revealed by statements like the following:

> LUCY: sorry, back :)
> LUCY: <scrolling>

Here Lucy was telling those around her to be patient; she was no longer afk, but needed a few moments to read through the chat history so that she could catch up on the conversation. Had Lucy logged off this would not have been possible, since chat was only recorded within a limited radius around a (logged-in) avatar.[25]

Afk could even be turned to economic uses, as in the case of "camping." For much of the period of my fieldwork, it was common to see a large number of green dots on the map, teleport to see what was happening, and find a group of people sitting on chairs or "dance pads" indicating how long a resident had been stationary and the amount of money to be paid as a result. This phenomenon—camping—originated in the notion of traffic. As noted earlier, traffic was a number attached to a piece of land based on how many people were spending time on that property: the more persons spending time on the property, and the more time each person spent there, led to a higher traffic score. Linden Lab would pay cash rewards to properties that received the greatest amount of traffic, based on the reasoning that high traffic reflected success in creating content attractive to Second Life residents. At some point in 2005, Second Life residents figured out how to script objects that would pay residents a token amount for spending time on a property (typically three lindens, or about one penny, every ten minutes); as a result, the property in question could in theory receive a high-enough traffic score to receive a cash reward from Linden Lab, only part of which went out to reimburse those camping on the property.[26] Persons who were camping—some for twelve hours or more—were typically afk for much of that time, but camping could also serve as a social venue where participants chatted with each other or caught up on their ims.

Afk is so fundamental to cybersociality that ways to regularize it are often woven into virtual worlds. Linden Lab programmed two forms of afk into the Second Life platform by providing commands to "set away" and "set busy." "Set away" caused the word "away" to appear over one's avatar, whose shoulders and head then drooped as if sleeping, in the same manner that occurred after not moving the mouse or typing for a period of time. This made one's avatar visibly afk immediately (for instance, at the moment one heard one's actual-world telephone ringing or one's actual-world kettle of water beginning to boil), avoiding the interval when one went afk but one's avatar still appeared unchanged. This was a form of courtesy to other residents, so that they knew the person in question was actually absent though virtually present. The second form of afk woven into the platform, "set busy," caused the word "busy" to appear over one's avatar: chat and ims were hidden, and teleport invitations and inventory offers declined. In effect, "set busy" acknowledged that a metaphorical form of afk could exist internally to Second Life—it was used, for instance, when a resident was building and might not be able to immediately respond to someone who approached them and said "hello." The distinction between these two commands reflects an understanding that someone could appear afk because in the actual world they had stepped away from their computer, or because they were engaging in some virtual-world task that took their focus away from their avatar's immediate environment. I was struck by how rarely these two built-in functions were used. Broad cultural understandings of afk, in particular a tolerance for persons not responding immediately to a greeting, made these built-in functions somewhat superfluous.

The phenomenon of afk revealed how in Second Life and virtual worlds more generally, people were not expected to always be "present"; they could be "away." Afk is not the same thing as walking out of a room in the actual world, because with afk one's avatar remains and contributes to the social situation. That is why residents who were afk could even become the focus of joking attention during my fieldwork. For instance, if at a dock fishing, an afk resident's friends might push the resident's avatar off the dock into the water (causing no lasting harm, but leaving the avatar submerged among the fish).[27] Another common practical joke was to arrange objects and other persons around an afk avatar so that it appeared the avatar was having sex, vomiting, or getting ready to stab someone with a knife. Snapshots of the hapless avatar could then be circulated to further tease the resident upon their return from being afk. Residents told stories of going afk to make dinner for their actual-world families, then finding that "they had made my bent-over avatar look like he was doing all sorts of evil things I won't mention, and took pictures!" Such jokes could also take place at the level of chat, as in the following excerpt, when I got up from my computer to snack:

> Joe: Tom are you here?
> Joe gets out a pen and draws all over Tom
> Joe: hehe
> Me: yes sorry was afk

This shows how the idea of afk can be put to conscious use. From the early days of MUDs, afk could be incorporated into forms of cybersociality: "This commonly understood fact of MUD life provides for the MUD equivalent of pretending not to hear. I know of players who take care after such a pretense not to type anything more to the MUD until the would-be conversant has left, thus preserving the apparent validity of their excuse" (Curtis 1992:133). During my fieldwork it was common for someone to simply stop typing in an uncomfortable situation, leading those around them to conclude they had "gone afk" due to some actual-world interruption. Residents sometimes explicitly scheduled mundane actual-world activities like laundry to coincide with events in Second Life, so that they could run back and forth to the washing machine: as one resident emphasized, "afk works so well because people do not know what we are doing [in the actual world]." Residents sometimes said they wished they could "go afk" in the actual world to escape uncomfortable situations, but knew this was not possible: "no one ever says 'afk' in real life." Such conscious uses of afk reflect the consequentiality and durability of the virtual/actual binarism: the boundary between virtual and actual is *constituted and reinforced* by movements between them. Like lag, afk reveals how virtual worlds are places in their own right, temporally linked to the actual world but constantly at risk of falling out of synch. Indeed what I term the "afk test" provides one of the clearest means for identifying virtual worlds: if you can go "afk" from something, that something is a virtual world.

IMMERSION.

Lag and afk are not just tardiness and daydreaming online; they are novel aspects of cybersociality that reveal how configurations of place and time constitute virtual worlds. These mundane phenomena illuminate implications of "immersion" and "presence," two common terms in the scholarly literature concerning online sociality (Castronova 2005:80). For instance, it has been possible for afk to be incorporated into cybersocialities since the rise of MUDs because afk persons are connected-but-idle in a specific sense: the person is absent but their avatar remains present. If both person and avatar go away, the person is said to be "logged off" or "offline," not afk. The idea of "*away* from keyboard" encodes assumptions about virtual agency and selfhood embedded in "awayness," the unacknowledged antonym to "presence." Afk ethnographically demonstrates the possibility—indeed, the constitutive ubiquity—of *presence without immersion.* This decoupling of presence and immersion—the appearance of a gap between them—is one hallmark of the virtual.

In the study of virtual worlds, "immersion" historically referred to a sense that sensory experience of the actual world was sufficiently muted, and sensory experience of a virtual world sufficiently heightened, so that persons felt they were no longer in the actual world. This notion of an "immersive virtual environment" (Blascovich 2002:128) has been associated with virtual reality technologies like visualization helmets and data gloves (Schroeder 1996). The ethnographic materials I have presented thus far indicate how this notion of immersion does not accurately characterize the dominant cultural logics at play in Second Life; it partakes of the "immersive fallacy" that "the pleasure of a media experience lies in its ability to sensually transport the participant into an illusory, simulated reality" (Salen and Zimmerman 2004:450). In virtual worlds, "virtuality" refers to sociality, not the senses.

The example of voice provides a useful example with which to consider these imbrications of virtuality, immersion, the senses, and the social. During the period of my fieldwork, communication in Second Life was primarily text-based. The virtual world was full of ambient sound (wind, footsteps, waterfalls, a typing sound as people chatted), and Internet radio or other sound could be streamed into specific parcels of land, but voice was not used for everyday communication. The question as to whether or not Second Life should acquire voice capabilities was the topic of heated debate and even protests (Au 2007c; Llewelyn 2007; see figure 4.3).[28] At times this debate touched upon questions of disability: people who had trouble typing wanted voice, while those who were hearing-impaired did not. (I never saw visual impairment discussed, reflecting how vision was a near-precondition for virtual worlds during the time of my fieldwork.) For the nondisabled, the controversy often touched upon questions of language. Many residents, particularly those living in countries where languages other than English

FIGURE 4.3. A sign protesting a proposal to add voice capabilities to Second Life (image by author).

dominated, understood spoken English only with difficulty, but could communicate effectively in written English. Residents sometimes described how "it's fun to convey nuance in typing," an attraction to textual communication that extended, for instance, to many dominant/submissive sexual relationships, where for the submissive partner carefully crafted chat could demonstrate obedience to their dominant partner.

What made debates about voice particularly impassioned were questions of presence and immersion that implicated the boundary between virtual and actual. Some residents felt voice would facilitate greater intimacy. For instance, Kimmy recalled how, after several months of increasing closeness to her Second Life boyfriend Jax, they decided to speak to each other using third-party software: "The first thing Jax said to me after he got his microphone working was 'can you hear me?' I said 'yeah' and he goes sweeeeeeeeeeeeeet lol. It was cool how he said it, cause right then I could tell he was the same person he was on Second Life. Just the whole tone of his voice."

However, other residents felt that voice would damage a border between the virtual and actual that they wished to maintain—that it would "destroy the fantasy." When one resident said "I think voice will be doom," it was to this border that he was referring. Many worried that even if voice were optional or one's voice could be electronically altered, the choice not to use it would have social implications. One resident who had participated in a different virtual world that had added voice capabilities described how her refusal to use voice was taken to mean that she was actually a man ("what are you hiding?" she was asked); another resident who had participated in a different virtual world emphasized how he "missed out on quite a bit because I didn't have voice [capabilities on my computer]." As one resident put it, "voicechat is an extension of rl"; as "a reminder of rl stuff some people would rather leave behind," it would blur the line between virtual and actual in an undesirable fashion: "for some people, it can break the illusions that they create in sl . . . to hear someone's real voice . . . it can ruin everything." In this view "if you introduce reality into a virtual world, it's no longer a virtual world: it's just an adjunct to the real world. It ceases to be a place, and reverts to being a medium . . . [and] voice is reality" (Bartle 2003a; see also Castronova 2005:89–90). Voice was thereby assumed to have a kind of direct link to the actual, a link assumed to be missing for visual phenomena (textures based on actual-world wood or stone, avatar skins derived from digital photographs of actual human skin) or physical phenomena (gravity, day and night, the distinction between land and water). Such phenomena were not necessarily "reality" when appearing in a virtual world, but voice was widely assumed to be irredeemably actual.

The debate over voice underscores how sensory input can be important even in virtual worlds that do not employ "virtual reality" technologies like helmets or data gloves, but it also shows how questions of sensory input have been subordinate to an understanding of immersion in social terms. Voice capabilities have not been needed for Second Life to form as a virtual world with its own culture, and could even lead to fragmentation: "I've found that voice chat splits people in two or three groups," one resident noted. "You'll have the ones who use only voice, the ones that use only text, and the people who don't care what they use." There is more than one way for a person to be "immersed": "Either the sensory inputs are so good that you actually think the crafted environment you're in is genuine, or, you become so involved mentally and emotionally in the [virtual] world that you stop paying attention to the fact that it is only [virtual]. *It turns out that the way humans are made*, the software-based approach seems to have had much more success. . . . As we head into the twenty-first century, the dominant paradigm for virtual reality is not hardware but software" (Castronova 2005:5, emphasis added).

While in the 1990s virtual worlds were commonly seen as "the form of reality that VR [virtual reality technology] enables" (Balsamo 1995a:348), it is now clear that virtual immersion is above all a social product, as Castronova's invocation of "the way humans are made" suggests. "Virtual" has come to index the cultural practices I term techne; only secondarily does it reference the striking graphics and creative possibilities that make such an impression upon the newcomer to online worlds. An entailment of this cultural logic is that single-player video games or three-dimensional design programs are less definitively virtual worlds, despite their graphic capabilities. What such video games and design programs lack is social immersion. At the intersection of place and time, social immersion comes into being as the constitutional ground for homo cyber.

As virtual worlds increase in size, questions of immersion will complexify. For instance, as my research progressed debates using phrases like "immersion versus augmentation" or "world versus platform" appeared with greater frequency (Bennetsen 2006; see also Almond 2005; Ondrejka 2004b). These phrases reflected a potential conflict between two cultural logics for virtual worlds. A logic of immersion predicated virtuality on a one-way transfer of analogies from the actual to the virtual. A logic of augmentation accepted analogical traffic between the virtual and actual; it presumed that virtual worlds could be one among many "platforms" for computer-enhanced sociality and work (in line with things like email or a web browser). In this view, virtual worlds could augment actual-world capabilities, social networks, and concepts. Like many binarisms, the dichotomy of immersion versus augmentation identifies two extremes that rarely manifested themselves in daily life. It marks stances toward virtual worlds that shade off into each other or even shift independently: more immersion does not necessarily mean less augmentation. Both assume a constitutive gap between the virtual and actual. Even an "augmentationist" understanding of virtual worlds acknowledges forms of immersion; indeed, it sees the actual world as becoming at least partially immersed in the virtual. In the Age of Techne, the most significant shift is not from augmentation to immersion or vice versa; it is the shift from sensory immersion to social immersion as techne's assumed effect.

PRESENCE.

Presence is often identified as a characteristic making virtual worlds "worlds" at all, even those that are solely textual (Markham 1998:17). Like the notion of immersion, the notion of presence is founded in a relationship to place and time: presence assumes both "the present" and conceptions of locality. It has been linked to immersion, so that an "immersive virtual environment" can be equated with virtual worlds "that organize sensory information in such a way as to create a psychological state in which the individual perceives himself or herself as being present or having 'presence' in" them (Blascovich 2002:129). As with immersion, most research on presence has focused on virtual reality rather than virtual worlds, but even in this literature there is a recognition that presence can result from "social richness" as well as "perceptual realism" (Schuemie et al. 2001:184; see also Heeter 1992; Lombard and Ditton 1997; Towell and Towell 1997:590).[29] As a result, "presence is one of the most elusive and evocative aspects of virtual systems—and yet it forms the very foundation on which immersion is built. . . . This grounding of presence not only consists of embodied practice, but of embodied *social* practice" (Taylor 2002:42, emphasis in original; see also Schroeder 2006).

The phenomenon of afk highlights the role of presence in virtual worlds. While afk is distinctive to virtual worlds, specifying this distinctiveness can be difficult: "people daydream, sleep, and imagine themselves in other settings even while in a given physical environment. . . . Individuals 'tune out' others in their physical presence all the time" (Blascovich 2002:129–30). The difference is that the afk person is not just daydreaming. They are *away*; they have shifted their presence to the actual world, or (in secondary meanings of afk) elsewhere in a virtual world.

Just as there are gradations of afk, so there are gradations of presence. For instance, during the time of my fieldwork there was a broad understanding that communication using ims involved less presence than communication within visual range using chat. Virtual place signified intimacy. For instance, one day I was im-ing a friend when they suddenly teleported to my location, saying "I just wanted to say hi in person—it feels so rude to only talk through ims."

While it has often been thought that emerging technologies will lead to inauthentic forms of placelessness (Relph 1976), it is clear that virtual worlds come into existence through a social field constituted by practices of place and time (Tuan 1977), even phenomena like lag and afk that are forms of breakdown in the thrownness of virtual place and time. These practices, even afk, are all forms of techne. The afk person leaves the keyboard in some sense; there is no equivalent way to leave one's body in the actual world, except perhaps as a ghost. It is thus no coincidence that an avatar which, due to a program error, remains after a person has logged off is often called a "ghost." The afk person haunts the virtual world of which they are a part. Afk straddles the border between online and offline; it is a kind of ghostly absent presence. In *Specters of Marx*, Derrida set forth the idea of a "hauntology," a theory of haunting (rather than an "ontology" or theory of being), linking it to the virtual and to techne: "the differential deployment of *tekhne* . . . obliges us more than ever to think the virtualization of place and time, the possibility of virtual events whose movement and speed prohibit us more than ever . . . from opposing presence to its representation" (Derrida 1994:169). Derrida wished to show that "the virtual is essential to the real, that 'ghosts' haunt the full presence of the real" (Poster 1999:50).

From such a hauntological perspective, afk is not a state of exception, but a specific "metaphysics of presence" (Derrida 1974:131). It can even be seen as the essence of culture in virtual worlds, the point where immersion and presence meet. When persons are in a virtual world, they are still embodied in the actual world and so are always already "away from keyboard," even when typing in front of their computer screens. The resolution of "be right back" is endlessly deferred: residents never completely "come back" to a virtual world because they were never completely there in the first place. This reveals the affinity between ethnography and the virtual, since ethnography is based upon the paradoxical method of participant observation, an "awkward presence" in the culture of those being studied (Strathern 1991:26–27). Phenomena like lag and afk indicate how "the ultimate lesson of the 'virtual reality' is the virtualization of the very 'true' reality: by the mirage of 'virtual reality,' the 'true' reality itself is posited as a semblance of itself, as a pure symbolic construct" (Žižek 1992:135). Virtual worlds show how we have always been virtually human.

Chapter 5

PERSONHOOD

The self—The life course—Avatars and alts—
Embodiment—Gender and race—Agency.

The self.

The self might seem to be the most obvious idea in the contemporary world. No one would say that speakers create language anew with each sentence they utter; what they say is obviously said through a language that precedes them and that they never know in its entirety. Yet a set of cultural ideologies associated with what is termed the Western Enlightenment, but now found to a surprising degree worldwide, contend that the individual is prior to society—be that the shopper who consumes, the citizen who votes, the worker who labors, or the intimate who loves.

This book has intentionally focused first on fundamental issues of history, method, place, and time. It is only now, in its fifth chapter, that I turn to the questions of identity that dominated many discussions of virtual worlds during the decade preceding my fieldwork. They dominated these discussions with good reason: of all concepts found in human societies, the notion we can gloss as "person," "self," or "individual" has been one of the most powerful but also one of the most obscure. Because concepts of personhood shape ideas of agency, desire, and possession, they have enormous consequences for what it means to be virtually human.[1]

An interest in selfhood extends back to early periods of anthropological thought. In his classic essay "A Category of the Human Mind: the Notion of Person; the Notion of 'Self,'" first published in 1938, Marcel Mauss traced the dominant Western conception of selfhood to the Latin term *persona*, which referred to a mask. Masks originally deindividualized by reducing the wearer to an "artificial role" (Mauss 1979a:81), but eventually "became synonymous with the true nature of the individual" (ibid.). With the rise of capitalism this "true nature of the individual" became linked to notions of productivity and possession (Macpherson 1962; Zaretsky 1976). This linkage has been crucial to the "creationist capitalism" that undergirded the political economy of Second Life during the period of my fieldwork (see chapter 8). A longstanding body of ethnographic research has demonstrated the provincialism of this now-dominant conception of selfhood, as summarized by the following quotation, known to many anthropologists: "The Western conception of the person as a bounded, unique, more or less integrated motivational and cognitive universe, a dynamic center of awareness, emotion, judgment, and action organized into a distinctive whole and set contrastively both against other such wholes and against its social and natural background, is, however incorrigible it may seem to us, a rather peculiar idea within the context of the world's cultures" (Geertz 1983:59). A few scholars still group residents of virtual worlds into a single category of "users," "gamers," or "players" (e.g., Beck and Wade 2004), but such generalizations have largely given way to more fine-grained categorizations, like Richard Bartle's 1996 four-way distinction between "achievers," "explorers," "socializers," and "killers" (Bartle 2003b:403). My ethnographic goal is not to seek a better typology but to investigate everyday senses of virtual personhood. What does it mean when residents say "in Second Life I find I can truly be myself, my inner self?"; "we wear our souls in here?"; and "I find it easy to be several selves here?"

The notion of the "role" has shaped conceptions of identity online. One important history to virtual worlds involves massively multiple online games, and in most of these players take on roles—elf, soldier, spaceship pilot, and so on. This idea of playing a role persists to varying degrees in many virtual worlds and has often been a focus of ethnographic interest (e.g., Schaap 2002:17). For instance, the very idea of a "screen name" different from one's actual-world name can imply a role. In addition, many places or subcultures within Second Life were based on roleplay. However, in comparison to online games that coexisted with Second Life during the period of my fieldwork, Second Life was not predominantly a role-playing environment. Most of those with whom I interacted felt that role-playing, in the words of one resident, "quickly loses its appeal; then you concentrate on 'being yourself,' since that's what most people are good at." For most residents, their primary mode of engagement with Second Life was as, in some sense, "themselves." Yet as another resident put it, "I always think that people behave a little differently in their online personas than for real, no matter what their intentions. I think that online activity is roleplay in every sense, even those who aren't roleplaying, because people just suppress certain aspects of their personalities and accentuate others." This reflects a broadly shared cultural assumption that virtual selfhood is not identical to actual selfhood. I have even heard this termed "persona-play" in distinction to "roleplay."

Given my argument that the gap between virtual and actual is foundational to culture in online worlds, it is not surprising that the continuity of selfhood between virtual and actual has been a robust area of debate and concern. Perhaps the earliest discussion of this issue appeared in the 1985 article "The Strange Case of the Electronic Lover," which recounted the story of Joan, a severely disabled young woman who became involved in a range of friendships and romances on a text-based virtual world (the CompuServe forums)—before it was revealed that "Joan" was actually "Alex," a male psychiatrist in his fifties (Van Gelder 1991; see also Stone 1995). An interest in the self continues to characterize scholarship on virtual worlds, but has increasingly questioned the primacy of the individual to ask how identities "are not produced by sovereign and autonomous subjects alone . . . identity-producing interactions take place in the use of communicative and signifying practices" (Fornäs et al. 2002:34). Such "identity-producing interactions" are "technologies of the self" (Foucault 1986), forms of techne turned inward to shape selfhood.

Since the early days of cybersociality, a crucial issue has been how the gap created by techne allows persons to have distinct identities in virtual worlds versus the actual world: "it seems to me that the most significant social factor in MUDs is the perfect anonymity provided to the players" (Curtis 1992:129). To take advantage of this possibility, many residents kept their actual and virtual selfhoods distinct during the time of my fieldwork. Somewhat extreme cases of this existed in the form of celebrities who spent time in Second Life without revealing their actual-world identities; they were thus able to gain a measure of everyday interaction unavailable in the actual world. One resident recalled how she discovered a friend of hers in-world was a Hollywood star: "last Christmas she finally revealed who she was—she even showed her face to me on webcam."

The gap between virtual and actual self could reverberate into everyday practices of identification and interaction. One resident noted how "the SL me and the RL me are two totally different people. I may appear strong in my online presence, but in RL I'm so weak it's not even funny." Another concurred by stating that "the personality I exude in SL is almost completely 180 degrees from what I show in public in RL." A third resident concluded that "Second Life is a chance to be someone else beside yourself, which you can't really do it in RL unless you want to lead a double life." For this resident, living a virtual-world and actual-world life was not a "double life"; with one self for the actual world and another self for the virtual world, there was no necessary sense of doubleness or overlap. Instead, in the words of one resident, the gap between virtual and actual "allows you to define your own role instead of being the one you are in RL (in my case, mother, wife)." In this understanding the *actual* world is more characterized by "role-playing" than virtual worlds, where one's self is open to greater self-fashioning and can be more assertive (no one during my fieldwork mentioned being outgoing in the actual world but shy in Second Life).

Alongside this notion of relatively separate virtual-world and actual-world selves, many residents saw varying forms of interpenetration and mutual constitution. The "immersion versus augmentation" debate discussed in chapter 4 with regard to place was relevant to questions of personhood as well. I recall hanging out with a group of residents when one person claimed "SL is all about just showing what you want to." He quickly encountered dissenting responses:

"I don't think ultimately anyone succeeds in concealing who they are."
"My appearance may change, but you're still talking to ME, my
     personality."
"I would imagine that the majority of the people who play here put in
     more of their personality than they'd like to admit."

For some, this sense of a permeable border between actual-world and virtual-world self was experienced in positive terms. Their online lives could make their actual-world self more "real," in that it could become closer to what they understood to be their true selfhood, unencumbered by social constraints or the particularities of physical embodiment. Common in this regard was the view that virtual-world experiences could lead to greater self-confidence: "I noticed yesterday that I had no problem talking to a complete stranger at the shopping center, simply because I have spent a lot of time in SL recently doing the same thing." Another described how: "People who are people-shy, after they have positive experiences here, move that into rl and go out more. I know one girl who has been housebound for years; she recently went out for coffee by herself [in the actual world]. Another person, a stroke survivor who was been in a wheelchair for a couple of years, found the strength to work toward walking again thanks to his involvement in Second Life: he's now walking using a walker sometimes."

When I asked this resident if such personal change could happen in text-only virtual worlds like MUDs, he replied: "I think the likelihood is considerably less, and here is why. In SL, you can develop parts of you that because of other constraints or expectations, you do not. And with that development, you can practice it in a natural way, every day, as much as you want. So if you have an inner desire, you get a chance to be supported, a chance to do it naturally. So it isn't from the outside. It is from the inside." Like many residents, this person saw nothing strange in referring to Second Life as a "natural" environment that allowed people to bring out something "from the inside." Against views of online technology as inevitably alienating, virtual worlds can provide contexts for self-fashioning—techne in its most basic sense. Some Second Life residents spoke of their virtual-world self as "closer to" their "real" self than their actual-world self. For this reason, Curtis's notion of "perfect anonymity" in virtual worlds has eroded. During my fieldwork not all Second Life residents knew that I was Tom Boellstorff, but all could see that I was Tom Bukowski. Screen names are by definition not anonymous, and the virtual selfhoods tied to them have become increasingly consequential. Just as it is possible to take virtual worlds in their own terms, so it is possible to take virtual personhoods in their own terms. In both cases, the virtual is shaped in powerful ways by referential and practical relationships to the actual world, but these relationships help constitute the virtual itself.

The life course.

One way cultures construct selfhood is by placing the self on a temporal trajectory or life course: "In order to exist in the social world with a comfortable sense of being a good, socially proper, and stable person, an individual needs to have a coherent, acceptable, and constantly revised life story" (Linde 1993:3). All humans are born, grow and age, and finally, die, but there are patterns to how people understand their life course, and these patterns are not biological pregivens; they are forged through culture, and this can now include culture in virtual worlds. Historically cultures often set forth a limited range of roles for their members, but although "until recently . . . traditions provided a relatively finite set of possible lives . . . [now] more persons throughout the world see their lives through the prisms of the possible lives offered by mass media" (Appadurai 1996:53). A body of work in the social sciences and beyond has examined how modern notions of selfhood now presume a personalized life course (Giddens 1991:145–49). During my fieldwork, residents would often say things like "she's only 19 weeks old" or "tomorrow is my second birthday" and be understood to refer to a life course specific to Second Life. Yet a person who had participated in Second Life for two years but switched avatars after one year would typically be understood to be *two* years old. What, then, might it mean to speak of a Second Life course?

During the time of my research, such a virtual life course began when someone in the actual world registered for a Second Life account. One of the few structuring principles for a Second Life course was the date when an account was created, sometimes termed a "Second Life birthday." This date could not be altered but did not definitively indicate a resident's status, since a resident could have other, older accounts. Choosing a screen name—which could only be composed of one first name and one last name—was central to this process. One could invent any first name but had to select a last name from a list. Once selected, the screen name could never be changed; as in many online worlds, it constituted the only immutable aspect of virtual selfhood (Reid 1996:328–29; Schaap 2002:41–46).[2] Screen names were important because most persons in Second Life gave out their actual-world names to few, if any, fellow residents. Since many residents had more than one account, and since two or more actual-world persons sometimes shared a single account, screen names indexed virtual life courses that could not necessarily be mapped onto actual-world persons. The screen name's importance throughout the history of virtual worlds is understandable given the significance of names in the dominant Western tradition from which virtual worlds emerged: "although most Westerners take their existence for granted, fixed, hereditary surnames are modern inventions . . . permanent surnames help to chart the human topography of any region. Names play a vital role in determining identities, cultural affiliations, and histories" (Scott, Tehranian, and Mathias 2002:6). Mauss noted how the rise of personalized names shaped concepts of the self (Mauss 1979a:80); as its title implies, screen names played a key role in the narrative of the 1981 novella "True Names" (Vinge 2001:244), one of the first works of fiction to represent a virtual world (see chapter 2).

Once a screen name was chosen, an avatar bearing that screen name would appear at a place called "Orientation Island," where the new resident could learn the basics of controlling avatar movement using keyboard and mouse. Orientation Island did not teach about social norms despite some calls for it to do so: this Linden Lab-controlled area encoded an assumption that mastering the basics of Second Life meant mastering a set of technical abilities.[3] After leaving Orientation Island, residents entered the "Welcome Area," a place located on the main continent of Second Life. From this point onward, residents were free to travel anywhere (excepting plots of land whose owners had banned general entry). There was no specific path to follow: one resident described a commonly experienced sense of "walking around in a daze when I started," and another described the typical sentiment that "I didn't have a 'class' or 'teacher' besides people I've met along the way." In virtual worlds with a more salient gaming component, residents often ascended through skill levels that structured their life course inworld. In such cases "leveling" or "skilling" provided a standardized measure of online experience.[4] In more open-ended virtual worlds like Second Life, the experience of being a "newbie" or "noob" (terms used in many virtual worlds; see Kendall 2002:31, 128–38) was more diffuse.

Newbie status was often revealed by facility with embodiment, social norms, and the interface. For example, controlling one's view, typically termed "camera movement," was often described as one of the hardest things for newbies to learn; it was important because of the emphasis on visuality in Second Life and the need for varied perspectives when building and socializing. Because the Second Life interface allowed one to build and script inworld, the interface was complex and mastering it could be challenging. I recall sitting with a group of residents when one asked "so how do you tell a newbie?" Another resident responded "by the box on their head!" This referred to the fact that commodities (shirts, for instance) were often sold within a prim, usually a box for simplicity's sake. Newbies often had difficulty extracting the box's contents, accidentally "wearing" the box once or twice before successfully removing the commodity.[5] When I began my fieldwork, I experienced several such frustrating experiences; for instance, going to an ice skating rink, purchasing ice skates that would animate my avatar so that it skated about on the rink, but repeatedly finding my avatar wearing the box in which the skates were sold, rather than the skates themselves.

During the conversation noted above about identifying newbies, two other residents emphasized "appearance, skin, animations" and "body language . . . behavior is a giveaway," while a third added "facility with chat and movement." These comments reveal how embodiment was part of the Second Life course. As discussed below, a wide range of embodiments were available to residents and the average resident spent more than an hour a week perfecting the look and movement of their avatars (Ondrejka 2004a:11). Newbies often did not yet have the skills to take advantage of these possibilities, so their avatars remained close to the default embodiment provided with a new account.

Newbies also had to learn the social norms of Second Life's culture. Some of these norms were specific to particular subcultures or communities, but others were widespread. A mundane example involved standing up before teleporting away or shutting down the Second Life program, so that nearby residents had a visual cue of one's immanent departure. Failure to provide such a warning was sometimes derided as "poofing." One resident who spent time in Second Life with an actual-world brother noted how "it's interesting having to learn the rules of society. When I log in, I used to appear inside our brother's house, which is not what we do in real life. So it took some time to figure out how to appear outside and ask to come in." Norms around social proxemics (for instance, how close to stand to another avatar while talking) were widely shared—and, like notions of everything from landscape to embodiment, drew upon cultural logics from the actual world (Au 2006g; Yee et al. 2007). Another common norm was virtual altruism: the tendency for residents to offer free advice, support, and objects. In the conversation about newbies discussed earlier, one resident noted that it was possible to identify newbies because "they are like OMG [oh my God] COOL when you give them landmarks to places with free stuff." Social norms also included familiarity with communicative conventions around chatting and instant messaging. One resident, speaking to a group of friends at a club, described how "I typed 'afk' for two months before I got the balls to ask what it meant—I didn't want to look like a noob."

Residents taught courses within Second Life on a range of topics: scripting, building, texturing, even more general courses on making money, land management, event management, or planning a virtual wedding. During most of the period of my fieldwork, Linden Lab paid some residents for hosting educational events. However, as in many virtual worlds, learning was mostly informal (Nardi, Ly, and Harris 2007; Gee 2003); this could be termed a "sandbox" model of learning. Residents would happily volunteer information about Second Life, as in the case of the following exchange, overheard at a dance club:

ELIOT: Hmm . . . How do I make what I'm wearing a set of clothes?
WALT: Right-click yourself and pick "appearance"
YOKI: Go to "appearance" and hit "make outfit" on the buttons on the bottom
ELIOT: I found it—thankies!

As persons spent more time in Second Life, their newbie status would fade and they would become known as residents, players, participants, or even "midbies." Midbie status was shaped not just by the absolute amount of time since the creation of an account, but by the cumulative amount of time spent inworld. A resident whose account was two years old, but was online just an hour a week, would typically be seen as more of a newbie than a resident who acquired an account only six months ago, but who had then spent roughly thirty hours a week in Second Life since that time. The amount of time a resident had spent inworld was not visible on their profile; this was a matter of judgment, based upon the apparent expertise and social networks of the resident in question. Some residents settled into a pattern of solitude—building, designing items to sell, or just enjoying a stroll through a virtual park, with few social activities or close friendships inworld. There is a need for a theory of cybersociality that takes into account how some people enter virtual worlds to be left alone. Yet for most residents, time with others was important to their virtual lives. A common sign one was no longer a newbie was that one had acquired intimates—friends, lovers, even kin—specific to Second Life. A significant decision for midbie residents was whether or not to acquire land. The decision to purchase or rent land for personal use (for instance, a home, park, or museum) and/or for commercial use (for example, a club or a store in a shopping mall) marked a greater investment in the virtual world, though some residents participated heavily in Second Life while remaining "homeless."

As residents accumulated more experience inworld, they would often become known as community leaders or notable figures to whom others could turn for advice. Given the novelty of Second Life and all graphical virtual worlds during the period of my fieldwork, even a few months inworld might qualify one as an "oldbie." Becoming known as an oldbie or community leader involved more than age; it was a matter of status as well. As in actual-world cultures, who qualified as a "leader" could be a matter of disagreement and debate. As noted in chapter 3, my Tom Bukowski account was older than over 99 percent of other accounts by the closing months of my research: ethnographers are usually not among the oldest members of the cultures they study.

In the actual world, every life course has an end, through notions like reincarnation complicate the issue. In Second Life, a resident could in theory be said to "die" every time they logged out of the Second Life program and their avatar disappeared from the virtual world, but I never encountered logging off described in this way. The gap between virtual and actual was not framed in terms of life and death. A much more common way in which Second Life courses came to an end was when residents stopped entering Second Life. The range of reasons for doing so was broad, but fell into two main categories. First, some residents felt that Second Life had started to detract from their actual-world lives, either because they were spending too much time in Second Life or because of a changed circumstance in their actual-world lives, like the illness of a relative. Such concerns underscore how time resists virtualization in a way that space does not—time spent in Second Life was for the most part time not spent in the actual world, though phenomena like afk trouble this neat binarism. In some cases, emotional intensity was the issue: residents might choose to leave because they felt a sexual relationship in Second Life was interfering with their actual-world marriage.

A second reason for leaving Second Life was dissatisfaction with the virtual world itself. Some residents stopped participating in Second Life soon after acquiring accounts: they found the interface too difficult to master, were seeking a more structured gaming experience, wanted to earn money but were failing to do so, or viewed the social activities as unfulfilling. In other cases, residents who had spent months or years in Second Life would stop participating due to disappointments with the Second Life platform and Linden Lab's governance of the virtual world: as one resident put it, "Linden Lab finally pushed me over the edge; this place is no fun for me anymore." Frustrations included bugs and more ongoing defects with the software that resulted in lag, missing items in one's inventory, and even crashes of the entire grid (compare Ito 1997). I recall, for instance, the sense of aggravation that broke out in late 2005 when Linden Lab updated the platform to add more detailed water "ripple effects," but did not appear to prioritize problems with lag that had become a serious concern. Other frustrations involved the apparent inability of Linden Lab to eliminate problems like offensive speech, inappropriate behavior, and unfair business practices. Some residents sympathized with the company's efforts to address these issues, but others felt that a hands-off approach to many dimensions of governance was leading to significant social disruption. Yet another source of frustration by the end of my fieldwork was that Second Life was becoming "too corporate" as more actual-world companies began moving into the virtual world in search of visibility and profit.

Regardless of the source, some frustrated residents would respond by reducing the amount of time they spent in Second Life. If they owned property this could include "tiering down," reducing the monthly tier fee paid to Linden Lab and selling off property in excess of the newly reduced tier. Some stopped owning land altogether and became "homeless" residents, or shifted from owning property to renting an apartment. A more drastic possibility was for residents to leave Second Life permanently. Particularly for "oldbie" residents who felt they had invested time and energy in Second Life and had friends they might never meet offline, this was a painful decision, charted on blogs and commemorated with farewell parties. Since Second Life accounts were free by the end of my fieldwork, residents leaving Second Life might not bother to terminate their accounts; a benefit of this was that ims sent to the account could be forwarded to an email account, allowing former residents to stay in touch with friends from Second Life. Particularly if an account had not been terminated, residents might be unsure if someone had left Second Life permanently or was just logging on infrequently, an uncertainty that could be an annoyance in itself, as in the following conversation at a dance club:

MAGAN: Hey, does anyone remember Rising Starr?
CARLL: Yes!

MAGAN: She isn't here no more
CARLL: whatever happened to her, anyway?
CARLL: I dunno
MAGAN: I am wearing a dress she made
CARLL: I still have a couple of her outfits.
MAGAN: I hate it when people just up and disappear.

Another kind of ending to a Second Life course occurred when some-one died in the actual world. For instance, one day I found a shirt by "Lila" for my avatar; I liked the shirt so much that I decided to search for Lila to see if she had any other shirts for sale. Her profile said: "Lila died on March 4th, 2006. Please forward any requests for shirts to Ian. Thanks and yes I miss her something terrible—Ian." I attended memorial services for residents who had died in the actual world, complete with mourners in black, roses, testi-monials, and actual-world photographs of the departed. The death of a per-son in the actual world was usually interpreted as bringing out the death of any avatars the person had.[6] For instance, in December 2004 I encountered a church with the following notecard attached to it: "I placed this church on my property to celebrate Christmas. Now it serves as a memorial to Tessie, my best friend in SL, who was killed instantly December 21, 2004 by a drunk driver. She enjoyed SL for all the things she could do here. I'm proud to have been a part of the time she spent in SL, but it was far too short." In theory, a different resident could take over the avatar of someone who had died in the actual world, resulting in a kind of virtual reincarnation. However, I did not hear of any cases of this happening during my fieldwork. Instead, the avatar would be rendered inactive as a memorial to the deceased person.

AVATARS AND ALTS.

Throughout this book I have been referring to the virtual embodiments of persons as avatars, a term used in many online worlds. This Sanskrit word originally referred to the incarnation of a Hindu god (particularly Vishnu). With reference to cybersociality, the term was probably first used in the virtual worlds Habitat and Ultima IV in the mid-1980s, as well as in Neal Stephenson's 1993 science fiction novel *Snow Crash* (Morningstar and Farmer 1991; Stephenson 1993:470).[7] While "avatar" ("avie" or "av" for short) historically referred to incarnation—a movement from virtual to actual—with respect to online worlds it connotes the opposite move-ment from actual to virtual, a decarnation or invirtualization. Even before the term was coined, observers of virtual worlds noted linkages between sociality, subjectivity, and embodiment: "people have a very proprietary feeling towards their image [i.e., their avatar]. What happens to it happens to them. What touches it, they feel. . . . A new kind of social situation is created" (Krueger 1983:127–28).

In Second Life during my fieldwork, the particular landscape you saw at any moment while online was the view from your avatar's proximity (though not its eyes, unless using "mouselook" mode). The virtual thirty-meter radius within which you "heard" the typed chat of other residents extended out from your avatar's body. Avatars, however, were not just abstract anchors of virtual perspective; they were the modality through which residents experienced virtual selfhood, "central to both immersion and the construction of community in virtual spaces" (Taylor 2006a:110; see also Hudson-Smith 2002:82). The idea of an avatar usually implies an embodiment that is intentionally crafted—the product of techne—and thus a "zone of relationality" between persons (Weinstone 2004:40). Avatars allowed residents to see if other persons were present and where their attention was directed; avatars could also express durable aspects of self-identity (Çapin et al. 1999:6; see also Damer 1998; Kushner 2004). Avatars are thus "one of the central points at which users intersect with a technological object and embody themselves, making the virtual environment and the variety of phenomena it fosters real" (Taylor 2002:41). Avatars make virtual worlds real, not actual: they are a position from which the self encounters the virtual.

A sense of total control over one's self-representation has been a striking feature of virtual worlds even when they were text-based (Markham 1998:124) and is, if anything, more significant in graphical virtual worlds. In Second Life embodiment could be changed for free, as often as one wished. The platform's "appearance" menu contained a range of sliders allowing residents to change nearly every aspect of their avatars, from overall height to the width of lips or the part of one's hair (figure 5.1; see Jones 2006:22–26). This slider self for the Age of Techne assumed near-total intentionality with regard to virtual embodiment: very little was randomized or left to chance.

In most virtual worlds during the period of my research, certainly including Second Life, residents lavished time and money on their avatars. The goal was typically not just an attractive or unusual avatar, but multiple embodiments, often across gender, race, even species (for instance, a handsome man, a wolf, and a robot). However, the most common modifications involved changing clothes or hair on a relatively stable human form. For instance, one resident recalled how "when I first started I alternated between two main avatars, and was planning on making more, but since I started actually meeting and hanging out with the same people I haven't

FIGURE 5.1. Using the "appearance" window (image by author).

really changed my basic look. . . . I started having static relationships, and wanted to remain a single entity." This link between avatar and sociality was widespread; other residents noted how "people treat you according to your avatar. It's a shame, but it's true," or "I sort of judge people based on their avatar appearance; I don't tend to like the tall skinny blondes."

In Second Life an avatar could be any age, gender, race, even species, but this very intentionality meant that avatars were interpreted as rather transparently indicative of resident selfhood: as one resident concluded, "I've come to observe that the outward appearance really does communicate a lot about who you are, because it's made up of conscious choices about how you want to present yourself." While as one resident put it, "you never really know who is on the other side of the mask," residents still judged each other based on avatar actions as well as appearance. Another resident described how "after a few weeks of SL, you 'learn' to watch other avatars. I don't necessarily mean 'animations reproducing RL body language,' but a SL-specific 'body language': knowing when someone is busy IMing, looking through scripts or inventory." A third resident recalled how "something interesting happened yesterday. I received an im from a complete stranger. It said 'Cheer up.' I couldn't figure out why he had sent it. I looked my av and noticed that I was sitting on a bench with my head down at an angle, like a sad-sack."

Such incidents reveal a perceived gap between actual-world self and virtual-world self; even residents who saw the two as in some way continuous or mutually informing would never, in my experience, claim they were self-identical. A controversy in 2006, when an intruder hacked into the Second Life platform, possibly gaining the ability to link avatars to actual-world names, exemplified a fear of closing this gap. While some concerns obviously related to compromised financial information, others were about selfhood, as in the case of the person who noted how "I make my living in SL as an escort. This is NOT the sort of thing I wish to have associated with my real self and would rather lose my account, its money, and the things I have worked pretty hard for, and just start all over again."[8]

During the time of my research, it was not really possible to have a fully automated avatar, but automated entities (often known as "bots," derived from "robot") were found in many virtual worlds, particularly those that were combat-based (or those with an educational emphasis, where the bots acted as guides or sources of information; Doyle and Hayes-Roth 1998; Turkle 1995). In the early years of Second Life, the term "bots" was not commonly used and there was little interest in the idea that residents might be automated. Toward the end of my fieldwork, there was increasing talk about bots, particularly "land bots" programmed to quickly purchase land that had mistakenly been set for sale at a low price. Volunteer helpers often found new residents of Second Life asking them "are you human?"—in other words, are you automated or not? Alieva noted how she was helping new residents when "the other day, I had to prove to someone that I wasn't a 'robot.' People with gaming experience tend to think that people willing to help are bots, not humans."

One factor complicating the relationship between self and avatar was an awareness that multiple persons could control a single avatar, as illustrated by the incident described in chapter 1, where Dara suspected there might be more than one person controlling my avatar Tom Bukowski. If a resident maintained a blog with lengthy daily postings, or was active with a range of business activities inworld, other residents might speculate that multiple actual-world persons were taking turns controlling the account. I recall when I was once playing Tringo with a group of about twenty residents in June 2005. While waiting for the next game to start, the following conversation took place between three residents seated near me:

GERI: Seth, you have amazingly muscley muscles
SETH: Little secret . . . I'm the wife playing for Seth til he gets home, lol

> LINA: Hiya Seth :)
> GERI: LOL
> LINA: awesome lol

In this example of a lack of one-to-one mapping between self and avatar, the avatar "Seth" is being temporarily controlled not by the person who originally created the avatar, but by the person's wife, but is still treated as "Seth" by Lina, albeit with a knowing emoticon smile.

This example demonstrates the isomorphism between person and avatar being thrown into question by the possibility of more than one person controlling a single avatar: multiple selves, one avatar. It was even more common for this isomorphism to be thrown into question from the other direction: single self, multiple avatars. This was the phenomenon of alternate avatars, known primarily as "alts," sometimes "nics" (from "nicknames"). Alts could be found in virtual worlds from their beginnings (Ito 1997:99; Rosenberg 1992; Stone 1995:120), and drew upon logics of technological multiplicity evinced, for instance, by the ubiquity of multiple email accounts.[9]

Alts were employed for many purposes. One kind of alt was the "banking alt," an alt whose account was used to hold funds, simplifying the work of bookkeeping. Another was the "building alt," used so residents could work at building or scripting without getting deluged by ims from their friends. Similar to building alts were "testing alts" with intentionally standard body shapes, used to try out clothing or animations. Some residents created "exploring alts" for wandering anonymously across the Second Life landscape. All of these kinds of alts were sometimes termed "escape alts," since they helped insulate residents from inworld social networks. For instance, while chatting with a group of friends in a park one day, "Mona" walked up to us and asked if she could hang out with us for a while. We invited her to sit down, remarking that none of us had met her before. She replied it was not surprising we did not know her, since, "This is a spare alt I have only used a couple of times. I was out on date from hell and had to get away. I met this guy; he seemed nice, but was set on taking me shopping. He had an ulterior motive I think. I'd had enough but I didn't want to go to bed yet. This alt is my getaway."

The most common kind of alt, however, was the "social alt," used to embody an alternative selfhood, and described by one resident as follows: "while the more fundamental personality of the real person is still driving in the background, it's filtered through a different surface persona." Another noted how "one reason I have alts is that I want to make people see past the avatar; a third observed that "some people like to explore different sides of themselves. The main account may be a proper housewife while the alt is a sexy escort!" Social alts could be used for more explicitly deceptive purposes, as in cases I encountered where residents created an alt in order to attempt seducing their Second Life spouse, so as to test the spouse's fidelity.

The concept of an "alt" only makes sense in opposition to the concept of a default avatar (often known as a "primary" or "prime" avatar),[10] typically the avatar created when a resident logged into Second Life for the first time. As one resident noted, "a lot of people have different avatars, but they have a main avatar they usually use, and their main avatar is usually designed by RL standards of beauty, or is a reflection of their RL self." This frequent imbrication between primary avatar and what was understood to be actual-world selfhood explains why it was that when residents referred to alts as "costumes" or "masks," or emphasized that they created alts that did not sound or look "like themselves," the implication was that the avatar in question was "alternative" to their primary avatar as much as their actual-world self. For instance, one resident described her alt as "very opposite to me [my primary avatar]. I type ('speak') differently on purpose when I'm her. I do different style things, like choose different laughing styles and other default animations. And my activities differ too—my alt, she works to make a living in Second Life, she's made over 300,000 lindens (about one thousand dollars) in the last couple of months."

Given how time resists virtualization in a way that space does not, it is understandable that alts could present temporal challenges. For instance, it could be difficult to maintain the social relationships of one's primary avatar and those of one or more alts. A means of coping with this issue of time was, as one resident observed, to "give your alt a persona that is 'busy in real life' and so cannot be online all that much. That way there isn't too much expectation, and your friends will cram into a couple hours a week's worth of fun and/or activities." Such a persona provided for an alt constitutes, in effect, the actual-world avatar of a virtual self.

During my fieldwork, alts were a widely accepted aspect of Second Life sociality. Since alts represented distinct accounts with their own passwords and histories, there was no way to absolutely determine if what appeared to be two residents were in fact alts controlled by the same person, short of the person volunteering that information. Oftentimes a resident's alts would be unknown even to their partner or closest friend in Second Life: many residents would have agreed with one person who concluded that "if my partner feels she needs to run around and get away with an alt I'm cool with that, and I don't need to know." In the absence of such information, residents would sometimes try to guess if two avatars might be alts based on things like idiosyncrasies of language use. One reason the plan to add voice to Second Life was so controversial was the belief that voice would make alts of the same actual-world person easier to identify. Despite such uncertainties, alts were not typically seen as deceptive, primarily because most residents did not reveal their actual-world identities even if they had only one avatar; an ethic of anonymity was pervasive in Second Life and most virtual worlds during my fieldwork.

EMBODIMENT.

That most graphical virtual worlds emphasized avatars by the time of my fieldwork indicated how embodiment had become central to online self-hood, largely displacing virtual reality technologies like data gloves and helmets (Biocca 1997) as well as forms of "textual embodiment" characteristic of text-based virtual worlds (Argyle and Shields 1996; Ito 1997; Markham 1998; McRae 1997; Reid 1996; Sundén 2003). It was increasingly the case that in graphical virtual worlds "presence enact[s] itself as an *embodied* activity" (Taylor 2002:44; see also Dourish 2001), an embodiment powerfully linked to vision (M. White 2006).[11] This emphasis on embodiment was significant because it challenged a longstanding presumption of cognition as disembodied. It represents a methodologically and theoretically significant convergence with ethnography, which is predicated on embodiment: rather than working as nineteenth-century "armchair anthropologists" who read the accounts of others, contemporary ethnographers are supposed to live in the places they study. Some scholars of virtual worlds have been suspicious of online embodiment, seeing virtual worlds as extending a Cartesian logic valorizing the mental over the physical: "the computer network simply brackets the physical presence of the participants, either by omitting or by simulating corporeal immediacy" (Heim 1991:74; see also Balsamo 1996:126; Jones 2006:12–13). But for many residents, Second Life had a corporeal immediacy that could not be reduced to a simulation of actual-world embodiment. Residents, for instance, might say that a particular animated chair caused their avatar to sit in an "unnatural" manner in comparison to the more "natural" animation they typically used. Virtual embodiment could even be understood as more authentic than actual-world embodiment; as one Second Life resident put it, "this is how I see myself on the inside."

I wish to challenge any "supposition conflating online interaction with bodily transcendence" (Campbell 2004:5) and argue for the reality of virtual embodiment. Actual-world embodiment certainly had consequences in Second Life: one saw or heard with actual eyes and ears, typed on a keyboard and moved a mouse with actual hands and fingers, even grew ill or died. Yet assuming that actual-world embodiment is the only real embodiment imputes "a fixity and integrity to bodily (pre-virtual) experience . . . fall[ing] back upon a rather romantic vision of the unmediated encounter between humans who are assumed in no way to be constituted by technologies of any kind" (Graham 2002:189). Embodiment can be physical, but "we are also bodies in a social and cultural sense, and we experience that, too" (Ihde 2002:xi; see also Graham 2002:187; Mitchell and Thurtle 2004).

This social and cultural experience of bodies is a form of techne, and it has long been noted that redeployments of techne can create "virtual" embodiment. In his 1935 essay "Body Techniques," Mauss noted how he erred in "thinking that there is technique only when there is an instrument. I had to go back to ancient notions, to the Platonic position on technique. . . . We are dealing with techniques of the body. The body is man's first and most natural instrument" (Mauss 1979b:104). In the Age of Techne, "when technique enters into every area of life, including the human, it ceases to be external to man and becomes his very substance" (Ellul 1964:6). Both virtual and actual embodiment are the product of techne, which is one reason why the notion of the posthuman inadequately characterizes virtual selfhood. Yet this very continuity also allows virtual embodiment to destabilize the human. This can be illustrated by examining cultural logics of embodied choice in Second Life, as well as the experiences of residents with actual-world disabilities.

Embodiment is often seen to be close to nature, and thus, it is assumed, something that "can't be helped," that lies outside choice, which is associated with culture. This understanding can persist even in the face of the many ways actual-world embodiment is shaped by human intentionality, from tattoos to plastic surgery. In many virtual worlds, including Second Life, embodiment was highly elastic, bringing notions of choice to the fore. As discussed in the previous section, during my fieldwork it was possible to alter, for free and at any time, any aspect of one's avatar except one's screen name (and the date the avatar's account was created). I recall walking up to a friend one day to find him looking like a cat. I complemented him on his animalistic avatar and he replied, "I wear this about 40 percent of the time." It was possible to purchase (or obtain for free) not just shirts, hair, and jewelry for avatars, but complete embodiment as an animal, child, robot, or anything else residents could imagine. One could understand "wearing" a whole embodiment in the same way one understood wearing a shirt or pair of shoes.

The cultural paradox was that as one resident phrased it, "being in SL means never having to be judged as the sum total of your appearance," yet as another resident noted, in Second Life "you can be who you are, not your [actual-world] body." That embodiment was framed in terms of choice meant it could be seen as a style or fashion, something only skin deep. Yet this ideology of choice also meant embodiment was seen to reveal something deeply true about the choosing self. In many virtual worlds "some users have even come to identify their avatar as 'more them' than their corporeal body" (Taylor 2002:54). This is one way that virtual worlds "change our notion of self because we will now be dynamic or unstable bodies" (Bolter and Grusin 1999:253). This instability was a source of pleasure for many residents, but could also lead to confusion. One resident, Icon, recalled when her friend Pente had returned from an actual-world vacation and so had not yet heard about "tinies," a new fashion where residents embodied themselves as three-foot high baby animals: "so me and my friend are these tiny foxes just chilling out and Pente comes around the corner and she goes WTF [what the fuck]????? I passed out laughing so damn hard."

The experiences of Second Life residents with actual-world physical disabilities throw into stark relief many of these issues around virtual embodiment.[12] The potential of virtual worlds to allow disabled persons to be embodied like the nondisabled has been noted from the earliest days of text-only chatrooms (e.g., Damer 1997:132; Van Gelder 1991:366). Incidental mentionings of temporary or permanent physical disability were common throughout my fieldwork, particularly if they effected one's ability to manipulate the Second Life interface. For instance, while chatting with a group of residents one day, one person interjected "Pardon the short sentences, I'm typing with one arm right now. I'll likely be out of work for around two months because of my broken arm." Another resident recalled attending a building class where the teacher had posted a sign stating "I have Parkinson's disease so the class may be interrupted briefly from time to time." Residents with arthritis spoke of difficulties in flying; those with visual impairment complained about small fonts; flashing particle effects could induce seizures in residents with epilepsy. Some residents even spoke of virtual disabilities, like the inability to type quickly or engage in the kind of abstract reasoning needed for scripting.

Most persons with disabilities embodied themselves in a manner indistinguishable from other residents, but a few created embodiments that referenced their actual-world disabilities, for instance by using a wheelchair. (Even I, with a very slight visual impairment, usually wore eyeglasses in Second Life.) This reflected a broader pattern in which some residents created avatars that resembled their actual-world embodiments, others created avatars differing in various ways from their actual-world embodiments, and still others created both kinds of embodiments (either to be worn by a single avatar, or by alts).

Many residents with actual-world physical disabilities found that Second Life broadened their social networks. One person who was deaf in the actual world described how "it's not easy for me to talk with everyone in RL, not everyone knows sign language . . . so because SL uses text chat, it gives me a good chance to make friends." His lover, sitting nearby, added "that's right. If I'd met him in RL, I don't think I'd ever know him as well as I do here, since I don't know sign language." Residents often noted with astonishment that they would interact with someone for weeks or months before learning they had an actual-world disability like hearing impairment or stroke-related paralysis. Occasionally the possibility of having more than one actual-world person control a single avatar permitted severely disabled persons to participate: in one case, nine disabled persons controlled a single avatar in this manner (Au 2004a).

Residents with short-term or newly acquired disabilities often claimed that Second Life could provide a venue for emotional support and information-sharing (for instance, about breast cancer). It could even help in the process of healing. For example, many residents contended that the hand-eye coordination needed to function in Second Life sped recovery from a stroke, as well as "the involuntary movements you make: when you walk or fly in Second Life, your physical body moves imperceptibly, like swimming as recovery therapy." For such residents, online embodiment could act as a means to regain agency: as one stroke survivor put it, "you lose your role and sense of control in real life; in Second Life you can take the bits of you that work and forge a new one."

Residents with more permanent physical disabilities also found new possibilities in Second Life's potential to allow them to experience different forms of embodiment: "there is the advantage of not being body bound, being able to be yourself." Such residents spoke of the pleasures of activities like flying (which cannot be done in the actual world by anyone) and dancing, skydiving, and swimming (which are possible in the actual world but cannot be done by many disabled people; see Ford 2001). One disabled resident summed up the impact of Second Life for those with permanent disabilities by stating that it "allows you to be free to explore yourself." It was for this reason that some residents with actual-world disabilities feared that "one of the first things that people will do when computers get faster is voice chat and person-to-person video . . . which will make disabilities more visible again."

This concern reflects how residents with actual-world physical disabilities found that discrimination did not disappear with virtual embodiment.

One issue was rejection when residents without actual-world disabilities discovered that their friend who might appear as a sturdy tall man or a winged dragon was disabled in the actual world: "sometimes they run away, and I think it bothers me more in here. It's like they are looking for the perfect person. It happens here just as easy as in the real world, so many here don't tell they have a disability."

One of the most potent conceptions of technological embodiment has been that of the cyborg, which in the work of Donna Haraway acts as an "imaginative resource" for theorizing hybridities between human and machine (Haraway 1991:150). The virtual human partakes of this cyborg logic but cannot be reduced to it. Cyborg selfhood is predicated on a prosthetic continuity between human and machine; it "relies on a reconceptualizations of the human body as a boundary figure belonging simultaneously to at least two previously incompatible systems of meaning—'the organic/natural' and 'the technological/cultural'" (Balsamo 1995b:215). In contrast, virtual embodiment is predicated on a discontinuity, the gap between virtual and actual. A cyborg implant is physically connected to the body it modifies; but it was never assumed that one could have a virtual arm grafted onto a physical arm, any more than one person in Chicago at 1:00 p.m. could be in Second Life simultaneously with another person in New York at 5:00 p.m.

GENDER AND RACE.

I had known Pavia for over a year as a woman with a beautiful female avatar on the day she sat me down for a talk in my virtual home:

Tom, I'm not the person you have gotten to know. But at the same time I am. I'm a man in real life, but about three weeks ago I learned that I'm transsexual. I've pretty much known that I was different all my life. . . . Here in Second Life I created something new in myself that I never realized was there before. At first it was just role playing, but then I grew to love Pavia. I kept infusing myself into her, but then something unexpected started to happen: Pavia started coming out in the real world. I became her, she became me.

Anthropologists have long known that selfhood is not a generic category. Just as there is no universal "Language" but historically specific languages, and just as there is no universal "Culture" but historically specific cultures, so "the notion that the essence of what it means to be human is most clearly revealed in those features of human culture that are universal rather than in those that are distinctive to this people or that is a prejudice we are not necessarily obliged to share" (Geertz 1973a:43). Gender and race are salient examples of such variation, and given that my work in Indonesia has focused on sexuality and nationalism, it should be clear that I could happily write an entire book on gender and race in Second Life. In largely confining my discussion of these domains to one section of a chapter on selfhood, I do not mean to diminish their significance. I subsume my discussion of them to my overarching goal of charting out the incipient cultural logics of virtual selfhood that occupy the dim interstices between the brightly shining controversies, benchmarks, and novelties that dominate contemporary debates about cybersociality.

Gender has been a topic of interest in virtual worlds from their beginnings, and continues to be a major focus of research (Balsamo 1996; Bartle 2004:527–56; Bruckman 1996; Curtis 1992; Edwards 1990; Fornäs et al. 2002; Kendall 2002; McRae 1997; O'Farrell and Vallone 1999; Paasonen 2002; Plant 1997; Roberts and Parks 1999; Rosenberg 1992; Schaap 2002; Stone 1995; Taylor 2006a; Turkle 1995). This salience of gender reflects how virtual worlds emerged in the 1980s and 1990s, a period during which feminist scholarship was gaining a stronger foothold and a cohort of young scholars—most of them women—took the risk of making gender the focus of their work. However, linkages between virtuality and gender have a much more extended history. This is reflected in an association between women and computers going back to the Jacquard loom, used for weaving cloth (Plant 1995). The term "virtual" comes from the Latin *virtus*, which also gives us modern English "virtue" and "virtuoso" (implying moral and technical excellence). *Virtus* refers to "manliness, valor, worth"; it shares an etymology with "virile." The notion of virtuality etymologically links masculinity and effectivity, and this masculinist vision of techne persists, associating maleness with technology and femaleness with nature (Halberstam 1991). This is a history in which "skilled men were seen as those who used to invent and fabricate new things, and the more they did so, they created the virtual phenomena of culture" (Fornäs et al. 2002:29).[13] At the same time, feminist theorists have discussed how women are "constituted as always already virtual" in modern regimes of power (Wise 1997:179).

In 1950, the British mathematician Alan Turing proposed a test to determine if a computer could converse in a manner indistinguishable from a human. This "Turing Test" is often described as an experiment in which a human and a machine are placed in separate rooms and allowed to communicate solely by text with a human judge. If the judge cannot determine which messages are coming from the human respondent and which from the computer respondent, then the computer can be said to have passed the Turing Test.[14] However, this test is based upon a parlor game that revolves around gender: "a significant choice, given the 'game' Turing, who was homosexual, was forced to play with prevailing social attitudes towards his sexuality. The game was simple. The player would interrogate two people in separate rooms. One person was a woman, the other a man. Both would, through written answers to questions asked by the player, try to prove that they were women" (Woolley 1992:104–5; see also Halberstam 1991:441–45; Schwartz 1996:357–62). The Turing test is also significant because whether determining gender or humanity, it is predicated upon reducing sociality to a textual form, anticipating early text-based virtual worlds like MUDs. Indeed, the Turing test was a popular topic for researchers of text-based virtual worlds, who noted that many such worlds (like WaterMOO and WolfMOO) provided for up to ten genders:

> neuter: it, it, its, its, itself
> male: he, him, his, his, himself
> female: she, her, her, hers, herself
> either: s/he, him/her, his/her, his/hers, (him/her)self
> Spivak: e, em, eir, eirs, eirself[15]
> splat: *e, h*, h*,h*s, h*self
> plural: they, them, their, theirs, themselves
> egotistical: I, me, my, mine, myself
> royal: we, us, our, ours, ourselves
> 2nd: you, you, your, yours, yourself (Rosenberg 1992; see also Sundén 2003)

These "genders" are less radical than they first seem: they refer to linguistic gender and assume a lack of visual embodiment. Theoretically "in cyberspace the transgendered body is the natural body" (Stone 1995:180), but even in early MUDs resident profiles revealed that recognizable male or female gendering predominated (Rosenberg 1992). Few residents switched gender on a regular basis (about 10–15 percent of residents, according to one survey; see de Nood and Attema 2006:19–20), or embodied themselves as transgendered (Roberts and Parks 1999). Virtual worlds thus "both erode gender and bring it to the fore" (Reid 1996:337).

During the time of my fieldwork, the male/female binarism continued to predominate in graphical virtual worlds. Destabilizations of gender worked upon the ground of this binarism, which in most cases was embedded into the platform. When creating a new avatar in Second Life, one had to choose male or female gender. Unlike a screen name, gender could be changed at any time, but both the initial choice and the subsequent limitation of choice to the male/female binary were unavoidable—despite, for instance, occasional resident requests that gender be undefined, or on a sliding scale with male at one pole and female at the other. Like many virtual worlds, the Second Life platform worked in various ways, large and small, to reinforce gender norms.[16] For instance, the default animations for sitting differed for women and men; men sat with their legs spread apart slightly, while women's legs were closer together.[17]

Yet gender subjectivity in Second Life and other online worlds was subject to reconfiguration. The reason for this was that in the actual world, gender is strongly conflated with embodiment, despite all of its disembodied modalities—linguistic, sartorial, relational. In Second Life, the fundamental fact that residents could *choose* to be embodied as a male or female, regardless of their actual-world gendering, made thinkable not only forms of transgendering (as exemplified in Pavia's narrative above), but also the possibility that actual-world women and men could embody manhood or womanhood in new ways. The lack of necessary linkage to actual-world gender could raise a host of issues. For instance, I once encountered a newbie woman asking some longer-term residents, "could I make an all-women space?" One resident replied "you could make an all-female avatar space, but you can't ask to check that people are RL women, that's against disclosure TOS [Terms Of Service]." Forms of transgenderism, gender-switching, and cross-dressing were quite common in Second Life during the period of my fieldwork, as exemplified by the following discussion between a group of residents:

ADAM: I'll be putting the truth out by asking this question, but who thinks it's wrong to portray yourself as the opposing sex here?

BRENDA: Some of my closest lesbian friends are men, lol

YAKER: Not only do I think it's not wrong, I think EVERYONE should do it

TROY: I keep switching sexes in SL.

YAKER: I have a male avie now, and I feel very enlightened!

FLO: You will find that most people don't have a problem with it.

FRANKIE: Unless you are trying to get involved with someone on a deeper level: then I think it is important to be honest

YAKAR: I agree, and I think I speak differently with a male avatar

GROG: Personally, I get creeped out when I find out someone I thought was female is male.

BRENDA: Some of the most fulfilling relationships have little gaps

Such "gender swapping" allows people to "experience rather than merely observe what it feels like to be the opposite gender or to have no gender at all" (Turkle 1997:152; see also Bruckman 1996:320–23), and goes back to the earliest days of virtual worlds, as indicated by the "Joan/Alex" controversy on the CompuServe forums in the early 1980s, discussed earlier in this chapter. Probably the most common "transgendered" state of affairs was for residents to participate in Second Life with a male avatar if they were an actual-world woman, or a female avatar if they were an actual-world man, and not tell other residents of their actual-world gender. Since these residents did not reveal their actual-world gender their number was impossible to ascertain, particularly because many had one or more alts; they might have, for example, a primary avatar with the opposite gender from their actual-world gender, and an alt with the same gender as their actual-world gender. In some cases, an actual-world husband would ask his wife to participate in Second Life as a man or vice versa, in an attempt to forestall potential jealousies from engaging in sexual or romantic relationships with a virtual competitor. Yet I also recall how one resident, who usually appeared as a woman but was a man in the actual world, refused to show his actual-world wife how he looked in Second Life because "I'm kind of worried she'll be jealous. My avatar is one part an expression of myself, one part expression of my desire. Half my idea of myself, half my idea of the woman."[18]

For some residents like Pavia, Second Life provided an opportunity to reflect upon and transform their actual-world gender. For others, the mutability of virtual gender allowed for forms of play specific to the online world, as evinced by event advertisements like the following: "Pick just that perfect outfit, and you may win $250 for Best Female as A Male, or $250 for Best Male as a Female! Rules are: you CANNOT change your avatar's gender. You must remain female and dress as a male, or be a male, and dress as a female!! Guys, you know it is that perfect time to put on your woman's panties and say 'It's only for the contest, I don't really like to wear them, I swear!'"

Forms of everyday gendering in Second Life could reflect a similar experimentation, as in the case of a resident who noted "I'm a male crossdresser, but I'm a female in real life." One rationale heterosexually identified residents provided for participating as the opposite gender was, as one man expressed it, "I like something nice to look at while I'm sitting there for eight hours with my eyes bleeding—and dwarves don't do it for me." Normative sexuality could motivate transgressive gendering. A few residents used the flexibility of virtual embodiment to experiment with having no gender at all. While the Second Life platform required avatars to be either male or female, it was easy to take on an embodiment that did not clearly mark gender (a box, for instance, or a blue ball of light, or an androgynous figure).

In graphical virtual worlds, discussions of gender have tended to focus on embodiment, reflecting how visuality had become powerfully constitutive of the virtual by the time of my fieldwork. Yet as in the actual world, gender in online worlds is also secured through a range of social practices. For instance, note how heterosexual masculinity is shaped in the following scene. This interaction took place as part of a bachelor party preceding the wedding of two Second Life residents. I and a group of other men were at a casino, playing the card game "Texas Hold'em" thanks to an automated dealer program:

> JORDAN: RL wife is playing tringo [elsewhere in Second Life]. I have some time [to play cards].
> SERLO: My girl asked me to marry her today lol
> TEXAS HOLD'EM TABLE WHISPERS: Colin calls.
> MICK: Cool. Did you say yes, Serlo?
> SERLO: lmao [laughing my ass off] I said maybe
> TEXAS HOLD'EM TABLE WHISPERS: Luke calls.
> TEXAS HOLD'EM TABLE WHISPERS: Dealing the Turn
> MICK: lol, maybe
> TEXAS HOLD'EM TABLE WHISPERS: The Turn is: (8 of Clubs).
> SERLO: But I will.
> JORDAN: I may need to take a shit break at some point
> TEXAS HOLD'EM TABLE WHISPERS: Peter bets.
> TEXAS HOLD'EM TABLE WHISPERS: Colin raises.
> MICK: lol, I'm down with a shit break man
> SERLO: lol
> TEXAS HOLD'EM TABLE WHISPERS: Peter raises.
> COLIN: Yeah, piss run sounds good
> TEXAS HOLD'EM TABLE WHISPERS: Colin wins L$589 with Two Pairs, 8s over 3s with a Queen kicker
> MICK: You guys almost ready to go out and get crazy? The kind of crazy that gets you divorced in rl?
> COLIN: You're going to the stripper show, right?

References to girlfriends and wives, joking about bodily functions, and talk of "getting crazy" by going to a stripper show all reinforced the idea that these residents were heterosexual men in the actual world. There was no way to verify this, but none expressed an interest in making the attempt; nor, when we went to the stripper show, was any concern expressed that the nude women strutting across a virtual bar might be men in the actual world. Taking the gap between the virtual and actual created by techne on its own terms, what mattered was that "male" and "female" acted as heuristically stable referents for online selfhood.

Race and ethnicity have received less attention than gender in the study of virtual worlds, though by the time of my fieldwork a literature on the topic was beginning to appear (e.g., Beckles 1997; Bleecker 1994; Kendall 2002:198–216; Kolko, Nakamura, and Rodman 2000; Nakamura 2002; Rodríguez 2003). Indeed, "while gender and sexuality have been crucial to theories of both cyberspace and the posthuman, the absence of race is usually perfunctorily remarked and of little consequence to these analyses" (Weheliye 2002:22). One reason for this was that due to unequal access, "people of color were functionally absent from the Internet at precisely that time when its discourse was acquiring its distinctive contours" (Nakamura 2002:xii). Few virtual worlds require choosing a race as one chooses a gender (Nakamura 2002:36); indeed, in more combat-oriented virtual worlds "race" often signifies "species," like elf or dwarf, indirectly signifying actual-world conceptions of race. This does not mean that race is irrelevant to virtual worlds. It may be more fundamental because more taken for granted; "the explicit acknowledgment need not be made" (Bleecker 1994:210).

Throughout the history of virtual worlds and continuing during my research in Second Life, the most basic way race shaped cybersociality was the assumption that residents were white unless stated otherwise. That Second Life's default embodiment was white reflected how "the power value of whiteness resides above all in its instabilities and apparent neutrality" (Dyer 1997:70). Theorizations of cybersociality that fail to address this state of affairs "enable the evasion of the race question, underwriting the whiteness of cyberspace" (McPherson 2000:120; see also Lockard 1997:226–27). Particularly in text-based virtual worlds where race was described, if at all, through screen names, narrative descriptions, and patterns of speech, researchers have noted forms of "identity tourism" in which, for instance, white men participated as Asian men, often through redeploying mass-mediated stereotypes (Nakamura 2002; González 2000). This can be linked to the metaphor of surfing and the idea that "cyberspace is a place where travel and mobility are featured attractions" (Nakamura 2002:40). Questions of race have taken on new forms with the movement to graphical virtual worlds in which an emphasis on place renders metaphors like "surfing" less relevant (I rarely saw this metaphor used in Second Life, since one "surfs" a network, not a place). With the rise of graphical virtual worlds it is possible for understandings of race to rediscover their association with notions of visual perception (Foster 2005), so that race can be framed in terms of "visible signs such as skin color, eye color, or bone structure . . . decorative features to be attached or detached at will" (González 2000:29).

In Second Life there was no specific "check box" for race, but by controlling skin tone, facial and other body features, and hair, it was possible to appear racialized in any way one wished. Though there was a sense in which one chose to appear African, Asian, or any other race, whiteness acted as a kind of default, so that as in other virtual worlds, "nonwhite identity positions [became] part of a costume or masquerade" (Nakamura 2002:47). Once during a group discussion, Nara, a resident who had embodied himself in what appeared to be an Asian manner, asked: "not for nothing, but am I the only dark-skinned person here? If there is such tolerance for diversity then why are there so few dark skinned people here?" Another resident replied: "Does a black person have to have a 'dark' skin for non-black people to recognize them as black; is that a bias?"

This mentioning of skin reflects how throughout my fieldwork, "skins" were highly prized items. It was possible to change one's skin tone using a slider built into the Second Life program, but it was also possible to create a skin texture that could be applied to one's avatar. Often known simply as a "skin," such textures could not be altered but could include stubble, moles, even fine wrinkles that together provided a highly realistic look. Many residents who designed skins for sale worked to create a range of skin tones, but white or near-white skins predominated and persons seeking darker skins complained of the difficulty in finding them. Some residents who tried wearing nonwhite skins reported racist responses, including friends who stopped answering ims and statements that nonwhite persons were invading Second Life (Au 2006h). It is not surprising that some residents who were nonwhite in the actual world engaged in forms of racial passing (Nakamura 2002:32–36), so that at least one of their avatar embodiments was white (Au 2003b).

Race showed up in ways other than avatar embodiment. Many screen names had ethnic connotations, including Linden Lab-controlled last names (from my own avatar's last name of "Bukowski" to last names like "Mfume" and "Chung"). Builds could also have racial overtones, from Gothic castles to Japanese tea gardens. They could also invoke race more explicitly, as in the case of builds with a Confederate theme that could be found in Second Life from the beginning of my fieldwork. By displaying Confederate flags, images of Robert E. Lee and other Confederate heroes, and by not mentioning African-Americans, such builds recalled a "cyber-Dixie" with a significant history online (McPherson 2000). Such builds were not common and often linked to residents with a background in combat-oriented virtual worlds that had a Civil War theme. Their existence is nonetheless significant, particularly when one could find events like "Slave Auctions" where residents could sell themselves into slavery with the explanation that "Slavery is a voluntary and self-imposed state in SL. You decide what services you offer and for how long when you put yourself up for sale." Such events were typically linked to certain dominant/submissive sexual communities, but could not but have racial connotations.

Race and ethnicity did not only appear in Second Life in negative terms; they could also act as resources for selfhood and rubrics for community. Many nonwhite avatars could be found in Second Life and ethnic-specific groups existed; for instance, a group for African-American women, or a group sponsoring a Kwanzaa celebration. An ethic of antiracism predominated and racist speech usually led to swift censure. For instance, an attack against a build used to raise awareness about the Darfur conflict in Sudan and the construction of an "SS Training Camp" were both quickly decried by many residents. In July 2004, soon after I started my research, the exchange recounted below involving "Trac" took place over the group im for the "Fun Times" group. (As discussed in chapter 7, groups could have collective instant messaging windows only their members could see.) This group had over one hundred members, making it a large group at the time; for concision, I reproduce only some of the group members' comments:

Trac: DEATH TO NIGGERS
A: wtf
B: no way
C: fuck off ass hole
D: You have just been reported
E: kick him off
F: You are ignorant!
Trac: DEATH TO NIGGERS
G: get a life
H: somebody get a linden [staff]
A: hey Trac where do you live
Trac: ALABAMA
I: That is messed up Trac
J: Fucking die.

TRAC: ohh scary

K: Already reported him

L: please stop this

M: Why did he say that?

C: because he's a complete jackass

D: You still have been reported, have a good day :D

O: He is saying this to get everyone upset. Please don't humor him

N: what a knuckle dragging neolithic twit

D: he had been reported with a screen shot and copy of the chat

N: Which group is this?

P: This is the Fun Times group

N: Does this group approve of that kind of talk?

P: No—it looks like someone tried to do a hit and run and was reported. All the members seemed quite upset and advocated he be reported and banned, yes it was disturbing. Well, we know that there are some immature and troubled folks in sl as well as in rl.

AGENCY.

Throughout this chapter I have touched upon questions of selfhood in Second Life, any one of which could be the subject of a book in its own right. In exploring the life course, embodiment, disability, gender, and race, I have turned ethnographic attention to the constitution of personhood online. A broader hypothesis I am willing to set forth is that virtual worlds presume a self who can discover its interests and desires and respond to them through acts of creativity. One way to explore such virtual agency is to consider how Second Life was important for many persons with psychological disabilities, not just the physical disabilities discussed earlier.

Forms of autism (including Asperger's Syndrome) have held a special place in Second Life and other virtual worlds. Autism is a neurodevelopmental disorder characterized by difficulty in social interaction, often including a reduced ability to read facial expressions. Not all persons with autism see it as a disability or disease; it has been noted for some time that many "are very high functioning and computer literate" and "have embraced online communities as a way to communicate."[19] Second Life's reliance on textual chat instead of voice during the period of my fieldwork, the limited capacity for avatar facial expression, and a general tolerance for delayed or unexpected responses (for instance, because persons were often afk) made it possible for many residents with autism to be competent social actors to a significantly greater degree than in the actual world. Even residents with what were typically seen to be more minor psychological disabilities, like Attention Deficit Disorder, often found that Second Life enabled new forms of selfhood. Afk and the ubiquity of multitasking (for instance, chatting with a group of nearby residents while iming a distant resident) already constituted forms of "attention deficit"; as a result, many persons with Attention Deficit Disorder found that in Second Life they were perceived like any other resident, analogous to the manner in which a person who could not walk in the actual world could walk like anyone else while inworld.

In cases of severe psychological disability, Second Life could enable significantly new forms of selfhood. Suzee's brother, Joseph, suffered from debilitating schizophrenia. She explained that in the actual world Joseph (like Suzee, in his mid-thirties) "is a recluse and rarely communicates." But in Second Life:

> Joseph and I explore places for hours, spend time talking, create things. It is amazing to watch him do things in here that he could never do in RL. For instance, in RL he lives with my mother for obvious reasons. Soon after he came into SL, Joseph put a cabin on a piece of land and decorated it with a few small items. I visited him and he said "This must be what it feels like to move into a college dorm for the first time." It broke my heart, but made me happy at the same time—because in RL he will never get to experience that, but here he can. If it were not for Second Life I would never have this experience with my brother because of his disability.

Cases like this represent contexts where virtual worlds could be seen as more "real" than the actual world, but the difference may be of degree rather than kind. Even residents who were simply shy or withdrawn in the actual world often found that the anonymity and control of a virtual world, where one did not have to give out one's actual-world name and could log off at any moment, allowed them to be "more outgoing," a trait that could then transfer back to the actual world. One resident noted how "experimenting with appearance or behavior in Second Life potentially opens up new ways to think of things in real life." Another emphasized how "despite everything, who I am still seems to come out, so perhaps I discover my essential nature [through my avatar]"; a third observed that "my offline self is becoming more like my avatar, personality-wise. It's like SL has grown on me and looped back." This theme of Second Life permitting access to an interior self that in the actual world is masked by an unchosen embodiment and social obligations was common. In some cases residents might unleash a hostile self who engaged in "griefing"—"you hear about people who are pretty fair offline but act like jerks in here," as one resident noted—but more often it implied intimacy and altruism. Residents often linked these transformative possibilities to the experience of avatar embodiment. Avatars were not just placeholders for selfhood, but sites of self-making in their own right: "through avatars, users embody themselves and make real their engagement with a virtual world" (Taylor 2002:40). One resident, Joe, observed that "Joe is my alter ego; he allows me to do and see things I might not do in RL"; Kipp, another resident, concluded that his avatar was "an extension of me, like icing on cake," while still another believed that "the Essential Me is in SL as well as RL, but the trappings are different, which I love."

Yet the dynamic was more complicated than residents controlling agentless avatars. Many felt that avatar appearance affected their behavior. Under the influence of what Nick Yee terms the "Proteus Effect" (Yee et al. 2007), they might act in a more risqué manner if dressed in more revealing clothes, or if they were embodied as a twentysomething athlete rather than a blue-skinned alien. New theoretical frameworks are needed to grapple with statements like that by Wendy, a resident who was male in the actual world but usually female in Second Life: "one day, I realized that my avatar had the hots for a lesbian girl's avatar. I mean it, it wasn't me—I just realized that it fitted the part."[20] Wendy's dramaturgical metaphor of "fitting the part" recalls Mauss's analysis of the persona as theatrical mask, as well as performative theories of selfhood (e.g., Butler 1990). What implicit understanding of agency lies behind Wendy's statement that "it wasn't me?" Is the avatar acting as a kind of persona, or even a person, in such contexts? Frameworks that allow for nonhuman entities to be agents in a social field, like actor-network theory (Latour 2005), have been influential in the anthropology of technology; how does this play out on a virtual plane? If Timothy Mitchell can expand upon Gayatri Spivak's question "can the subaltern speak?" to ask "can the mosquito speak?" (Mitchell 2002; Spivak 1988), then must not our question be: Can the avatar speak?

The nascent or complicit agency of avatars was heightened by the prevalence of alts. Many residents did not like to log off of one alt's account and then immediately reenter Second Life as another avatar; it could be disconcerting to move between embodiments, as well as personalities and social networks. One resident described how "I take a breath and prepare myself into whatever 'mode' I'm logging in as, because both alts are very real—my second alt is very much a part of me, the part I choose not to express here on my main account. I am still 'me' on either, just different facets." Is there a common cultural logic of agency behind this resident's statement that each avatar was "a part of" his self, whereas for Wendy her avatar, in some contexts at least, "wasn't me?"

The beginnings of an answer may lie in the striking fact that for most residents, having alts was not cognitively dissonant, despite the lack of any real parallel in the actual world (where it is rare indeed to have multiple embodiments, each with independent social networks). Alts operationalized the gap between actual and virtual into a resource for fractal subjectivity, into a kind of "dividual" (rather than "individual") selfhood for which persons are "constructed as the plural and composite site of the relationships that produced them" (Strathern 1988:13). Perhaps the most glaring examples of such dividual selfhood appeared when residents embodied more than one alt at once. Since they were controlled by a single resident, alt accounts were not usually online at the same time. However, some residents would log on two or more alts simultaneously, either using multiple computers in the same actual-world room or opening multiple copies of the Second Life program on a single computer. This permitted forms of fractal subjectivity. What theory of agency is in play when Frank logs in two alts at once "to have company," so that "Nancy" is sitting with "Ray" in Frank's virtual house? What theory of intimacy is in play when a resident logs in two alts to have sex with herself? Embodying multiple alts at once instantiates a discontinuous self—there is a clear gap between where one alt ends and the next begins, a gap that can be temporarily narrowed but not erased by having sex with oneself or keeping oneself company. As Brenda noted earlier in this chapter, "some of the most fulfilling relationships have little gaps." Such gaps were comprehensible to residents because as a virtual world, Second Life was already constituted by the gap between actual and virtual. Such a gap is the product of techne, and a precondition for homo cyber, the virtual human.

Chapter 6

INTIMACY

*Language—Friendship—Sexuality—Love—
Family—Addiction.*

LANGUAGE.

Intimacy is predicated on language's ability to mediate selfhood, the topic of the previous chapter. Anthropologists and others have long noted the centrality of language to human cultures. Forms of techne in ancient Greek thought "were above all . . . ways with language" (Lyotard 1991:47), and language may prove even more crucial in the future. To the degree its symbolic systematicity is irreducible to sound and inscription, language has always been virtual; it is thus a key element of the techne that both constitutes and bridges the gap between virtual and actual. Some virtual worlds (particularly early ones, such as MUDs) were entirely text-based; graphical virtual worlds still depend upon computer programs that are forms of language, so language can be said to act as a material foundation for them. Given language's importance and my background in linguistics, I could easily have devoted an entire chapter to language.[1] Due to space limits I examine but a few key aspects of language with regard to Second Life, building upon earlier scholarship on language and virtual worlds (e.g., Aarseth 1997; Baty 1999; Bolter 2001; Cherny 1999; Hayles 2005; Jacobson 1996; Reed 2005; Ryan 1999; Sundén 2003). During my fieldwork, the three most consequential aspects of language were the predominance of text over voice, the distinction between "chat" and "instant messages" (ims), and the preponderance of American English. In identifying these three factors, I deemphasize neologisms (like "newbie"), acronyms (like "rl" for "real life" and "afk" for "away from keyboard," many of which date from MUDs; see Cherny 1999:92), and emoticons (like ":)" for a smile). All these have attracted attention, but they are less central to culture in virtual worlds.

Toward the end of my fieldwork, Linden Lab announced that voice capabilities would be added to Second Life. This was a controversial decision, and debates over voice extended back to the earliest days of my research.

For the period of Second Life's history during which I conducted field-work for this book, voice had not yet been added; almost all language was textual. This included not only chat and ims, but one's inventory of objects, the world map, the search function, associated websites, even the Terms of Service agreement each resident had to accept before logging on for the first time. The ubiquity of text made Second Life particularly accessible to persons with impaired hearing in the actual world, but made it near-impossible for visually impaired persons to participate. More broadly, residents spoke of the predominance of text as having a distancing effect, keeping the actual world and Second Life distinct—so that, for instance, men could participate as women, or one could not prejudge the actual-world age of a resident. Text could act as techne, its mere use separating the virtual from the actual.

The distinction between "chat" and "ims" was pivotal. Chat was the primary mode of communication during my fieldwork. If one pressed the "enter" key while logged on, a small "chat window" would appear at the bottom of the screen. Typing at the keyboard produced text that would not appear inworld until one pressed the "return" key. While typing, one's avatar's hands would move as if typing on an invisible keyboard and a typing sound could be heard, signaling to nearby residents that one was preparing to say something.[2] Once the "return" key was pressed, the chat would be visible as white text at the bottom of the screen for any resident whose avatar was within thirty virtual meters.[3] After a few seconds the chat would fade, but all chat encountered by an avatar while logged on could be reviewed by opening the "history" window.

Since communication took place through chat that was prepared one line at a time, multiple threads of conversation were the norm when many were present. While one resident was preparing a response to statement A, another resident would raise topic B and yet another resident might respond to topic B before the resident responding to topic A had finished their own reply. As had long been the case in virtual worlds, developing linguistic competency within Second Life required learning how to parse multiple overlapping threads of talk, often by using the history window to disentangle the discussion (Curtis 1992:134). This differs from most actual-world sociolinguistic contexts, where "turn-taking" is a major concern and multiple threads of conversation are more likely to be perceived as tangents or interruptions (Duranti 1997:248–63).

In addition to chat, residents of Second Life (and many virtual worlds) could send "instant messages" to individuals or groups. In Second Life instant messages were composed in a separate window from the one used for chat; one's hands did not move as if typing and there was no typing sound. Ims could be sent to a resident anywhere inworld, and an option existed to have ims forwarded to an email address if a resident was offline. Ims thus allowed residents to communicate across virtual distance, but what I found interesting was the widespread use of ims when residents were in close proximity. For instance, a group of four avatars—call them John, Paul, George, and Ringo—might be within thirty virtual meters and so could chat with each other. At the same time, John and Paul could be exchanging ims (perhaps commenting on something George said), and also George, Ringo, and Paul could be exchanging ims as a group of three. This kind of layered conversation, made possible by the simultaneous use of chat and ims, represents a novel linguistic form. There is really no analogous way in the actual world to, within a single room, talk and whisper at the same time, or talk to everyone in the room and also engage in a distinct conversation with a subset of persons in the room, and also with others outside the room.

I noted in the previous chapter that in some cases chat could be seen as more intimate than ims, because chat presupposed virtual embodiment. In other cases the reverse could hold: the fact that ims were directed to specific persons, rather than specific locations as in the case of chat, could give ims a greater sense of intimacy, particularly with someone whose avatar was already nearby. This is why when a discussion turned to matters deemed sensitive, residents would sometimes switch from chat to im even if no one else was around. In the following example, for which I number the lines of chat, I was talking to Yuko with no other avatars nearby. Yuko was drinking beer in the actual world as we discussed the settings for the Second Life program:

1. YUKO: I cut my network usage slider down pretty tight. Got tired of massive lag spikes from rezzing objects
2. ME: Okay, I'm gonna go to bed—don't sit there drinking too long!
3. IM: Yuko: Can I ask you a question, do you sometimes feel overwhelmed at all the . . . hmm . . . guess I'll call it sex on tv and stuff?
4. ME: Don't stay up all night buzzed lol
5. YUKO: Hehe—I'm a few shots away from being beyond buzzed
6. IM: Yuko: I mean . . . we get bombarded by it everywhere
7. IM: Yuko: Always seeing these "perfect" people
8. IM: Yuko: Therapist today was not happy when I brought that subject up. lol

In this example, Yuko switched to ims at (3), when shifting the topic from technical issues to sexuality. When responding to my chat statement (4) at (5), Yuko returned to chat, then went back to ims at (6) when revisiting the topic of sexuality. Yuko used ims not to address different persons, but to create topic-specific intimacy. Sociolinguists refer to this as codeswitching (Heller 1988), but whereas most actual-world codeswitching involves different languages or registers (for instance, formal versus slang speech), codeswitching in Second Life could operate with regard to modalities of textual language.[4]

Because ims were directed to specific avatars and saved if the avatar was offline, many residents would find themselves deluged with accumulated ims when they logged on. Residents often made a point of "checking their ims" to review these stored messages. Because one's "friends" (see below) would be notified whenever one was inworld, residents also often found themselves receiving large numbers of im greetings immediately after they logged on. While this was an important way to stay in touch, it could also be overwhelming, and many residents spoke of being "stuck in ims" or even in "im hell." One major reason for having alts in Second Life was to be able to log in anonymously, so that one could focus on building, shopping, or other more solitary activities, without being flooded with ims.

It was also common for residents to engage in ongoing im conversations, leaving their im window open at the top or bottom of their screen as they moved from place to place within Second Life. One resident spoke about how she "usually juggled a live convo and 10 ims at the same time." In such cases iming could be seen as constituting virtual places in its own right, recalling MUDs and other textual virtual worlds. This was particularly the case for ims sent out to groups whose membership could number in the hundreds. Such "group ims" or "channels" constituted distinct textual spaces for community within Second Life. I recall when I once sent an im to a group that was not in line with that group's focus. Joe, a leader of the group, responded with an im sent to the entire group (numbering over two hundred members), admonishing me not to send such an im again. I sent a personal im to Joe apologizing for my transgression, but asking if—should such an incident recur—he could im me directly, rather than embarrassing me in the textually virtual presence of the group. Joe responded with a personal im of his own: "I am sorry if that was too public. I have found if I don't respond in the channel [that is, to the whole group], people complain that 'you let him do it.'" Group ims can act as a virtual site for social control.

In addition to the prevalence of text over voice and the distinction between chat and ims, the dominance of American English was a linguistically significant aspect of Second Life culture. Like the Internet as a whole, American English has dominated Second Life and most virtual worlds. Based in California, Linden Lab designed Second Life around an interface that was entirely in English, although the technical ability to communicate in languages other than English and to have a non-English interface increased during my fieldwork. As the number of residents grew, there appeared an increasing number of places—from individual residences to entire regions—where residents used languages other than English (the most common were Chinese, French, German, Italian, Japanese, and Korean). In August 2006, a resident even designed an inworld device that could translate between a number of languages (Au 2006i).

However, English remained the dominant medium of communication; as in the actual world during the period of my fieldwork, a globalized English often acted as a lingua franca even between, say, a speaker of Japanese and a speaker of French. The form of English that dominated Second Life was American, and speakers of British or Australian English sometimes found themselves using American-English terms (Au 2006l). Some nonnative speakers of English enjoyed its ubiquity because it allowed them to practice English in an environment where grammatical and typographic errors were the norm (just as some English speakers sought out residents with whom they could practice communicating in other languages). Nonnative speakers of English also drew attention to forms of inequality fostered by its dominance. One such person appealed to her fellow residents, reminding them that being a nonnative English speaker could be "a great handicap in relationships, because sometimes when you speak like a 14 year old people get impatient and leave rather than help. So, when you meet a player that 'speaks strange,' please consider that he/she might not be stupid; give her/him some time to express." Despite the high tolerance for spelling and grammatical errors in chat and ims, nonnative English speakers often experienced communication difficulties—as in the following exchange, which took place at an event for the opening of a club:[5]

ROLAND: You look great in that dress, real sexy
AUDRA: TY. i made it.
ROLAND: i envie you for that. Wish I could.
AUDRA: awwww. Well, i havent made anything new 4 a while now.
ROLAND: Dont need new stuff for your shop
AUDRA: I dont? Rich, I dont??
ROLAND: Sorry? What do you mean?
AUDRA: u said i dont need new things 4 my shop
ROLAND: Dont you? You said you havent made any for quite some time.
AUDRA: i haven't, in a long time
ROLAND: So, I asked, dont you need new clothes for the shop every
    once in a while?

AUDRA: oh. I misunderstood u. hehe.
ROLAND: Its me. Sorry
AUDRA: no, its me.
ROLAND: English is not my native tongue
AUDRA: well u type it well.
ROLAND: yeah but i have to translate it first. I think in French

Turning to languages other than English could even act as a linguistic resource for challenging the America-centric sociality of Second Life. For instance, one year when attending a Fourth of July celebration, complete with virtual fireworks, I encountered the following exchange:

HANNA SHOUTS: Brought to you courtesy of the red white and blue
MAHON: Wat is dit hier? Ik mag een wens doen ik sta tussen 2 mooie vrouwen. [What is this here? My wish is coming true; I'm standing between two beautiful women.]

Another speaker continued speaking to Mahon in Dutch, wresting the discussion away from the topic of (American) Independence Day. These kinds of contestations over the dominance of English, as well as the effects of the ubiquity of text rather than voice and the distinction between chat and ims, all represent ways in which language shaped Second Life sociality during the period of my fieldwork, with consequences for the most intimate aspects of selfhood and interpersonal relationship.

FRIENDSHIP.

Since the early days of the Internet, a widely disseminated dystopic narrative has portrayed virtual worlds as engines of isolation, the pastime of techno-hermits firmly ensconced in lonely rooms, consoled only by the deceptively warm flicker of a computer screen. Given the resilience of this narrative, one of the most surprising and consistent findings of cybersociality research has been that virtual worlds can not only transform actual-world intimacy but create real forms of online intimacy. Observers of virtual worlds have long noted that persons engaging in forms of computer-mediated communication often "come to feel that their very best and closest friends are members of their electronic group, whom they seldom or never see" (Hiltz and Turoff 1978:101, cited in Reid 1999:113). Even early virtual worlds could thus be "powerfully conducive to intimacy" (Van Gelder 1991:366); reflecting such conclusions, Second Life residents often saw it as "an intimacy-making culture." This was a positive aspect of the disinhibition that, as I discuss later, could manifest itself as griefing. Desirable intimacies often took sexual forms, and I turn to sexuality in the following section. However, the prevalence (and sometimes, heated tone) of discussions regarding cybersex has obscured that for most residents of virtual worlds, nonsexual friendships are the most important aspect of their lives online.[6] Friendships are the foundation of cyber-sociality; the friend is the originary social form for homo cyber.

Residents of Second Life and other virtual worlds expended enormous amounts of time and energy in finding, making, and maintaining friends (Jakobsson and Taylor 2003), a goal which extended beyond virtual worlds to locations for Internet-mediated friendship like MySpace, Facebook, and Friendster (Boyd 2006b). In the Western traditions that dominated the cultures of cyberspace during the period of my research, and in other traditions as well, there existed a range of hierarchical models for social relations—husband and wife, parent and child, teacher and student, employer and employee—and others that were quite egalitarian, like siblings, coworkers, and neighbors. Yet the cultural concept of "friend," defined by its two key characteristics of choice and egalitarianism, represented the dominant rubric residents of Second Life (and beyond) drew upon as the default category for social relations.

One possible interpretation of this predominance of friendship is that it is congruent with the "creationist capitalism" I discuss in chapter 8, and with the overall ethic of individualized choice and intentionality that is a key element of techne. In this interpretation, friendship is the ultimate form of "pure relationship" associated with modern selfhood, in which "a friend is defined specifically as someone with whom one has a relationship unprompted by anything other than the rewards that relationship provides" (Giddens 1991:90). However, it is also possible to see friendship as a more subversive "way of life" that questions naturalized categories of kinship, ethnicity, and nation (Foucault 1997a). Perhaps friendship is not just "pure relationship," but "virtual relationship," built through techne rather than any received biological or social arrangement. Were this the case, then one reason for the ubiquity of friendship online might be that like ethnography, friendship anticipated the emergence of virtual worlds.

Some residents did not seek friendship online; their sociality was oriented around what they saw as superficial shopping and entertainment, or meaningful but solitary creative activities like building or designing clothes, saying things like "I've been trying to keep the 'knowing someone' down to a minimum here." For most residents I encountered during my fieldwork, however, friendships were a primary reason for their participation. Residents spoke of making life-long friends in Second Life. For many, it was friendships, not sexual relationships, that were the social core of their virtual lives: as one resident noted, in Second Life you could get together with friends and go to a club or concert or some other activity "without spending an hour getting ready and 100 bucks at the bar." Residents sometimes entered Second Life to meet actual-world friends, or friends from another virtual world who also had a Second Life account. The majority of any resident's friendships, however, originated within Second Life itself. Residents could make friends in a range of locales, from more private places like an apartment or home to more public events like "Combat Cards," a game first created within Second Life in 2004, which allowed residents to acquire and exchange cards that not only described combat moves (swinging a sword, for instance) but animated one's avatar to execute the depicted move.

Whenever meeting a new person, most residents would read the person's "profile." As mentioned in earlier chapters, the profile was a window which could be accessed by right-clicking on an avatar or by using the "find" menu to search for an avatar by name.[7] The profile window was composed of several pages or "tabs." The first tab, "2nd Life," provided basic information, including groups to which the avatar belonged and a box in which one could type up to 500 characters (two or three sentences) of information. The second tab, "Interests," allowed residents to identify what they liked doing (building, exploring, meeting people, selling objects, etc.), what skills they possessed (texturing, scripting, etc.), and in later updates to the platform, what languages they spoke. A tab called "Picks" allowed residents to identify their favorite places or groups. The distinction between actual and virtual self was encoded in the Second Life platform with a tab entitled "1st Life," which provided 250 characters for residents to talk about their actual-world selves, as well as a place to post an image. This tab was often left blank, or filled in with statements such as "Like anyone really wants to know?"

Because Second Life (like all virtual worlds) was not really a form of mass media that "mediated" two or more locations but a place in its own right, residents could make friends that were exclusive to that virtual world. As one resident noted, "I have a number of really close friends online, but have never thought of contacting them any other way, and they haven't asked me either. It seems natural to keep things here." Friends might eventually share aspects of their actual-world lives beyond the minimal information provided on the "1st Life" tab of their profile, but it was possible to have close friends about whom one knew very little in actual-world terms. In other cases friends would provide some detail about their actual-world lives—the nation in which they lived, their occupation, their actual-world hobbies, and so on, without necessarily revealing their exact identities. Many spoke of the pleasure of making friends from different countries whom they never would have met were it not for Second Life, and also persons from different social backgrounds: one resident observed how "I've made friends online with whom I'd never have had even the first conversation in real life." Friendships in Second Life were not always seen as poor approximations of their actual-world analogues: their intensity reveals that it is incorrect to assume that virtual worlds produce only "loose" social ties. Many residents insisted that they had built friendships in Second Life that were as real as their friendships in the actual world—even more real, since one did not prejudge persons based on factors like gender, race, and age. As one resident put it: "in real life, you get to know someone from the outside in, but in Second Life you get to know them from the inside out." Another said that in Second Life "you get to know someone for personality alone; it's almost a spiritual connection, sans body." A third resident emphasized that "when you meet someone online and you don't have the whole real-world environment, you get to know someone's personality on a much greater level. . . . When all you look at is their avatar, you can only go on personality and the things they say. So you aren't as quick to judge. . . . You can only go based on someone's heart."

A common sentiment among Second Life residents was that "time goes faster online." This phrase did not refer to virtual sociality in general—for which lag, not acceleration, was a common experience. This sense of speeded-up time was above all in reference to friendship; as one person noted, "it is very intense here. The emotions and feelings are magnified. . . . The time you spend with someone here is more, and you can feel it." Another resident noted that "I think you can get a good judgment on people just by talking to them. If you are boring in rl, then chances are you are in sl too." A third spoke about "feeling the essence of who people are behind the keyboard." I recall one day when I imed my friend Vonda and could tell by her reply that she was not feeling well. I was not surprised when she added: "ims are not enough right now; I want to be held. Can you come see me?" I teleported to Vonda's location to find her on the ground floor of her home, which she had designed as an area for dancing. "Let's hold each other," Vonda said. "I'm kinda down and out and need a friend. A slow dance would be nice; I've been lonely." We each clicked on a pair of "slow dance" pose balls in one corner of the room, objects with scripts inside that animated our avatars so that we swayed to the music with our arms wrapped around each others' shoulders. "I can feel you," Vonda typed. "You are a nice man. I've been having a hard time and I need time to relax with a friend. Hold me tight, don't let go. I need friends now."

What kind of intimacy is at play in this scene, which reveals the inadequacy of earlier theorizations of online intimacy that contended "You can't hold your lover [or your friend] in cyberspace" (Suler 1996)? Language and embodiment intersect to instantiate a hierarchy of virtual intimacies: ims, which as noted earlier can sometimes be seen as more intimate than chat, are seen in turn to be less intimate than an embrace.

Sexuality.

The lap dancer, one of many at the club, was wearing only a beaded thong around her waist; she caressed her bare breasts as she looked at the man below her. "I'm feeling something growing as I grind myself down on your lap . . . my hands moving down my sides and around to my wet pussy . . . spreading my lips, my finger tracing up and down my slit mmmmmm . . . lifting my finger to my mouth and sucking on it slowly just like I was sucking your dick."

Scenes like this were not rare during my fieldwork: sex was an important aspect of Second Life, though portrayals of the virtual world as little more than an avenue for sexual expression were inaccurate (e.g., Stein 2006). For some residents, sex was the main reason they logged on; others engaged in sexual activity only on occasion or not at all—seeing it as being "like licking honey through the glass," or viewing Second Life as a place for creativity and friendship but not sexual expression. Sex online has an extensive history, even in text-only virtual worlds (Branwyn 1994; Campbell 2004; Carlstrom 1992; McRae 1997; Reid 1999:114; Rodríguez 2003). Long before my fieldwork, it had become so pervasive that the ostensibly generic term "cybering" had become a synonym for sex, rather than for chatting, building a structure, or any other activity (Mills 1998). For many, homo cyber was always already cybering.

Just as many residents of Second Life said that inworld friendships could be more "real" than actual-world friendships, so many found sex online deeply meaningful. They sometimes spoke of "sex in virtual places" rather than "virtual sex" to underscore this sentiment. Sex in Second Life often had an exploratory character; it is not coincidental that by the time of my research the term "play," originally used in reference to games, often referred to transgressive forms of online sexuality—"age play" (with youthful or childlike avatars), "domination play," and so on. Despite the emphasis on vision in Second Life, sex often had a strong linguistic component. One resident referenced this view when stating that "looking at two avies humping each other like programmed automatons is a waste of time; meaningless gimmickry. But two people, painting pictures of sights, sounds, emotions and feelings in intense words, can be very personal, and very deep. In a strange way, you can be more expressive about things that aren't expressed easily in rl, but to do that in a way that comes over with grace and beauty takes practice and a fluent use of descriptive vocabulary" (see LeFleur 2006). In theory two or more residents could have virtual sex using ims while their avatars were in different locations; such purely textual sex would recall the sex found in text-only virtual worlds like MUDs. This appeared to be quite rare during the time of my fieldwork; despite the importance of language, sex usually implied contact between avatars. Through clever animations, avatars could engage in a wide range of sexual practices, from embracing and kissing to oral, vaginal, and anal sex. The default embodiment for avatars did not include genitalia, but many forms of genitalia were created and sold by residents, who also created beds, bondage devices, and even whole landscapes for sexual encounters.[8]

Because sex usually involved virtual embodiment, it was linked to place. The "PG" versus "M" distinction discussed in chapter 4 designated broad swaths of land as "mature" and thus appropriate for sexual content (though sex often occurred in PG areas too). An issue for some residents was that they wished to have sex undisturbed. During the time of my fieldwork it was not possible to make one's avatar invisible on the world map; two or more green dots would reveal the presence of avatars, and someone could always teleport to the location and find sexual activity taking place.[9] One solution was a "skybox" or "sky build," which as noted in chapter 4 could be constructed hundreds of meters above ground level. Since avatars could only fly to a height of 200 meters without the aid of a scripted object (anything from a jetpack or plane to a belt buckle or giant bird), and since residents typically set the Second Life program to rez objects no more than a 128-meter radius from their avatar so as to reduce lag, skybuilds were relatively secluded. One would see green dots on the map but teleport to the location to find no one present. A determined resident could eventually solve the mystery, but the cultural norm was not to make the attempt, on the assumption that persons in a skybox wished to be left alone.

Sex was not always private. Because residents could keep their actual-world identities secret and could keep online activities hidden from the actual world (for instance, by logging on when no one else was nearby), Second Life offered the opportunity to experiment with sexual practices and relationships. This could include sex work (prostitution), forms of group sex, or sexualized environments like strip clubs. Many large builds, even entire islands, were dedicated to sexual themes, and sexual-themed events were common.[10]

Some of these one-time events could shade off into persistent communities of sexual practice. During the time of my research BDSM communities were the most common form of sexual community. The portmanteau acronym "BDSM" refers to bondage, discipline, domination, submission, sadism, and masochism; in reference to these last two terms, the contraction "s/m" was widely used, as was d/s to refer to "doms" (dominants) and slaves. The ability to create buildings, objects (like restraints to tie an avatar to a bed), scripts, clothing, animations, and genitalia allowed for a range of BDSM communities to form during my fieldwork with a built environment that would have been expensive to acquire in the actual world.

Some residents saw actual-world ramifications from their experiments with BDSM. For instance, one person recalled how "I have this friend in SL who's a dom. Hanging out with her and her SL slave, I've realized that there's this really cool bond between master and slave. So I want to try it here in SL to see if I can learn anything and bring it into RL." For others, virtual BDSM was a distinct form of sexual expression with little bearing on the actual world. For instance, residents who participated in BDSM were aware that a key characteristic of BDSM sex in the actual world, "the erotic use of pain and domination," was "replaced with *representations* of pain and domination" in Second Life (Bardzell and Bardzell 2006:4). Yet these were not second-best approximations; they had their own meaning and efficacy, just as a beautiful texture on a shirt was not just an imitation of actual-world fabric but a source of pleasure (and income) in its own right.

BDSM communities took many forms during my fieldwork, from gay BSDM to furrie BDSM, and could include everything from pornography magazines with sexually explicit images of avatars to group orgies. The largest BDSM community in Second Life during my fieldwork was probably the "Gorean" community, based on a series of novels (beginning with *Tarnsman of Gor* in 1967 and continuing twenty-five novels later with *Witness of Gor* in 2002) by John (Lange) Norman, a professor of philosophy at Queen's College in New York.[11] Because I identified as an anthropologist during my research and did not use alts, I did not conduct participant observation with roleplaying communities, including Gorean ones, but did interview residents who belonged to Gorean communities. One such resident summarized Norman's vast science fiction narrative as follows:

> Gor is a fictional planet that is in the same orbit as the Earth, but opposite, always obscured by the sun. It is inhabited by an advanced race of aliens, who for some reason, choose to populate the planet with humans, initially abducted from earth. The aliens impose restrictions on human

activities, particularly technology, so in some ways, the society is medieval. The aliens are otherwise irrelevant to most of Gorean "culture." The result is a society based strongly on honor, trust, survival of the fittest, strength. Broadly, people are divided into three groups. The Free Men, who are subdivided into many castes of different ranks. The Free Women, who are normally very subordinate to Free Men, but are Free. And the female slaves, who are "owned," treated as property.

Norman set forth a ruggedly heteronormative and sociobiological vision in which men "naturally" desire to dominate women and women "naturally" desire to be dominated by men: "part of the correct treatment of a woman is treating her as you wish; she has genetic dispositions for submission bred into every cell of her body, a function of both natural and sexual selection" (Norman 1978:10). Despite controversy, Norman's novels have sold millions of copies since the late 1960s and continue to draw an avid following, including persons who attempt to live out Gorean fantasies of female sexual slavery in the actual world. Gorean communities have also existed in a number of virtual worlds, particularly Active Worlds, and were a significant presence in Second Life even before I began my fieldwork. In Second Life, members of Gorean communities—many of whom had differing ideologies of how to interpret the novels and were not always on speaking terms—maintained a series of islands (with a lesser presence on the mainland as well). On these properties, they built cities and landscapes based on descriptions in the Gor novels and created avatars reflecting Gorean themes.[12]

As with BDSM more generally, Gorean communities were controversial. Angie, for instance, had been involved in Gorean communities in Second Life and other virtual worlds for over four years by the time of my research. She noted that "Gor is a 'man's world' if taken literally, and offends a lot of people. And with reason: a lot of the bad press is fully justified." Such "bad press" has included accusations that Gorean communities prey upon women with low self-esteem.[13] In some cases, participants in Gorean or other BDSM communities would take their relationships into more public areas—for instance, going to a shopping mall with one's partner on a leash and asking permission to speak. This was sometimes a source of conflict: even if the mall in question were in a mature-rated area, other residents might feel that public space was being sexualized in an undesirable way.[14] Residents knew that an actual-world man could be controlling the nubile slave woman avatar before them, or that an actual-world woman could be controlling a barechested male avatar, but some still felt that Gorean communities provided a venue for female subordination that could transfer to actual-world contexts, particularly since some fans of the Gorean novels tried to live a "Gorean lifestyle" in the actual world (Fate 2006a, 2006b).[15] Other residents felt that forms of BDSM (including Gorean forms) could "liberate" women. One female resident noted how: "my 'character' as a Gorean slave is far closer to my rl character than I like to admit. I am talking about getting a thrill from being thought well of, from 'service' in a broad sense, and enjoying much more being 'led' than doing the 'leading,' mostly non-sexually."

Other controversial forms of sexuality, sometimes grouped together under the label "edgeplay" (Pettus 2006), included "child play," also known as "age play," which involved residents embodying themselves as children and having sex with adult avatars. Second Life was technically restricted to adults, with a separate "Teen Grid" for persons from 13–17 years old.[16] Yet for many residents virtual pedophilia was highly discomfiting, not least because in some jurisdictions even simulated sex with minors could be a crime (Teriman 2006). Reflecting how "for over a century, no tactic for stirring up erotic hysteria has been as reliable as the appeal to protect children" (Rubin 1993:6), fears over ageplay tapped into fundamental questions of agency, power, and propriety with regard to sexuality—as did other forms of edgeplay, such as roleplaying scenarios involving rape or even dismemberment.

Debates over both edgeplay and BDSM exemplified a much broader question about the nature of representation and ultimately the gap between the virtual and the actual. Clearly a murder in Second Life was a representation of a murder; no actual-world person was harmed. But sex in Second Life, even forms of BDSM and edgeplay, *were* forms of sexual expression for many residents, leading to orgasm and even to long-term relationships. What about a house in Second Life? Was it a representation of a house, or (as I would claim) a real house within the virtual context? Is it possible to rape someone in a virtual world, given my stance on virtual homes? Answers to questions like these were strenuously debated in Second Life during my fieldwork, tapping into vital issues of selfhood, community, and the meaning of the virtual. Historically binarisms like material versus representational mediated these kinds of distinctions. In the Age of Techne, such binarisms are reconfigured—not eliminated, but transformed in myriad ways.

In providing examples of BDSM and edgeplay, I have touched upon boundary-pushing aspects of sexual culture in Second Life in which most residents did not engage. More common were forms of sexual expression in the context of serial monogamy and romance. These romances and relationships were not solely heterosexual. Given my notion of the virtual human as "homo cyber," it only makes sense that I should discuss "cyber homos"—gay, lesbian, and bisexual subjectivities online. Since homosexuality has been the primary focus of my research in Indonesia, I could have written an entire book on queer Second Life—which, as one resident noted, is "queer along axes we don't even have in first life." Since this book aims for a more holistic perspective, I here provide only a preliminary analysis.

Because nonnormative sexualities remain stigmatized (if not illegal) in much of the actual world, there has been a tradition of interpreting them as "virtual" or "apparitional" (e.g., Castle 1993; Sullivan 1995; Vaid 1996; Weston 1997). Homosexuality has been a feature of virtual worlds from their very beginnings; the first moment of cybersociality may well have been an incident in 1970 when one man drew away from the virtual touch of another man's hand (see chapter 2; figure 2.6). Homophobia is far from unknown online (one study found over 80 percent of gamers encountering homophobic speech [Glover 2007]), but there is also a long tradition of cyberlibertarian tolerance. In Second Life during the period of my fieldwork, gay and lesbian communities flourished, including entire islands complete with clubs, clothing stores, and residential areas (Jones 2007). These highly visible venues were occasionally the target of griefing, as when a lesbian-themed island was attacked and objects on the island deleted, but for the most part homosexually themed areas were left alone. Many communities in Second Life had gay or lesbian subcultures within them, the best-known example probably being "gay furries." Some gay and lesbian residents participated in these communities rarely or not at all, socializing instead with mixed groups while perhaps cohabiting with a same-sex lover in a virtual home.

Since sexual orientation was typically not seen to be embodied online (or offline) in the way that gender, race, age, and disability were, the sexual orientation of residents was often unclear. For some, Second Life provided a virtual closet where they could live out same-gender desires they were unable or unwilling to enact in the actual world. For instance, I encountered many cases of bisexual men and women who were heterosexually married, had chosen to be monogamous with their opposite-gender spouse in the actual world, but with their spouse's blessing pursued same-gender sex and even relationships in Second Life. For other residents, Second Life could act as a venue to grow comfortable with a gay or lesbian identity before coming out in the actual world.

LOVE.

> For suddenly, I saw you there
> And through this foggy SL world

> The sun was shining everywhere,
> There's this place in me where your fingerprints rest,
> your kisses linger,
> and your whispers softly echo.
> It's the place where a part of you
> will forever be a part of me.

During the time of my research there were two primary models for social relation in virtual worlds—the friend and the partner—but friendships were clearly more basic to online culture.[17] Almost every resident developed friendships, but many avoided relationships. For others, romance was extremely important, and in this section I examine the words and actions of those who spoke of having an online lover, partner, boyfriend, girlfriend, spouse, husband, or wife.

As suggested by the poem above (which appeared in a resident profile), love could be the most meaningful aspect of life online, the thing that made the virtual real. I noted in chapter 3 how Heidegger identified a separation in the Western tradition between episteme (knowledge) and techne (art, craft), claiming that this separation inaugurates one important sense of a distinction between the actual—for which the human goal is knowledge—and the virtual, constituted by humans through craft. As mentioned in chapter 2, a key origin point for this notion of episteme in the Western tradition is the story of the Tree of Knowledge: episteme is linked to heteronormative notions of desire and the subordination of women. Foucault noted how the separation between episteme and techne was linked to changing ideologies of love in Greek thought: "the traditional erotics laid strong emphasis on the polarity of the lover and the beloved and on the necessary dissymmetry between them," but with the separation of episteme and techne "it is the double activity of loving, by the husband and the wife, that forms the essential element" (Foucault 1986:208–9). Love emerges as a form of techne, of that distinct form of human activity crafting a social world. While taking a range of forms over the centuries and across the globe, by the twentieth century, love had become an essential characteristic of the modern self and was strongly linked to notions of placemaking and social belonging (Boellstorff 2005; Coontz 2005; Freeman 2002). Those who cannot understand how persons can fall in love online without "knowing" their partner in the actual world confuse episteme with techne. What operationalizes love in virtual worlds is not knowing who someone is in the actual world, but crafting a relationship within the virtual world.

Love has long been present in virtual worlds and the Internet in general (Ben-Ze'ev 2004; Jacobson 1996; Stone 1995; Sveningsson 2002), as one element in a broader history of technologically mediated intimacy going back even to love letters (Ahearn 2001).[18] The first wedding in a graphical virtual world probably took place in May 1996 (Damer 1998:133; see also Curtis 1992:135; Reid 1999:114), and lovers were creating shared virtual homes even in text-only virtual worlds (Reid 1999:114). By the time I began my research, using the Internet to find romance—for instance, via an on-line dating service—was no longer considered an aberration, just as going online to purchase a book, read up on a medical condition, or reconcile a bank account had become increasingly mundane. What did seem new was that virtual worlds could be the location for the love relationship, as in the case of Chancie: "I met my Second Life boyfriend the first week I was here. I came to an event at his club, and I was so impressed with him right away, thought what he did there was so incredible. I would come back every day and looked forward to his events. And I began to have feelings for him. I wasn't sure what they were at first: respect, admiration, and then they became deeper. Then he started having an interest in me. I couldn't believe it. Such a noob was I, not able to build or script, just an explorer."

Like many residents, for Chancie Second Life was not a communications tool allowing her to meet someone with shared actual-world interests. Second Life was the place where shared interests were forged and experienced, and they had no plan to meet in the actual world: "If things were different I would, but our RL paths are very different. I am older, my path set. He is just starting his. . . . That is why SL is so important to me. It gives me an avenue to explore what I cannot in first life. It helps me enhance what I already have: my adventurous spirit, my openness, my ability to change all the time."

The role of Second Life as a venue for love continued for most partners beyond the initial romance; they traveled through the virtual world as a couple, sharing the joy of discovery and a mutual network of friends. Some such couples moved together to Second Life from another virtual world and continued to spend time in other online worlds—for instance, going together to Worlds of Warcraft for some combat-based fun before returning to Second Life to listen to a musical performance. Many would build or rent a home together, and eventually sought to formalize their relationship. Weddings were some of the most elaborate events in Second Life, as exemplified by the wedding of Dax and Cynd, one of many I attended during my fieldwork. It was held on a property whose owners earned money hosting weddings: the land featured a chapel and a club for celebrating after the ceremony. One of the owners, Drake, worked as the officiant. After sitting down (in my best tuxedo) with several friends and iming each other with comments about the lovely flowers and trays of virtual food that decorated the chapel, we turned our attention toward the couple before us, Drake standing between them as he began to speak:

DRAKE: Welcome everyone. Ladies and gentlemen, we have gathered today to bear witness to Cynd and Dax's declaration of love . . . You two will be sharing your love and energy with your friends, chosen family, and God. At this time I would like to ask Dax to lead and share his words now.

DAX: Today we make a commitment to one and other. . . . I promise to be your confidant, your best friend and to share in your hopes and dreams. With these vows we face new responsibilities together, and I promise to love you in all circumstances.

CYND: ty baby :) Shall i go? I'm bawling :)

DRAKE: And now Cynd, please share your love and vows with Dax and us all

CYND: Dax, you have made this "second life" for me. . . . When I played There, I never could find anyone who could understand me, care for me, and treat me the way that you do. You make every day on here a joy and I find myself just counting the minutes till I can see you again. I never thought I could really truly let myself love someone on a "game" but you have broken down the walls, and with that you have gained my full and complete respect. Never in a million years did I think I would be standing here in this beautiful chapel in a white gown saying all of this.

DAX: I love you baby :)

DRAKE: Dirk, do you take Cynd to be your Secondlife Wife

DAX: I do

DRAKE: And do you Cynd take Dax to be your Secondlife Husband

CYND: I do

DRAKE: Then it is my true heartfelt pleasure to pronounce you partners and present you to the world. May no man, woman, or lag do you under.

Same-sex partnerships were permitted in Second Life and there was a broad tolerance for them, particularly because one's actual-world gender was not necessarily known. Same-sex relationships could be celebrated just as heterosexual ones—as in the wedding of Freddie and JohnRay, who had never met in the actual world, officiated by their friend Lola:

LOLA: Dear friends, we have gathered today to witness a truly special moment. In a world of our own making, two men have come together to affirm their love. . . . There is not only a deep love in this relationship, but a mutual respect and understanding of life's boundaries. At this time, Freddie and JohnRay have vows to speak to each other. Freddie, would you please speak first?

FREDDIE: Our love is no game, no roleplaying; it's a very real, deep and abiding love. . . . I shall always remember the moment my heart realized it had found its home in you. Thank you for loving me through a very difficult year in real life.

LOLA: JohnRay, would you please speak to Freddie.

JOHNRAY: I take you to be my husband and I will love you always. . . . You truly are the love of my life.

LOLA: These two men have shared their love and their friendship with each other and with all of us. By the power vested in me by virtue of being a Citizen in the World of Second Life, I wish you many more years of happiness.

Many noted the rapidity with which falling in love and establishing a relationship could take place. One resident recalled how "in my experience, relationships in online communities often become a lot more intense in the early stages than in the real world"; another exclaimed "two weeks to a wedding!" Newbies were often struck by this intensity; during a game of Tringo, I once overheard the following exchange between Alice (who had just obtained a Second Life account the previous day) and Leeza (a longer-term resident):

ALICE: I see there are a lot of people on here pairing; is that the thing?

LEEZA: Pairing? Like hooking up? omg yes

ALICE: I need a man then lol. Because all of you are having great conversations. Is it easy to do that with everyone being so far apart? This is a game; how can you trust on here?

LEEZA: Well Alice, it takes a lot of time to build up that trust. I met my boyfriend on The Sims Online and then we spent the next year getting to know each other here in Second Life before we decided to take it to RL. I'm moving in with him in about a week!

Because Alice was new to Second Life, she thought of it as a game and saw residents as "far apart" rather than copresent in a virtual place. Her concerns about trust were not necessarily shared inworld. Unlike Leeza, who was soon to share an actual-world home with her formerly virtual-world boyfriend, for many residents Second Life was the only site where a virtual romance ever existed. The virtual romance was complete within its online parameters: it was real, because the intimacy, care, and desire were real. One member of a couple expressed this sentiment by stating that "we are real to each other. Second Life and real life don't make a difference for us"; another noted that "when you love somebody, it doesn't matter where: you want to be able to do anything for them. So with my boyfriend the whole online factor doesn't matter. I care just as much for him as anyone I know in real life." What Alice did not yet understand was that trust could be internal to the virtual world. It was not an issue of trusting that the person told the truth about their actual-world gender, age, marital status, or occupation; one typically hoped for such honesty, but it was honesty about one's words and deeds inworld that was paramount. Many residents refused all actual-world contact with their online lovers; I knew a couple who had never exchanged actual-world photographs of each other after three years of a close and meaningful online marriage. In response to the claim that love could not be sustained without physical contact, one person replied in a manner many residents would find intelligible: "You can be blind and be in love; the brain compensates fully for the lack of sensorial input. So the Second Life experience doesn't need to be perfect. It just needs to be good to a certain degree, and from there on, the brain takes over. Aren't we holding back things in RL as well? The SL marriage is within the SL context, so how is it fake?"

For some, Second Life romances were *more* real than actual-world romances, because as one resident observed, "in a virtual environment we get to meet the person before we can judge their physical appearance." In one case, two women carried on a lesbian relationship for several months even knowing that both were heterosexual men in the actual world: Second Life had fostered a form of intimacy that would probably never have otherwise occurred (Au 2005a). Those without experience in online worlds might find it hard to grasp how it could be pleasurable, even erotic, to have virtual relationships distinct from those in the actual world. One resident suspected his online lover was someone with whom they "probably would not click in real life;" another emphasized how "I take people as they present themselves online, and the less I know about rl the better."

Ignorance about the actual-world life of one's online partner could be pleasurable because it reinforced the gap between virtual and actual, establishing the online world as a site for intimacy in its own terms. This reveals a link between techne and episteme: that ignorance could keep clear the distinction between the virtual and actual implies that knowledge could act as the human agency bridging this gap. Yet I encountered cases during my fieldwork where this desire to maintain the gap between virtual and actual could backfire, as in the following example:

> I have a friend in Second Life named Susan, and I've known her and her companion George for some time now. For about a year and a half Susan and George talked in Second Life every day, they were extremely close, but they had never even seen each other's picture and didn't know each other's real-life names—they had an agreement. One day George tells Susan he's going to log off of Second Life for a moment to clean the snow off his car. He doesn't come back on for days, weeks. Susan's a wreck. Suddenly it's like the real-life disappearance of a loved one, yet you are powerless to do anything. Did he die? Did he have a stroke? I comforted her every day. She took me to the [virtual] house they had built and would recall things they had done together. Susan started piecing together conversations over the year and a half, checked obituaries online, trying to figure out who George was in real life and what had happened. After a month he arrives one day back in Second Life. His mother had taken deathly ill in another country where there he couldn't get internet service. He had left as quickly as possible and didn't think to leave her a message. He's apologized profusely since, but it was very hard for her.

Stories like this, which have parallels in other virtual worlds (Kendall 2002:148–53), led some Second Life residents to leave instructions in a sealed envelope so that their actual-world spouse could contact their Second Life partner in an emergency.[19] This example illustrates how some residents found the gap between virtual and actual undesirable or even painful. Sometimes this was linked to a belief that residents of virtual worlds "hide behind an online identity" or were "always holding something back" because Second Life was "the proverbial shared hallucination." More often—as in the case of Leeza above—it was not a matter of denigrating virtual romance, but believing its success indicated that the relationship could be extended into the actual world. Residents told many poignant stories of "crossing over" to meet their Second Life lovers offline. One man recalled first meeting his Second Life wife: "It was fabulous! She is so sweet and really just like she is in here. She's beautiful, warm, curvy and has the most delicate hands. The only difficulty was my not knowing

American Sign Language: she is deaf, and like everyone else we communicate in Second Life through typed chat. So when we met in the real world, we just wrote on a pad and paper, back and forth." Some actual-world marriages had begun as romances within Second Life.

Some residents who fell in love online were single in the actual world, but for those in a committed relationship, the issue of fidelity threw into sharp relief the question of what kinds of human activity could sustain or threaten the gap between actual and virtual.[20] One person talked about how "in RL, I am married, but not happily. I have formed a special relationship with GB. She and I are having a virtual affair. I have admitted this to my RL wife, and explained that it was better to get my urge to have an affair out in a virtual world, rather than in RL. The challenge is keeping the 'affair' to SL. I have sent GB pictures of myself in Hotmail—crossed a boundary there. And we have talked on the phone." Other residents felt that it was "worse to cheat in Second Life than in rl. In rl it's a physical thing, but here it's your mind." Yet another possibility was that the actual-world partner did not know about Second Life, or only partially understood the idea of virtual romance: one resident joked about how she had told her husband about her online relationship, but "not all the sex and cuddling."

While some actual-world partners did participate in Second Life as a couple, others fell in love with separate online lovers. In such cases, one actual-world partner might even attend the others' virtual wedding and become friends with their partner's virtual-world lover. One resident talked about how his actual-world wife had become good friends with his virtual wife and even "attended our wedding. And she has been crying for me ever since she heard the news that my sl wife was leaving me." Even when only one member of an actual-world couple participated in Second Life, the partner uninterested in becoming a resident might tolerate or support the other partner's virtual-world romance, often with the condition that the virtual lover not be provided any information about the couple's actual-world lives. In some instances a frustrating result of such agreements was that one member of a virtual romance might know much more about their partner's actual-world life than the other way around. Jonco and his online lover Mark each had male partners in the actual world, but Mark had never told Jonco his actual-world name or address, despite the fact that Jonco had provided such information to Mark. One day, Jonco described how: "Mark really did something that amazed me. He actually sent a Valentine's Day card to my [actual-world] home address. No return address of course. So I can't send him one lol, I still don't know his real name. I'm damn curious to see a picture of him after two years but I guess that's asking too much. He's been with this guy for 10 years now, and he wants his world with me totally separate. He still refers to me by my online name, which I find interesting because he knows my real name."

On more than one occasion I encountered residents who had used images of other people when asked for an actual-world photograph of themselves, which could lead to strong feelings of betrayal if discovered. David had been a good friend of mine when he imed me to his house to talk about a crisis with his girlfriend Emma:

> I led her to believe I was a whole other person for a year and a half . . . not personality-wise, but a different picture and occupation and everything. I know, really stupid and a BIG mistake. How do you look past that? . . . It started off so small. I was going through a hard time in rl, and I just sent a fake picture. I was scared to tell her it wasn't me, so I just kept going with it, and it kept getting bigger and bigger. . . . I didn't think I was gonna meet someone here I wanted to spend the rest of my life with. I guess at first part of me thought it was just a game. When I really started to develop feelings for this woman I was too scared to tell her the truth, so I kept going with it. She's asked me a million and a half times to fly out to see her. I never could cause she thought I was a different person. If I was myself the whole time I would have been able to in a heartbeat. What I wouldn't give to have her trust back.

When a relationship like David and Emma's came to an end, the sense of loss could be as intense as with an actual-world relationship. One Second Life resident noted that "I can honestly say I feel more crushed about losing my girlfriend than I ever have about any of my real life girlfriends. I still cry about it and it still hurts. I was convinced she was the one for me." It could be hard for residents to wear certain pieces of virtual clothing, go to certain places, socialize with certain friends, or even look at certain snapshots, because they all evoked memories of the lost relationship. Yet despite the risks of heartache and betrayal, risks that were "real" and could have implications in the actual world, love in Second Life remained an important source of support and meaning. One resident who lived in Europe and had a relationship with a person living in the United States, eight time zones away, recalled how "one day, we were hanging here just snuggling, and he sent me a site where I could see a webcam of a highway in his town, and we watched the sunset together." In making the virtual real, love could act as the purest form of techne.

FAMILY.

During my fieldwork it was still common to see residents of virtual worlds portrayed as loners neglecting social ties. Yet there is strong evidence that from the earliest days of virtual worlds there have been greater-than expected numbers of actual-world friends and family who participate together online (Damer 1998:224; Nardi and Harris 2006; Nardi, Ly, and Harris 2007; Taylor 2006a:52–56). On many occasions I encountered multiple members of an actual-world family meeting in Second Life, engaging in projects together and visiting each others' virtual homes despite being separated by thousands of miles in the actual world. Satin and Gretel, for instance, were actual-world sisters who resided in Second Life together with three other siblings. When I asked them if they did things together online, they replied:

> GRETEL: Yes! Shopping, roller-skating all over the place. We even had a birthday party for Satin.
> SATIN: We enjoy building together too.
> GRETEL: I find the email has slowed a lot since Second Life.
> SATIN: Second Life adds a creative dimension to our interactions.

Second Life could also be the site for new, online families. Some Second Life couples had automated children, with scripted sounds of crying and the occasional demand like "I'm hungry!" More common, however, were forms of "child play." As discussed earlier, there were residents who participated in Second Life as children for sexual purposes. Most of those who participated in Second Life as children, however, did so to create forms of virtual kinship. Appearing as a child was their primary virtual embodiment, and they also used language and social practice to enact their subjectivities as children—for instance, not swearing while using a child avatar. Wendy, one of several virtual children I came to know during my fieldwork, would refer to me as "Mr. Bukowski" and ask me to take her out to play after she had asked permission from her parents. She wished to engage only in children's activities, a wish facilitated by the existence of groups and places dedicated to child play, from malls selling cribs, wood blocks, and children's clothing to an elementary school complete with classes, recess, and a school nurse. One day, while Wendy and I were sitting together, she decided to "break character" and speak with me as an adult about her online life as a child:

> I've been fascinated by a few things. One, the ability to explore alternate life experiences by use of various avatars. Two, the nature of created

families here. Three, the differences in the way people interact with me socially depending on my avie. In my [online] family, there are some RL connections as well as the SL ones, and it is interesting to see how those play out. One of the kids in our family is a very close RL friend of mine. Our mommies are RL sisters, and so on. This is more about letting my inner child out to play than anything. The family I'm in is made up of over 60 people. Five generations. I had no idea it was so large when I was asked to be adopted. But that it is so big has been one of the most fascinating aspects. I've had to start doing a family tree as I meet people, just to keep things straight.

Most people participating as children found that having parents was "almost essential" to their subjectivities. Child play was fundamentally relational, a subset of what could be termed kin play: residents participating as children but also as husbands, wives, grandparents, aunts, uncles, cousins, and friends, as exemplified by Wendy's large family. Virtual families could be important sources of intimacy, and as in Wendy's case could include members who were related in the actual world. That what is at issue was kin play rather than child play was demonstrated by virtual families with adult children. Arlen had a daughter and a son in Second Life: "My Second Life children are adults in RL, and in Second Life they play as adult children. My son on here is even engaged. They both never had a father figure in RL and I am happy to give them what they need from that type of bond. . . . I have seen a lot of closeness, a lot of support, a sense of belonging and purpose that travels to RL."

Whether involving persons participating as adult children or youngsters, kin play raised the possibility for new forms of intimacy that wove together preexisting actual-world families and emergent virtual world families, and could loop back to transform relationships in the actual world. Kin play could also involve kinship-specific forms of conflict, including parental discord and abandonment. Like other forms of intimacy, the intimacies of family life, for all their significance, were constituted through mundane social interaction as much as authoritative practice. One of many poignant moments during my research occurred when chatting with Wendy one evening, outside the context of a formal interview. We were talking about the little rituals that characterize family ties and she turned to her experiences with her Second Life family: "One of the big ones is being tucked into bed for the night. Mommy will come up to my room, we'll talk a little about our day, give hugs, I'll hop up into bed, she'll usually sing me a song or otherwise comfort me, I'll say my goodnights, and right then log off."

Pondering Wendy's words as we sat together looking out over a Second Life sunset, the virtual water lapping up against our feet, I began to realize their significance. I turned to Wendy and said "so what you're saying is that when you go to bed in Second Life, at the moment Wendy closes her eyes in this virtual world, you log off the Second Life program on your computer?" "Uh huh," Wendy replied. "So the actual world is Wendy's dream, until she wakes up again in Second Life?" I could have sworn a smile passed across Wendy's avatar's face as she said "Yup. Indeed."

ADDICTION.

By the time I began my research, fears about "Internet Addiction Disorder" were common in the mass media and extended to virtual worlds, despite the fact that scholars of cybersociality had long cautioned against analogizing biological dependency to virtual contexts: "It is striking that the word 'user' is associated mainly with computers and drugs" (Turkle 1995:30; see also Baty 1999; Curtis 1992:137; Turkle 1997:150; Yee 2002, 2004, 2005, 2006c). I did not find the notion of addiction etically useful; it did not transparently diagnose an existent psychological disorder. Emically, however, it was symptomatic of anxieties about selfhood, agency, and intentionality that lie at the core of discourses of the virtually human.

Many residents questioned the accuracy of the term "addiction." One resident emphasized that "I think part of the problem is that we're using too broad a brush. Saying 'Second Life is addictive' is just like saying 'real life is addictive.' Real life is a broad category. It could entail riding motorcycles, watching movies, even masturbating." The language of addiction was often linked to the view that Second Life was a game; one entrepreneurial resident recalled how "everyone I know stopped joking about me being 'addicted' to SL when it started paying my bills. So was I ever 'addicted'?"

Consider how virtual addiction differed from "identity theft," another well-known term during the period of my fieldwork. Identity theft was seen to occur when one person claimed to be someone else for economic gain. The term came into existence in the twenty-first century because it presumed the misuse of online networks that did not exist in earlier decades (Poster 2006:90). It presumed an avatarization of the self difficult to imagine prior to the emergence of virtual worlds; identity theft could be said to involve one person's virtual self becoming the alt of another. Isolated incidents of identity theft in Second Life—where one person took control of another's avatar—occurred during my research but were not termed "addiction." This was probably because the damage identity theft caused was framed in economic terms; the notion implied that identity is "external to the consciousness of the self" and "consists of a series of numerical indicators" like credit card numbers and dates of birth (Poster 2006:113).

When residents spoke of themselves as "addicted" or "hooked on" Second Life, they typically meant they were spending too much time online; the harm caused by virtual addiction was almost always understood in temporal terms. With surprising consistency in Second Life and beyond, the harm of "virtual addiction" was assumed to effect the temporality of the *actual* world: "any time you spend online is time not spent on other parts of your life" (Greenfield 1999:64; see also Castronova 2005:64–65; Turkle 1997:150). Even self-help books for Internet addiction spoke of the "one more minute" syndrome or the "Terminal Time Warp" (Young 1998:35–58). Since time is particularly resistant to virtualization, it is not surprising that losing control over time could be seen as both symptom and effect of virtual addiction.

For most residents of Second Life, two things made their inworld activities definable as addiction. First, the activities began to take up what was felt to be a disproportionate amount of time. Second, this was seen to detract from time that could be devoted to actual-world activities. This could include everything from raking leaves in one's actual-world yard to tasks at one's actual-world job. Some residents spoke of sleeping less so as to have more time in Second Life, and lack of sleep was often interpreted as a sign of addiction; others claimed that Second Life simply replaced television viewing, and thus need not take time away from actual-world activities. Above all, the issue of detraction referred to actual-world intimacy, to spending less time with one's actual-world family and friends, particularly one's partner: "I found sl before my rl partner did, and I became very—and I mean very—addicted. I withdrew from rl, it left my wife feeling unloved. I worked from 7am to 4pm, came home, got on around 4:30pm, and was on until midnight."[21] During a discussion, when one resident asked "why must sl replace something else?" another resident replied "time is finite. Everything one does replaces something else." A third resident added, "I don't think it's addiction until you're spending the whole evening or weekend here, jumping up every three hours or so to get food or use the bathroom." Since all Second Life activities took up time, any activity could be seen as addictive. However, it was social relationships—particularly love relationships—that were commonly described in such terms (Greenfield 1999). During my research I encountered statements like "I'm addicted to people" or "it's the social part of SL that gets me hooked" far more often than statements about being addicted to building, scripting, or other activities.

There emerges a highly significant parallelism that underscores the place of culture in the constitution of homo cyber: friendships and relationships were the source of addiction and the thing most harmed by that addiction. It was a logic of substitution and commensurability made possible by the striking fact that what led residents to label certain activities "addictive" was quantitative, not qualitative. It was not the character of an activity, be it shopping, sex, games, or listening to a poetry reading, that led residents to classify it as addictive. It was possible to gamble in Second Life, but if residents found themselves too involved in that activity, they would speak of being addicted to gambling, not addicted to Second Life. Some residents thought it possible to become addicted to games played within Second Life (Tringo, for instance), but this was also not equated with being addicted to Second Life. The concern was time itself: any activity could be seen as addictive if it took up too much time. At issue was human activity taken generically, the human capacity for intentional creation I term techne.

Concerns about addiction were thus concerns about compromised agency—about the need for a self that is self-controlled, creative, and intentional—reflecting broad cultural assumptions about the character of homo cyber. They reflected the belief that the human online is created and sustained through acts of techne; an apparent loss of agency over these deployments was interpreted as "addiction." Culture in Second Life emerges as an interplay between forms of selfhood and community on the one hand, and place and time on the other, all meeting under the rubric of intimacy. Generalizing outward, to be virtually human might itself constitute an ethnographic project, in the sense that it involves a dialectic of participation and observation, a self-reflexive crafting of one's point of view.

Chapter 7

COMMUNITY

*The event—The group—Kindness—Griefing—Between
virtual worlds—Beyond virtual worlds.*

THE EVENT.

Eleven of us sit in a row on stone benches amidst a green sloped meadow. A
forested hill rises into the distance; before us shimmers the endless expanse
of the Second Life ocean. A twelfth resident stands in front, one hand extended as he builds in silence, prims taking form and changing shape before
our eyes. The rest of us type out words:

body
person
man
woman
soldier
ghost
shade
spirit
no, that's too easy . . .
spectre
afterlife
wraith
fig leaf
sheriff badge
gender
chaste
genitals
knob
chakra
thrush lol
chi
* * * STOP!! * * * WE HAVE A WINNER!

acupuncture
George gets CHAKRA!
:(
yow.
wowie
holy moley
Nice one

This innocuous game of "primtionary" is only one of myriad possible examples of an "event." In the previous chapters I discussed selfhood and intimacy in Second Life. But if what makes virtual worlds "worlds" is that they are places, what makes them sites of culture—and thus amenable to ethnographic investigation—is that people interact in them. Some scholars of the online have contended that the term "community" is of questionable utility because virtual worlds engender a "faceless community" that is less authentic and meaningful than actual-world sociality. In this view, a person will "reach out to the Internet to make connections while never really connecting with the other person in a meaningful, real-life way" (Young 1998:96; see also Guimarães 2005).

Such interpretations are not supported by the ethnographic evidence. It has long been noted that virtual worlds "do become true communities after a time" (Curtis 1992:137; see also Ducheneaut, Moore, and Nickell 2004). Often negative assessments of online community originate in misunderstandings of actual-world sociality: "pundits worry that virtual community may not truly be community. These worriers are confusing the pastoralist myth of community for the reality. Community ties are already geographically dispersed, sparsely knit, connected heavily by telecommunications . . . and specialized in content" (Wellman and Gulia 1999:187). These myths of physical proximity and cultural homogeneity resemble the stereotypes of classic anthropology that shaped the assumption that the "field" of ethnographic fieldwork must be a small-scale, "traditional" community (e.g., Redfield 1955). Many contemporary anthropologists have critiqued this assumption (Gupta and Ferguson 1997); for instance, in my research on sexuality I took "Indonesia" (rather than an ethnolocalized group like "Javanese") as the unit of ethnographic analysis (Boellstorff 2002). The anthropological critique of locality finds its analogue in game studies scholarship that questions Huizinga's classic notion of the "magic circle" within which a game-space is defined and its rules of play are efficacious (Huizinga 1950:57).

What these critiques share is an appreciation for how community has never been reducible to locality: "that communities do not presuppose that members have to be spatially copresent or temporally simultaneous in their activities has been known for ages: already the early civic public sphere in the late eighteenth century revolved not only around bourgeois salons but also around press and book publishing" (Fornäs et al. 2002:35). This invocation of the public sphere recalls the work of Jürgen Habermas on the rise of the "lifeworld" in Western Europe, "the transcendental site where speaker and hearer meet" (Habermas 1989:171; see also Habermas 1970a), raising the possibility that virtual worlds could be "Third Places" (Oldenberg 1989; Steinkuehler and Williams 2006) that stand outside the dichotomy of public and private (Ducheneaut, Moore, and Nickell 2004). In this sense "all communities are virtual communities" (Silverstone 1999:104); for this reason, virtual worlds "compel conversations about the nature of community itself" (Turkle 1997:152). One reason these conversations are important is that, as discussed in the following chapter, debates over what counted as community and its place in governance were frequent in Second Life during my fieldwork. This was sometimes triggered by a Linden Lab claim that an alteration to the platform or Terms of Service reflected "community sentiment," without a clear explanation of who constituted or spoke for the community in question.

It might be possible in theory to have a virtual world with only one inhabitant, but most of those I met during my research would not term something a "virtual world" unless it had multiple residents.[1] A few residents came to Second Life for solitude, but socializing with other residents was the most common activity inworld. Since the first days of MUDs, there has been a remarkable degree of consensus across a range of virtual worlds that social relationships are their most important aspect: as one Second Life resident put it, "people wouldn't be here without other people; they are here for social reasons. No matter how fancy the tool, it comes back to connecting with people." Things like "getting crazy with my friends" or "the life I've built with my sl partner" were frequently highlighted by residents as what motivated them to spend time in Second Life.

"Events" were one way Second Life residents interacted, and thus one way I engaged in participant observation. The range of events I attended represents a small fraction of the total number of events held in Second Life during my fieldwork, but is still so large and varied that a firm typology would be counterproductive. Events in which I participated included everything from teaching elementary school for a group of thirty residents living in Second Life as children, to a fashion show complete with models on a catwalk, to performances of live music (streamed onto a parcel of land, while the performer appeared as an avatar before the crowd), to philosophy discussions, to religious meetings at houses of worship, to different kinds of games and contests, including Tringo (which, as one resident noted, "is not just a game; it is a place to meet people"). Some events had a fairly clear distinction between performer and audience, while others were more egalitarian. As part of my participant observation, I also hosted a regular event, the "Digital Cultures" discussions, where groups of ten to forty residents would talk about current issues in Second Life; this allowed me to experience firsthand the process of posting and hosting events.

As noted in chapter 1, during my fieldwork the Second Life map showed the location of each online resident with a green dot. It was common to see pairs of dots—two residents talking or even having sex—and clusters of dots hinted at larger social interactions. Pavel Curtis termed this "social gravity": "If more than a couple of players are in the same room, the presumption is that an interesting conversation may be in progress there; players are thus more attracted to more populated areas" (Curtis 1992:132). Areas of the map without green dots, or views across the Second Life landscape without visible residents, remained part of Second Life sociality. On their own residents could do anything from shopping to visiting an art gallery or walking through a park. In general, however, the aspects of Second Life that were most important to residents were social places. As one Second Life resident put it, "an empty virtual world is a truly sad sight to see," recalling how in virtual worlds more generally, residents often say that "inworld locations devoid of avatars feel empty and abandoned" (Taylor 2002:47). The presence of other persons was key to a sense of place; no amount of dazzling graphics could compensate for the role of sociality in filling an otherwise "empty" virtual world. As one resident explained, "the people that inhabit this space are what make it real."

In general terms, an "event" in Second Life involved a conjunction of place, time, and sociality. Forms of asynchronic sociality, like several residents working at different times of the day on a single building, would not typically be seen as events, nor would two or more persons communicating by im, but not in the same virtual location, typically be seen as participating in a single event.[2] For instance, I once attended a "round-robin storytelling" event, where a group of residents got together in a circle and took turns contributing a paragraph to an evolving story. Such a story could have been constructed over instant messaging, or asynchronically, with one person writing a paragraph and leaving it in a note card for another person to find several hours later, but in neither case would such forms of social interaction have been considered an event by most residents. The concept of "event" was formalized from the beginning of my fieldwork, and by the end of my research over one thousand events took place each day. When I first became a resident, the virtual world was small enough that Linden Lab staff would make hourly announcements of upcoming events: "Hey all, in the 4pm hour we have four events! An advertising opportunity, a discussion of aliens, an offer of free animations, and a new business!" Later, events were listed within the "find" menu and also on the Second Life website and other websites. Some of these were little more than advertisements for stores, but many events were never officially listed, being announced by ims in a form of virtual word of mouth. Often events were not listed because they were not open to all residents—for instance, a wedding ceremony limited to invited guests.

During the period of my fieldwork, limitations of server and broadband technology meant that most events involved five to fifteen residents: events with 100,000, 1,000, or even 100 participants were technologically impossible. Most sims could accommodate a maximum of forty avatars; as server technology improved, some sims could accommodate seventy-five avatars or more, but no matter what the location, it was difficult to have more than about twenty-five avatars present without experiencing significant lag. Second Life's culture, involving a vast landscape and tens of thousands of residents by the end of my research, was thus constituted through many relatively intimate instantiations of sociality. This is not unlike the everyday constitution of actual-world cultures.

THE GROUP.

The phrase "massively multiple" is misleading because it implies an atomized sociality where individuals aggregate into an undifferentiated whole. In contrast, collectivities or subcultures standing between the individual and the society have been important to virtual worlds from their beginnings (Jakobsson and Taylor 2003), often under names like "guild" or "group," the term most often used in Second Life. Events can be understood as groups temporarily formed in time and place. As less delimited collectivities, "groups" were important to how many residents understood selfhood and community online. In this book I focus on Second Life as a whole, but in this section I briefly turn to the place of groups in Second Life culture.

The notion of "group" had two primary meanings in Second Life during the period of my research: a formal sense, linked to the Second Life platform, and an informal sense of association. In formal terms, "groups" were named networks of residents; for instance, "Club Rama Fans," "Nerds with Attitude," or "Women's Support Group." Any resident could join a number of these groups (up to twenty-five by the end of my fieldwork). Groups could be free to join, or could require an invitation and even the payment of a fee. Once a resident joined a group, the resident could, if they wished, have the title of that group appear above their screen name for others to see. Groups could be organized around almost anything, including places (a club, a store, a home); topics (helping newbies, scripting, architecture, poetry, Second Life history); and identity categories (disabled persons, educators, vampires, gay men, music lovers).

Although "groups" in this first sense were integrated into the Second Life platform, their formality varied greatly. Since it was possible to im an entire group at once, some functioned as little more than conduits for communication; for instance, used by clubs to announce upcoming events. Groups could also be highly formalized, including a range of official roles and leadership positions. Residents could even contribute "tier" (the right to own a certain amount of land, tied to a monthly payment), allowing members of a group to co-own large parcels they could not afford on their own. Linden Lab encouraged this by allowing groups to own 10 percent more land than individual residents; for instance, if four residents formed a group "Nice Girls" and each was allowed to own 250 square meters of land based upon their monthly payment, the "Nice Girls" group would have the right to purchase 1,100 square meters of land. Groups could develop complicated organizational structures, shaped by the changing possibilities afforded by the Second Life platform. Because groups were listed on each resident's profile, perusing them was an important way to learn about someone's sense of selfhood.

A second meaning of "group" during the time of my fieldwork was informal and expansive, often described as a "community" or "subculture." Most groups in this second sense (for the sake of clarity, I will term these "communities") usually had many formal groups within them. "Furries" are an example of a well-known community in Second Life during the time of my fieldwork. In overly simplistic terms, Furries are persons who identify as animals or animal-like, and often wish to be embodied as animals in some fashion. Furrie culture, which for some but not all participants had sexual aspects, predates and exists outside of virtual worlds. In a sense it links up to forms of "totemic" identification with animals that date back to the earliest recorded cultures and have been a classic topic of anthropological interest (Durkheim and Mauss 1902; Lévi-Strauss 1962). Furrie culture has long been incorporated into virtual worlds—even when they were solely textual, as in the case of the "FurryMUCK" MUD, which opened in 1990 (Koster 2003:452; Reid 1996:339, 1999:111) and Furcadia, a furry-based graphical virtual world, which opened in 1996.[3] Furrie groups have often been a source of controversy, due to outsider discomfort with a sense such persons are "role-playing" (that is, exhibiting an inauthentic self in a virtual context that expects authenticity) or with sexual aspects of Furrie identity (Kendall 2002:45–46). Furrie culture was widespread in Second Life, with some residents living entirely as animal-like creatures and others embodying themselves as Furrie in more circumscribed contexts.[4] Many formal groups existed for Furries, and there were a range of properties (including multiple islands) devoted to Furrie culture, often with builds suggesting forests or other natural landscapes. Toward the end of my research it was estimated that at least 15,000 residents owned Furrie avatars.[5]

Religious groups are another example of communities or subcultures in Second Life, reflecting the associations between religion and technology harking back to the invention of writing and the Gutenberg Bible. Religion has been present since the early days of the Internet, and "the notion of cyberspace as some kind of Heaven runs rife through the literature" (Wertheim 1999:20; see also Apolito 2005; Dawson and Cowan 2004; Schroeder, Heather, and Lee 1998). However, the presence of religion was quite minimal in Second Life at the outset of my research, possibly due to the low religious participation of those who were its early adapters. I recall one resident asking "Has anyone noticed how God seems left out of SL?" Another answered, "God in SL seems like an absurdity. When you can fly, create objects out of thin air, etc., what meaning does a God have?"—an answer foreshadowing the ideology of "creationist capitalism" I discuss in the following chapter. Yet builds with a religious theme did exist from the beginning of my fieldwork, and by its end there were a range of religious communities, from Bible study groups to builds with Muslim, Jewish, or Buddhist themes (Au 2007d), to groups creating new religions within Second Life, such as "Avatarians."

As Second Life grew throughout the period of my fieldwork, there were increasing debates as to whether or not groups were becoming the primary form of socialization, to the extent that an overarching sense of community was at risk (Llewelyn 2005). I take seriously the statements of some residents who felt that "there is most undoubtedly a balkanization of the 'SL culture'—people logging onto SL to engross and involve themselves with a subculture." Yet just as it is possible to be "American" or "Indonesian" and also identify with a range of subcultures and localities, so the existence of communities did not prohibit a sense of simultaneously belonging to Second Life as a whole. As one resident noted, "people gain strength by being in groups. SL (like rl) is large and disorienting."

KINDNESS.

In the section following this one I discuss "griefing"—participation in a virtual world with the intent of disrupting the experience of others. Before doing so, however, I wish to underscore the predominance of kindness and altruism in virtual worlds. While griefing was often a source of complaint (and even notoriety) during my fieldwork, it can be a source of disproportionate debate and complaint, making it appear more salient than is actually the case (Taylor 2006a:36). As one Second Life resident noted, "people are very vocal about 'he shot me in the face,' but aren't so vocal about 'he helped me get dressed.'" Many residents I met during my research insisted they had never been directly griefed, and I experienced little griefing during my fieldwork.

Without minimizing the emotional, social, and financial damage wrought by griefing, the ubiquity of virtual altruism demands explanation. Researchers have been struck by a strong ethic of kindness and mutual aid in virtual worlds, often without any possibility of financial compensation: "on social MUDs cooperation is encouraged by the opportunity to extend the virtual world, not by the necessities of survival in it" (Reid 1999:129; see also Nakamura 2002:52). Acts of kindness in Second Life could take many forms. It was common to give items away (clothing for avatars, healing spells, "how-to" texts, furniture for a virtual home, even weapons), known in some virtual worlds as "twinking" (Jakobsson and Taylor 2003; see also Nardi and Harris 2006). Residents were typically quick to invite others to events and generally to see that those around them felt welcome.

Aside from the issue of actual-world universities or other educational institutions holding classes in Second Life, there were many educational activities for the benefit of residents. Educators involved in such activities taught—for minimal pay or for free—courses on everything from building and scripting, to designing clothing, hosting an event, or learning the virtual real estate market. Since learning the full capabilities of the Second Life interface was relatively difficult, this educational work was important. Indeed, in many cases this education worked not to produce knowledge, episteme, but the capacity for techne that in the actual world is often denigrated as "vocational-technical" learning. Education could also be more informal, as in the case of residents who answered resident questions. At some points during my fieldwork, Linden Lab formally labeled some of these persons as "Greeters" or "Mentors," but many residents helped others without receiving official recognition.

Entire groups took form on several occasions during the period of my fieldwork whose purpose was to provide a location and team of residents to help newcomers. I recall my experience teaching a class at an elementary school, mentioned in the previous chapter. Meeting in the school gym because there were too many students to fit in the regular schoolhouse, I taught the basics of the Indonesian language to about thirty virtual children.

I was astounded that after an hour, these virtual children (adults in the actual world) were typing out basic sentences in Indonesian. It was a virtual environment of kids together in a gym, throwing virtual wads of paper at each other and laughing about recess, yet real learning was taking place. How did this virtual environment of carefree childhood facilitate a form of learning that could not really be termed "distance education?"

Altruism could shade off into friendship: often I encountered residents struck by the willingness of persons not just to explain how to fly or build a house, but also to listen to personal problems—from frustrations with an actual-world job to troubles with an inworld lover. One resident reflected on the ubiquity of this ethic of generosity by stating that "I don't think the way SL works is exactly like RL. Most of the people I've met here are very considerate and helpful. In RL, often we're so overloaded with what we have to accomplish just to get to the end of the day that we aren't as generous."

GRIEFING.

It has long been noted that persons involved in virtual worlds (and other forms of online interaction, from email to blogs) can experience forms of "disinhibition." Such disinhibition can have positive aspects, from the kindness and altruism discussed above to the friendships and relationships explored in the previous chapter. During the time of my fieldwork, it was also widely recognized that disinhibition could have negative effects; as one Second Life resident put it, "people think they can shoot and run." A range of factors contributed to this disinhibition, including the ability to keep one's actual-world identity secret (though not all virtual worlds use screen names, and screen names can become part of personal identity); the ability to create groups bringing together people with shared interests who might never meet in the actual world; the ability to save, edit, and forward the communications of others; and the difficulty in knowing the size of one's audience (Carnevale and Probst 1997:238–40). However, "being disinhibited is not the same as being uninhibited. [Virtual world residents] experience a redefinition of social inhibitions; they do not experience the annihilation of them" (Reid 1999:112).

When residents acted to disrupt the experience of others, this was most often known as "griefing."[6] One resident defined griefing to a newbie as "deliberately doing something that interferes with other users' Second Life experience." In Second Life as in other virtual worlds, the question of when an act counted as "griefing" was debatable. One resident complained that: "'Griefing' has become a useless umbrella term; it used to be reserved for the people that filled sims with junk and bombed events and built giant dildos in the Welcome Area. Now a griefer is anybody you disagree with. It's gone from someone who's threatened the stability of the grid to someone who says your shirt's a funny color." One survey of respondents from five different virtual worlds (not including Second Life) found that "a perception that griefing has occurred" typically involved the resident verbalizing malicious intent, engaging in additional antisocial behavior, and repeating the act after being asked to stop (Foo 2004). A useful three-part definition of griefing is that "the griefer's act is intentional; it causes other [residents] to enjoy the [virtual world] less; [and] the griefer enjoys the act" (Foo 2004; see Mulligan and Patrovsky 2003). While some forms of griefing can have terrible consequences (including financial and emotional harm), griefing is not without social contexts of its own. For instance, some forms of griefing can represent a motivation for persons to participate in virtual worlds and a foundation for sociality with other griefers (Malaby 2006d; Yee 2006a). This recalls the long history of work in anthropology and beyond demonstrating how forms of conflict contribute to sociality, showing the limitations of theories of culture that presume it to depend upon consensus (Gluckman 1955).

While not being named as such, the concept of griefing dates back to the earliest virtual worlds, which as I define them in this book date to the telephone: "The first telephone operators of the Bell system were ... telegraphic messenger boys. . . . Within its very first year of operation, 1878, Bell's company learned a sharp lesson about combining teenage boys and telephone switchboards. . . . The boys were openly rude to customers. . . . And worst of all, they played clever tricks with the switchboard plugs: disconnecting calls, crossing lines so that customers found themselves talking to strangers, and so forth" (Sterling 1992:13). Another example of griefing in an early virtual world occurred in the mid-1970s, when the CommuniTree computerized bulletin board "collapsed under the onslaught of messages, often obscene, posted by the first generation of adolescent school children with personal computers and modems" (Reid 1999:107; see also Stone 1995:112–17). Griefing was well-known in textual virtual worlds like LambdaMOO, in which:

> [the] protective anonymity [of virtual worlds] also encourages some players to behave irresponsibly, rudely, or even obnoxiously. We have had instances of severe and repeated sexual harassment, crudity, and deliberate offensiveness. In general, such cruelty seems to be supported by two causes: the offenders believe (usually correctly) that they cannot be held accountable for their actions in the real world, and the very

same anonymity makes it easier for them to treat other players imper-
sonally, as other than real people. (Curtis 1992:130)

Julian Dibbell's essay "A Rape in Cyberspace," originally published in
1993, describes a sexual and verbal assault in LambdaMOO (Dibbell 1998;
Koster 2003:456; see also Ito 1997:97–98). Another early instance of griefing involved JennyMUSH, a MUD created for female survivors of sexual
assault: a person hacked into the system as a male and sent sexually threatening messages to every user logged on at the time (Reid 1999:115).[7] Similar kinds of incidents occurred in Second Life during my fieldwork; one
resident recalled "someone coming to a support group meeting for people
recovering from sexual abuse, and playing sex animations with his avatar."
Such acts of sexual violence led some Second Life residents to ponder questions of selfhood, as in the following interchange, debating the idea that an
avatar could "feel raped":

RHONDA: So rape is impossible in SL, great
ISAAC: No it's not: use a freeze weapon and make lewd suggestions.
    The avatar will feel raped
RHONDA: Just thought of that. Is that rape though?

While sexual assault provoked understandably strong reactions, other
forms of griefing were more common and, I would argue, more consequential for Second Life sociality. Verbal harassment was a typical form of griefing; for instance, one or more residents surrounding someone and typing
profanities at them. The Second Life program allowed residents to "mute"
others, so that they could not see their typed chat, but by using alts a determined griefer could at least temporarily get around this capability. More
serious forms of harassment involved sending multiple ims to a resident, or
using the Second Life map to "stalk" someone across the virtual world.[8]

From the early days of graphical virtual worlds, forms of vandalism and
inappropriate building have constituted another form of griefing (Damer
1998:130). Since visuality was so important to Second Life, unattractive
builds constituted a widely recognized form of griefing. Extreme examples
of this included gigantic sex organs or sexually explicit images on the sides
of buildings, particularly when placed next to residential or commercial
venues. Large prims with offensive images could be rezzed onto a property,
for instance while a resident volunteer was trying to teach a class to a group
of newbies. The controversy over Zazzy's store described at the beginning
of chapter 4 was seen by many residents as griefing even though no obscene
images were involved. In such instances, what made a build inappropriate

FIGURE 7.1. The "Freedom-O-Matic" (image by author).

was not how it looked in isolation but its placement in a landscape. Had the store been built between two shopping malls, it probably would not have been interpreted as an act of griefing.

One day I looked outside the window of my Second Life home to discover that someone had purchased a tiny plot of land next to mine and rezzed upon it a cube with the name "Freedom-O-Matic" (figure 7.1). Clicking on the cube—which had been carefully placed next to my window to block my view—activated a script informing me that "as a neighbor-friendly measure, the Freedom-O-Matic can be made invisible for a small donation of $10L per day." While not much money in actual-world terms (about four U.S. cents), this added up to about twenty percent of the weekly stipend provided to "premium account" holders at the time. When I contacted a member of the group listed as owning the Freedom-O-Matic, she responded that another resident was the actual owner of the cube, that "he exercises his right to free speech" (in fact, the owner later claimed he was trying to make a statement to Linden Lab), and that I could pay it to make it disappear if I chose to do so. (The owner later removed the cube.)

Most residents would have considered the Freedom-O-Matic a form of griefing, as indicated by the larger-scale "Jacey" controversy. Jacey was

FIGURE 7.2. Trying to hide visual blight (image by author).

a resident who, like the owners of the Freedom-O-Matic, purchased small plots of land and put up large boxes with political slogans on them. He then charged inflated prices for the plots (about ten times the normal price), leaving frustrated neighbors no choice but to pay in order to reclaim their view, or to construct walls around the boxes in an effort to hide them (figure 7.2). Neither the Freedom-O-Matic nor Jacey's boxes technically went against the Terms of Service; property owners were free to build anything they wished on their land so long as they did not engage in openly derogatory behavior, block a neighbor's access to their own land, or have explicit sexual content if in a PG sim. During the months in which controversy raged over Jacey's boxes, it was clear that most residents saw Jacey as griefing the Second Life landscape: as one resident put it, "I would gander that not a second goes by that one of these boxes does not make someone somewhere feel like they have been griefed."

Forms of fraud or misleading advertising would often be placed within the category of griefing during my fieldwork. This included scams in which a griefer would pose as an entrepreneur and ask for resident password accounts (so as to drain the money from those accounts, or to hijack the account to use for other forms of griefing). "Mafias" of residents sometimes tried to extort protection payments from owners of clubs or whole islands, or threatened to reveal embarrassing information about them, a more organized form of group griefing. Another genre of griefing involved bumping, pushing, or shooting residents outside areas specifically designated as sites for combat. Just walking up to an avatar and pushing it with one's own avatar could be seen as griefing if done to intimidate or trap the resident in question. That a resident thus cornered could simply teleport away did not always lessen a sense that griefing was occurring. "Shooting" did not always involve the use of an object that looked like a gun, but did involve the use of scripts that could push an avatar so far into the Second Life stratosphere that it would take hours to fall back to ground level, forcing the resident to restart the Second Life program.

Other uses of scripts for griefing included creating scripts that would cause residents to see a false "you have been ejected from this land" message, which could be used to disrupt events. Some griefers would go to locations with large numbers of residents (like a club) and then rez scripted objects that produced high numbers of light particles or other effects; the processing power needed to manage these effects would produce high levels of lag. Such "lag bombs" (which have been seen in other virtual worlds; see A. Smith 1999:147) could occasionally crash a server, causing a region to become temporarily inaccessible. Scripts could also be used to animate avatars against the wishes of their owners, as in the case discussed in "A Rape in Cyberspace." One resident recalled how she "was talking with some people, and somehow one of them was able to animate my avatar. All of a sudden I'm walking toward him." A more serious use of scripts was to create self-replicating objects that would spread like a virus across the Second Life landscape. On more than one occasion this caused Second Life to crash for several hours. Such "grid attacks" had serious social and economic consequences, and have precedents in other virtual worlds (as when a griefer rezzed over 85,000 objects, crashing the Active Worlds server [Hudson-Smith 2002:81]).[9]

Why grief? This question was certainly discussed during my fieldwork, particularly in the wake of egregious or widespread attacks, as in this interchange between a group of residents:

> FARLEY: There are so many interesting things to do here and so many really nice people, why would anyone waste the brain cells and time to be annoying?
>
> SAL: Sometimes it's fun to be annoying
>
> NORTON: Good question to ask the griefer community, Farley! To some that is "fun"

SAL: I think it's fun to poke fun at people who take themselves too
seriously

NORTON: Fun for whom, Sal? Not the one being annoyed. There's a
sense of power in annoyance

FARLEY: I don't agree Sal. Any idiot can be annoying. There's no challenge and no pride in it.

ALIEVA: Well, Farley, that is one reason for those "attacks." Getting
attention, being part of a group, showing off intellectual skills. The
higher the risk, the bigger the adrenaline rush.

In this discussion, both Norton and Alieva emphasized how griefing is
not solely an individual act, but linked to a "griefer community." Griefers
sometimes spoke of this sense of community. Through my fieldwork I came
to know several persons who saw themselves as griefers in some sense of the
term, though they often preferred terms like "goon" and defined what they
did as "messing around" with residents.[10] As an anthropologist I worked
to understand the cultural logics behind their actions, without in any way
condoning them. Ethnography is often used to understand the lifeworlds of
the "repugnant other" (Harding 1991); for instance, to explore how forms
of racism or sexism are culturally reproduced over time in specific historical contexts.

One day, I noticed someone in combat fatigues, with a machine gun,
walking down the slope toward my home. As he approached me, the resident, "Mack," said "Achtung. This is a robbery. Give me 1,000 dollars to live."
After politely explaining to him that I would do no such thing, we fell into a
conversation and I asked Mack why he was engaging in behavior that could
lead to his being banned from Second Life. After joking that he "needed to
work on my robbery skills," Mack complained "I wish you could do rob-
beries and whatnot in SL. . . . My group has a ton of weapons, uniforms, a
destroyer, some landing craft. The group got banned by Linden Lab though;
they didn't quite appreciate us."

The following exchange with "Ralph," a griefer, took place over email
because he feared the conversation would be discovered by Linden Lab
were it to take place within Second Life, even via instant messaging. Ralph
recalled the circumstances leading to a major grid crash I experienced during my fieldwork:

I witnessed it first hand. It happened on land owned by a short-lived
goon group. . . . Ozzy, one member of this group, was scripting objects
called griefspheres, which were basically spheres that scanned for an

avatar and moved to that position, causing people to get pushed around by them. Someone then told him about self-replication and showed him how to do it, claiming that it would be a lot funnier if they replicated. The griefspheres weren't meant for a large-scale grid attack, they were just meant for screwing with some of our neighbors on that land we owned at the time, and they contained a mechanism to quickly kill them all off if things got out of control. So the first test of the griefspheres happens. Everyone thinks it's hilarious, and a few goons take it upon themselves to start shooting the griefspheres. Once the griefspheres escaped the sim they were in, the shit hit the fan. At this point Ozzy is frantically yelling the magic word to kill the griefspheres, and they are gone, and things settle down. A minute or two later, we get an im from someone in the goon group chat who is asking Ozzy what the hell is going on. I mapstalk this person, and they are on the other side of the grid. This is when we realize that things are going to get really, really bad. Ozzy starts getting hundreds of ims, from private islands too. It turns out because of the large scale replication, the griefspheres were warping across the grid and hitting places that wouldn't normally be affected. The grid then went down, and a lot of people in this small goon group were banned from SL.

I have no way of verifying this narrative's accuracy, but it is useful for what it reveals about griefing as a social phenomenon. In particular, in some cases at least griefers link their actions to notions of "play" that within game studies are cited as a major motivation for participating in virtual worlds like Second Life. It is clear that there are a range of motivations for griefing—from boredom, reputation, or a sense of power, to testing the limits of the platform in question—and that griefing links up to actual-world forms of "dark play" like teasing and bullying (Schechner 1988:12; see Foo and Koivisto 2004). Ralph's narrative pairs a sense of pranksterism with a claim that the griefing in question was partially unintentional. Both themes resurface in a discussion of how a corporate event (the opening of a "Big Brother" reality contest within Second Life) was attacked by several "griefer groups." In the excerpt below, a reporter from an independent Second Life newspaper anonymously interviewed a member of a "griefer crew" about what transpired:

INTERVIEWER: So why did you want to grief this event?
ANONYMOUS: I didn't go there to grief it just all kind of happened
INTERVIEWER: I see. Well, would you classify yourself as a griefer?

ANONYMOUS: I have an alter ego, yes. But I'm not a full griefer in that sense. I do have some respect for this world.[11]

This linkage between griefing and "respect for this world" recalls how "griefing," as a form of deviant behavior, only makes sense in the context of a code of conduct (Talin 2003:348). This includes formal codes of conduct—all virtual worlds to my knowledge have some kind of Terms of Service (ToS) or end-user license agreement (EULA). It also includes informal norms for social interaction, and both could serve as resources for responding to griefing, including making the griefing impossible from a technical standpoint, disincentives, deterrence, ostracism, vigilantism, and even incorporating the griefing behavior into the virtual world (Talin 2003:357–59). Formal responses to griefing involved action by Linden Lab against the offending griefer, and are thus linked to the questions of governance that I examine in chapter 8. The Second Life program allowed residents to file "Abuse Reports." It testifies to the often unacknowledged prevalence of kindness over griefing that during the time of my fieldwork, only about 6.5 percent of residents who regularly logged into Second Life filed one or more Abuse Reports per month, a percentage that apparently remained stable even as the population grew.[12] Filing a frivolous Abuse Report could constitute a form of griefing, since it could damage a resident's reputation or have economic repercussions if their account was suspended.

While not ubiquitous, griefing (and the forms of conflict and misunderstanding into which griefing shaded) were too numerous to be addressed in every case by Linden Lab, a source of frustration to many residents. Residents thus found other ways to respond to griefing. Since griefing took place in a virtual world, one could not be physically harmed (but could suffer economic damage if involved in business activities that were disrupted due to griefing). It was always possible to teleport away from a griefer or log off of Second Life entirely, depriving the griefer of an audience and placing oneself beyond the griefer's reach. For some, the fact that griefing was a virtual phenomenon helped them ignore it. As one resident said, "it's easier to laugh at someone cursing you out in type than it is when they're RL shouting at you." Laughing at or ignoring griefers was often an effective response, as in the following example from a resident: "There was this one time I and my partner were in a building, testing out some new [sex] animations and such, wink wink, and in the middle of it, we saw like five guys hovering right outside, and they started jeering and everything. So my friend and I got the idea and we rezzed a bunch of cubes for them to sit on and gave them all prim popcorn. They all left though. It was funny that once they didn't get the reaction they wanted, they just up and went."

When a resident felt griefing could not be ignored, there were ways to respond to it short of filing an Abuse Report. Residents could "mute" other residents, which meant that they would not see chat typed by them. Those who owned land could ban particular avatars from entering their land, but the banned person could still shout abuses from outside the land's border, or could use an alt to gain entry. "Ban lists" began to circulate during my fieldwork without any clear method for appealing being placed on them, recalling a "frontier ethic of taking the law into one's own hands" that emerged in several virtual worlds (A. Smith 1999:147).

In general, griefing could be a highly emotional issue for residents, and if anything its frequency and severity increased during the period of my fieldwork. It was seen to be a form of behavior threatening Second Life's social fabric and with the potential for serious emotional and financial consequences, which could on occasion even extend into actual-world harassment. Without wishing to understate or overestimate its significance, it is clear that griefing could be seen as diagnostic of many challenges faced by residents of emerging virtual worlds. In my research in Indonesia, I examined cases of "political homophobia," where violent attacks against gay men, while reprehensible, were still important to understand because they provided important information about how masculinity was linked to national belonging (Boellstorff 2007). In an analogous manner, griefing reveals how cultures in virtual worlds often contain within them suppositions about selfhood and society that are vulnerable to antagonistic reinterpretation, but nevertheless intelligible.

BETWEEN VIRTUAL WORLDS.

While attending the bachelor party of a friend who was about to get married in Second Life, I recall chatting with Tallis, the best man, and two women who had come to the party, Gari and Cailyn. We were exchanging pleasantries when Gari turned to Tallis and said:

> GARI: Tallis, you didn't happen to play The Sims Online before did you?
> TALLIS: In [the city of] Interhogan, yes
> GARI: I knew someone named Tallis
> TALLIS: Yes, that was me
> CAILYN: I know you too from The Sims Online, Tallis. You remember Sabina?

TALLIS: Name rings a bell, yes
CAILYN: Hehe, that's me hun

While some Second Life residents participated in only one virtual world at a time, this moment of mutual recognition exemplifies how it was probably more common for residents to move between virtual worlds.[13] This replicated at the level of community the phenomenon of alts discussed in chapter 5. One could have multiple selfhoods within a single virtual world, and one could also have selfhoods in multiple virtual worlds. Just as most Second Life residents had a "primary" avatar and then one or more alts, so most residents of virtual worlds had a primary virtual world and additional virtual worlds they visited in more circumscribed contexts. Temporality became a major issue in relationship to alts in Second Life—many residents found setting aside the time to maintain multiple avatars to be challenging. Similarly finding the time to participate in multiple virtual worlds could become a major issue. Both alts and multiple virtual worlds raised questions of fractal or dividual selfhood (see chapter 5), of a plural self forged through the same practices of techne that sustained the gap between actual and virtual.

The ability to move between multiple virtual worlds dates back to MUDs (Turkle 1995:12). During the time of my research, many residents had relatively stable levels of participation in online worlds other than Second Life. For instance, many residents also spent time in World of Warcraft, a virtual world oriented around role-playing and combat. Second Life residents who were friends or romantic partners would often travel to other virtual worlds together, maintaining their relationship across platforms. "Metaguilds" and groups of friends represented larger-scale examples of such conjoint movement between virtual worlds. During my fieldwork I also encountered several examples of residents who had lost touch with a friend they had come to know in an early MUD or graphical virtual world, only to stumble upon the friend many years later in Second Life. As in the narrative above, one factor facilitating such reunions was the tendency for residents to choose similar screen names in multiple virtual worlds.

A special kind of movement between virtual worlds is virtual diaspora, which occurs when a virtual world goes out of existence and some of its residents flee to other virtual worlds. One of the best-documented cases of this involved Uru, the first of the series of Myst games designed with a virtual world component. When discontinued by the company that owned it, former residents of Uru moved to several other virtual worlds, particularly Second Life and There, working to recreate visual and social aspects of the virtual world they had lost (Pearce 2006a, 2007). Lesser forms of virtual diaspora can take place when a virtual world becomes less popular. For instance, one Second Life resident talked about how he "pretty much brought all my friends over from The Sims Online."

Experiences in other virtual worlds often led residents to reflect on the strengths and weaknesses of Second Life. For instance, residents might comment that The Sims Online allowed residents to see a "friendship network" map that did not exist in Second Life, note that Worlds of Warcraft had less lag, or observe that Second Life residents were gregarious. This recalls the classic anthropological conceit of "making strange" one's own culture by encountering other cultures. Moving between virtual worlds made Second Life residents into their own virtual anthropologists, traveling to the shores of strange new cybercultures and challenging their own beliefs about selfhood and community online.

BEYOND VIRTUAL WORLDS.

Wishing to understand Second Life's culture in its own right, and recognizing the impracticality of conducting ethnographic research in multiple virtual worlds within one time frame (just as I could not conduct ethnographic research in, say, Indonesia and Thailand within one time frame), my fundamental methodological conceit was to conduct research entirely inside Second Life, using the avatar Tom Bukowski. However, I soon recognized that for many residents, "entirely inside Second Life" included participation in a range of websites external to the Second Life program.[14] To my knowledge no one would think of themselves as a resident if they only used a web browser to visit websites associated with Second Life, never logging into the virtual world itself. The platform was the primary social form and thus the location of my participant observation research. Nonetheless external websites were not inconsequential to Second Life; analyzing them thus constituted an additional research strategy.

All virtual worlds during the time of my fieldwork had official websites associated with them. Linden Lab maintained a website that, among other features, allowed residents to freely download the (frequently updated) Second Life platform, obtain basic information about Second Life, link to media coverage, and see which of their friends were currently inworld.[15] At the beginning of my fieldwork, the official website also contained a forum to which residents and Linden Lab staff could post messages. This forum was divided into over forty sections (including some for languages other than English),[16] covering topics ranging from "announcements and news" to "land management" and "resident answers." Not all Second Life residents visited "the forums," as they were known, but thousands certainly did, many on a regular basis.[17] During my fieldwork, Linden Lab began phasing out the forums. The decision was controversial because, as one resident noted: "the forums are a thriving part of the SL culture. Who here hasn't found out about a benefit event for RL issues? Who here hasn't learned a way to fix settings for avies, computers, networks, or SL functions, to better enjoy their time in SL? Who here hasn't been spurred to action, debate, or thought by the posted thoughts of others?" Despite such support, by the end of my research Linden Lab had largely replaced the forums with a collective blog to which only Linden Lab staff could post; residents were limited to commentary and could be banned if staff felt that griefing was taking place.

From the beginning of my fieldwork, the presence of Second Life "beyond the platform" was not limited to this official website. Second Life residents created and maintained thousands of websites that formed a "blogosphere" around Second Life (some residents termed this the "SLogophere"). These included diary-like blogs in which residents chronicled their experiences in Second Life (often without revealing their actual-world identity). Some of these blogs included reflective and even theoretical writings on Second Life culture and technology (compare Reed 2005). During the time of my fieldwork there were also many periodicals that could be accessed without logging into Second Life.[18] Another common kind of website was the commercial website, which might advertise products by a single entrepreneur or a number of content creators. Such sites were popular because they allowed residents to shop without logging onto Second Life, and because they often had more user-friendly search functions. There were also a range of more iconoclastic websites, ranging from sharing snapshots and movies produced within Second Life, to producing physical versions of virtual items, to websites associated with Second Life groups, including a "nature preserve," local governments, and supporters of live music events.[19]

Collectively these forums and other websites constituted a kind of virtual Second Life, a virtual virtual world. Indeed, when the Second Life grid was down for an update or due to a crash, many residents would go to the forums or other websites to feel like they were in Second Life and to exchange messages with their friends. This could even represent a means for overcoming griefing: as one resident noted, "I had to laugh in talking with many of my friends yesterday, to note how many of us, during the grid attack, edited our personal webpages, or posted to the forums. It was like 'I'll find other ways to be in my virtual world.' We were not going to let a moron hacker do us in." Even when the grid was operative, some residents found the forums an important aspect of their sociality; one resident noted how "I'm mostly a hermit inworld, but I lurk a lot on the forums."

In addition to these linkages between Second Life and other Internet technologies, in every chapter of this book I have charted how the virtual and actual interpenetrate, from notions of place and selfhood to afk and lag. For instance, the forms of virtual altruism discussed earlier could have ramifications in the actual world. From the beginning of my fieldwork, there were activities held within Second Life to raise awareness and money for actual-world nonprofit activities (for instance, for cancer research or the crisis in the Darfur region of Sudan). In the wake of Hurricane Katrina, which struck during my fieldwork, parts of New Orleans's French Quarter were recreated within Second Life, allowing a few of those affected by the hurricane to meet online, as well as a venue to memorialize damaged landmarks and hold fundraising events. Many places were designed by residents to have tight referential relationships with the actual world, from a spaceflight museum to an Iraqi War Memorial and recreations of the Twin Towers destroyed in the 9/11 attacks. Such forms of imbrication have been a source of confusion in the literature on virtual worlds because of the assumption that such traffic blurs or even erases the gap between the virtual and actual, rather than working to define and sustain that gap.

Another way residents could build community beyond the virtual world was by meeting in the actual world. This was not a major social form during my fieldwork. Many residents did not wish to meet other residents in the actual world because it would "shatter the illusions." In addition, even when I began by fieldwork (and certainly by the time I ended it) it was clear that there were so many residents in Second Life, from so many parts of the actual world, that meeting more than a handful of them was impossible. For some residents, however, the possibility of meeting a few Second Life acquaintances in the actual world was a source of fascination (or fear), as it has been from their earliest days of virtual worlds: "there is a tradition within Internet communities for online friends and gaming partners to get together for face-to-face meetings" (Taylor 2006a; see Van Gelder 1991). I attended one such event, the 2006 Second Life Community Convention (held in San Francisco), and Second Life residents sometimes told me of occasions when they would meet an online friend or lover (there were cases of actual-world weddings resulting from Second Life romances). Toward the end of my fieldwork, a handful of "alternate reality games" appeared in Second Life, combining inworld and actual-world events.[20]

These forms of movement between virtual and actual are less consequential than they might first seem. As virtual worlds grow in size to the point that they have tens of thousands of residents from across the globe, it becomes infeasible for actual-world socializing to constitute more than a tiny percentage of the overall interpersonal interactions in any particular virtual world. Even social networking websites like MySpace and Facebook had, during the time of my fieldwork, become so large that it was not practically possible for members to meet all of their online friends offline. Virtual worlds will continue to draw cultural assumptions and social norms from the actual world, but this influence is primarily indirect. An exaggerated concern with actual-world meetups reflects an unfounded suspicion that cybersocialities are not legitimate or sustainable places of human culture in their own right. Virtual worlds are not secondary representations of the actual world. They require actual-world computers and bodies to exist, and draw upon many elements of actual-world sociality, but through techne residents reconfigure these elements in unforeseen ways.

PART III: THE AGE OF TECHNE ▶

Chapter 8

POLITICAL ECONOMY

Creationist capitalism—Money and labor—Property—
Governance—Inequality—Platform and social form.

CREATIONIST CAPITALISM

In Part 3 of this book I increasingly step back from my ethnographic materials to set forth hypotheses about culture in virtual worlds. Ethnography, which derives its strength from engaged attention to the everyday, cannot allow other approaches to monopolize the big questions by claiming a privileged access to the general or the global. For instance, in my books *The Gay Archipelago* and *A Coincidence of Desires* (Boellstorff 2005, 2007) I discussed the lives of gay and lesbian Indonesians, but also made general claims about the relationship between sexuality and nationalism. As I moved outward from data collected firsthand and engaged with wider literatures, my claims became more provisional, often taking the form of questions rather than assertions. This book examines Second Life during a period in which quite different virtual worlds also existed—just as Indonesia, fourth most populous nation and home to more Muslims than any other, was quite different from neighboring countries like Vietnam and Australia. Yet as some aspects of my Indonesia research had broader relevance, so some lessons learned from Second Life have consequences for understanding virtual worlds more generally. Such a "continuous dialectical tacking between the most local of local detail and the most global of global structure in such a way as to bring them into simultaneous view" is a classic ethnographic strategy (Geertz 1983:68).

This chapter's goal is to examine the political economy of Second Life. The topic of political economy (like many explored thus far) could easily be the subject of a book in its own right, the focus of many excellent studies (e.g., Castronova 2005; Dibbell 2006). It is precisely due to its importance that I have held off discussing political economy until the eighth of nine chapters. I hope to exploit the linear strictures of the book form, contextualizing my analysis in light of the preceding discussion. I address politics and economics together because I see them as aspects of the same cultural domain; indeed, until fairly recently "the economy" was not seen as distinct from the political (Foucault 1991:99; Mitchell 2002:4–5). In my research in Indonesia, I addressed how governments have significant power in shaping the subjectivities of their citizens. Under contemporary conditions of globalization, capitalist forces—transnational corporations, for instance—also have great influence. However, no corporation or government body directly controlled social structures in Indonesia. A pivotal difference between virtual worlds and the actual world is that virtual worlds can be *owned*. Despite the fact that there have been virtual worlds that were created and managed for free, that parts of the Second Life platform became "open-source" during my fieldwork, and that wholly collaborative virtual worlds might well appear in the future, at the time of my research most virtual worlds, including Second Life, were owned by companies, backed by venture capital and prioritizing cash flow (Lastowka and Hunter 2004:59; Taylor 2006a:125; Thomas 2005:1).[1] Politics and economics were fused online at the most basic level. These companies never had total control and faced various indeterminacies (Malaby 2006a). Yet through coding the platform and managing many aspects of social interaction, they enjoyed influence most actual-world governments could only dream of attaining.

In terms of its economics and politics, Second Life was predicated upon and exemplified what I term "creationist capitalism." During my fieldwork this was becoming recognized as a globally predominant mode of production, often phrased in terms of a "creative class" or "creative industries" (Caves 2000; Florida 2002; Hartley 2005). It was a central tenet of what is often termed neoliberalism, evident in concepts like "crowdsourcing" (Howe 2006; Llewelyn 2006a). Neoliberalism is an ideology founded in the use of market mechanisms and personal responsibility as principles of governance. Large-scale graphical virtual worlds came into being in this context, and the consequences of this historical juncture were "particularly powerful because they set precedents for the networked future in which spaces and experience come to be mediated primarily through commercialized systems of authorship and exchange" (Taylor 2006a:126).

"Creationist capitalism" is a mode of capitalism in which labor is understood in terms of creativity, so that production is understood as creation. Techne is the modality this creation takes; self-fulfillment becomes a means of production—a Robinson Crusoe-like fantasy of the individual working outside social relations, critiqued by Marx himself as masking the social character of labor (Marx 1976:169–71). Aspects of this constellation of creation, techne, and value are novel, but it also draws upon an Western association of techne and creation extending back to the Greek myth of

Prometheus (see chapter 2). This "participatory culture," in which producers and consumers interact in new ways (Jenkins 2006:3), depends on imbrications of market capital and sociocultural capital, so that persons "draw on obligations through their social networks as a resource just as they do their material resources" (Malaby 2006b:146).[2]

While I intend the idea of creationist capitalism to speak to "how status, expertise, and the market are all interrelated in Second Life" (Malaby 2006b:144)—an interrelationship that has been characterized as recalling the Medicis of Renaissance Italy (Neva 2007c)—I also see Second Life as exemplifying, even concentrating, notions of creationist capitalism that are not unique to virtual worlds. For instance, the social theorist Mary Poovey concludes that a logic of commodification—what Lisa Rofel terms "consumer fundamentalism" (Rofel 2007:164)—"provides the primary terms in which residents of the modern world imagine value, register sensations, and experience time and space" (Poovey 2001:399). It is not coincidental that she recommends in its place a culture that "promotes and preserves human creativity" (Poovey 2001:421). This, I would claim, is not really an alternative, for it remains squarely within the logic of creationist capitalism. Indeed, it could be argued that ethnography itself has become increasingly predicated on creativity since the acknowledgement of ethnographer as "writing culture" (Clifford and Marcus 1986). This very book can be seen as within the logic of creationist capitalism, a product of creativity made possible by Second Life itself. It is also not coincidental that in December 2006, as I was completing my fieldwork, *Time* magazine announced that their person of the year was "You." The magazine cover featured a computer terminal with a reflective surface: the editors justified their selection by claiming that online technologies were setting the groundwork for a new chapter in human history that will "change the way the world changes" (Grossman 2006:40). This emphasis on "you" reflected the pronominal logic of customization seen in the ubiquity of "my" in Internet discourse (as in MySpace, MyYahoo, etc.), as well as the shift in "i" from signifying "Internet" (as in the original meaning of "iMac") to meaning "me" (as in "iPod" and "iPhone"). "Custom," that hoary term of longstanding anthropological interest identified by Tylor as central to culture, here bridges its earlier sense of habitual practice to its later sense of self-fashioning—as indicated by the English term "costume," derived from "custom." In creationist capitalism, selfhood is understood as the customization of the social.

Creationist capitalism draws structuring principles from the individualistic ethos of contemporary capitalism—specifically its Silicon Valley variant, which can be termed the "Californian Ideology" (Barbrook and Cameron 2001; see also Turner 2006). Given that Linden Lab was based in California and its CEO, Philip Rosedale, grew up in San Diego, it is not surprising that Second Life was particularly shaped by assumptions of this ideology, which "has emerged from a bizarre fusion of the cultural bohemianism of San Francisco with the high-tech industries of Silicon Valley. . . . [T]he Californian ideology promiscuously combines the free-wheeling spirit of the hippies and the entrepreneurial zeal of the yuppies. This amalgamation of opposites has been achieved through a profound faith in the emancipatory potential of the new information technologies" (Barbrook and Cameron 2001:364).

This ideology, by no means limited to California, is an economic model of "prosumption" where capitalist subjects produce what they consume, turning consumption into a form of production (Toffler 1980). This "technological imagination" (Balsamo forthcoming) presumes, I claim, a capitalist imagination. Understanding creationist capitalism therefore requires "a nondichotomous processual model of culture and capitalism" that "treats capitalist action as culturally produced and, therefore, always infused with cultural meaning and value" (Yanagisako 2002:6). In terms of this cultural meaning and value, creationist capitalism is, as its name implies, a mode of production constituted through a Christian metaphysics—despite the fact that not all residents of Second Life (and other virtual worlds) are Christian or even religious, and despite the fact that (as noted in the previous chapter) overt religious practice was a relatively minor aspect of Second Life culture during my fieldwork. This metaphysics shapes even notions of the virtual, in the sense of a savior who is physical and not-physical, virtually present whenever persons gather in his name (Wilbur 1997:10). Early traces of creationist capitalism can be seen in the Western view that property results from the mixing together of human labor with the products of nature, as set forth in John Locke's influential essay "Of Property," first published in 1690: "it being by him removed from the common state nature hath placed it in, it hath by this *labour* something annexed to it, that excludes the common right of other men."[3] This notion of labor began to take on a more explicitly creationist tone; by the early twentieth century Max Weber identified how a "Protestant Ethic" combining self-denial with worldly success shaped capitalist production, which became linked to a Romantic ethic of consumerism as a means to self-discovery (Campbell 1987; Weber 1992). Creationist capitalism builds upon this earlier formulation, but departs from it in that under the Protestant ethic, worldly success was taken to index God's favor in a cosmology where human fate was predestined. In creationist capitalism, the prosumer has become a kind of minor god, and we find not predestination but a performative notion of production that assumes the relationship between the economic and the social is "one of complicity rather than analogy" (Joseph 1998:25). In creationist capitalism it is persons who create, not God; it is a vision of "people inhabiting specialized online communities" where "every creative act is no more or less than the reenactment of the Creation" (Purdy 2001:357). Through conflating labor and creation, production itself becomes a form of spectacle in which "reality considered partially *unfolds*, in its own general unity, as a pseudo-world apart" (Debord 1983:2).

This is a deeply Western vision of human life as "consist[ing of] a need of creation" (Bergson 1911:251), founded in a "culture of improvement" (Friedel 2007) and predicated on a kind of "partible personhood" (Golub 2005:525) where embedding one's creative self into (virtual) objects is the assumed means of turning labor into value. This creationist capitalism is, indeed, a millennial capitalism "that presents itself as a gospel of salvation" (Comaroff and Comaroff 2000:292). Just as Christ is seen in dominant Christian traditions to unite the human and the divine, so creationist capitalism unites production and consumption. At the core of creationist capitalism is the idea of the self as a creator. Production is reinterpreted as creation; for the first time, techne becomes a mode of production, a kind of "high techne" (Rutsky 1993:3). In this understanding, workers are not just sellers of labor-power, but creators of their own worlds: "the ontological conditions-of-being under millennial capitalism [are linked to] epochal shifts in the constitutive relationship of production to consumption, and hence of labor to capital" (Comaroff and Comaroff 2000:293). This presumes the possibility, indeed the necessity, of production without alienation; it equates creation with the species being of the human. That millennial capitalism can be seen as "the Second Coming of Capitalism—of capitalism in its neoliberal, global manifestation" (Comaroff and Comaroff 2000:294) reveals the religious connotations of "Second Life," a virtually resurrectional sociality born again through the creative machinations of techne.

There is a history to this valorization of creativity in virtual worlds and online technology more generally: "Before the modern era all ethics used to begin with 'Thou shalt not.' During the industrial age, the ethical code shifted to the idea of 'Be productive.' The ethics of the computer time world is 'Be creative'" (Rifkin 1987:157). While the first MUDs tended to be programmed by a small number of persons who usually controlled overall access, many of these text-only virtual worlds soon developed the ability for residents to create their own objects, so that one way for residents to become known was "through displaying the products of their imagination" (Reid 1999:129).

The Sims Online was probably the first graphical virtual world to draw substantially upon creationist capitalism, with the parent company claiming in 2001 that about 80 percent of the objects in the world were resident-created (Ondrejka 2004a:6). Second Life took the implicit rubric of creationist capitalism further than any virtual world before it; creativity operated as its primary mode of production, governance, and subjectivation (self-making). Persons affiliated with Linden Lab, in particular Cory Ondrejka, its vice president of product development until December 2007, have used rhetorics of nature and freedom to frame creativity as a pregiven desire of all human beings. Already by May 2004, one month before I began my research and one year after Second Life first went online, residents were creating over 99 percent of the more than one million objects inworld (Ondrejka 2004a:10). From its beginnings, Second Life was predicated on "user created content" (Ondrejka 2004a:1). The valorization of creation was key to Linden Lab's business model, for it provided a way to get around the "large teams and lengthy development cycles" needed to design and update large graphical virtual worlds (Ondrejka 2004a:5). In place of in-house teams, Linden Lab could draw upon what was seen as an almost biological "need to create" (Ondrejka 2004a:5) to produce content, which Ondrejka linked to everything from machinima (films created inworld) to customized cellphone ringtones and weblogs (Ondrejka 2004a:7–9). The correct tools, it was assumed, would harness this need to create to the maintenance of the world itself: residents would produce the content they and other residents consumed, the prosuming model that is one aspect of creationist capitalism.

Assuming a need to create is fundamental to creationist capitalism: "some type of distributed creation is needed if there is to be any hope of creating an online world that dwarfs the complexity of [the] real-world" (Ondrejka 2004a:5–6). During my fieldwork, Linden Lab held an annual contest in which residents tried to produce the best machinima in Second Life; the winner got to have their film used to promote the virtual world. It is the cultural logic of creationist capitalism that renders intelligible a state of affairs where consumers labor for free (or for a nominal prize) to produce advertising materials for a product they have already purchased.

This ideology of creation remained in force even when making money was not directly at issue. For instance, I did not have the time to try earning money, but like many I found great pleasure in building my home, using the well-named "create" command and the same assumptions about place and presence that undergirded building for profit.

What made all this creationist capitalism rather than just creativity was that in Second Life, creativity could be a way to make money. Even for those who did not seek to make money or who were not successful in doing so, that same creativity served as a means to self-knowledge and social efficacy.

As one resident put it, "creativity becomes the primary asset" (see Weber, Rufer-Bach, and Platel 2007). Creativity was linked to self-expression and thus to freedom: when residents would say things like "there is a lot of freedom here, in many more ways than rl," the freedom to create was what they usually referenced. Residents often said they spent time in Second Life because they found other virtual worlds lacking opportunities for creativity. Terms like "creativity" and "creation" were common when residents talked about why they liked Second Life; for instance: "I am a creative person. I love the open structure that SL provides me, where I can try to create things within restrictions." Another resident stated, "I just like being immersed in so darn much creativity;" a third explained that "what appealed to me was that there were no goals, and freedom to do what you wanted."[4]

MONEY AND LABOR.

Place and time are the foundations of virtual worlds, but during my field-work money was the more sensational phenomenon leading many to conclude virtual worlds were real: "the blurring of real and virtual is perhaps nowhere more obvious than in the pricing of goods and services that exist only in [virtual] worlds" (Castronova 2005:149). Creationist capitalism was forged by Linden Lab and Second Life residents through understandings of money and labor.

It was not obligatory to labor for wages within Second Life. By the latter part of my fieldwork it was possible to obtain an account for free, and many residents explored Second Life without purchasing anything or earning any money. Since many objects were given away, residents could acquire a basic wardrobe without paying, and could also build for free in sandboxes; one's creations would be temporary, but residents could save them in their inventories. Most importantly, residents could socialize for free, building up a network of friends and intimates. By becoming members of landowning groups, some residents could even build permanent structures on land they did not own directly. Another option was to use a credit card to convert actual-world money into linden dollars (see below), financing Second Life activities through actual-world labor. Since one U.S. dollar exchanged for many linden dollars during the time of my research, exchanging just a few dollars a month could finance a substantial amount of shopping and other pursuits.

Many residents, however, sought to earn money by laboring within Second Life. For many, this troubled the boundary between the virtual and actual—as one resident noted, "I don't think you can get much more real than that"—but it was nonetheless attractive to many residents; one of the most common questions newbies asked was "how do I make money in here?" At the time of my fieldwork, Second Life was known as one of the only virtual worlds that freely allowed one to work for wages inworld, as well as permitting free currency exchange and full intellectual property rights: "As a user-*created* digital world, the ultimate success of Second Life is coupled to the innovation and *creativity* of its residents, not to ownership of their intellectual property" (Ondrejka 2004d, emphasis added). The existence of labor within Second Life was part of this broader political economic reconfiguration, shaped by emergent forms of cybersociality, that I term creationist capitalism.

During the time of my research, not all virtual worlds had true currencies within them; particularly if structured as games, they might have at most scoring systems, leveling, or other quantitative measures. Many, however, included some kind of monetary form (for instance, "simoleans" in The Sims Online). Many companies that owned virtual worlds tried to prevent exchange with actual-world currencies or other virtual-world currencies, but black markets typically took root, illustrating how understandings of money in virtual worlds were not simply imposed from above. I am less concerned with money's semantics—its meaning, the knowledge (episteme) produced by its existence—but its pragmatics (Maurer 2006:16), its use as a form of techne within the horizon of creationist capitalism.

Second Life's currency was the "linden dollar," known colloquially as the "linden" (its symbol was "L$"). In its Terms of Service, Linden Lab defined the linden dollar as a "in-world fictional currency" or "limited license right,"[5] but since version 1.2 of the platform (released in December 2003), linden dollars have been freely convertible with U.S. dollars and by extension any actual-world currency.[6] During the time of my fieldwork, the linden dollar exchange rate fluctuated between approximately 265 and 300 to one U.S. dollar. This convertibility permitted some residents to engage in forms of banking (including savings accounts with interest) and finance (including currency speculation). It also meant that if one worked in Second Life, one's linden-dollar income could be turned into United States dollars.

The level of economic activity in Second Life grew throughout my fieldwork, though changes in permitted activities (like a ban on gambling) and shady financial practices threatened economic stability. By December 2006, over one million U.S. dollars were being exchanged between residents daily. Over 2,000 residents were making more than US$1,200 profit a year; 58 were earning more than US$60,000 a year, and one entrepreneur claimed to have Second Life assets worth over one million U.S. dollars, often based upon large numbers of micropayments ($0.10–$2.00) for virtual goods. Creativity became a form of exchange value, not just a form of use value.[7]

A few residents were making their actual-world living from labor within Second Life. More often, resident incomes were more modest. One culturally significant threshold was "paying one's tier"—earning enough money to pay for the monthly fees on land one owned. Other residents might make the equivalent of just five or ten dollars a month from their work. In a traditional Marxist analysis this would be seen as a form of superexploitation where workers are unable to reproduce their needs for existence. Within a logic of creationist capitalism, such labor could been seen to have both exchange value and use value as a form of self-fulfillment. As one resident noted, "when I stay up for two nights in a row programming my virtual pet, trying to get it to do something new, it sure isn't for the L$. It's bringing something into existence." Creationist capitalism allowed labor to acquire value as a form of leisure. Creativity was no longer only that what labor allowed one to do during "leisure time"; it was a form of labor in its own right. This reflected a broader "blurring of work and play" in virtual worlds, so that "they may soon become indistinguishable from each other" (Yee 2006b:68; see also Wittel 2001:68–69), a playful capitalism or "ludocapitalism" in which "production is melting into play" (Dibbell 2006:299, 25; see also Pearce 2006b). The dichotomy of public and private, which only took form with the rise of industrial capitalism, may be in danger of collapsing under the influence of creationist capitalism.

One way Second Life residents could work was by making commodities to sell, a form of "building" I discuss in the following section. Linden Lab's "Guide to Jobs in Second Life" listed building as one form of skilled labor that had emerged inworld, alongside texturer, fashion designer, scripter, animator, event hoster, and DJ—a fairly accurate typology.[8] Textures (designed offline using programs like Photoshop) were important to residents because they allowed prims to appear as anything from glass windows to satiny bed sheets.[9] During my fieldwork it was typical for a package of 9–30 textures to sell for 300–1,200 linden dollars. "Fashion designers" were essentially texturers, but had to consider how clothing would fit on an avatar body. Fashion design was a competitive business composed primarily of residents discovering their fashion talents for the first time: one resident remarked "I can be a clothing designer in here; all I need is Photoshop and a little creativity. But in rl I'd need degrees and experience." It was also possible to design skins, eyes, and hair for avatar bodies. These kinds of bodily modification were understood to be an aspect of fashion; they were often created by the same designers and sold in the same stores as for clothing (I never, for instance, saw skins sold at a store specializing in textures, despite the fact that skins were essentially textures for avatar bodies).

Persons with computer programming skills could use the Linden Scripting Language to craft a range of devices, including intruder warning systems that notified owners of visitors to their property, radios that would tune a parcel of land to a station broadcast over the Internet, and inworld computers providing news and even screensavers. Scripts were rarely sold alone, but embedded within objects, so that scripters usually worked in collaboration with builders (Llewelyn 2004). "Animations" were scripts applied to avatars so they appeared to engage in almost any behavior: dance, sit, stroll, have sex, drink from a cup. Unlike scripts, animations could not be designed within Second Life during the time of my fieldwork; they were thus fairly difficult to produce and in high demand because the range of default animations provided by the platform was limited.

All of these forms of skilled labor were fairly solitary and oriented around commodity creation. Residents engaging in such labor sometimes found it could "pad their resume" in the actual world—for instance, work in textures or fashion might demonstrate graphic design skills. However, these forms of labor also raised questions of intellectual property, ownership, and law (Castronova 2005; Herman, Coombe, and Kaye 2006; Humphreys 2004; Lastowka and Hunter 2004). An important aspect of creationist capitalism in Second Life was that after November 2003, Linden Lab allowed residents to retain intellectual property rights over anything they created (Dibbell 2006:191–93; Ondrejka 2004a). The most celebrated example of this during my fieldwork concerned the game Tringo, designed by a resident inworld, the concept for which was eventually sold to an actual-world corporation for over 10,000 U.S. dollars, without any profit going to Linden Lab (Au 2005b, 2006a; Malaby 2006b; Walsh 2005).

One controversial issue during my fieldwork concerned reselling objects made by others. A particularly complicated example concerned textures: if Resident A created a chair using wood textures purchased from Resident B, did Resident B deserve a portion of the sales every time the chair was sold? Some texture sellers explicitly permitted purchasers to incorporate their textures in new objects created for sale, so long as the textures were not resold in isolation. In other cases, residents told stories of a designer selling skins with moles or details that betrayed the fact that the skin was created by someone else. These concerns reached a fever pitch toward the end of my fieldwork, when a group of programmers working on an open-source version of the Second Life platform released a program called "CopyBot," which allowed residents to copy information about objects without permission. This led to several days of controversy, during which some designers stopped selling their wares and there was heated debate on a range of forums, as well as several inworld protests. It was seen an attack on copyrights and trademarks, but also an attack on creativity itself.[10] This controversy, which some compared to debates over the copying of music and movies over the Internet, was part of a broader phenomenon in which "technology is detaching information from the physical plane, where property law of all sorts has always found definition. . . . Law protected expression, and with few (and recent) exceptions, to express was to make physical" (Barlow 1996a:10–11).

The two other forms of skilled work mentioned in the "Guide to Jobs"—event hosting and DJing—were forms of service labor rather than commodity production. (Second Life itself was defined by Linden Lab as a service, not a commodity.) Residents engaging in these lines of work made money by hosting and playing music at events (discos, games, even sex parties). Event hosters and DJs were sometimes paid a (quite minimal) wage by the club's owner. They were worth this investment because good event hosters and DJs helped ensure a larger turnout, increasing one's traffic. For most of the period of my research, Linden Lab paid incentives to properties receiving the most "traffic," which also affected where a property appeared in the "find" menu.

Most other kinds of labor within Second Life—listed as unskilled on Linden Lab's "Guide to Jobs"—could be classified as aspects of the service economy. Probably the highest-paying such job was sex worker—rates during my fieldwork typically ran at 500–1,000 linden dollars for 30 minutes of sex (Bainbridge 2006). Sex work often shaded into jobs like "dancer" and "escort," though by no means did all dancers and escorts engage in prostitution. In theory a sex worker could be freelance, but most worked in specific locations because they relied upon furniture containing scripts that animated avatars in a sexual manner. Some residents found employment as a model, provided one had an attractive avatar (with high-quality prim hair, for instance) and good animations for walking down a catwalk (Llewelyn 2004). Store owners might hire residents as attendants to facilitate sales. Larger clubs would sometimes employ residents as "bouncers" to warn or ban potential griefers, freeing owners to look after their guests.

Property.

The forms of labor discussed above involved selling commodities or services. The economic system of Second Life, however, was predicated on property. Only by owning property could residents build objects with permanence: this was an economic model in which property made the virtual "real." Linden Lab's primary source of income was resident fees paid to own land, and selling land was a key source of income for many residents themselves. This recalls my thesis that virtual worlds are fundamentally places; Linden Lab wove a recognition of this fact into the Second Life platform and their business model. Attending to the consequences of the model underscores how "like workers, capitalists are always constituted as particular kinds of persons through historically specific cultural processes" (Yanagisako 2002:5).

Second Life originally featured a object-based economy where residents were taxed per prim they created. This system led to widespread protests, in particular because of a sense that persons creating large builds that could benefit the broader community were being inhibited (Au 2003a; Grimmelmann 2003; Ondrejka 2004d). With version 1.2, released in December 2003, Linden Lab shifted Second Life to a property-based economy. While a few parcels remained the property of Linden Lab (for instance, roads that cut through the virtual landscape), the company sold almost all land to residents, who were then free to resell the land at any price they could attain. In order to own land, it was necessary to have a "premium account" costing U.S.$9.95 a month. This allowed a resident to own up to 512 square meters of land. To own larger parcels of land, a monthly "tiering fee" had to be paid in addition to the ten-dollar basic fee; for instance, U.S.$5 for an extra 512 square meters, U.S.$40 for an extra 8,192 square meters, U.S.$195 for an extra 65,536 square meters, and so on.[11]

In shifting from an object-based economy to a property-based economy, Linden Lab operationalized the assumption that place lies at the core of the virtual, drawing upon a history of linkages between landscape and capital: "It is precisely the relationship between. . . attitudes to land on the one hand, and the transition to capitalist forms of material production on the other, that . . . lies at the root of the landscape idea" (Cosgrove 1998:6). One resident suggested to a confused newbie that they "think of Linden Lab as '3D content hosting providers.' They run a farm of servers, and you can hire 'bits' of those farms to deploy your persistent content there." Yet land in Second Life was not just a metaphor for storage capacity on a server: it was a form of place with political and economic consequences. It was the foundation (not effect) of creationist capitalism: as one resident observed, "talking about property in here always leads to talking about creating."

Given the importance of property, it is understandable that the most lucrative forms of work in Second Life involved real estate. Such residents, the most successful of whom were termed "land barons," purchased land as it became available from Linden Lab or other residents, then resold it for a profit ("flipping" it, in the words of residents who found land barons distasteful) by subdividing the land (or joining together plots to create a larger one should a buyer request it), or by finding land to meet the desires of specific residents (say, a plot on a mountaintop, or near a body of water). Some land barons also retained plots of land, building apartments and renting them out to residents who did not wish to buy land outright (one such resident felt that "now that I have a place I can call 'my own,' even if I don't own it, I feel a lot more at home here. A virtual place to hang my hat, I suppose"). More successful land barons purchased entire islands from Linden Lab, which in the most extreme cases were aggregated into entire continents.[12] Managing such large properties required significant social engineering, usually including zoning, organizing events, and identifying whole areas with specific communities: languages other than English, Furries, gay men and lesbians, Victorian or Mediterranean-themed landscapes, and so on.

Commodities, like land, were forms of property. It was possible to set any object one created (whether composed of one prim or multiple prims) to be "for sale," for any amount desired. If this option was not selected, avatars could interact with the object in question—for instance, if a chair, avatars could sit on it—but it would not circulate as a commodity. Three additional settings could allow the consumer to "modify," "copy," or "resell/give away" the object. Some creators did not select the "modify" option, thereby working to protect their commodity's integrity. Many, however, did so, allowing purchasers some limited ability to modify the commodity (and thus bringing a sense of consumer creativity to objects created by another). For instance, my avatar usually had tattoos on his arms; I preferred modifiable long-sleeved shirts because I could shorten the sleeves to reveal my tattoos. Because clothing items like shirts and pants were in effect textures applied to the outside of an avatar, they could be set "no modify" and would still wrap themselves around an avatar in an aesthetically pleasing manner. However, clothing items made from prims (jewelry, shoes, hair) were almost always modifiable because of the need to resize them for differently sized avatars. In 2004, early in my fieldwork, I encountered the following exchange at a club:

> LEIGH: I love your shoes, Irisa. Did you make them?
> IRISA: Ohhh, these are tintables from, let me look, Sassy Walsh made them!!
> LEIGH: I haven't seen tintable shoes like that
> IRISA: I can give you the landmark—they are only 150 lindens—full mod
> LEIGH: Wow, thanks
> IRISA: I got the stilettos too. Basically my attempt at making prim shoes went horribly wrong lmao

LEIGH: They are difficult

IRISA: Indeed—I leave that to the experts now rofl

In this conversation, Irisa acknowledged the limits of her own creativity, which made her interested in purchasing shoes as a commodity. The shoes she liked (and that attracted Leigh's interest as well) were "full mod," or fully modifiable. Not only could they be sized to an avatar's foot; they were "tintable," meaning the color could be changed to fit whatever outfit the avatar was wearing.

A second option, "resell/give away" (known in earlier versions of the platform as "transfer") allowed a seller to prevent the consumer from reselling the commodity or gifting it to another resident. Even when "resell/give way" was permitted, only one copy of the object would remain in circulation; it would thus remain a commodity object sustaining creationist capitalism. A third option allowed commodities could be set so that the next owner could copy the object. When this option was selected, the virtual good would in a sense be removed from commodity circulation and become a free item contributing to the prevalent altruism in Second Life.

These dynamics of commodity circulation illustrate how the economic system under consideration is better termed "creationist capitalism" than "capitalism" in the abstract, due to the centrality of creativity to its operation—creativity was the form of labor producing value. If a resident designed a chair and sold it for 300 lindens, what was sold was information about a concatenation of prims, textures, and possibly scripts, so that a consumer could rez a particular configuration of prims in the shape of a chair on a plot of land they owned, co-owned, or rented. The chair was not being produced as such. No raw materials were needed for its manufacture, and the labor to sell 1,000 chairs was no different than to sell 10, reflecting "a larger trend where the status of information as a commodity is becoming undeniable" (Malaby 2006b:149). This recalled how a song or text could be copied endlessly using online technology, except that the chair had virtual materiality: avatars could sit on it. Even shopping could be seen as a form of creation: as one resident observed, "picking furniture is pretty creative, even if you buy it all"; another resident added that "creativity doesn't just mean creating from the prim up."

The dynamics of commodity circulation were further transformed as actual-world corporations began to take an interest in Second Life. One of the first such companies was Wells Fargo, who in September 2005 created "Stagecoach Island" with the idea of teaching young people about banking.[13] In the second half of 2006 the corporate presence in Second Life

increased rapidly, including businesses ranging from the telecommunications company TELUS and the clothing company American Apparel to
America Online, the British Broadcasting Corporation, Coca-Cola, Dell,
General Motors, IBM, NBC, Nissan, Pontiac, Reuters, Starwood Hotels,
the Sundance Channel, and Sun Microsystems. Typically aided by marketing firms that specialized in introducing businesses to the possibilities of
virtual worlds,[14] these corporations all purchased property, which almost
always took the form of islands rather than parcels on the mainland. Most
of these businesses were interested in marketing actual-world products to
Second Life residents conceived as a demographic niche. Some, however,
began investigating the possibility that Second Life could become a space
for commodity production and consumption in its own right. For instance,
the idea of "avatar-based marketing" linked classic notions of advertising to
the idea of the alt, and more broadly to the avatarization of the self: "advertising has always targeted a powerful consumer alter ego: that hip, attractive, incredibly popular person just waiting to emerge (with the help of the
advertised product) from an all-too normal self" (Hemp 2006:54). Persons
involved in "immersive marketing"—a nascent field during the time of my
research—used phrases like "the consumer is also the creator" and "the key
to reaching today's end users in this marketing space can be summed up in
the words: don't sell to me, play with me."

Resident reactions to this corporatization of Second Life varied, ranging from contempt to enthusiasm, recalling debates a decade earlier about
the commercialization of the Internet. Some residents feared corporate
intrusion because, paradoxically, corporations could be seen to threaten a
key tenet of creationist capitalism: that the consuming self and producing
self should be the same person. It was not unusual to encounter comments
like that of the resident who, upon encountering a series of corporate islands, complained that Linden Lab had betrayed its slogan "Your World,
Your Imagination": "This is not our world. They used our imaginations and
free labor to create this wonderful playland they sell to corporate America. Linden Lab used us and is now throwing us away." Despite such fears,
many residents noted how during the time of my fieldwork, the graphically stunning corporate areas of Second Life were not popular: there was
often a sense that corporate activities in Second Life lacked the creativity
characterizing resident activity (Au 2006d). One reason for this may have
been that these companies did not comprehend the character of creationist capitalism. Corporations who simply saw Second Life as "interactive"
misrecognized interactivity for creation: the cultural logic in play was not
that residents interacted with a commodity and its producer, but that they

literally produced what they consumed through self-actualizing acts of creation. The idea of interacting with a company and its products assumes a model of consumer feedback, the goal of which is knowledge. Creationist capitalism is predicated not on episteme, but techne.

GOVERNANCE.

Linden Lab's influence upon Second Life's economy and culture was hotly debated in the virtual world and its associated "SLogosphere" during my research. Concerns over governance were driven in part by a venerable "tension between the imagined transformative capacities of technology, on one hand, and the countervailing suspicion that digital society simply replicates offline social processes" (Malaby 2006a), including fundamental questions of access, openness, and control (Kelty 2005; Lessig 2000; Lovink 2002; Ludlow and Wallace 2007).

To address governance in virtual worlds it is crucial to consider what Foucault identified as a shift from "sovereignty" to "governmentality" that accompanied the rise of the modern nation-state. The key distinction is that while sovereignty is self-justifying and "possesses its own intrinsic instruments in the shape of its laws," governmentality "resides in the things it manages . . . the instruments of government, instead of being laws, now come to a range of multiform tactics" (Foucault 1991:95). These tactics are forms of techne; their target is "the population," which becomes "the ultimate end of government" (100). In this regard "it is both striking and important to recognize how relatively little the premodern state actually knew about the society over which it presided. State officials had only the most tenuous idea of the population under their jurisdiction" (Scott, Tehranian, and Mathias 2000:7). In contrast, modern governmentality is concerned with an infinitely knowable and improvable population—seen, for instance, in the invention of mass education and public health.

With the rise of virtual worlds, techniques for controlling populations can potentially be augmented to an unprecedented degree. As many scholars of cybersociality have noted, by the mid-twentieth century Norbert Wiener had coined the term "cybernetics" in reference to "control and communication." As discussed in chapters 1 and 2, cybernetics was developed in the context of a post–World War II "control revolution," which sought technocratic means to produce a social homeostasis that would obviate violent conflict (Beniger 1986; Shapiro 1999; Wiener 1948). This cybernetic rubric, extending modern governmentalities of surveillance and social control, has been applied to online communities since the days of ARPANET, developed by the United States Department of Defense (Stone 1995:117). In the 1990s, as virtual worlds as I define them in this book came into broader being, debates over their governance became heated, as exemplified by Timothy C. May's "The Crypto Anarchist Manifesto," first circulated in 1988, and John Perry Barlow's "A Declaration of the Independence of Cyberspace," first circulated in 1996. The opening of Barlow's Declaration became something of a classic in the study of virtual worlds: "Governments of the Industrial World, you weary giants of flesh and steel, I come from Cyberspace, the new home of Mind. . . . You are not welcome among us. You have no sovereignty where we gather. . . . This governance will arise according to the conditions of our world, not yours" (Barlow 1996b:28).

Despite such declarations and manifestos, during my fieldwork it was broadly assumed that Linden Lab had total control over their virtual world. For instance, it was widely believed that there was, as one resident put it, "no real privacy in Second Life." There was substantial privacy with regard to actual-world identity—anyone could obtain an account anonymously, providing only a screen name and password—but there was no privacy for avatars.[15] Residents knew that every word they typed, indeed their every movement, was potentially recorded and stored on Linden Lab servers. They often assumed they were being monitored, as when I was sitting with three residents as they discussed a way to circumvent the maximum allowable size for prims:

> ZEV: I know someone who can teach me how to break the 10 meter limit on size.
> LORI: lol—how do you do that?
> ALBA: Satellite cams lol
> ALBA: Lindens are watching
> LORI: lol
> ALBA: Hi out there

This kind of jesting about an invisible but pervasive presence reflected how direct contact with Linden Lab staff was minimal. Staff would occasionally host a "Town Hall" meeting inworld, but these were structured in a question-and-answer format rather than a dialogue; since most sims could hold only forty residents, even if the event was held at the border of two or more sims it was difficult to have more than thirty residents present without significant lag. Even when these events were broadcast on "repeaters" so that residents elsewhere inworld could read the chat (or listen in, on occasions when voice was used), most could not participate. Residents might encounter individual staff inworld (they all had the last name "Linden," making them easy to recognize), and some Linden staff would hold "office hours," but as the virtual world grew such encounters became increasingly rare.

The two main ways residents encountered Linden governance were filing Abuse Reports when encountering griefing, and experiencing changes to the Second Life platform, a topic I address later in this chapter. When first acquiring their accounts, residents signed Terms of Service. They had no opportunity to negotiate the "terms" of these Terms of Service; as in all virtual worlds, one had to "take it or leave it" (Castronova 2005:208). It is debatable if such Terms of Service, built upon a notion of private contractual agreement, can serve as effective charters for public behavior (Fairfield 2007). These Terms of Service set out obligations of Linden Lab to residents, but also resident obligations to Second Life.[16] This included upholding the community standards, summarized in terms of the "big six" transgressions of intolerance, harassment, assault, disclosure (of personal information), indecency, and disturbing the peace.[17] If a resident experienced a violation of these principles or saw someone else being victimized, they could file an "Abuse Report" using a menu function in the Second Life program (accessible also by right-clicking on the offending resident or object). This did not have any immediate effect, and residents often complained that it could take days or weeks for Linden Lab staff to react. If they decided the report had merit, Linden Lab had a range of possible responses. This could range from removing offending objects and issuing a warning to the accused resident, to temporary or permanent suspension.[18] For more severe transgressions, particularly attempts to crash the Second Life grid or gain actual-world information about residents (like credit card numbers), Linden Lab staff might refer the case to authorities for actual-world prosecution, though if the accused person lived outside the United States, enforcement could be difficult. Linden Lab staff maintained a "police blotter" on the Second Life website that detailed some of their enforcement activities (without providing screen names); they would also ban residents temporarily or permanently from the website and its associated blog if they decided a resident's postings were abusive or inflammatory.[19]

Since Second Life was owned by Linden Lab, its authority was absolute; as noted earlier, such total control over virtual worlds is one of the most consequential aspects of emerging models of governance for them, raising the prospect of virtual dictatorships (Doctorow 2007; see also Chun 2006). In regard to deciding which Abuse Reports to act upon and the appropriate punishment to be meted out, Linden Lab acted with unbounded authority, with no court of appeal or governing body to review their decisions. Linden Lab staff claimed to forward some Abuse Reports to groups of residents as a kind of jury, but they were under no obligation to do so, and details of cases were kept secret. This omnipotence with regard to Second Life's governance was a source of concern to many residents. Those accused of transgressions had no way to face their accusers or appeal a decision. This led to complaints about selective enforcement. For instance, one of my neighbors left Second Life after Linden Lab forcibly removed billboards she had set up promoting her business, yet did not take action against other entrepreneurs who she felt had forms of advertising just as intrusive upon the Second Life landscape.

From the beginning of my fieldwork, Linden Lab tried to mitigate the controversy engendered by its authority in two ways. First, the company emphasized that because Second Life depended upon resident creativity, Linden Lab staff would hesitate to act against residents unless the company could document a clear violation of the Terms of Service.[20] The company claimed to employ a laissez-faire mode of governance, which can be seen to reflect a "virtual governmentality" (Thomas 2005:6) combining modern logics of governmentality, creationist capitalism, and the "Californian Ideology" that is predicated upon "an impeccably libertarian form of politics" (Barbrook and Cameron 2001:364). When I first joined Second Life in June 2004, I spent seven days flying over the entire world. By the end of my fieldwork such a survey have taken ten times as long or more; in addition, new land was being added so quickly that it would have been impossible to keep up. Philip Rosedale (Linden Lab's CEO) estimated that at some point in 2005 Second Life passed an "event horizon" after which it became an unknowable entity, even to Linden Lab itself (Wallace 2006). Thus, a fundamental factor Linden Lab faced in its governance of Second Life was that the virtual world was growing quickly and was full of indeterminacies—social formations that were not directly created (or even predicted) by the company. Linden Lab's "user-content" model of world-building found its governmental analogue in a "form of governance [that] tends to be implicit, for it is constituted by (cultural) convention" (Malaby 2006a). This had consequences for governmentality, because it meant that much of Linden Lab's governance operated at the level of setting norms, rather than managing everyday interaction.

A second way Linden Lab worked to deflect dissent over its governance practices was by offloading authority to residents, exemplifying a notion of "participatory design" that could be found in many virtual worlds at the time (Taylor 2006b), but also an increasingly laissez-faire, libertarian vision of creationist capitalism (Llewelyn 2007b). Even the system of Abuse Reports reflected this aesthetic: large-scale attacks on the Second Life grid might be detected independently by Linden Lab, but for the most part the company learned of transgressive behavior only when receiving resident-filed Abuse Reports. As discussed in chapter 7, there were many groups in Second Life and it was possible for land to be owned by a group. There were cases during my fieldwork of elaborate experiments in local governance, complete with constitutions, elections, campaigning, political parties, and council meetings. More common were relatively informal rules and procedures, typically distributed via note cards, for managing a property—for instance, for ensuring that a club had a DJ on duty each night, that stalls in a shopping mall were properly allocated, or that buildings did not encroach upon someone's view. During the time of my fieldwork Linden Lab staff expressed a desire to delegate more of the labor of governance to residents, for instance, through the notion of "covenants" on land. While such local forms of governance were not immune from controversy (and were often oriented around a leader who was the primary landowner), residents often pointed to them as models for grassroots governance. As one resident put it, "we don't need big government—we just need tribal, or village government." Another resident concurred: "We have to police ourselves. Linden Lab's job is to maintain grid stability, not intervene with squabbles between users."

Many residents thus shared with Linden Lab a cultural model of governance drawing upon creationist capitalism and the Californian Ideology—a virtual neoliberalism linked to broader open-source and prodemocracy movements online. Other residents felt that Linden Lab should acknowledge their ultimate control over the virtual world and take a more proactive role in governance. These debates reflect how the project of governmentality fundamentally includes "the question of the government of oneself" (Foucault 1991:87), the transformation of governmental techniques of management and control into internalized forms of techne.

Another way in which questions of governance intersected with Second Life was in regard to actual-world governance. Since during my research Linden Lab was located in the United States and a majority of residents had their actual-world homes in the United States, such issues of actual-world governance primarily concerned the United States government, but Second Life internationalized significantly during the course of my research.[21] In the months leading up to the November 2004 national elections, a number of residents put up yard signs for John Kerry (or more rarely, for George W. Bush), importing images of actual-world campaign signs into Second Life as textures. There was even a "headquarters" for the Kerry campaign, but like the other political images and texts used up to this point, it was not produced by the campaign itself.

Toward the end of my fieldwork, more politicians started appearing in Second Life or sponsoring a headquarters there (like John Edwards, a candidate for the U.S. presidency for 2008). By the end of 2006 a newly elected Democratic majority in Congress had created a virtual Capitol

Hill on two islands in Second Life (Au 2006k, 2007a; Neva 2007a). However, I was responsible for the first use of Second Life in direct connection
with an actual-world political campaign. This underscores how the ethnographic method of participant observation does not require pretending
that researchers have no impact upon their fieldsites. It asks instead that
researchers acknowledge and theorize this impact, without underestimating or overstating its significance. In my case, Brian Ulaszewski, a neighbor
and friend, was running for city council in Long Beach, California, where
I lived. I was involved in his actual-world campaign and suggested we try a
"meet-and-greet" event in Second Life as an experiment. He had organized
an actual-world art exhibit in support of his candidacy, and by importing
images from this exhibit into Second Life I could recreate the exhibit within
Ethnographia, my Second Life home (Au 2006e).

Beyond campaigns lies the possibility of more intensive military and
government activity in Second Life. The United States military has been
involved in virtual worlds from their beginnings, and while I did not have
access to definitive information, it appeared that military and government
bodies may have owned islands in Second Life from early in its history (Au
2005d). Second Life residents wondered about these possibilities. One recalled how "the week I started Second Life, my first thought was that the
U.S. government was now trying an experiment, looking for people with
social skills." As my fieldwork progressed, there was increasing talk that
the U.S. Congress might investigate the possibility of taxing Second Life
income, or of regulating questionable content. Whether in regard to Linden
Lab, residents, or actual-world politics, questions of governance in Second
Life strike at the center of struggles over its political economy. These struggles will be of enormous consequence for the future of virtual worlds.

Inequality.

Virtual worlds have often been presented as sites of untrammeled freedom,
where humans are released from the shackles of physical embodiment and
can reinvent themselves as they choose. I have already explored many ways
in which this assessment is inaccurate. Perhaps nowhere is this more clear
than with respect to social inequality. The idea of governance assumes some
kind of power differential between the governed and those with authority
over them. Anthropologists have noted that no human society has existed
without some form of inequality; forms of status and authority exist even in
"primitive" societies without private property (Collier 1988). To be human,
including to be virtually human, is to live in social contexts structured by

inequality, though the form and severity of that inequality vary greatly. Even Plato's allegory of the cave envisioned some persons chained to the floor of a cave and others casting shadows. More recent imaginings of virtual worlds, like the "metaverse" of Neal Stephenson's *Snow Crash*, also imagined online distinctions between rich and poor, empowered and powerless (Stephenson 1993; see also Williams 1996).

Inequality has been integral to virtual worlds (Jakobsson and Taylor 2003). All text-based virtual worlds have had ranked statuses, typically including "gods" and "wizards" who had privileged access to the platform and could do things like remove residents (Curtis 1992:130–32; Kendall 2002:65; Kollock and Smith 1999:7; A. Smith 1999:139). In Second Life, the equivalent to gods or wizards were the staff of Linden Lab. The terms "god" and "wizard" were not commonly used: Linden Lab staff simply bore the last name "Linden," but some were known to also participate in Second Life using alts. Collectively they were known as "the lindens," a moniker identical to the colloquial term for Second Life's currency save the definite article. A source of concern to many residents was that unlike the "wizards" of most earlier text-based virtual worlds, "the lindens" were not just administrators but salaried employees of a company that owned the virtual world in question. As one resident put it: "there's a godlike quality to the lindens. They have power we don't; they ultimately control the world." Another worried that the lindens could act "like Grand Wizards in god mode."

Below the lindens there existed a class of elite residents. This has antecedents going back to the earliest days of text-based virtual worlds, where a class of "privileged users" (Reid 1999:110) had some kind of favor with the gods and wizards of the virtual world in question. This "'power elite' was a symbolic category that centralized much debate about community ideology and the location of power" (Cherny 1999:273). Such persons were "treated differently by other players" (Curtis 1992:131); often they would "become 'acolytes' who serve as helpers in the community and have a higher status than regular members" (Kollock and Smith 1999:8). In Second Life there was no specific label for such privileged status, but about a year after I began my fieldwork the term "Feted Inner Core" was coined and became well-known.[22] Often persons presumed to be privileged in this manner were seen as "content creators" who actualized the ideology of creationist capitalism. This recalls how even in text-based virtual worlds, economic dynamics could add "another form of social stratification, creating virtual millionaires as well as beggars" (Kollock and Smith 1999:8; see also Damer 1998:161–88).

These privileged users were sometimes invited by Linden Lab to participate in focus groups, or given special treatment in terms of access to the platform (one, for instance, was allowed to edit proposals other residents had written for the "Feature Voting" page of the Second Life website [Neva 2006c]). A few members of this class were even hired by Linden Lab, "leveling up to become lindens," as one resident put it. Note that since my ethnographic approach in this book is descriptive, not prescriptive, I am not passing judgment on these actions here. I am simply noting the existence of a privileged class of Second Life residents and underscoring how this dynamic contributes to ideologies of creationist capitalism and thus a political economy of techne. Many residents did complain of what they saw as preferential treatment given to this class. One day I was talking to Sandra, a resident who was a skilled texturer but worked informally for her friends, when she expressed her frustration that:

> They need to upgrade the platform so that people like me have more things to play with. But instead they say fuck the people who don't own businesses and tons of land in SL. They give those people everything they want because they feed LL tons of cash every month. . . . They don't care about us, Tom. You and me. The people who don't produce anything and give to the economy. They don't care. . . . They lie to us, and don't give us direct answers to simple questions. Second Life is no different than real life. The rich get richer while the poor stay poor.

This recalls a darker side of the "Californian Ideology" that shaped the ethos of Second Life's creationist capitalism: that ideology celebrates creativity and freedom, but depends upon "a willful blindness toward the other, much less positive features of life on the West Coast—racism, poverty, and environmental degradation" (Barbrook and Cameron 2001:364). For instance, residents debated if those who did not own or rent property were truly "free," since such "homeless" residents could not build or display commodities permanently: as one noted, "what good is stuff if you don't have a place to put it?"

While there was no single criterion for becoming a more privileged resident, Linden Lab did structure the world so as to have social classes within it, and this structure became more elaborate as my fieldwork progressed. These social classes were Second Life's equivalent to the classes of "basic users" and "guests" that undergirded earlier virtual worlds (Reid 1999:110). During the early period of my fieldwork, all Second Life accounts required a monthly U.S.$9.95 fee, paid via a credit card, which thereby confirmed the identity of the person holding the account. All accounts received rights to a small (512 square meters) plot of "first land." Acquiring additional land involved paying a monthly "tiering fee," which, as noted earlier, could reach thousands of dollars a month. In June 2006, a shift in the Second Life platform offered the possibility of acquiring an account without any monthly fees, but such an account could not own land unless converted to the $9.95 account requiring credit card verification, renamed a "Premium Account." Without such an account, the only option was to rent land from a landlord with a premium account.[23]

Second Life did not have "leveling," a system with which many combat-oriented virtual worlds marked status, but it did have a ratings system. Before version 1.2, any resident could be rated positively or negatively, for a charge of L$1. After version 1.2, this charge was changed to L$1 per rating among three options: "behavior," "appearance," and "skill at building." This system, in place when I began my research, was so inexpensive that a common event was the "ratings party," where residents would gather at a club to listen to music and give each other positive ratings. Such parties were technically against the Terms of Service, because ratings were specifically designed to produce a kind of reputation system within Second Life, a form of social inequality that would reward behaviors beneficial to the world as a whole. Since ratings parties and a general willingness to rate other residents rendered the ratings system relatively ineffective, version 1.7.0 of the platform (released in October 2005) removed negative ratings and raised the cost of a positive rating to L$25 (it had earlier been briefly raised to L$5). These changes ended ratings parties but made ratings largely irrelevant as a measure of social status; residents simply no longer rated each other with any frequency. The information provided by, for instance, the groups to which a resident belonged carried more significance than the decontextualized quantitative information provided by ratings. In response to the relative infrequency of ratings usage, and the contribution (albeit relatively small) ratings made to lag, the ratings system was discontinued in April 2007.[24] Reputation and rating systems have become extremely important in many virtual worlds, as on the Internet more generally (for instance, on EBay or Amazon.com), a state of affairs foreseen from the beginnings of virtual worlds themselves: "reputations will be of central importance, far more important in dealings than even the credit ratings of today" (May 1988:62). While the official ratings system of Second Life had been discontinued by the end of my fieldwork, some residents had developed systems to rate residents, so it seemed unlikely ratings would disappear entirely.

Other, less formal forms of inequality based upon status and reputation also existed in Second Life during my research. The "life course" of avatar selfhood produced a kind of inequality, since newbies tended to have less status than those with more experience inworld. As one resident noted, "sometimes I feel there is a status differentiation between 'seasoned' SLers and newcomers." Some residents also spoke of "appearance status." Looking like the default avatar provided when first obtaining an account marked one as a newbie—or if an older account, someone who was not active inworld. More expensive skins and clothing, including jewelry, shoes, and other attachments, could act as forms of "conspicuous consumption" (Veblen 1899) marking status, as could a large or well-designed residence. Other forms of inequality were produced in terms of skills inequality. The ability to script, for instance, created a status that those without computer programming skills lacked. Linguistic skills (particularly in English) also raised resident status.

Despite all of these forms of status differentiation in Second Life, it is important to point out the existence of widespread forms of egalitarianism, a characteristic found in other virtual worlds as well (Nardi and Harris 2006). Because of the relative anonymity provided by most virtual worlds and the additional factor of alts, residents of virtual worlds like Second Life could befriend persons with whom they might not associate in the actual world due to differences in social status. The example of celebrities mentioned earlier is an extreme case, but it was not unheard of to find a group of friends in Second Life who in the actual world might be a thirty-year-old white gay automobile mechanic, a twenty-year-old Latina university student, and a seventy-year-old Asian male retiree.

Although a common stereotype presents virtual world residents as privileged computer geeks, working-class persons participated in Second Life quite often during my fieldwork, and would sometimes find support inworld for the difficulties they faced in their actual-world jobs. Such support could range from an ongoing relationship or friendship network to incidental side chatter. In the following example "Jacqui" is hosting a game of Tringo, and "Sanders" has just returned from being afk to help Jacqui make musical selections for the group to enjoy:

SANDERS: Hello all
JACQUI: wb, Sanders.
VELMA: hey sanders
JACQUI: Gonna play some Rolling Stones for me, Sanders?
SANDERS: Depends if I cheer up
JACQUI: What's wrong, hon. Tell ol' Jacqui all your problems.
SANDERS: Just having a bad day. Burned myself 7 times at work and got the marks to show for it
JACQUI: Owch.
SANDERS: You know the metal bars in the ovens that heat them up
JACQUI: Yeah

SANDERS: Imagine an industrial oven, and my arm colliding with the
  metal bar in an industrial oven.
JACQUI: The smell of burning flesh.
SANDERS: Not burning
SANDERS: It melted
JACQUI: Ouch. Shit. Hurts just hearing about it.

This example recalls how creationist capitalism exists alongside other
capitalisms and forms of noncapitalist economic exchange (Gibson-Graham
1996). A greater attention to creationist capitalism in virtual worlds might
reveal important clues as to how political economic formations in the Age
of Techne will present opportunities and dangers for human freedom.

PLATFORM AND SOCIAL FORM.

In this chapter I have noted how many issues in regard to the political economy of Second Life are not unique to online contexts. This reflects a broader
pattern, evident in everything from heated debates over gender and race to
largely implicit notions of place and time, where parallels and interchange
sustain rather than collapse the distinction between the virtual and actual.
Second Life extended and elaborated an ideology of creationist capitalism
that, as one aspect of what was often termed neoliberalism, was gaining
prominence in the actual world during the time of my fieldwork: virtual
worlds thus represented "a fascinating test bed for ideas about how to gov-
ern" (Castronova 2005:207). It was not trivial that Philip Rosedale saw Linden Lab as "building a country" (some residents also referred to Second
Life in terms like "a country outside countries").[25] It was through governance that economics and politics intersected in Second Life and other virtual worlds during my fieldwork, so that creationist capitalism within them
could take on the appearance of a national economy (Malaby 2006b:145).
    I have emphasized that the sharpest distinction between the virtual
and actual with regard to the question of governance is that virtual worlds
can be owned; open-source or nonprofit virtual worlds existed during
my research, but most were the property of companies. Second Life was
fundamentally a "program," a concept that "first appeared in the seventeenth century for public notices but which in the past 150 years has spread
through other organizational and informational technologies. . . . [it] has
come to mean any prearranged information that guides subsequent behavior" (Beniger 1986:39). This question of how virtual world platforms
guide behavior constitutes a crucial emerging topic of interest in the study

of cybersociality: "the relation between design and culture . . . cannot be overstated" (Taylor 2006a:65).

In my fieldwork in Indonesia, I saw how individuals, communities, and institutions (including the Indonesian state) shaped cultural logics, but none had the absolute power to "program" them into being. In the actual world, governments influence the societies over which they have authority: this was, for instance, what Foucault meant by a "discourse" and what Marxist thought has meant by "ideology" and "hegemony" (e.g., Althusser 1971; Foucault 1970; Gramsci 1971). Virtual worlds raise the possibility of a whole new degree of control over culture. The platform can literally encode assumptions about the virtual world: "the technology does not wholly determine the nature of the society, though it may determine the parameters within which that society may develop" (Reid 1999:109). An actual-world government could ban slot machine gambling, but a virtual-world government could, in theory, disable all random-number generating scripts in the virtual world, an act for which is there no true actual-world parallel. Anthropologists and others have long asked how language might shape thought (Lucy 1992; Sapir 1949; Whorf 1956). How, for instance, might conceptions of gender be influenced by the fact that some languages (like English) obligatorily mark gender on pronouns (he/she) while others (like Indonesian) do not (dia/dia)? Virtual worlds are sites of culture constituted through computer languages, shaped by menus, commands, and windows all designed and modified by the virtual worlds' owners, administrators, and open-source contributors, raising possibilities for social engineering of which any actual-world ruler could only dream.

How, then, does the platform shape the social form?

Throughout this book I have examined many aspects of Second Life culture that were encoded into its program. For instance, the idea of private property shaped sociality with regard to everything from land and commodities to "intellectual property." Any resident could right-click on any of the millions of prims in Second Life or on any square meter of virtual land, and in all cases see the owner—but there was no option for the ownership field to be left blank. Historically the Western notion of property is quite idiosyncratic. One could imagine a virtual world in which land and objects were held in common or framed in terms of caretaking rather than ownership, but such imaginings lay beyond the horizon of the Second Life platform during my fieldwork.

The notions of place so fundamental to Second Life were also shaped by the platform. For example, as discussed in chapter 4 Linden Lab had at one point designed Second Life so that one could teleport only to "telehubs."[26]

Throughout my fieldwork, residents could "offer a teleport" to other residents; under the telehub system this was the only way to teleport to an exact location (other than one's home). Residents who had arrived at an event would "offer a teleport" to others, and offering teleports to guests was an important aspect of hosting events. The importance of offering teleports declined dramatically after telehubs were abolished and the platform was recoded to allow free point-to-point teleporting. This also transformed land use: proximity to a telehub was no longer a source of value and meaning.

Building was another example of Second Life sociality powerfully influenced by the platform. Residents could shape and transform prims in a range of ways, but even as small changes were made to the building tools (ghostly rulers, for instance, making it easier to judge the a prim's size), many residents found the tools difficult to use and a barrier to being seen as fully competent members of the social world. One resident who was disabled in the actual world recounted appealing to the lindens to make the building tools more accessible: "it's what I am fighting for; the build feature does not work properly for me. They made SL for people who are 'perfect,' with no thought to those of us who have special needs."

Even something as basic as embodiment was shaped by the Second Life platform. For instance, via a function termed "mouselook," residents could see the virtual world as if through the eyes of their avatar. It was more common, however, for residents to select the partially disembodied view which allowed residents to see their virtual body. This was termed the "camera" view, not because it included any representation of a camera, but because it placed one's point of view at a distance from one's avatar. The ability to "set away" and "set busy" represented attempts to encode the "afk" (away from keyboard) phenomenon into the platform, as well as a recognition that afk could operate with respect to the gap between a virtual world and the actual world, or internally to a virtual world itself.

Friendship was so central to Second Life that it was integrated into the platform, in that one could "offer friendship" to as many residents as one wished.[27] As noted in chapter 1, upon becoming friends with someone both persons would receive a brief notice whenever the other logged on or off, each could see the exact location of the other on the map, and each could see if the other was online via the Second Life website. In December 2006, an update to the platform allowed residents to provide each of these capabilities only to specific friends, and also to grant certain friends the right to modify objects one owned. This introduced implicit degrees of closeness between friends, yet there was still no category of "best friend": one was a friend, or not. Yet notions of intentionality remained highly encoded into the social construction of friendship online. Rarely in the actual world do persons become friends by asking each other "would you like to be my friend" and then receiving a positive reply (such a scenario recalls nothing more than schoolyard banter). Yet such a contractual, formalized notion of friendship was common to Second Life and many other virtual worlds. One could imagine a virtual world platform in which, after spending a certain number of hours in a certain proximity to someone's avatar, one would gradually become labeled the "friend" of that person—but no such encoding of emergent friendship existed in Second Life during my research.

The other encoded category of social relation was "partner"; this provided no privileges except that one's partner was listed on one's profile. One could have a partner of any gender but only one partner at a time, reflecting the Californian Ideology where homosexuality was acceptable so long as it respected the norm of serial monogamy (Barbrook and Cameron 2001; Rubin 1993). "Friend" and "partner" were the only two categories of recognized social relationship in Second Life, recalling how in other virtual worlds as well, forms of inequality "were 'hard coded' into the software" (Hudson-Smith 2002:79). How might Second Life sociality have worked differently if other kinds of social relationship were possible? How would sociality have been effected if, say, one could have as many partners as one wished, but was permitted only one friend?

Beyond the dyadic relationships of friend and partners, "groups" were important to Second Life sociality. When I began my fieldwork, one could join a maximum of five groups. This was seen by many residents to impose limits on sociality, particularly as the number and range of groups expanded—for instance, some for a shared interest, others to manage shared land. Later in my fieldwork, the maximum number of groups a resident could join was raised from five to fifteen and then to twenty-five, reshaping the possibilities for sociality. Had the number of groups been kept at a smaller number, membership in any particular group would have carried significant meaning; joining a group would almost always have meant leaving another. With the number raised to twenty-five, it was often possible for residents to join groups that did not function as social collectivities, but, for instance, provided news about upcoming events at a favorite club.

Just as significant as the increase in number of groups residents could join was a radical expansion of "group tools" with the August 2006 (version 1.12) upgrade to the platform. Prior to that time, groups were composed of just two categories, officers and members. This two-tiered system had consequences for the social form of groups; someone who succeeded in being named an officer could do things like expel other members or sell the group's land. When the number of groups a resident could join was raised to twenty-five, the ability to create a range of group roles with specific abilities was added as well. For example, it became possible to create a role—say, "manager"—and specify that only managers could create new roles for the group or move objects on group land. This change to the platform reflected Linden Lab's recognition of the importance of organizational dynamics; it offered residents greater freedom in how groups were structured, but also created new possibilities for inequality and social differentiation.

Tools for social control and combating griefing were also encoded into the platform, as exemplified by the ability to file Abuse Reports, as well as the ratings system. The ability to ban any resident from one's land, as well as the ability to "mute" residents so that one would not hear their chat, represented attempts to encode means of defusing social tension into the platform. Other changes to the platform to combat griefing included the version 1.11 modification allowing landowners to disable "push" scripts on their land (the scripts used to create, for instance, most kinds of guns that could shoot avatars into the air).

Linden Lab could even effect Second Life sociality indirectly, as with the example of "update Wednesdays." During most of my fieldwork, the platform would be shut down nearly every Wednesday from about 6am to noon for an update of the Second Life program. Some Second Life residents found this disruption beneficial, a time when they could do actual-world chores like laundry without feeling they should be doing something in Second Life as well. Others used this downtime to read or post messages to the many websites (including forums and blogs) devoted to Second Life.

All these examples of the platform shaping the social form only hint at the extensive new possibilities for social control that have accompanied the emergence of virtual worlds. However, they also indicate how forms of resistance could challenge, reshape, or work around these encodings of sociality. This reflects how in many online worlds, residents have reworked the available tools to make objects or engage in activities (like sex work) that the owners of the virtual world never intended (Ondrejka 2004a:6–7; Thomas 2005:10). As noted earlier, the ratings system was modified over time to make ratings more expensive and to remove negative ratings, but residents largely lost interest in the ratings system after it was revised.

Another example of resident resistance involves categories of membership. On June 6, 2006, Linden Lab modified the process for obtaining free accounts so that it was no longer necessary to provide credit card or other identifying information: all that was needed was a name and password. Under this new system, credit card information was only necessary to obtain a "Premium Account," needed to own land. The company had noted that about one-half of potential registrations were lost at the point where credit card information was requested, a particular hardship for persons in nations where credit cards were not commonly used. The new process for obtaining accounts led to an approximately fourfold increase in the rate of persons signing up for Second Life accounts, including an increase from 25 percent to 50 percent in the percentage of persons signing up from outside the United States (Au 2006f).[28]

However, the ability to join Second Life without providing any identifying information made many residents concerned; they complained that the grid was being flooded with persons bent on griefing, and also that it would be easier for children to enter Second Life, raising issues of ethics and legal liability. Complaints about the new registration system culminated in a protest on Friday, June 23, 2006, at the area set aside for Second Life's third anniversary. By June 28, a proposition to "bring back identity verification for new registering accounts" (Proposition 1503) had become the top vote-getter on the "Feature Proposals" webpage, despite the fact that it had been added only nine days earlier. The explanation for the feature stated simply: "we have seen the results; now let's fix it. Some form of identity verification is necessary. Go back to credit cards now! It may not be the best way but it was better than this chaos." Linden Lab, of course, was not beholden to this request, but did seek a way to make verifying identity easier. Their response appeared in the Release Notes for the June 28 upgrade to the Second Life platform (version 1.10.5.1): "Each resident's profile now includes a field revealing . . . one of three status entries: (1) 'No Payment Info on File'—account was created with no credit card or Paypal; (2) 'Payment Info on File'—account has provided a credit card or Paypal; (3) 'Payment Info Used'—credit card or Paypal on account has successfully been billed. We plan to provide features in future updates to mark specific parts of the Second Life world (or allow residents to mark their own land) as accessible only to accounts with payment information."

One way of interpreting this state of affairs is in terms of responding to resident concerns, but changes to the platform could also be seen to co-opt resident creativity and consolidate Linden Lab control over Second Life. Some residents termed this getting "gommed," a reference to Gaming Open Market (GOM). This website was one of the first allowing the exchange of virtual world currencies with each other and with U.S. dollars (Castronova 2005:164). As more companies owning virtual worlds prohibited residents from exchanging their inworld currencies, GOM's sphere of exchange shrunk until it exchanged only linden dollars. However, in September 2005 Linden Lab added a "Currency Exchange" feature to the official Second Life website, a feature eventually incorporated into the platform, appearing as a small "L$" symbol on a resident's computer screen. This feature soon drove GOM and similar websites out of business, leading some residents to complain that Linden Lab had a double standard—encouraging creativity as the foundation of the virtual world, but then coopting resident success stories, rather than allowing them to continue to earn a profit.

Another example of being "gommed" concerned the "God Mode" program, created in 2006 by a Second Life resident. This program fooled the Second Life servers into thinking that any resident had "God Mode" privileges typically reserved for the lindens, including being able to see the location of any resident inworld (not just "friends"), the ability to detach one's camera view from the location of one's avatar, and many other features. At first some residents feared this God Mode would allow residents to engage in destructive activities like taking over the land of other residents, but it soon became clear that it provided only "client-side" privileges accessible through resident computers. That the God Mode program did not threaten the platform was underscored by the version 1.12 (August 2006) update to the Second Life platform, which allowed any resident access to almost all of these client-side features, rending the "God Mode" program useless.

These examples illustrate the complex give-and-take between Linden Lab and residents over questions of Second Life's governance. While most residents I encountered during my fieldwork saw the lindens as a rather benign, hard-working group of individuals, frustrations and suspicions toward them were far from rare. These frustrations and suspicions might concern anything from a minor incident where a resident felt an Abuse Report was not addressed, to major concerns over an update to the platform or favoritism expressed toward certain individuals, groups, or businesses. All these frustrations and suspicions reflected pervasive dynamics of governance inworld. Game studies analyses sometimes characterize virtual-world governance in terms of "players" agreeing to a set of "rules" that describe how a game is played. This structuralist conception of social action might be applicable to some contexts of gaming, but is of limited utility for understanding governance in virtual worlds, because it assumes that a description of a social world has a different ontological status than social action in that world. Such views are deeply engrained in Western thought—recalling notions of a sovereign who rules over society while standing apart from it (on the model of the Christian God's separation from the profane world). However, they fail to explain how forms of governance participate in the cultural realities they otherwise seem merely to control (Strathern 1985:128; see Venera 2006). Struggles over governance will play a pivotal role in determining the possibilities for culture online in the Age of Techne.

Chapter 9

THE VIRTUAL

The virtual human—Culture and the online—Simulation—Fiction and design—The massively multiple—Toward an anthropology of virtual worlds.

The virtual human.

> Technologies are artificial, but . . . artificiality is natural to human beings. Technology, properly interiorized, does not degrade human life but on the contrary enhances it.
>
> —Ong 1982:82–83

In the quotation above, Walter Ong is discussing a widespread belief that a shift from oral to written culture transformed selfhood and society. Culture in virtual worlds may be monumental in its own way, but as speaking did not disappear with the emergence of text, so the actual world will not become irrelevant as it becomes possible to live parts of our lives online. At hand is not a Virtual Age that sweeps the actual aside, but an Age of Techne in which there is continuity and change. There is continuity because humans are virtual whenever they engage in techne: "the virtual is essential to the real" (Poster 2001:127). The story of Prometheus describes one mythic moment when humans, receiving the gift of techne, became fully human for the first time. Since humans are always crafting themselves through culture, they have always been virtual (Clark 2003). *The virtual is the anthropological.* This makes it possible to study virtual worlds with the same flexible, underdetermined ethnographic tools used to study human cultures in the actual world.

Alongside this continuity there is change. In the Age of Techne, human craft can—for the first time—create new worlds for human sociality. Human imaginings enabled by techne are not all interchangeable: I cannot meet a lover inside a novel and invite friends for a wedding ceremony there, nor can I and a group of like-minded persons buy joint property inside a television program. Not all new technologies are virtual worlds as I define them (for instance, I would not classify social networking websites like MySpace or Facebook as they existed during my research as virtual worlds). Virtual worlds are not necessarily any more significant than these other new technologies; at issue is simply that virtual worlds have unique characteristics and social significance that does not hinge on a direct relationship to the actual world. Virtual worlds remain linked to the actual world, and questions of political economy, inequality, community, and selfhood remain just as pertinent. Yet my conclusion as an ethnographer of Second Life is that virtual worlds are distinct domains of human being, deserving of study in their own right.

It is this dialectic of continuity and change that motivates the polysemy of this book's title. In virtual worlds we can be virtually human, because in them humans, though techne, open up a gap from the actual and discover new possibilities for human being. At the same time, virtual worlds highlight the virtuality that has always been part of the human condition. This is why it is mistaken to temporalize this virtual human into the figure of the "posthuman." Rather than inaugurating the posthuman, virtual worlds make us *"even more human"* (Lévy 2001:216, emphasis in original). It is not true that theories of the virtual must shed their "anthropocentric associations" (Plant 1996:34). The association between the virtual and the human must, if anything, be more deeply theorized and delinked from the white, male, heterosexual, middle-class self that has too often stood in for a generic human being, online and offline. The Age of Techne marks a worldview in which aspects of selfhood formerly seen as natural or derived from group membership can be seen as produced through creativity. During my fieldwork in Indonesia, I learned that while forms of homosexuality had existed there since time immemorial, the modern Indonesian identities *"gay"* and *"lesbi"* had their own unique characteristics. Similarly online worlds draw upon a capacity for the virtual that is as old as humanity itself, but aspects of selfhood and society within them are novel. Virtual worlds do not lead to an erasure of the human: as one Second Life resident observed, a virtual world can act as "another platform for the human OS [operating system]." They do, however, transform what being human can mean, recalling how "we have used our relationships with technology to reflect on the human" (Turkle 1995:24).

In this ethnography I have focused general attention on one specific virtual world during a particular period of time. I have purposely employed the most "traditional" ethnographic methods possible, and the fact that I have found them so useful is one piece of evidence indicating that virtual worlds are robust locations for culture. Part of this methodology has been to produce the "traditional" product of ethnography, the ethnographic monograph. I see it as an advantage of the book form that I cannot update this text;

it will stand as an analysis of the early years of Second Life and a set of theoretical and methodological frameworks for understanding culture in virtual worlds. Websites and blogs can be constantly revised, and such commentary can be insightful, reflecting a history of "Commentaria" dating back to the Middle Ages, "when philosophers and theologians literally surrounded texts with commentary on the same page" (Fabian 2002:777). In the future, I may well use websites and blogs to further analyze cybersociality, but for this experiment I have explored the benefits and limitations that accompany using the book form to investigate culture in virtual worlds.

Throughout my research I was struck by the banality of Second Life. Exotica could certainly be found, from castles in the sky to alts, furries, and gender transformations. Yet everyday Second Life was also mundane creativity, conversation, intimacy, shopping, entertainment, even tedium. As one resident put it, "that's the dirty secret of virtual worlds; all people end up doing is replicating their real lives." While qualifying his statement by noting he was "being a bit facetious," caution as to the novelty of cybersociality is certainly justified; during the time of my research "breathless reports of an Immanent Shift in the Way We Live® [did] not seem to be accompanied by much skepticism" (Shirky 2006). Yet significance and novelty are not the same thing. It is appropriate to be weary toward cyberhype and also cyberdismissal; virtual worlds do not change everything, but neither are they reducible to what came before them.

As indicated by the epigraph above as well as the discussion in chapter 2, there is a history of correspondences between the human, technology, and creativity. At the beginning of the twentieth century, the philosopher Henri Bergson claimed in the aptly titled *Creative Evolution* that:

> As regards human intelligence, it has not been sufficiently noted that mechanical invention has been from the first its essential feature, that even to-day our social life gravitates around the manufacture and use of artificial instruments. . . . If, to define our species, we kept strictly to what the historic and the prehistoric periods show us to be the constant characteristic of man and of intelligence, we should say not *Homo sapiens*, but *Homo faber*. In short, *intelligence, considered in what seems to be its original feature, is the faculty of manufacturing artificial tools, especially tools to make tools, and of indefinitely varying the manufacture.* (Bergson 1911:138–39, emphasis in original)

The idea of an Age of Techne challenges the assumptions of the "Information Age," predicated on a conflation of the human with *homo sapiens*, the "knowing man," which thereby equates "civilization's new horizon" with a "knowledge space" (Lévy 1997:8). In contrast, Bergson's analysis locates the human in techne rather than episteme, in crafting rather than knowing. His universalizing framework defined *homo faber* in terms of the human capacity for techne: in the words of Adriano Tilgher, whose book *Homo Faber* extended Bergson's analysis, it is in crafting that humanity "begins a new cycle in the history of life" (Tilgher 1930:95). The French anthropologist Claude Lévi-Strauss, the most significant figure in twentieth-century structuralist anthropology, saw Bergon's analysis as demonstrating that "every human mind is a locus of *virtual* experience where what goes on in the minds of men, however remote they may be, can be investigated" (Lévi-Strauss 1962:103, emphasis added). Yet Bergson's notion of humans as "indefinitely varying" their tools, and thus the worlds made by those tools, opens a space from which to consider how online selfhood cannot be reduced to the seamless implementation of a social order coded into the platform. In this regard, Bergson himself was heavily interested in notions of the virtual (Friedberg 2006:141–46).

In working to theorize the virtual human, it is crucial to avoid both utopic and dystopic narratives that posit a unilinear trajectory for the Age of Techne. Some Second Life residents were attracted to the work of futurologists like Ray Kurzweil, who argued that we are on the brink of a "technological singularity," a total fusion of human and machine (Kurzweil 2005); a few residents even expressed a desire to someday be able to "download" themselves into Second Life. Other observers of virtual worlds and video games have seen them as "perfect training for life in fin de siècle America, where daily existence demands the ability to parse sixteen kinds of information being fired at you simultaneously" (Herz 1997:2). One resident predicted that "a lot of baby boomers are coming up on retirement soon and I think a lot of them don't have that magical retirement nest egg that they were supposed to have when they retired. So things like SL are going to be where these people start going instead of cruise ships or having dozens of cats." Both viewpoints reflected debates over emerging relationships between the virtual and the human—as one resident noted, "Second Life is part of real life"—but this relationship was predicated upon the gap between the virtual and actual, rather than heralding its dissolution.

CULTURE AND THE ONLINE.

This book demonstrates the importance for those interested in researching culture in virtual worlds to familiarize themselves with theories of culture originating in anthropology and other disciplines, and also to understand that "ethnography" is not the same thing as any qualitative method, includ-ing interviewing in isolation. One of the key conceits I have taken from "traditional" ethnographic methods has been to treat Second Life as a culture—albeit one that, like all cultures, has many subcultures within it. I have addressed a range of topics, many of which could easily be the subject of an entire book in their own right. What one gains from the traditional approach is a holistic understanding of the constitutive intersectionality of cultural domains. This is quite different from cultural studies scholarship that tends to focus on gender, ethnicity, class, religion, language, or some other topic in relative isolation, gesturing at intersections in an additive rather than constitutive manner. For instance, it is possible to see a shared cultural logic of multiplicity behind alts, participation in more than one virtual world, and the practice of iming multiple friends while chatting. Creationist capitalism effected everything from screen names and friend-ship lists to virtual real estate and "prim hair." The idea that virtual worlds are places shaped conflicts over a ruined view, assumptions about value, and the idea that a resident could be "away from keyboard."

The notion of virtual worlds as social forms "in themselves" is a fun-damental theoretical conceit of this book. Anthropologists have long be-rated themselves (and been berated by others) for assuming that cultures are bounded wholes. This tendency is by no means limited to anthropol-ogy, of course. It can be seen, for instance, in the work of social theorists going back at least to Emile Durkheim, who used the analogy of societies as organisms to underscore both functional interdependence (any one part of society—religion, law, etc.—serves to sustain the society as a whole) and discreteness (societies are organized wholes, such that it is possible to speak of French society, German society, and so on). The idea that anthropol-ogy assumes cultures are discrete wholes has always been somewhat unfair; even schools of thought considered the worst offenders, like functionalism and structuralism, were often characterized by a notable savvy in this re-gard. For instance, in *Argonauts of the Western Pacific* Malinowski empha-sized that his ethnographic object was a "trading system, the Kula": that is, a distributed network rather than bounded place (Malinowski 1922:2). At present, contemporary conditions of globalization, migration, and technol-ogy make it seemingly self-evident that cultures are not now hermetically sealed entities; our understanding of colonialism and precapitalist histories of trade and settlement indicates that they never really were.

Yet it is also clear that persons around the world understand themselves to belong to cultures that are discrete even if their boundaries are porous. For instance, I used the notion of "dubbing culture" to capture how *gay* and *lesbi* Indonesians were aware that the terms *gay* and *lesbi* originated in some sense beyond Indonesia's borders, even as they felt the terms had been transformed into Indonesian categories of sexual selfhood (Boellstorff 2005). The idea of dubbing—taken from the dubbing of foreign movies into the Indonesian language—was a technological metaphor highlighting how in a dubbed movie, the words one heard spoken and the lips of the actors one saw moving never quite matched up. It could be said that they *virtually* matched up. Where translation seeks to eliminate any distinction between the original and its translated product, dubbing is predicated upon productively sustaining the gap between a dubbed soundtrack and the moving lips on the screen with which it can never unify. Both the Indonesian case and the case of virtual worlds speak to juxtapositions of cultural discreteness and cultural interchange in an era of globalization. Indeed, Second Life residents typically understood it as a discrete virtual world and at the same time as having a porous "membrane" (Castronova 2005:147). This porosity took three forms: the nebula of online content surrounding Second Life (forums, blogs, webpages); relationships between Second Life and other virtual worlds and video games; and the relationship between Second Life and the actual world. It is with a deep appreciation of these porosities that I am interested in what happens if we take cybersociality on its own terms rather than as a signifier for another mode of sociality. What happens if we return, even heuristically, to Huizinga's notion of the magic circle and see virtual worlds as meaningful in themselves? How might porosity and interchange, in what some might see as a paradox, work to shore up notions of discreteness, in Second Life and elsewhere?

Simulation.

One important history of virtual worlds links them to U.S. military interest in simulation as a means of training soldiers (Herz 1997:197–213; Poole 2000:219–20; Stone 1995:27). For instance, soon after the release of Battlezone—as noted in chapter 2, the first video game using first-person perspective—"a group of retired Army generals contacted Atari. The officers wanted to license a more realistic version of the game to be used for training soldiers" (Kent 2001:153–54). "Military Battlezone" was created as a result; this was probably the first use of a video game for military purposes, a phenomenon that continues unabated. In addition, some virtual worlds that coexisted with Second Life during the time of my fieldwork, like The Sims Online, framed themselves as simulations to some degree; a "culture of simulation" was widespread (Turkle 1995:19; see also Poster 1999:47; Schwartz

1996). Many popular interpretations of virtual worlds portrayed them as simulations, often dystopic ones (as in the *Matrix* movies).

Despite these linkages, the ethnographic materials presented in this book indicate that is it misleading to characterize virtual worlds as simulations: "they don't simulate anything. They approximate aspects of reality—enough for the purposes of immersion—but that's all" (Bartle 2004:474). Objects, actions, and ideas in virtual worlds might appear to refer back to the actual world—water in an ocean, the smile on an avatar's face, a friend listed in one's inventory. Yet experientially these things as signs referred to signifieds internal to the virtual world. Thus, while "it might appear that the terms 'simulation' and 'virtual reality' are equivalent, each suggesting a sign system in which cultural objects are divorced from their references" (Poster 1999:45), they are distinct. It is likely, for instance, that "Second Earth" platforms combining a virtual world like Second Life and a simulation like Google Earth will appear, but such platforms would simply extend the referential relationships already evident in things like gravity, water, and green grass in Second Life. Even if such a place looked more like the actual world, if it was a place of human sociality it would be a virtual world, not a simulation. In virtual worlds, cultural objects are not divorced from their referents, because both object and referent are within the virtual world. Both are constituted and kept distinct from the actual through techne, whereas simulation typically implies an nostalgic attempt to replicate the actual and close that gap, as Jean Baudrillard argued in *Simulacra and Simulation* (Baudrillard 1994). Key to this distinction is that virtual worlds are those from which humans can log off; in contrast, the actual is that from which they cannot. Humans can fall asleep, lose consciousness, hallucinate, even die, but none of these things are equivalent to the dialectic of logging on and logging off that is the originary boundary-marker between virtual and actual. Philip K. Dick, a key figure in cyberpunk literature, once recalled how a college student asked him to define reality: "I thought about it and finally said, 'Reality is that which, when you stop believing in it, doesn't go away'" (Dick 1985:3). By that definition virtual worlds are real, an assessment I share with many Second Life residents.

While Second Life was not a simulation, per se, there were examples of simulation within it. For instance, early in my fieldwork a group of university researchers created a virtual psychiatric ward that allowed residents to simulate the experience of having schizophrenia (see Au 2004c). Some objects created by residents tried to simulate aspects of the actual world, from boats that would sail on the Second Life "wind," to books with pages that made a sound when turned. Residents sometimes pondered in what ways Second Life culture drew upon notions of simulation, as in the following conversation:

> KARY: Perhaps the formation of communities in SL is limited by our acclimation to notions of RL, much like how folks in SL add sinks and bathrooms to their houses, even though such things are perfectly useless.
> RIMA: And roofs, etc., creating a model of a perfect rl?
> MARKY: I never understood the homes in sl with kitchens.
> JEEN: I remember I saw a laundromat once, and it made my day!
> RIMA: Almost as if SL is a simulation of RL rather than its own true world.

I recall once visiting the home of Tandy, an acquaintance who was an accomplished builder in Second Life. The two of us walked through the home, with its immaculately "baked" textures simulating light and shadow, but what drew my attention was a circular mirror in the hallway. It showed a reflection of the room behind us, but with without us present. As I walked past the mirror its reflection changed in a jerky manner. I asked Tandy about the mirror and he reminded me that "there is no way to currently make a mirror in Second Life." Opening the closet behind the mirror, he showed me an elaborate device: a ball with only one side facing out into the hall, scripted to rotate as an avatar walked near so that the "mirror's" reflection would appear to change. I was impressed by Tandy's creativity, but leaving his house, wondered about the implications of a world without reflections. Using the "camera" function to separate one's screen view from the exact location of one's avatar, it was always possible to look back on oneself, but a true reflection was not possible. I knew that some day, an update to the Second Life platform would probably make mirrors possible. In the meantime, I was struck by a culture that did not prioritize simulating or "mirroring" reality, but assumed human creativity produced its own realities.

FICTION AND DESIGN.

The Myst series of virtual worlds were predicated on the idea that writing can create a new reality, a metaphor for the transformative power of technology pointed out by Walter Ong at the opening of this chapter. The metaphor also highlights how humans can now use computer programs to create worlds that are both "virtual" and "real." This represents yet another way in which ethnography has anticipated the emergence of virtual worlds, since "anthropological writings are . . . fictions, in the sense that they are 'something made,' 'something fashioned'—the original meaning of *fictio*—not that they are false, unfactual, or merely 'as if' thought experiments" (Geertz 1973b:15). To be fashioned in this sense is to be the product of techne. Such artifice is not always intentional, despite the ideology of creationist capitalism, which sees conscious creation as producing value. Languages are human inventions, but no one person or group of people invented English in a deliberate sense, though neologisms and attempts at language planning exist. Similarly the cultures of virtual worlds are the product of techne—fictions, just like the ethnographic attempt to describe them—but they are not solely or even primarily the result of conscious intention.

This distinction between conscious intention and emergent crafting is important because the concept of "design" continues to distort understandings of culture in virtual worlds. Since most virtual worlds are the property of companies, there has been great interest in questions of design (e.g., Bartle 2004; Koster 2004; Salen and Zimmerman 2004). This interest in design is completely legitimate but often pushes discussions in prescriptive rather than descriptive directions; the goal of foreseeing an unknowable future leads to misunderstandings of the present. Design presumes intentionality and is linked to Christian-inflected ideologies of creationist capitalism, as exemplified by the phrase "intelligent *design*," often used in popular culture to signify an opposition to evolutionary theory. "Design" is a structuralist concept presuming a distinction between creation and implementation; it recalls de Saussure's distinction between grammar and speech, *langue* and *parole*, a distinction that founds structuralism itself (de Saussure 1959). Only within this conceptual horizon does the idea of "emergent design" hold any fascination; the term's analytical purchase inheres in its implicit opposition to a notion of intentional design.

By setting aside the notion of design in favor of fiction, it is possible to circumvent the question of emergence versus intention; the more consequential issue is how human crafting creates social worlds that are both fictional and real. It appears that virtual world design is expanding in three ways: self-contained "bubble worlds" for children, businesses, or specific topics; general platforms that allow persons to create their own virtual worlds (examples that emerged during the time of my research were Multiverse, Croquet, and VastPark, harking back to the GURPS platform from the mid-1980s [see chapter 2]); and the further growth and segmentation of large-scale virtual worlds like Second Life. What makes these virtual worlds real is that relationships, romance, economic transactions, and community take place within them—in short, that they are places of human culture. It is this social reality that links virtual and actual. On the one hand, the virtual is actual: "the virtual is not completely unreal or detached from materiality. . . . it still has a fully physical and tangible basis: computer chips are as material as are recorder pickups" (Fornäs et al. 2002:29–30).[1] On the other hand, the actual is virtual: "the real world consists of much more than what can be seen or sensed. . . . [S]ymbolically expressed and intersubjectively shared meanings belong to human reality even though they cannot be measured in length or weight" (Fornäs et al. 2002:29–30).

Such linkages from the virtual back to the actual sometimes manifested themselves to residents in terms of "blurring" or "bleed-through." During my research these terms were almost never used to refer to ways that the actual world manifested itself in Second Life; residents did not use these terms to refer to the fact that Second Life had a sun and water, or that most Second Life residents used humanoid avatars. Instead, these terms were used with regard to how Second Life manifested itself in the actual world. One resident recalled spending several minutes looking for a favorite shirt—rifling through his dresser drawers, even checking the washing machine—before remembering that the shirt he had in mind was located only in Second Life. Another noted how "once in a while I try to right-click things in the real world, expecting a user interface to pop up." Other residents would accidentally sign the name of their avatar to an actual-world check, or drive past a home and wonder "how many prims did it take to build that?" Linda, who participated in Second Life as a child, recalled how:

> I have a friend, Brenda, who I have known in rl for many years, and who is my cousin in Second Life, a kid like me. She came by my [actual-world] house the other night. There was a slightly different dynamic, given that we have both been kids in Second Life. Probably as a result, we ended up having a moment of playing a bit of "Miss Mary Mack" in a real life space. Which was one of those bleed-through moments. Now, there's nothing wrong with two grown women playing a kids' clapping game. It's not that I'm gonna start thinking of myself as a preschooler in real life, but it's interesting to note that dynamic.

THE MASSIVELY MULTIPLE.

Prior to the time of my fieldwork, notions of the "massively multiple" were commonly used to conceptualize virtual worlds. Terms like massively multiple online role-playing game (MMORPG), massively multiple online game (MMOG), and massively multiple online world (MMOW) were first coined to distinguish video games that one played alone (or in a two-to-four player configuration) from online worlds in which hundreds, thousands, or millions of residents played online at the same time.

I find the notion of "massively multiple" of limited use, because it implies that virtual worlds are composed of masses of individuals: it frames the social in terms of aggregate individualism, rather than in terms of intersubjective cultural logics that cannot be reduced to personal thoughts and feelings (just as no language exists entirely in the head of any particular speaker). However, one benefit of the concept is that it may provide another conceptual framework with which to approach the notion of "network" that has been developed with the goal of theorizing current conditions of globalization (e.g., Castells 2000; Riles 2000; Strathern 1996; Latour 2005). The notion of social networking has become commonly used to describe websites like MySpace, Facebook, and Friendster, and virtual worlds like Second Life have sometimes been described as three-dimensional social networking websites. What this interpretation misses is how virtual worlds are places, not networks: the transition from the "2D web" to the "3D web" heralded during the period of my fieldwork was really an addition of online places to online networks. Graphical capabilities were salient but not fundamental to this transition, which was not really a transition at all but the layering of new online possibilities to preexisting ones. One connects relationships "through" networks, but lives relationships "in" places. In my research in Indonesia I found the archipelago concept to be a useful metaphor for conceptualizing complex topographies that appeared network-like but were really places. It may prove helpful to conceptualize Second Life and other online worlds as virtual archipelagos, recalling how Second Life itself appears as an archipelago of islands and continents on a blue sea.

This may also provide new ways to conceptualize resistance to forces of domination. Linden Lab's official slogan was the highly individualizing "Your World, Your Imagination," but most residents saw the company as maintaining a firm grip over Second Life; the slogan represented an invocation of creationist capitalism more than a statement of ownership. Residents often resisted this individualizing notion of belonging through various forms of community building and coalition, recalling how techne "obliges us to think . . . another space for democracy" (Derrida 1994:169). Could the "massively multiple" represent an online analogue to the concept of "the multitude" posited as a source of resistance to contemporary capitalism (Hardt and Negri 2001)? One danger is that oftentimes "the analytic resources developed by progressives have insisted on the necessary domination of technics and recalled us to an imagined organic body to integrate our resistance" (Haraway 1991:154). How might we develop a politics not just "for" virtual worlds, but "of" virtual worlds: a politics that sees virtual worlds as one site for social struggle and justice?

Toward an Anthropology of Virtual Worlds.

Throughout this book I have referred to the "actual world" rather than "actual worlds." However, anthropological inquiry has long demonstrated that there are many forms of human being—many ways to live a human life. In a sense there are many actual worlds, and now many virtual worlds as well. In this book I have examined one such virtual world for what it can teach us about what it means to be virtually human. I have worked to provide an extended portrait of Second Life as it existed during my fieldwork, and at the same time a series of analyses and hypotheses with regard to virtual worlds more generally. In its double goal of ethnographic detail and theoretical framework, this book stands squarely within the traditions of anthropological inquiry. It is in the effort to bring together everyday detail and broad pattern that anthropology has a special contribution to make to the study of virtual worlds. If anthropology has typically worked in service of knowledge, but in virtual worlds we find an ascendancy of techne over episteme, then could an anthropology of virtual worlds produce a technology, rather than an epistemology, of the human itself?

Within the static pages of a book there is no way I can do justice to my adventures within Second Life, or the experiences of the residents who so generously shared their activities and thoughts with me. A book cannot capture the beauty and joy of a virtual world, nor its anger and heartbreak. But that is not what a book is for. What I hope *Coming of Age in Second Life* can do is instill a sense of *wonder* regarding virtual worlds. "Wonder" is a stance toward experience quite different from that of knowledge, closer in spirit to the artfulness of techne. In the Western tradition, wonder is associated with the Renaissance discovery of the "New World" (and its "Indian" inhabitants) that played an important role in the history of anthropology. As Foucault argued, conceptions of knowledge are deeply linked to forms of social control (Foucault 1978), but "wonder stands for all that cannot be understood, that can scarcely be believed. It calls attention to the problem of credibility and at the same time insists upon the undeniability, the exigency of experience" (Greenblatt 1992:20, cited in Weschler 1995:77). I hope to have left the reader with a sense of wonder at the emergence of our New Worlds, a sense of wonder at how they draw upon our oldest traditions while presenting new possibilities. As Vernor Vinge noted at the dawn of cybersociality, an important reason many people participate in virtual worlds is that it is "simply a

hell of a lot of fun to live in a world as malleable as the human imagination"
(Vinge 2001 [1981]:272). Virtual worlds can be sites of griefing and inequality, but they can also produce new ways of living, including a kind of empa-
thy that recalls the ethnographic project itself: as one resident put it, "In SL,
you can get some marginal experience of what it's like to be fat, or black, or
female. It can lead to a better understanding of other people."

Through culture, humans are always already virtual; ethnography has
always been a kind of virtual investigation of the human, and can therefore play an important role in understanding cybersociality.[2] While, as
Arturo Escobar has observed, some scholars of cybersociality claim that the
"human-centred foundation of anthropological discourse ... must be displaced" (Escobar 1994:61), I argue it is imperative to focus more, not less,
attention on the place of the human. Understanding virtual worlds is important because "we increasingly live in a world in which opting out of technological systems is more and more difficult and yet participation within those
systems pushes us to accept structures we might oppose" (Taylor 2006a:135).
This is an important point for interdisciplinary collaboration between the
social sciences, the humanities, and the arts. For instance, the science fiction
author Philip K. Dick noted that "the two basic topics which fascinate me are
'What is reality?' and 'What constitutes the authentic human being?'" (Dick
1985:2). Dick saw virtual worlds as linking these questions: "my two topics
are really one topic; they unite at this point" (Dick 1985:6).

An anthropology of virtual worlds can be understood as a study of
techne, even an exercise in techne: "what 'missing' realities are already contained within the way people think about virtual reality? We can use ethnographic methods to find out. But the result will be, so to speak, a description
that is *inside* virtual reality rather than outside it" (Strathern 2002:304). One
useful definition of "virtual" is "a philosophical term meaning 'not actually, but as if'" (Heim 1998:220). The ethnography of virtual worlds is, in a
sense, the ethnography of the "as if," a state of being in which "the world of
the 'unreal' is just as important as the world of the so-called real or actual"
(Vaihinger 1924:11).

Since I began this book with a quotation from Bronislaw Malinowski—
in line with my wish to take ethnography seriously as a powerful tool for
investigating virtual worlds—it is only proper that I end with Malinowski's
insistence upon "the final goal, of which an Ethnographer should never lose
sight. This goal is, briefly, to grasp the native's point of view, his relation to
life, to realize *his* vision of *his* world" (1922:25). In realizing the vision of
virtual worlds, ethnography holds the promise of better understanding how
it is that we, all of us, online and offline, are virtually human.

Terms marked with an asterisk (*) are acronyms or contractions of words or phrases. These terms are used most often when chatting; most are found in virtual worlds in addition to Second Life, and some date back to the 1980s or even earlier.

actual world: a place of human culture not realized by computer programs through the Internet.

*afk: away from keyboard.

*alt: alternative (avatar).

avatar: a graphical representation of a virtual world resident.

*av: See avatar.

*avie: See avatar.

*brb: be right back.

camping: spending time on a parcel of land, often afk, to earn money.

chat: text typed in a virtual world that can be read by those in the vicinity of one's avatar.

*cu: see you.

cyberworld: See virtual world.

dwell: See traffic.

emoticon: typographic characters used to represent emotion, like :) for a smiling face (turned on its side).

*fl: first life.

grid: the Second Life virtual world (or the platform that undergirds Second Life).

griefing: behavior in a virtual world intended to disrupt the experience of others.

*im: See instant message.

*imho: in my humble opinion.

instant message: typed text that can be read only by the resident or residents to whom it is addressed, and that is not limited by the proximity of the addressee's avatar.

inworld: See online.

*irl: in real life.

lag: an experienced slowdown in time inside a virtual world.

lindens: (1) Second Life's inworld currency. (2) as "the lindens," Linden Lab staff.

*lmao: laughing my ass off.

*lol: laugh out loud.

MMOG: massively multiple online game.

MMORPG: massively multiple online role-playing game.

MMORT: massively multiple online real-time strategy.

MMOW (massively multiple online world): See virtual world.

MOO: MUD Object Oriented.

MUCK: multi-user chat kingdom.

MUD (multi-user domain/dimension/dungeon): See virtual world.

MUG: multi-user game.

MUSH: multi-user shared habitat.

newbie: someone relatively new to a virtual world.

noob: See newbie.

*np: no problem.

*prim: See primitive.

primary: one's actual-world self; more rarely, one's default avatar.

primitive: the basic building blocks of the Second Life world, used to build objects.

profile: basic information about a resident displayed in a separate window.

rez, to: to appear on a resident's screen, because the information has downloaded over the Internet.

*rofl: rolling on the floor (laughing).

*rl: real life.

*sl: Second Life.

Second Life: a virtual world, owned by the company Linden Lab.

*sim: See simulator.

simulator: a region of land in Second Life, contained on server in the actual world.

teleport: to move instantaneously from one location to another within Second Life.

tier: the amount of land a resident can own in Second Life.

*ToS: Terms of Service.

*tp: See teleport.

traffic: a measure of the amount of time avatars are present on a piece of property. Before January 12, 2005, with the release of version 1.5.13, traffic was known as "dwell."

*ty: thank you.

*tyvm: thank you very much.

virtual world: a place of human culture realized by a computer program through the Internet.

*wb: welcome back.

*yw: you're welcome.

CHAPTER 1.
THE SUBJECT AND SCOPE OF THIS INQUIRY.

1. Malinowski 1922:4. While many anthropologists have played an important role in the discipline's history, I will take Malinowski as exemplifying classical anthropology (see Bunzl 2004:438).

2. Following the style guide of the American Anthropological Association and the practice of most anthropologists, citations appear at the end of sentences in parentheses, with the author and year of publication (and after a colon, the page number, if a specific page is cited). Malinowski has been rightly critiqued for his theoretical shortcomings and failure to take an explicit stance against colonialism. His functionalist theory of culture was quickly discredited for its inability to address issues of history and power, and his views on colonialism, while shifting over time, tended to frame anthropology as a tool for more humane colonial rule rather than undermining colonialism itself (see Kuper 1996; Malinowski 1945).

3. In the game studies literature, video game titles are often italicized. For ease of reading I do not italicize "Second Life," and also because I approach Second Life as a culture (I thus see it in some ways as closer to "Indonesia" than "*Space Invaders*").

4. The question of the exact number of Second Life residents was difficult to ascertain during my fieldwork and a source of controversy. This was because residents could have more than one account (these were known as "alts"; see chapter 5) and because residents could stop participating in Second Life without canceling their account. Since anthropologists often study communities with only a few hundred members and from such studies learn things of broad importance and validity, the equation of significance with population size is spurious. It is undeniable that Second Life's population grew rapidly during my fieldwork. Second Life passed 100,000 registered accounts in December 2005, one million registered accounts in October 2006, three million registered accounts in January 2007, and ten million registered accounts in October 2007. A more accurate metric of participation is concurrency, that is, how many persons are inworld at once. At one point or another, this number exceeded 8,000 in June 2006, 13,000 in October 2006, 25,000 in January 2007, and 50,000 in July 2007. It is for this reason that I speak of "tens of thousands" of residents. See, inter alia, Nino 2006. One study conducted in May 2007 found that 1.3 million persons had logged into their account during the month of March 2007, so concurrency may significantly underestimate the number of active residents (James 2007).

5. During the time of my fieldwork, last names had to be picked from a limited list. As discussed later, the only exception to this methodological approach is that I analyze some blogs, websites, and other texts produced by Second Life residents.

6. I include a few citations and events that took place between the end of my formal fieldwork in January 2007 and the submission of the final manuscript in November 2007.

7. See, for instance, Boellstorff 2002; Brenner 2001; Gupta and Ferguson 1997.

8. This method has been used effectively by other researchers (e.g., Castronova 2005:29–44). For introductions to Second Life, see the "Unofficial Complete Fool's Guide to Second Life" (http://www.sldrama.com/index.php?page=2, accessed September 29, 2006); Guest 2007; Rymaszewski et al. 2007; and B. White 2007.

9. The Second Life platform began as a program for the Microsoft Windows operating system; during the time of my fieldwork, versions for the Apple and Linux operating systems were added. Regardless of the operating system used, the interface allowed for "windows" with information (inventory, instant messages, maps, and so on) to float over the main screen.

10. To explain specialized terms and acronyms, ethnographies of virtual worlds have from the beginning often used a glossary (e.g., Rosenberg 1992; Taylor 2006a), and I provide one at the end of this book as well.

11. I have omitted Castronova's clause "represented graphically in three dimensions" because, as discussed in chapter 2, under the definition of virtual world I use, there can exist textual virtual worlds that have no graphical component. Linden Lab refers to Second Life as a "multi-user environment, including software and websites" (Terms of Service, June 28, 2006).

12. My thanks to Maria Bezaitis for helping me develop this point.

13. See Castronova 2005:9–11 for another discussion of terminology with regard to virtual worlds. Ryan's notion of "possible world" includes everything from dreams to novels; while suggestive, it is too expansive for my purposes here.

14. Oxford English Dictionary, http://dictionary.oed.com/cgi/entry/50278111?single=1&query_type=word&queryword=virtual&first=1&max_to_show=10, accessed July 3, 2006.

15. During the time of my fieldwork, virtual worlds had little to do with artificial life, artificial intelligence, or artificial worlds. "Artificial life" refers to computer programs that self-replicate and often "evolve" (Hayles 1996a; Helmrich 1998), while "artificial intelligence" refers to attempts to create computer programs that can think (Mazlish 1993). Second Life residents have created "artificial life" objects that self-replicate, including "bots" or automated avatars, and also "artificial intelligence" mock-ups of thinking machines, but both are distinct from virtual worlds themselves. At the time of my research, virtual worlds were distinct from artificial worlds, based upon notions of artificial life, in which programs replicate and "evolve" within a computational environment (Helmrich 2004; see also Galison 1996), though some Second Life residents did create artificial life environments inside Second Life.

16. There is some debate as to the term's origin, but it appears to have been coined in the early 1980s by Jaron Lanier. See Heim 1995, and also http://en.wikipedia.org/

wiki/Jaron_Lanier#_note-0, accessed August 22, 2006. Two of many examples of fiction that conflate virtual reality and virtual worlds are Cadigan 1998 and Williams 1996.

17. "First Life" is the term used by Linden Lab and is part of the Second Life interface.

18. Oxford English Dictionary, http://dictionary.oed.com/cgi/entry/50002233? query_type=word&queryword=actual&first=1&max_to_show=10&sort_type=alpha &search_id=eLA4-KqbBCd-9831&result_place=2, accessed September 26, 2006.

19. In the introduction to *Argonauts of the Western Pacific*, Malinowski commented that anthropology was in a "sadly *ludicrous*, not to say tragic, position" because "native" cultures were ostensibly disappearing (Malinowski 1922:xv, emphasis added).

20. Michael Rosenberg, who probably conducted the first ethnography of a virtual world (Bartle 2004:491), observed that the virtual world he studied was "more of a pastime than a game in the usual sense" (Rosenberg 1992).

21. One reason virtual worlds are sometimes confused with games is that from their beginnings they have had games inside them. For instance, participants in text-only virtual worlds from the early 1990s used keyboard characters to play games like Scrabble, backgammon, reversi, Monopoly, chess, and Go (Curtis 1992; Rosenberg 1992).

22. Like much of the philosophically inflected work on games and play, *Homo Ludens* takes a prescriptive rather than descriptive approach to defining its object of study. It is not difficult to find play that is not voluntary: children, for instance, are compelled to play all the time, and adults often find an ideology of "leisure time" that pushes them to play. Compare with Schechner 1988; Turner 1982.

23. It is also crucial to distinguish virtual worlds from electronic mass media, though they often have mass media associated with them (blogs, virtual newspapers, and the like). Virtual worlds do not mediate between different sites, but are sites for social relations in their own right: "virtual worlds are not a medium. Well, let's put it this way: If they are, so is the world. . . . You can play in a virtual world without communicating with any of the other players" (Bartle 2004:475). Second Life is not a form of mass media, because it does not mediate two places; it is a place in its own right, which as Heidegger notes, foregrounds issues of power: "suppose now that technology were no mere means, how would it stand with the will to master it?" (Heidegger 1977:5).

24. The correct transcription for this originally Greek term is *technē*, but for purposes of readability I render it as "techne."

25. In an early study of virtual worlds, Pavel Curtis noted that "Social behavior on MUDs is in some ways a direct mirror of behavior in real life, with mechanisms being drawn nearly unchanged from real-life, and in some ways very new and different, taking root in the new opportunities that MUDs provide over real life" (Curtis 1992:125).

26. Claims that anthropological researchers have lost their objectivity and "gone native" have been common since the early days of the discipline and took on new valences as more and more anthropologists started studying communities to which they "belonged" in some sense (Abu-Lughod 1991).

27. See, for instance, Boyd 2006a; Harrison 2007; Jenkins 2007; Reuters 2007; Reynolds 2006; Semuels 2007; Shirky 2007; Walsh 2007; http://www.ihatesecondlife

.blogspot.com, accessed December 24, 2006; http://www.getafirstlife.com, accessed January 24, 2007.

28. See also Nguyen and Alexander 1996.

29. I first encountered this quote on the blog of Prokofy Neva, http://secondthoughts .typepad.com.

30. See, for instance, Malinowski 1935:324–30, 452–82.

CHAPTER 2.
HISTORY.

1. See http://en.wikipedia.org/wiki/Alan_Kay, accessed January 3, 2007.

2. My thanks to Geremie R. Barmé for introducing me to this text.

3. The worldwide spread of cellphones indicates how the cybersocialities created by telephone technology are by no means disappearing (Ito, Okabe, and Matsuda 2005; Rafael 2003).

4. Stephenson originally intended *Snow Crash* to have a computer-generated component, providing for the possibility of multiple endings (Stephenson 1993:470). Many of those associated with Linden Lab draw explicitly upon Stephenson (e.g., Ondrejka 2004a:2–3).

5. Andy Wachowski and Larry Wachowski (writers and directors), *The Matrix*. USA, Warner Bothers, 1999; Andrew Niccol (writer) and Peter Weir (director), *The Truman Show*. USA, Paramount Pictures, 1998. There are too many films involving virtual worlds to enumerate in detail; other examples include *Ghost in the Shell* (Kazunori Itô and Masamune Shirow, writers, Mamoru Oshii, director, Bandai Visual Co. Ltd., Japan, 1995), *Lawnmower Man* (Brett Leonard, director, USA, New Line, 1992), and *The Village* (M. Night Shyamalan, writer and director, USA, Touchstone, 2004).

6. See http://en.wikipedia.org/wiki/Cosmic_Osmo, accessed November 4, 2007.

7. See Herman 2001:6; Herz 1997:5; Kent 2001: 18–22; http://en.wikipedia.org/wiki/ History_of_computer_and_video_games#References, accessed July 9, 2006. The first patent for a video game was filed by Ralph Baer in 1968 (Herman 2001:7).

8. http://en.wikipedia.org/wiki/Doom, accessed July 19, 2006.

9. See http://en.wikipedia.org/wiki/First-person_shooter#History, accessed May 8, 2007; http://www.digibarn.com/history/04-VCF7-MazeWar/index.html, accessed March 12, 2007.

10. Another important example is Sonic the Hedgehog, first released in 1991 (Herman 2001:161). A "game engine" is "the core software component of a computer or video game or other interactive application with real-time graphics" http://en.wikipedia.org/ wiki/Game_engine, accessed July 19, 2006.

11. See http://en.wikipedia.org/wiki/Hunt_the_wumpus, accessed August 20, 2006.

12. See http://members.chello.at/theodor.lauppert/games/hamurabi.htm, accessed August 20, 2006. The game is spelled "Hamurabi" (with only one "m") so that it could fit the eight-character limit for file names that existed at the time.

13. See http://en.wikipedia.org/wiki/Zork, accessed July 19, 2006. As noted earlier, I played Adventure around 1982, when I would have been about thirteen years old.

14. See http://en.wikipedia.org/wiki/Colossal_Cave_Adventure#History, accessed December 27, 2005, and http://www.rickadams.org/adventure/a_history.html, accessed December 27, 2005, for more information.

15. See http://www.classicgaming.com/museum/intellivision, accessed December 27, 2005. *Utopia* was designed and programmed by Don Daglow (http://en.wikipedia .org/wiki/Utopia_(video_game), accessed December 27, 2005).

16. See Doyle 2003 and http://en.wikipedia.org/wiki/SimCity, accessed July 9, 2006; http://en.wikipedia.org/wiki/SimEarth#Play_options, accessed December 27, 2005; http://en.wikipedia.org/wiki/Simlife, accessed May 17, 2007; http://en.wikipedia.org/ wiki/SimFarm, accessed July 9, 2006; and http://en.wikipedia.org/wiki/SimAnt, accessed July 9, 2006. These were all designed to some degree by Will Wright and produced by the company Maxis (by Electronic Arts after it acquired Maxis in 1997).

17. Bartle notes that "Contrary to what many people assume, [the term "dungeon"] has nothing to do with the role-playing game Dungeons & Dragons and does not mean that the game world had a dungeon setting. Instead, it is due to the fact that the version of ZORK Roy played was a Fortran port called DUNGEN. Roy wanted something that was like a multi-user DUNGE(o)N, and the acronym MUD immediately presented itself" (Bartle 2004:5).

18. Some of the best-known MUDs (or classes of MUDs) include AberMUD, released in 1987 and the first MUD to run on UNIX systems (Bartle 2004:8; Koster 2003:450; Shah and Romine 1995:7), Club Connect (Nakamura 2002), DikuMUD (Shah and Romine 1995), ElseMOO (Cherny 1999), Legends of Terris, KobraMUD, MicroMUSE (A. Smith 1999), TrekMUSE (Turkle 1997), WaterMOO (Sundén 2003), and WolfMOO (Rosenberg 1992).

19. Other early virtual worlds with a graphical component include Meridian 59 (which first appeared in 1996), Virtual Places, and WorldsAway. For a discussion of Meridian 59, see Schubert 2003. For discussions of Virtual Places, see Damer 1998:237–98, and also http://en.wikipedia.org/wiki/Virtual_places. For discussions of WorldsAway, see Damer 1998:161–88; Kollock and Smith 1999:8.

20. It was based upon the single-computer virtual world The Sims (first published in 2000), which sold more than 6.3 million copies. See http://en.wikipedia.org/wiki/ The_Sims, accessed July 9, 2006; http://en.wikipedia.org/wiki/The_Sims#The_Sims_ Online, accessed July 9, 2006.

21. See http://history.secondserver.net/index.php/Main_Page, accessed October 5, 2006.

22. My additional debts to research outside this domain is evident throughout this book, as a perusal of its bibliography indicates.

23. For this transgression Prometheus was chained to a rock by Zeus—where every day an eagle would eat out his liver, only to have it grow back again—until he was freed by Hercules.

24. For clarity, I am using "techne" as an equivalent for what Stiegler terms "tekhne" or "technics."

CHAPTER 3.
METHOD.

1. See Holmes 1987:7; Orans 1996:19.

2. Mid-twentieth-century structuralists, for instance. See Kurzweil 1980; Lévi-Strauss 1963.

3. My "first land" and the first Ethnographia was built in the Kane sim; in February 2005 I moved to the Dowden sim, where I built four different versions of Ethnographia, partially because I learned how to make interior spaces work better for interviews and discussions, but primarily because I enjoyed building.

4. Toward the end of my fieldwork, Linden Lab began distinguishing "the grid" from "the world," "the grid" referring to the platform that could be used, in theory, to create virtual worlds other than Second Life.

5. One aspect of Second Life "beyond the platform" that I do not draw upon in this book are "meetups" residents would occasionally hold in the actual world. Such meetups were rare and only a tiny fraction of Second Life residents ever attended them. The only exception to this was that I attended the 2nd "Second Life Community Convention" in San Francisco in August 2006 (an event sponsored by Linden Lab, composed primarily of expert panels discussing various aspects of Second Life).

6. I did not pay residents for their involvement in interviews or focus groups, and was never asked for such compensation.

7. In a sense, leaving an actual-world fieldsite is like going offline, but since one can always log back into a virtual world, one never has to take permanent leave of one's fieldsite. I found that in order to write this book I had to drastically reduce my presence in Second Life for several months, which frustrated many of my fellow residents.

8. This has become a fairly standard procedure in ethnographic work on virtual worlds; see, for instance, Campbell 2004:48; Kendall 2002:241.

CHAPTER 4.
PLACE AND TIME.

1. For the purposes of my analysis I treat "place" and "space" as synonyms, although some geographers and others create analytical typologies that distinguish them.

2. As virtual worlds have become more graphical they have drawn more extensively from video games: the term "video" (from Latin *videre*, "to see") signals the importance of vision in their constitution. Only some virtual worlds aimed at children remained two-dimensional, perhaps because of their similarity to cartoons.

3. At this point what Crary termed "fabricated visual 'spaces'" (1990:1) were best-known through video games. There have been many conventions for representing place in video games, from "one screen, contained, with wraparound" formats used in video games like Asteroids (where a object disappearing off one side of the screen reappears on the other side), to various forms of "scrolling" (one of the first examples of which

was the video game Defender) where the screen moves from side to side or even in four directions, to a truly "interactive three-dimensional environment" (Wolf 2001:65). At the time of my research into Second Life there were some popular two-dimensional graphical virtual worlds, but three-dimensional environments were already the norm. See Wolf 2001 for a detailed typology, and also Poole 2000.

4. Since virtual worlds always exist in relation to the actual world, they can be seen as examples of what Foucault termed a "heterotopia," a place seen as set apart from everyday life and so "a sort of place that lies outside all places" (Foucault 1997b:352). In the relation between utopian ideals and a heterotopia "I see myself where I am not, in an unreal space . . . a sort of shadow . . . allowing me to look at myself where I do not exist" (ibid.).

5. The first such "snow sims" were added on July 19, 2004.

6. See Neva 2006b. Islands had become popular for a range of reasons, including the fact that guidelines concerning landscape were easier to enforce (residents of islands typically rented parcels from a single landlord or group of managers, who could ban avatars if they wished).

7. See Ondrejka 2004c:5. PG sims were supposed to be free of anything inappropriate for a PG movie (particularly in terms of sexual context and violence), while "anything goes" was the rule for an M sim. While this was a vague distinction and not actively enforced, land in M sims was worth more than land in PG sims. The absence of "G" sims reflected the larger absence of children from Second Life, save the segregated "Teen Grid."

8. See Ondrejka 2004d and http://history.secondserver.net/index.php/Telehub, accessed October 17, 2006.

9. A handful of telehubs were created in the air. It was possible (and remained possible throughout the period of my fieldwork) to have someone "offer a teleport," which would teleport the invited person directly to a specific location.

10. Mainland telehubs were renamed "infohubs" and were to be used as information kiosks, but were not popular.

11. As of January 12, 2005, with the release of version 1.5.1 of the Second Life program, dwell was renamed "traffic," but the term "dwell" was still used quite often. The system of awarding financial incentives to property owners based on dwell/traffic was phased out entirely as of June 13, 2006.

12. Occasionally residents whose properties were partially or wholly on a sea or other waterway would build a structure under the water for the same reason, covering the outside of the structure to camouflage it. During the time of my fieldwork it was not possible to build underground.

13. An update during the final phases of writing this book (1.16) allowed for "sculpted" prims that could take a range of shapes determined by the textures applied to them. Residents also found ways to create a limited range of prims much larger than the official limit of ten meters on a side.

14. Such internal programming languages have been available in some virtual worlds since the early 1990s; LambdaMOO, for instance, had such an "embedded programming language" (Curtis 1992:122).

15. To count toward the prim allocation of a particular parcel, such additional land, sometimes called "prim land," had to be located in the same sim.

16. Basic clothing like shirts and pants were not created from prims, but were a kind of texture applied to the body of an avatar.

17. Strathern and Pottage are obviously also drawing upon traditions of Marxist thought in this analysis. For readers without a background in social theory, it bears emphasizing that social scientists find Marx's analysis of capitalism useful without thereby endorsing communism, just as psychologists and others can draw upon Freud's thought without accepting his quite dated understanding of the human psyche.

18. Gwyneth Llewelyn, personal communication, April 20, 2007.

19. To reduce lag, some aspects of the Second Life virtual world (for instance, the location of the sun and moon) were "client side." The ability of prims to be "flexible," a feature added to Second Life in May 2006 and used in everything from skirts to flags, was also client-side: a flexible-prim flag waved in the breeze slightly differently for each resident.

20. Another form of lag, "client-side" lag, was caused by the actual-world personal computer a resident used to log into Second Life: for instance, an inferior graphics card or slow processor could cause lag. Still other sources of lag existed (for instance, asset server responsiveness). Most Second Life residents did not have high levels of expertise in computer technology, and so these various forms of lag were usually experienced as the same phenomenon.

21. Sometimes events like town hall meetings would be held at the intersection of four sims, or would have "repeater" events where the text or audio from the event would be streamed to another location, but this was due to the limit of about forty avatars on any one sim during most of the period of my fieldwork, not to issues of time.

22. Celia Pearce, personal communication. By the time I completed the final version of this book (November 2007), the presence of Europeans was quite pronounced; by July 2007 Americans already constituted only 29 percent of resident accounts (Au 2007e). In some cases, persons living outside the United States (where all servers for Second Life were initially located) might experience lag due to their being more distant from the servers. However, I did not encounter this form of lag discussed with any frequency.

23. During the time of my fieldwork, some residents developed ways to disable this feature (first through the "God mode" third-party software, and then directly via the "client" menu).

24. "Brb" was also sometimes used when residents planned on logging out of the Second Life program and then relogging on within a few minutes.

25. Exceptions to this are that another resident could have cut-and-pasted the chat that took place while Lucy was afk and given it to her in the form of a note card, or if the conversation took place on land owned by Lucy or a group to which Lucy belonged, she could have placed an object on the land with a script that would have recorded the chat even while she was logged off.

26. As noted in chapter 8, even after such incentives were discontinued, camping could be used to increase a property's dwell score and thus how high up it appeared on the "find" window.

27. Residents often sat on an object before going afk so that their avatar would be less vulnerable to being pushed in this manner.

28. Second Life acquired broad voice capabilities in August 2007. I hope to address this in a future publication.

29. See chapter 1 for a discussion of the distinction between "virtual reality" and "virtual world."

CHAPTER 5.
PERSONHOOD.

1. For an example of resident discussions about selfhood, autonomy, and governance, see the "Flack Attack" collective's "Issue #1: Flack Attack on Autonomy," www .flackattack.org, accessed May 17, 2007.

2. Toward the end of my fieldwork, Linden Lab announced they intended to make it possible for residents to purchase unique last names by the end of 2007. In other virtual worlds it has been possible to change one's screen name (going back at least to LambdaMOO [Curtis 1992:124]), but even in such contexts screen names remain consequential.

3. Toward the end of my fieldwork, Linden Lab started permitting select organizations and companies to create their own orientation areas, in essence contracting out the labor of teaching newcomers about Second Life.

4. The phenomenon of "farming," where actual-world persons were paid to play an avatar inworld to raise its skill level, so that the skilled avatar could then be sold to a different actual-world person, represented a way to accelerate through such a structured life course (Dibbell 2006).

5. The version 1.7 update to the Second Life program (October 2005) added an "open" command when right-clicking on a prim, to make it easier to extract anything placed inside it and reduce the possibility of a resident inadvertently wearing the prim.

6. During my research a company, Virtual Death, began offering services in Second Life and other virtual worlds to inform online friends in the event of one's actual-world death. See http://www.virtualdeathllc.com, accessed November 24, 2006; *Metaverse Messenger* 2(13):22 (November 21, 2006).

7. See Stephenson 1993; http://en.wikipedia.org/wiki/Avatar_%28virtual_reality %29, accessed July 19, 2006.

8. nwn.blogs.com/nwn/2006/09/open_forum_secu.html, accessed September 11, 2006.

9. In some virtual worlds alts have been mandatory; for instance, during the period of my fieldwork, The Sims Online required persons to create three avatars. In other virtual worlds (including Second Life), residents could add alts through the same process by which they created their original account. In Second Life, for a period of time there was a limit of five alts per credit card; when the requirement of a credit card was abolished, this limit was effectively abolished as well.

10. Linden Lab referred to this as a "principal" account. See http://secondlife.com/corporate/cs.php, accessed January 2, 2007.

11. Even building could be understood as a kind of embodiment, since prims and avatars were both ultimately constructed by residents from the same virtual resources (in the early testing stages of Second Life, avatars were built directly from prims and were known as "primitars").

12. I discuss psychological disabilities later in this chapter.

13. Linkages between visuality and virtuality are also gendered (Haraway 1997: 173–212). See Fornäs et al. 2002:29; Oxford English Dictionary, http://dictionary.oed .com/cgi/entry/50278117?query_type=word&queryword=virtual&first=1&max_to_ show=10&single=1&sort_type=alpha, accessed January 12, 2006.

14. On one island in Second Life during my fieldwork, residents had created an in-world version of "Alice," a program that would try to simulate a therapist responding to questions posed by a patient, an early example of a program designed to pass the Turing test. See http://en.wikipedia.org/wiki/Artificial_Linguistic_Internet_Computer_Entity, accessed December 2, 2006.

15. "Spivak pronouns" do not refer to the literary theorist Gayatri Chakravorty Spivak, but were invented by the mathematician and author Michael Spivak (Sundén 2003:28).

16. In The Sims Online during the period of my fieldwork, female avatars could not use urinals, but had to sit on toilets.

17. A greater distinction between male and female sitting styles was introduced in version 1.2 and was somewhat controversial; see Au 2004b.

18. Some evidence from other virtual worlds has suggested that men participate as women more than the other way around, but this data often comes from more combat-oriented virtual worlds where actual-world male players greatly outnumber actual-world female players. One independent study released in the final stages of writing this book indicated that as of May 2007, 61 percent of residents identified as male in the actual world and 39 percent as female (James 2007).

19. See http://braintalk.blogs.com/brigadoon, accessed August 23, 2006.

20. See Au 2007b.

Chapter 6.
Intimacy.

1. See Boellstorff 2007; Leap and Boellstorff 2004.

2. It was possible to override these features and chat without one's avatar's hands moving or the typing sound, but relatively few residents did this. Residents also created and sold keyboards or typewriters that would appear temporarily when an avatar was typing, so that the avatar did not appear to be typing "in thin air."

3. One hundred meters if using the "shout" option. Beginning with version 1.6, it was also possible to have chat appear as "chat bubbles" near the avatar who "spoke" them, as in a comic book.

4. Communities within Second Life that emphasized role-playing in some fashion often admonished their members to "take it to ims" if they wanted to discuss matters out of character.

5. Since I am interested in questions of language, I have edited this exchange only lightly, preserving punctuation and grammatical errors.

6. Only about 35 percent of respondents to one survey conducted within Second Life indicated that sex was important to them, while about 65 percent indicated that friendship was important (de Nood and Attema 2006:6).

7. Profiles or "descriptions" have been important since the days of text-based virtual worlds (Reid 1996:329–31).

8. An idea in existence since the 1980s has been of "teledildonics," or actual-world devices like dildos that could be controlled by computer. Only a few residents experimented with such devices during my fieldwork.

9. It was possible to ban all avatars save a select list from any parcel of land, but unless the parcel was very large, any avatar could see into the land using the camera controls, even if their avatar could not enter the land. Only on islands one owned was total exclusion possible.

10. In June 2004 the ability to label events as "mature" was added to the platform.

11. Not all members of Gorean communities would define them as BSDM communities; here I use the term in an etic sense.

12. In the Gorean novels Free Women outnumbered female slaves, but in most virtual interpretations of Gorean culture, including those in Second Life, most female avatars appeared as slave women.

13. Part of a "collaring" ritual often used to link a slave to her Master involved asking the slave if she had any alts, to ensure that the slave avatar was her only avatar inworld (Bardzell and Bardzell 2006:3).

14. This question of sexuality moving beyond acceptable boundaries extended to the gap between Second Life and the actual world. For instance, I encountered cases of cyberstalking during my fieldwork: one beleaguered resident described how she had met a man who "keeps hitting on me, and giving me unwanted compliments. I'm having a hard time figuring out how to gently tell him to stop. What makes it complicated is that the compliments aren't directed at my avatar, they're directed at ME."

15. Visitors to Gorean islands were usually expected to enter only a small area of the island unless wearing an "observer" tag, and members of the community were expected to remain within their roles—talking about actual-world issues only in ims, if at all. Some Gorean communities within Second Life were "full roleplay," expecting complete participation. Others were less intensive, permitting participants to venture out to other parts of Second Life or were looser in their interpretation of Norman's novels—for instance, the "Panther women," who were only vaguely described by Norman but in Second Life have become a subculture of warrior women who enslave men. See Manen 2006; Witte 2006.

16. I did not study Teen Second Life as part of my research.

17. Both models were incorporated into the Second Life platform. As noted earlier, one could exchange "calling cards" to become officially recognized friends with as many

persons as one wished. It was also possible to designate a "partner" in one's profile, but one could partner with only one person at a time and either could revoke the partnership at will.

18. In fact, physical proximity has never been a prerequisite to relationships: "a married couple is no less a married couple if they happen to live in two separate towns" (Fornäs et al. 2002:36).

19. See my discussion of the company "Virtual Death" in footnote 6 to chapter 5.

20. There were even persons in Second Life who hired virtual detectives to ascertain the fidelity of their virtual lovers (Au 2005c).

21. For an example of this issue with regard to another virtual world (Everquest), see Hayot 2005.

CHAPTER 7.
COMMUNITY.

1. For instance, the "Myst" series of virtual worlds, with the exception of Uru Online.

2. A partial exception to this were activities like a "Big Brother" reality show event held during my fieldwork over a period of a month. This could be seen as a single extended event, but could not be listed as a single event on the "Events" list.

3. See http://en.wikipedia.org/wiki/Furcadia, accessed August 22, 2006.

4. See Deeeep Witte, "The SL Way to Wear Furs: Brings out the Animal in You!", *Slatenight* 1(2):45 (September 2006), www.slatenight.com, accessed December 17, 2006.

5. Of course, this would represent only one possible embodiment of any resident's avatar, and many residents also used alts. Yet it was clear that the population of residents who identified as Furrie in some fashion numbered in the thousands. See http://nwn .blogs.com/nwn/2006/10/finding_fur.html#more, accessed October 28, 2006.

6. "Trolling" and "flaming," earlier terms associated with email listservs, were occasionally used as well (Donath 1999:45; Kiesler, Siegel, and McGuire 1984:1129; Millard 1997; Reid 1999:114; Tepper 1997).

7. In this case, the offender's account was frozen in place by an administrator of the system, allowing other residents to engage in "virtual revenge. They described all the most violent punishments they would like to enact on this and all other attackers" (Reid 1999:116).

8. Normally only the designated "friends" of a resident could see their exact location, but griefers sometimes found ways around this restriction. After the version 1.13 (December 2006) update to the Second Life program, residents had to specify which friends would be able to see their inworld location.

9. Another kind of griefing not applicable to Second Life is using alternate accounts to gain an unfair advantage in turn-based conquest games (Mulligan and Patrovsky 2003: 286–87).

10. This term comes from the Something Awful Forums, a "group of general discussion internet message boards which accompany the humor website Something Awful," http://en.wikipedia.org/wiki/Something_Awful_forums, accessed October 28, 2006.

11. See *The Second Life Herald*, "Big Brother Opening Hypervent Griefed for 4 Hours," December 3, 2006, http://www.secondlifeherald.com/slh/2006/12/big_brother_ope.html#more, accessed December 3, 2006.

12. See http://secondlife.com/newsletter/2006_10/html/police_blotter.html, accessed October 5, 2006. However, a Linden Lab staff claimed in 2007 that about 1.5 percent of residents report abuse on a given day, a somewhat different figure (Neva 2007b).

13. Other virtual worlds during the time of my Second Life research included Active Worlds (formerly known as Alphaworld), A Tale in the Desert, A World of My Own, Barbie Girls, City of Heroes, Club Penguin, Cyworld, Dubit, EVE Online, Everquest, Faketown, Furcadia, Gaia, Habbo Hotel, HiPiHi, IMVU, Kaneva, Lineage I and II, Millsberry, Mokitown, Neverwinter Nights, Neopets, Playstation 3 Home, Project Entropia, Red Light Center, Star Wars Galaxies, The Sims Online, Sociolotron, There, vSide, Webskinz, Whyville, Worlds.com, Worlds of Warcraft, and Zwinktopia. Many of these included additional virtual worlds within them or developed from them, such as A Land Far Away (ALFA) in the case of Neverwinter Nights.

14. It sometimes also included the use of other programs. All residents to my knowledge used email, and it was possible to instruct the Second Life platform to forward instant messages from Second Life to an email account. Particularly with earlier versions of the platform that did not allow residents to selectively mute ambient sound (footsteps, the typing sound made while chatting, wind, etc.), some residents attending, say, a music performance would mute Second Life entirely and listen via a separate audio program like WinAmp or RealPlayer. While the building features internal to the platform were quite powerful, they were not all-inclusive, and some residents would use programs like Photoshop (for creating textures) or Poser (for creating animations).

15. See www.secondlife.com.

16. By the end of my fieldwork, languages with forums other than English included German, Japanese, Korean, and Spanish.

17. In his research on Star Wars Galaxies, Douglas Thomas found that residents who visited the forums tended to have a more negative view of the virtual world, largely because they were more aware of flaws in the platform (Thomas 2005:7), a finding that I suspect is valid for Second Life as well.

18. For instance, *New World Notes*, the *Metaverse Messenger*, *In the Grid*, and *The Second Life Herald*. Toward the end of my fieldwork, a number of actual-world media agencies (such as Reuters and the British Broadcasting Corporation) began to establish a presence in Second Life and report on events within the virtual world.

19. See, for instance, the Second Life Parks and Recreation Service website: http://www.gabrielguyer.com/slparksandrec, accessed December 31, 2006.

20. The best-known example of an alternate reality game during my fieldwork was Watching Cassie. See, for instance, http://www.youtube.com/profile?user=cassieiswatching, accessed January 7, 2007.

CHAPTER 8.
POLITICAL ECONOMY.

1. Open-source virtual worlds in existence during my fieldwork included Ogoglio and Croquet. See, inter alia, http://www.opencroquet.org, accessed January 7, 2007; http://www.secondlifeherald.com/slh/2007/01/interview_with_.html#more, accessed January 7, 2007. On January 8, 2007, Linden Lab made the Second Life client source code available on an open-source basis, but did not release the code used for servers (see http://blog.secondlife.com/2007/01/08/embracing-the-inevitable, accessed January 8, 2007).

2. For my limited purposes here, I treat social capital and cultural capital as aspects of the same thing, recognizing their blurring in the history of anthropology and social theory more generally (see Malaby 2006b:148).

3. Locke 1690, section 27.

4. For other examples, see Lapointe 2006.

5. Section 1.4, Second Life Terms of Service, http://secondlife.com/corporate/tos .php, accessed December 30, 2006.

6. The first virtual world to allow conversion with actual-world currency was probably Project Entropia, whose owners announced this intention as early as 1999 (Koster 2003:463).

7. See "Anshe Chung Becomes First Virtual World Millionaire" (November 26, 2006), http://www.anshechung.com/include/press/press_release251106.html, accessed December 26, 2006; Reuters 2006.

8. See Jesse Linden, "Guide to Jobs in Second Life," http://secondlife.com/knowledge base/article.php?id=077, accessed December 30, 2006.

9. As noted in chapter 4, textures mimicking repeating building materials (bricks, wood slats, panes of glass, and so on) were particularly desirable because they could make one prim stand in for many, reducing lag and avoiding using up the prim allocation on one's land.

10. See, inter alia, Au 2006b, 2006c; Doctorow 2006; Harper 2006; Llewelyn 2006b; Ondrejka 2006b; Rice 2006; Sipress 2006; Takashi 2006; and *theKonstrukt* special issue on CopyBot (Issue 5, November 27, 2006), http://www.theKonstrukt.com/magz/ Konstrukt5.pdf, accessed December 31, 2006.

11. Islands were acquired under a slightly different system; toward the end of my fieldwork, the tier fee for private islands raised to $1,675 for the initial purchase and a $295 fee thereafter (from $1,250 and $195, respectively). Since many residents were passionately attached to their land, many would make small actual-world sacrifices to afford their properties. One person claimed to have quit smoking to justify paying forty dollars a month in tiering fees; another discontinued a DVD rental plan to compensate for a larger tier.

12. The largest of these during my fieldwork was Anshe Chung Studios. See http:// www.anshechung.com, accessed December 30, 2006.

13. After a few months, Wells Fargo moved to the virtual world Active Worlds, becoming one of the first corporations to leave Second Life.

14. Some of the best-known such marketing agencies during my fieldwork were Rivers Run Red, The Electric Sheep Company, and Millions of Us.

15. In September 2006, there was a security breach that underscored the possibility of residents accessing the credit card information of other residents (Au 2006j).

16. The other requirement when signing up was to choose a screen name: in chapter 5, I linked this to the rise of permanent surnames in the actual world, which "represents a relatively recent phenomenon intricately linked to the aggrandizement of state control over individuals" (Scott, Tehranian, and Mathias 2002:6).

17. See the official Second Life Community Standards, http://secondlife.com/corporate/cs.php, accessed December 6, 2006. There have been cases of harassment related to griefing extending into the actual world: see Neva 2006a.

18. This could take the form of banning a computer's Internet Protocol (IP) address, so that any alts the resident had would be banned as well, but of course there was no foolproof way to prevent a determined resident from registering for a new avatar using a different computer. A more unusual possibility for punishment was the "Corn Field." This was a simulated corn field, complete with aged tractor and a television set playing a 1940 film *Boy in Court*; residents exiled here were only able to log into the Corn Field, not the main grid of Second Life itself, and could not log into any other part of Second Life while the punishment was in effect. See "Hidden Virtual-World Prison Revealed," *Clickable Culture*, January 3, 2006 http://www.secretlair.com/index.php?/clickableculture/entry/hidden_virtual_world_prison_revealed, accessed December 6, 2006. See also "Misbehavior in Second Life Game Punished by Exile to 'The Corn Field,'" *Boingboing*, January 4, 2006, which notes the existence of a similar space in the virtual world WorldsAway known as "the Void" http://www.boingboing.net/2006/01/04/misbehavior_in_secon .html, accessed December 6, 2006.

19. Several features of the official website served the cause of governance, including the forums and the "Linden Blog" that largely replaced it (and allowed Linden Lab staff more control over postings). During my fieldwork, a "Feature Voting" capability was added to the webpage, allowing residents to vote on their favorite proposed improvements to the platform. This was seen to be of limited success due to questions about its design and oversight (Neva 2006c, J. Linden 2006). In any case, like the Linden Blog and other aspects of the website, the Feature Voting tool was not incorporated into the virtual world itself, and those residents who did not visit the website could not access it.

20. The company stated that "Linden Lab does not exercise editorial control over the content of Second Life, and will make no specific efforts to review the textures, objects, sounds or other content created within Second Life. We may, however, remove any materials that violate the Community Standards, or which, in our sole discretion, may be illegal, or which may subject us to liability according to our Terms of Service." Section 1.2, Second Life Terms of Service, http://secondlife.com/corporate/tos.php, accessed January 2, 2007.

21. The French National Front, a right-wing party in France, opened an office in Second Life in December 2006. See http://www.secondlifeherald.com/slh/2006/12/another_sl_firs.html, accessed January 5, 2007.

22. The term was coined by Prokofy Neva in April 2005. See, inter alia, Au 2005e, 2005f, Neva 2006d, and, for an example of a spoof, http://www.fetedinnercore.com, accessed January 7, 2007.

23. "First Land" was discontinued in February 2007.

24. There were some protests against the end of the ratings system, particularly by older residents who had accumulated a significant number of ratings.

25. See Bennetsen 2006; Keen 2006; Llewelyn 2005.

26. Prior to this system point-to-point teleporting had existed, but residents had to pay for each teleport.

27. Prior to version 1.6 this was known as "exchanging calling cards."

28. Philip Linden claimed "four to five times as many people signing up." See Philip Linden, "Third Anniversary Thoughts" (June 23, 2006), http://secondlife.blogs.com/philip/2006/06/third_anniversa.html, accessed June 29, 2006.

CHAPTER 9.
THE VIRTUAL.

1. During my fieldwork, some persons were seeking to extend this linkage by making physical versions of objects from Second Life. See, for instance, http://www.objectsofvirtualdesire.com and http://www.recursiveinstruments.com, both accessed January 16, 2007.

2. It was already the case during my fieldwork that "ethnographic research—both on Linden Lab's corporate culture and many on the residents and world of Second Life—has led to greater understanding of Linden Lab's development processes" (Ondrejka 2006a:113).

Works Cited

Aarseth, Espen J. 1997. *Cybertext: Perspectives on Ergodic Literature*. Baltimore: Johns Hopkins University Press.

Abbate, Janet. 1999. *Inventing the Internet*. Cambridge, MA: Cambridge University Press.

Abu-Lughod, Lila. 1991. "Writing against Culture." In *Recapturing Anthropology*, ed. Richard Fox, 137–62. Santa Fe: School of American Research Press.

Ahearn, Laura M. 2001. *Invitations to Love: Literacy, Love Letters, and Social Change in Nepal*. Ann Arbor, MI: University of Michigan Press.

Almond, Paul. 2005. "Taking the Virtual out of Virtual Reality" (March). Available at: http://www.paul-almond.com/TakingTheVirtualOutOfVirtualReality.htm (accessed December 31, 2006).

Althusser, Louis. 1971. "Ideology and Ideological State Apparatuses (Notes Towards an Investigation)." In *Lenin and Philosophy and Other Essays*, trans. Ben Brewster, 121–73. New York: Monthly Review Press.

Anderson, Benedict R. O'G. 1983. *Imagined Communities: Reflections On the Origins and Spread of Nationalism*. London: Verso.

Aneesh, A. 2006. *Virtual Migration: the Programming of Globalization*. Durham, NC: Duke University Press.

Apolito, Paolo. 2005. *The Internet and the Madonna: Religious Visionary Experience on the Web*. Chicago: University of Chicago Press.

Appadurai, Arjun. 1996. "Global Ethnoscapes: Notes and Queries for a Transnational Anthropology." In his *Modernity at Large: Cultural Dimensions of Globalization*, 48–65. Minneapolis: University of Minnesota Press.

Argyle, Katie, and Rob Shields. 1996. "Is there a Body on the Net?" In *Cultures of Internet: Virtual Spaces, Real Histories, Living Bodies*, ed. Rob Shields, 58–69. London: Sage.

Asad, Talal, ed. 1973. *Anthropology and the Colonial Encounter*. New York: Humanities Press.

Au, Wagner James. 2003a. "Tax Revolt in Americana!" *New World Notes*, (September 12). Avaliable at: http://nwn.blogs.com/nwn/2003/09/tax_revolt_in_a.html (accessed December 30, 2006).

———. 2003b. "White Like Me." *New World Notes*, (October 28). Available at: http://nwn.blogs.com/nwn/2003/10/white_like_me.html (accessed November 10, 2006).

———. 2004a. "The Nine Souls of Wilde Cunningham." *New World Notes*, (December 15). Available at: http://nwn.blogs.com/nwn/2004/12/the_nine_souls_.html (accessed May 13, 2006).

———. 2004b. "Sitting Pretty." *New World Notes*, (February 18). Available at: http://secondlife.blogs.com/nwn/2004/02/sitting_pretty.html (accessed October 24, 2006).

Au, Wagner James. 2004c. "A Lever to Move the Mind." *New World Notes*, (September 9). Available at: http://nwn.blogs.com/nwn/2004/09/a_lever_to_move.html (accessed January 12, 2007).

———. 2005a. "Man and Man on Woman on Woman." *New World Notes*, (January 10). Available at: http://nwn.blogs.com/nwn/2005/01/man_and_man_on_.html (accessed June 12, 2005).

———. 2005b. "The Tragics of Tringo." *New World Notes*, (March 8). Available at: http://nwn.blogs.com/nwn/2005/03/the_tragics_of_.html (accessed December 31, 2006).

———. 2005c. "Watching the Detectives." *New World Notes*, (March 22). Available at: http://nwn.blogs.com/nwn/2005/03/watching_the_de.html (accessed August 12, 2005).

———. 2005d. "Homeland Security Comes to Second Life." *New World Notes*, (October 19). Available at: http://nwn.blogs.com/nwn/2005/10/homeland_securi.html (accessed February 12, 2006).

———. 2005e. "The Feted Inner Core, Revealed!" *New World Notes*, (April 27). Available at: http://secondlife.blogs.com/nwn/2005/04/_sl_explorers_l.html (accessed January 7, 2007).

———. 2005f. "Feted Inner Chomsky." *New World Notes*, (June 29). Available at: http://nwn.blogs.com/nwn/2005/06/feted_inner_cho.html (accessed January 7, 2007).

———. 2006a. "The Triumph of Tringo." *New World Notes*, (April 12). Available at: http://nwn.blogs.com/nwn/2006/04/the_triumph_of_.html (accessed December 31, 2006).

———. 2006b. "Open Forum: Copybot Controversy." *New World Notes*, (November 14). Available at: http://nwn.blogs.com/nwn/2006/11/open_forum_copy.html (accessed December 31, 2006).

———. 2006c. "Copying a Controversy." *New World Notes*, (November 15). Available at: http://nwn.blogs.com/nwn/2006/11/second_life_clo.html (accessed December 31, 2006).

———. 2006d. "The Mixed Success of Mixed Reality." *New World Notes*, (October 23). Available at: http://nwn.blogs.com/nwn/2006/10/why_mixed_reali.html (accessed December 31, 2006).

———. 2006e. "Building Walls, Building Platforms." *New World Notes*, (April 10). Available at: http://nwn.blogs.com/nwn/2006/04/building_walls_.html (accessed October 29, 2006).

———. 2006f. "A Day without Screenshots." *New World Notes*, (June 23). Available at: http://nwn.blogs.com/nwn/2006/06/a_day_without_s.html (accessed June 29, 2006).

———. 2006g. "The Spaces between Us." *New World Notes*, (August 9). Available at: http://nwn.blogs.com/nwn/2006/08/the_spaces_betw.html (accessed October 10, 2006).

———. 2006h. "The Skin You're In." *New World Notes*, (February 23). Available at: http://secondlife.blogs.com/nwn/2006/02/the_skin_youre_.html (accessed November 10, 2006).

———. 2006i. "A Brother-HUD of Man." *New World Notes*, (August 23). Available at: http://nwn.blogs.com/nwn/2006/08/a_brotherhud_of.html (accessed September 2, 2006).

———. 2006j. "Open Forum: Security Breach and True Names." *New World Notes*, (September 9). Available at: http://nwn.blogs.com/nwn/2006/09/open_forum_secu.html (accessed September 14, 2006).

Au, Wagner James. 2006k. "Governor Mark Warner Comes to Second Life." *New World Notes*, (August 30). Available at: http://nwn.blogs.com/nwn/2006/08/governormark _w.html (accessed November 20, 2006).

———. 2006l. "Walk Like an American?" *New World Notes*, (June 2). Available at: http:// nwn.blogs.com/nwn/2006/06/walk_like_an_am.html (accessed November 4, 2006).

———. 2007a. "Virtually Democratic." *New World Notes*, (January 4). Available at: http:// nwn.blogs.com/nwn/2007/01/virtual_democra.html (accessed January 4, 2007).

———. 2007b. "The Agency of Avatars." *New World Notes*, (January 4). Available at: http:// nwn.blogs.com/nwn/2007/01/the_selfactuali.html (accessed January 26, 2007).

———. 2007c. "Losing Voice." *New World Notes*, (March 19). Available at: http://nwn .blogs.com/nwn/2007/03/losing_voice.html (accessed March 23, 2007).

———. 2007d. "The Mosque of Chebi—and Muslims in Second Life." *New World Notes*, (March 20). Available at: http://nwn.blogs.com/nwn/2007/03/the_world_from_1 .html (accessed April 2, 2007).

———. 2007e. "Social Circles." *New World Notes*, (May 16). Available at: http://nwn .blogs.com/nwn/2007/05/social_circles.html (accessed May 16, 2007).

Auden, Wystan Hugh. 1968. *Secondary Worlds: Essays by W. H. Auden*. New York: Random House.

Bainbridge, Sandi. 2006. "Escorting 101." *theKonstrukt* 4 (October 25):14–15. Available at: http://www.theKonstrukt.com/magz/Konstrukt4.pdf (accessed December 31, 2006).

Balsamo, Anne. 1995a. "Signal to Noise: On the Meaning of Cyberpunk Subculture." In *Communication in the Age of Virtual Reality*, ed. Frank Biocca and Mark R. Levy, 347–68. Hillsdale, NJ: Lawrence Erlbaum Associates.

———. 1995b. "Forms of Technological Embodiment: Reading the Body in Contemporary Culture." In *Cyberspace/Cyberbodies/Cyberpunk: Cultures of Technological Embodiment*, ed. Mike Featherstone and Roger Burrows, 215–37. London: Sage.

———. 1996. *Technologies of the Gendered Body: Reading Cyborg Women*. Durham, NC: Duke University Press.

———. Forthcoming. *Designing Culture: The Technological Imagination at Work*. Durham, NC: Duke University Press.

Barbrook, Richard, and Andy Cameron. 2001. "Californian Ideology." In *Crypto Anarchy, Cyberstates, and Pirate Utopias*, ed. Peter Ludlow, 363–87. Cambridge, MA: MIT Press.

Bardzell, Shaowen, and Jeffrey Bardzell. 2006. "Sex-Interface-Aesthetics: The Docile Avatars and Embodied Pixels of Second Life BDSM." Available at: http://www.ics.uci .edu/~johannab/sexual.interactions.2006/papers/ShaowenBardzell&JeffreyBardzell -SexualInteractions2006.pdf (accessed November 15, 2006).

Barlow, John Perry. 1996a. "Selling Wine without Bottles: The Economy of Mind on the Global Net." In *High Noon on the Electronic Frontier: Conceptual Issues in Cyberspace*, ed. Peter Ludlow, 9–34. Cambridge, MA: MIT Press.

———. 1996b [2001 reprint]. "A Declaration of the Independence of Cyberspace." In *Crypto Anarchy, Cyberstates, and Pirate Utopias*, ed. Peter Ludlow, 27–30. Cambridge, MA: MIT Press.

Bartle, Richard A. 2003a. "Not Yet, You Fools!" *Game Girl Advance*, (July 28). Available at: http://www.gamegirladvance.com/archives/2003/07/28/not_yet_you_fools.html (accessed October 26, 2006).

———. 2003b. "Hearts, Clubs, Diamonds, Spades: Players Who Suit MUDs." In *Developing Online Games: An Insider's Guide*, ed. Jessica Mulligan and Bridgette Patrovsky, 397–435. Indianapolis: New Riders.

———. 2004. *Designing Virtual Worlds*. Indianapolis: New Riders.

Bateson, Gregory. 1972. "A Theory of Play and Fantasy." In *Steps to an Ecology of Mind: Collected Essays in Anthropology, Psychiatry, Evolution, and Epistemology*, 150–66. New York: Ballantine Books.

Baty, S. Paige. 1999. *Email Trouble: Love and Addiction @ the Matrix*. Austin: University of Texas Press.

Baudrillard, Jean. 1994. *Simulacra and Simulation*. Ann Arbor, MI: University of Michigan Press.

Baym, Nancy K. 2000. *Tune In, Log On: Soaps, Fandom, and Online Community*. Thousand Oaks, CA: Sage Publications.

Beck, John C., and Mitchell Wade. 2004. *Got Game: How the Gamer Generation Is Reshaping Business Forever*. Boston: Harvard Business School Press.

Beckles, Colin. 1997. "Black Struggles in Cyberspace: Cyber-segregation and Cyber-Nazis." *Western Journal of Black Studies* 21, 1(Spring):12–19.

Benedict, Ruth. 1946. *The Chrysanthemum and the Sword: Patterns of Japanese Culture*. New York: Houghton Mifflin Co.

Benedikt, Michael. 1991. "Introduction." In *Cyberspace: First Steps*, ed. Michael Benedikt, 1–25. Cambridge, MA: MIT Press.

Beniger, James R. 1986. *The Control Revolution: Technological and Economic Origins of the Information Society*. Cambridge, MA: Harvard University Press.

Benjamin, Walter. 1955. "The Work of Art in the Age of Mechanical Reproduction." In *Illuminations: Essays and Reflections*, ed. and introd. by Hannah Arendt, 217–52. New York: Schoken Books.

Bennetsen, Henrik. 2006. "Immersion vs. Augmentation." Available at: http://www.slcreativity.org/wiki/index.php?title=Augmentation_vs_Immersion&oldid=2149 (accessed December 7, 2006).

Ben-Ze'ev, Aaron. 2004. *Love Online: Emotions on the Internet*. Cambridge: Cambridge University Press.

Berger, Arthur Asa. 2002. *Video Games: A Popular Culture Phenomenon*. New Brunswick, NJ: Transaction Publishers.

Bergson, Henri. 1911. *Creative Evolution*. New York: Henry Holt and Company.

Biocca, Frank. 1997. "The Cyborg's Dilemma: Progressive Embodiment in Virtual Environments." *Journal of Computer-Mediated Communication* 3, 2 (September).

Biocca, Frank, Taeyong Kim, and Mark R. Levy. 1995. "The Vision of Virtual Reality." In *Communication in the Age of Virtual Reality*, ed. Frank Biocca and Mark R. Levy, 3–14. Hillsdale, NJ: Lawrence Erlbaum Associates.

Blascovich, Jim. 2002. "Social Influence within Immersive Virtual Environments." In *The Social Life of Avatars: Presence and Interaction in Shared Virtual Environments*, ed. Ralph Schroeder, 127–45. London: Springer-Verlag.

Bleecker, Julian. 1994. "Urban Crisis: Past, Present, and Virtual." *Socialist Review* 24, 1–2 (Winter):189–221.

Boas, Franz. 1887 [1940 version]. "The Study of Geography." In *Race, Language, and Culture*, 639–47. Chicago: University of Chicago Press.

Boellstorff, Tom. 2002. "Ethnolocality." *Asia Pacific Journal of Anthropology* 3, 1(April): 24–48.

———. 2005. *The Gay Archipelago: Sexuality and Nation in Indonesia*. Princeton: Princeton University Press.

———. 2006. "A Ludicrous Discipline? Ethnography and Game Studies." *Games and Culture* 1, 1:29–35.

———. 2007. *A Coincidence of Desires: Anthropology, Queer Studies, Indonesia*. Durham, NC: Duke University Press.

Bogost, Ian. 2004. "Asynchronous Multiplay: Futures for Casual Multiplayer Experience." Proceedings of the Other Players conference, Copenhagen, Denmark. Available at: http://www.itu.dk/op/papers/bogost.pdf (accessed October 27, 2006).

———. 2007. *Persuasive Games: The Expressive Power of Videogames*. Cambridge, MA: MIT Press.

Bolter, Jay David. 2001. *Writing Space: Computers, Hypertext, and the Remediation of Print, Second Edition*. Mahwah, NJ: Lawrence Erlbaum Associates.

Bolter, Jay David, and Richard Grusin. 1999. *Remediation: Understanding New Media*. Cambridge: Cambridge University Press.

Bourdieu, Pierre. 1977. *Outline of a Theory of Practice*. Cambridge: Cambridge University Press.

Boyd, Danah. 2006a. "On Being Virtual." Available at: http://www.zephoria.org/thoughts /archives/2006/12/15/on_being_virtua.html (accessed December 30, 2006).

———. 2006b. "Friends, Friendsters, and Top 8: Writing Community into Being on Social Network Sites." *First Monday* 11, 12. Available at: http://www.firstmonday.org/ issues/issue11_12/boyd/index.html#p2 (accessed December 24, 2006).

Brady, Ivan. 1983. "Speaking in the Name of the Real: Freeman and Mead on the Samoa (Introduction)." *American Anthropologist* 85, 4:908–9.

Branwyn, Gareth. 1994. "Compu-Sex: Erotica for Cybernauts." In *Flame Wars: The Discourse of Cyberculture*, ed. Mark Dery, 223–35. Durham, NC: Duke University Press.

Brenner, Neil. 2001. "The Limits to Scale? Methodological Reflections on Scalar Structuration." *Progress in Human Geography* 25, 4:591–614.

Bromberg, Heather. 1996. "Are MUDs Communities? Identity, Belonging, and Consciousness in Virtual Worlds." In *Cultures of Internet: Virtual Spaces, Real Histories, Living Bodies*, ed. Rob Shields, 143–52. London: Sage Publications.

Bruckman, Amy S. 1996. "Gender Swapping on the Internet." In *High Noon on the Electronic Frontier: Conceptual Issues in Cyberspace*, ed. Peter Ludlow, 9–34. Cambridge, MA: MIT Press.

Bukatman, Scott. 1994. "Gibson's Typewriter." In *Flame Wars: The Discourse of Cyberculture*, ed. Mark Dery, 71–89. Durham, NC: Duke University Press.

Bunzl, Matti. 2004. "Boas, Foucault, and the 'Native Anthropologist': Notes toward a Neo-Boasian Anthropology." *American Anthropologist* 106, 3(September):435–42.

Butler, Judith. 1990. *Gender Trouble*. New York: Routledge.

Cadigan, Pat. 1988. *Tea from an Empty Cup*. London: HarperCollins.

Cairncross, Frances. 2001. *The Death of Distance: How the Communications Revolution Is Changing Our Lives*. Boston: Harvard Business School Press.

Callois, Roger. 1961. *Man, Play, and Games*. Chicago: University of Chicago Press.

Campbell, Colin. 1987. *The Romantic Ethic and the Spirit of Modern Consumerism*. Oxford: Basil Blackwell.

Campbell, John Edward. 2004. *Getting It On Online: Cyberspace, Gay Male Sexuality, and Embodied Identity*. New York: Harrington Park Press.

Çapin, Tolga K. et al. 1999. *Avatars in Networked Virtual Environments*. New York: John Wiley and Sons.

Carlstrom, Eva-Lise. 1992. "Better Living Through Languages: The Communicative Implications of a Text-Only Virtual Environment, or Welcome to LambdaMOO!" Avaliable at: ftp://ftp.game.org/pub/mud/text/research/communicative.txt (accessed December 10, 2006).

Carnevale, Peter J., and Tahira M. Probst. 1997. "Conflict on the Internet." In *Culture of the Internet*. ed. Sara Kiesler, 233–55. Mahwah, NJ: Lawrence Erlbaum Associates.

Cascio, Jamais, Jerry Paffendorf, and John Smart. 2007. "Metaverse Roadmap: Pathways to the 3D Web." Available at: http://metaverseroadmap.org/MetaverseRoadmapOverview.pdf (accessed July 10, 2007).

Castells, Manuel. 2000. *The Information Age: Economy, Society, and Culture. Volume 1: The Rise of the Network Society*. Boston: Blackwell.

Castle, Terry. 1993. *The Apparitional Lesbian: Female Homosexuality and Modern Culture*. New York: Columbia University Press.

Castronova, Edward. 2005. *Synthetic Worlds: The Business and Culture of Online Games*. Chicago: University of Chicago Press.

———. 2006. "On the Research Value of Large Games: Natural Experiments in Norrath and Camelot." *Games and Culture* 1, 2(April):163–86.

Caves, Richard E. 2000. *Creative Industries: Contracts between Art and Commerce*. Cambridge, MA: Harvard University Press.

Chee, Florence. 2006. "The Games We Play Online and Offline: Making *Wangtta* in Korea." *Popular Communication* 4, 3:225–39.

Cherny, Lynn. 1999. *Conversation and Community: Chat in a Virtual World*. Stanford: CSLI Publications.

Chun, Wendy. 2006. *Control and Freedom: Power and Paranoia in the Age of Fiber Optics*. Cambridge, MA: MIT Press.

Clark, Andy. 2003. *Natural-Born Cyborgs: Minds, Technologies, and the Future of Human Intelligence*. Oxford: Oxford University Press.

Clifford, James. 1983. "On Ethnographic Authority." *Representations* 1, 2(Spring):118–46.

Clifford, James, and George Marcus, eds. 1986. *Writing Culture: The Poetics and Politics of Ethnography*. Berkeley: University of California Press.

Collier, Jane F. 1988. *Marriage and Inequality in Classless Societies*. Stanford: Stanford University Press.

Collier, Stephen J., and Andrew Lakoff. 2005. "On Regimes of Living." In *Global Assemblages: Technology, Politics, and Ethics as Anthropological Problems*, ed. Aihwa Ong and Stephen J. Collier, 22–39. Oxford: Blackwell.

Comaroff, Jean, and John L. Comaroff. 2000. "Millennial Capitalism: First Thoughts on a Second Coming." *Public Culture* 12, 2:291–343.

Consalvo, Mia. 2007. *Cheating: Gaining Advantage in Videogames*. Cambridge, MA: MIT Press.

Constable, Nicole. 2003. *Romance on a Global Stage: Pen Pals, Virtual Ethnography, and "Mail Order" Marriages*. Berkeley: University of California Press.

Coontz, Stephanie. 2005. *Marriage, a History: From Obedience to Intimacy, or How Love Conquered Marriage*. New York: Viking Press.

Cosgrove, Denis E. 1998. *Social Formation and Symbolic Landscape*. Madison: University of Wisconsin Press.

Coyne, Richard. 1994. "Heidegger and Virtual Reality: The Implications of Heidegger's Thinking for Computer Representations." *Leonardo* 27, 1:65–73.

Crary, Jonathan. 1990. *Techniques of the Observer: On Vision and Modernity in the Nineteenth Century*. Cambridge, MA: MIT Press.

———. 1999. *Suspensions of Perception: Attention, Spectacle, and Modern Culture*. Cambridge, MA: MIT Press.

Curtis, Pavel. 1992 [1997 reprint]. "Mudding: Social Phenomena in Text-Based Virtual Realities." In *Culture of the Internet*, ed. Sara Kiesler, 121–42. Mahwah, NJ: Lawrence Erlbaum Associates.

Damer, Bruce. 1998. *Avatars!: Exploring and Building Virtual Worlds on the Internet*. Berkeley: Peachpit Press.

Dawson, Lorne L., and Douglas E. Cowan, eds. 2004. *Religion Online: Finding Faith on the Internet*. New York: Routledge.

Debord, Guy. 1983. *Society of the Spectacle*. Detroit: Black & Red.

De Koven, Bernard. 1978. *The Well-Played Game: A Player's Philosophy*. Garden City, NY: Anchor Press.

de Nood, David, and Jelle Attema. 2006. "Second Life: The Second Life of Virtual Reality." Avaliable at: www.epn.net (accessed December 13, 2006).

Deleuze, Gilles. 2004. *Difference and Repetition*. London: Continuum.

Derrida, Jacques. 1974. *Of Grammatology*. Baltimore: Johns Hopkins University Press.

———. 1994. *Specters of Marx: The State of the Debt, the Work of Mourning, and the New International*. New York: Routledge.

de Saussure, Ferdinand. 1959. *Course in General Linguistics*. New York: McGraw-Hill.

Dibbell, Julian. 1998. "A Rape in Cyberspace." In his *My Tiny Life: Crime and Passion in a Virtual World*, 11–32. New York: Henry Holt and Company.

———. 2006. *Play Money: Or, How I Quit My Day Job and Made Millions Trading Virtual Loot*. New York: Basic Books.

Dick, Philip K. 1985. "How to Build a Universe That Doesn't Fall Apart Two Days Later." In his *I Hope I Shall Arrive Soon*, 1–23. Garden City, NY: Doubleday.

Doctorow, Cory. 2006. "Second Life Struggles with Copying." *Boingboing* (November 15). Available at: http://www.boingboing.net/2006/11/15/second_life_struggle.html (accessed December 31, 2006).

———. 2007. "Why Online Games are Dictatorships." *Information Week* (April 16). Available at: http://informationweek.com/internet/showArticle.jhtml?articleID=199100026&pgno=1&queryText= (accessed April 23, 2007).

Doel, Marcus A., and David B. Clarke. 1999. "Virtual Worlds: Simulation, Suppletion, S(ed)uction, and Simulacra." In *Virtual Geographies: Bodies, Space, and Relations*, ed. Mike Crang, Phil Crang, and Jon May, 261–83. London: Routledge.

Donath, Judith S. 1999. "Identity and Deception in the Virtual Community." In *Communities in Cyberspace*, ed. Marc A. Smith and Peter Kollock, 29–59. London: Routledge.

Dourish, Paul. 2001. *Where the Action Is: The Foundations of Embodied Interaction*. Cambridge, MA: MIT Press.

Doyle, Richard. 2003. *Wetwares: Experiments in Postvital Living*. Minneapolis: University of Minnesota Press.

Doyle, Patrick, and Barbara Hayes-Roth. 1998. "Guided Exploration of Virtual Worlds." In *Network and Netplay: Virtual Groups on the Internet*, ed. Fay Sudweeks, Margaret McLaughlin, and Sheizaf Rafaeli, 243–63. Menlo Park, CA: AAAI Press.

Dreyfus, Hubert L. 1991. *Being-in-the-World: A Commentary on Heidegger's* Being and Time, *Division I*. Cambridge, MA: MIT Press.

Ducheneaut, Nicolas, Robert J. Moore, and Eric Nickell. 2004. "Designing for Sociability in Massively Multiplayer Games: An Examination of the 'Third Places' of SWG." Proceedings of the Other Players conference, Copenhagen, Denmark. Available at: http://www.itu.dk/op/papers/ducheneaut_moore_nickell.pdf (accessed October 27, 2006).

Ducheneaut, Nicolas, Nick Yee, Eric Nickell, and Robert J. Moore. 2006. "Building an MMO with Mass Appeal: A Look at Gameplay in World of Warcraft." *Games and Culture* 1, 4(October):281–317.

Duranti, Alessandro. 1997. *Linguistic Anthropology*. Cambridge: Cambridge University Press.

Durkheim, Emile, and Marcel Mauss. 1902. *Primitive Classification*. Translated by Rodney Needhan. 1963 edition. Chicago: University of Chicago Press.

Dyer, Richard. 1997. *White*. New York: Routledge.

Edwards, Paul N. 1990. "The Army and the Microworld: Computers and the Politics of Gender Identity." *Signs* 16, 1(Autumn):102–27.

Ellul, Jacques. 1964 [1954]. *The Technological Society*. Trans. John Wilkinson and introd. by Robert K. Merton. New York: A. A. Knopf.

Escobar, Arturo. 1994. "Welcome to Cyberia: Notes on the Anthropology of Cyber-culture." *Current Anthropology* 35, 3(June):211–23.

Evans-Pritchard, E. E. 1940. *The Nuer: A Description of the Modes of Livelihood and Political Institutions of a Nilotic People.* Oxford: Clarendon Press.

Fabian, Johannes. 2002. "Virtual Archives and Ethnographic Writing: 'Commentary' as a New Genre?" *Current Anthropology* 43, 5(December):775–86.

Fairfield, Joshua. 2007. "Anti-Social Contracts: The Contractual Governance of Online Communities." Washington & Lee Legal Studies Paper No. 2007-20 (July). Available at SSRN: http://ssrn.com/abstract=1002997.

Fate, Artemis. 2006a. "The Problems of Gor, Part 1." *The Second Life Herald,* (November 27). Available at: http://www.secondlifeherald.com/slh/2006/11/the_problems_of.html (accessed December 2, 2006).

———. 2006b. "The Problems of Gor, Part 2." *The Second Life Herald,* (November 29). Available at: http://www.secondlifeherald.com/slh/2006/11/the_problems_of_1.html (accessed December 2, 2006).

Feinberg, Richard. 1988. "Margaret Mead and Samoa: *Coming of Age* in Fact and Fiction." *American Anthropologist* 90, 3(September):656–63.

Fernback, Jan. 1999. "There is a There There: Notes Toward a Definition of Cybercommunity." In *Doing Internet Research: Critical Issues and Methods for Examining the Net,* ed. Steven G. Jones, 203–20. Thousand Oaks, CA: Sage Publications.

Florida, Richard. 2002. *The Rise of the Creative Class.* New York: Basic Books.

Foo, Chek Yang. 2004. "Redefining Grief Play." Proceedings of the Other Players conference, Copenhagen, Denmark. Available at: http://www.itu.dk/op/papers/yang_foo.pdf (accessed October 27, 2006).

Foo, Chek Yang, and Elina M. I. Koivisto. 2004. "Grief Player Motivations." Proceedings of the Other Players conference, Copenhagen, Denmark. Available at: http://www.itu.dk/op/papers/yang_foo_koivisto.pdf (accessed October 27, 2006).

Ford, Paul J. 2001. "Paralysis Lost: Impacts of Virtual Worlds on Those with Paralysis." *Social Theory and Practice* 27, 4(October):661–80.

Fornäs, Johan, Kajsa Klein, Martina Ladendorf, Jenny Sundén, and Malin Sveningsson. 2002. "Into Digital Borderlands." In *Digital Borderlands: Cultural Studies of Identity and Interactivity on the Internet,* ed. Johan Fornäs, Kajsa Klein, Martina Ladendorf, Jenny Sundén, and Malin Sveningsson, 1–47. New York: Peter Lang.

Foster, Thomas. 2005. *The Souls of Cyberfolk: Posthumanism as Vernacular Theory.* Minneapolis: University of Minnesota Press.

Foucault, Michel. 1970. *The Order of Things: An Archeology of the Human Sciences.* New York: Vintage Books.

———. 1978. *The History of Sexuality, Vol. 1: An Introduction.* New York: Vintage Books.

———. 1985. *The History of Sexuality, Vol. 2: The Use of Pleasure.* New York: Vintage Books.

———. 1986. *The History of Sexuality, Vol. 3: The Care of the Self.* New York: Vintage Books.

Foucault, Michel. 1991. "Governmentality." In *The Foucault Effect: Studies in Govern-mentality*, ed. Graham Burchell, Colin Gordon, and Peter Miller, 87–104. London: Harvester/Wheatsheaf.

——. 1997a. "Friendship as a Way of Life." In *Ethics: Subjectivity and Truth (Essential Works of Foucault 1954–1984, Vol. 1)*, ed. Paul Rabinow, 135–41. New York: The New Press.

——. 1997b. "Of Other Spaces: Utopias and Heterotopias." In *Rethinking Architecture: A Reader in Cultural Theory*, ed. Neil Leach, 350–56. London: Routledge.

Franklin, Ursula. 1992. *The Real World of Technology*. Concord, Ontario: Anansi.

Freeman, Derek. 1983. *Margaret Mead and Samoa: The Making and Unmaking of an Anthropological Myth*. Cambridge, MA: Harvard University Press.

Freeman, Elizabeth. 2002. *The Wedding Complex: Forms of Belonging in Modern Ameri-can Culture*. Durham, NC: Duke University Press.

Friedberg, Anne. 2006. *The Virtual Window: From Alberti to Microsoft*. Cambridge, MA: MIT Press.

Friedel, Robert. 2007. *A Culture of Improvement: Technology and the Western Millen-nium*. Cambridge, MA: MIT Press.

Frykman, Jonas, and Orvar Löfgren. 1987. *Culture Builders: A Historical Anthropology of Middle-Class Life*. New Brunswick, NJ: Rutgers University Press.

Galison, Peter. 1996. "Computer Simulations and the Trading Zone." In *The Disunity of Science: Boundaries, Contexts, and Power*, ed. Peter Galison and David J. Stump, 118–57. Stanford: Stanford University Press.

Garfinkel, Harold. 1967. *Studies in Ethnomethodology*. Englewood Cliffs, NJ: Prentice-Hall.

Gee, James Paul. 2003. *What Video Games Have to Teach Us about Learning and Literacy*. New York: Palgrave Macmillan.

Geertz, Clifford. 1973a. "The Impact of the Concept of Culture on the Concept of Man." In his *The Interpretation of Cultures*, 33–54. New York: Basic Books.

——. 1973b. "Thick Description: Toward an Interpretive Theory of Culture." In his *The Interpretation of Cultures*, 3–32. New York: Basic Books.

——. 1983. "From the Native's Point of View": On the Nature of Anthropological Understanding." In his *Local Knowledge: Further Essays in Interpretive Anthropology*, 55–72. New York: Basic Books.

Gelernter, David Hillel. 1991. *Mirror Worlds, or, The Day Software Puts the Universe in a Shoebox: How It Will Happen and What It Will Mean*. Oxford: Oxford University Press.

Gibson, William. 1984. *Neuromancer*. New York: Ace Books.

——. 1988. *Mona Lisa Overdrive*. New York: Bantam Books.

——. 1993. *Virtual Light*. New York: Bantam Books.

Gibson-Graham, J. K. 1996. *The End of Capitalism (As We Knew It): A Feminist Critique of Political Economy*. Cambridge: Blackwell.

Giddens, Anthony. 1991. *Modernity and Self-Identity*. Oxford: Polity Press.

Giedion, Siegfried. 1948. *Mechanization Takes Command: A Contribution to Anonymous History*. New York: W. W. Norton and Co.

Giles, Jim. 2007. "Life's a Game." *Nature* 445(January):18–20.

Gleick, James. 2000. *Faster: The Acceleration of Just about Everything*. New York: Vintage.

Glover, Katherine. 2007. "Why Can't Gay Dwarves Get Married in Middle-earth?" *Salon .com*. Available at: http://www.salon.com/news/feature/2007/04/28/gay_dwarves/index .html (accessed April 30, 2007).

Gluckman, Max. 1955. *Custom and Conflict in Africa*. Oxford: Basil Blackwell.

Goffman, Erving. 1959. *The Presentation of Self in Everyday Life*. Garden City, NY: Doubleday Anchor Books.

Golub, Alex. 2004. "Copyright and Taboo." *Anthropological Quarterly* 77, 3(Summer): 521–30.

González, Jennifer. 2000. "The Appended Subject: Race and Identity as Digital Assemblage." In *Race in Cyberspace*, ed. Beth E. Kolko, Lisa Nakamura, and Gilbert B. Rodman, 27–50. New York: Routledge.

Goodenough, Ward H. 1964. "Cultural Anthropology." In *Language in Culture and Society*, ed. Dell Hymes, 36–39. Bombay, India: Allied Publishers Private.

Gottlieb, Nanette, and Mark McLelland, eds. 2003. *Japanese Cybercultures*. London: Routledge.

Graham, Elaine L. 2002. *Representations of the Post/human: Monsters, Aliens, and Others in Popular Culture*. New Brunswick, NJ: Rutgers University Press.

Gramsci, Antonio. 1971. *Selections from the Prison Notebooks*. Trans. and ed. Quintin Hoare and Geoffrey Nowell-Smith. New York: International Publishers.

Greenfield, David N. 1999. *Virtual Addiction: Help for Netheads, Cyberfreaks, and Those Who Love Them*. New York: New Harbinger Publications.

Greenblatt, Stephen. 1991. *Marvelous Possessions: The Wonder of the New World*. Chicago: University of Chicago Press.

Grimmelmann, James. 2003. "The State of Play: On the Second Life Tax Revolt." *Law-Meme*, (September21). Available at: http://research.yale.edu/lawmeme (accessed October 27, 2006).

Grossman, Lev. 2006. "Time's Person of the Year: You." *Time* 168, 26 (December 25): 40–41.

Guest, Tim. 2007. *Second Lives*. London: Hutchinson.

Guattari, Félix. 1995. *Chaosmosis: An Ethico-aesthetic Paradigm*. Bloomington: Indiana University Press.

Guimarães, Mário J. L. 2005. "Doing Anthropology in Cyberspace: Fieldwork Boundaries and Social Environments." In *Virtual Methods: Issues in Social Research on the Internet*, ed. Christine Hine, 141–56. Oxford: Berg.

Gupta, Akhil, and James Ferguson. 1997. "Discipline and Practice: 'The Field' as Site, Method, and Location in Anthropology." In *Anthropological Locations: Boundaries and Grounds of a Field Science*, ed. Akhil Gupta and James Ferguson, 1–46. Berkeley: University of California Press.

Habermas, Jürgen. 1970a. "Technical Progress and the Social Life-World." In his *Toward a Rational Society*, 50–61. Boston: Beacon Press.

Habermas, Jürgen. 1970b. "Technology and Science as 'Ideology.'" In *Toward a Rational Society*, 81–127. Boston: Beacon Press.

———. 1989. *Jürgen Habermas on Society and Politics: A Reader*. Ed. Steven Seidman. Boston: Beacon Press.

Hafner, Katie. 1997. "The Epic Saga of The Well." *Wired* 5, 5(May). Available at: http://www.wired.com/wired/archive/5.05/ff_well.html (accessed June 15, 2007).

Hafner, Katie, and Matthew Lyon. 1996. *Where Wizards Stay up Late: The Origins of the Internet*. New York: Simon & Schuster.

Hakken, David. 1999. *Cyborgs@Cyberspace? An Ethnographer Looks to the Future*. New York: Routledge.

Halberstam, Judith. 1991. "Automating Gender: Postmodern Feminism in the Age of the Intelligent Machine." *Feminist Studies* 17, 3(Autumn):439–60.

Haraway, Donna. 1988. "Situated Knowledge: The Science Question in Feminism as a Site of Discourse on the Privilege of Partial Perspective." *Feminist Studies* 14, 3(Fall):575–99.

———. 1991. "A Cyborg Manifesto: Science, Technology, and Socialist-feminism in the Late Twentieth Century." In her *Simians, Cyborgs, and Women: The Reinvention of Nature*, 149–82. London: Routledge.

———. 1997. *Modest_Witness@Second Millennium. FemaleMan_Meets_OncoMouse: Feminism and Technoscience*. New York: Routledge.

Harding, Susan. 1991. "Representing Fundamentalism: The Problem of the Repugnant Other." *Social Research* 58, 2:373–93.

Hardt, Michael, and Antonio Negri. 2001. *Empire*. Cambridge, MA: Harvard University Press.

Harper (Linden), Robin. 2006. "Copyrights and Content Creation in Second Life." (November 13). Available at: http://blog.secondlife.com/2006/11/13/copyrights-and-content-creation-in-second-life (accessed December 31, 2006).

Harrison, Randolph. 2007. "SecondLife: Revolutionary Virtual Market or Ponzi Scheme?" Available at: http://randolfe.typepad.com/randolfe/2007/01/secondlife_revo.html (accessed January 26, 2007).

Hartley, John, ed. 2005. *Creative Industries*. Malden, MA: Blackwell.

Harvey, David. 1989. *The Condition of Postmodernity: An Enquiry into the Origins of Cultural Change*. Cambridge: Basil Blackwell.

———. 1993. "From Space to Place and Back Again: Reflections on the Condition of Postmodernity." In *Mapping the Futures: Local Cultures, Global Change*, ed. Jon Bird, Barry Curtis, Tim Putnam, George Robertson, and Lisa Tickner, 3–29. London: Routledge.

Hayles, N. Katherine. 1996a. "Narratives of Artificial Life." In *FutureNatural: Nature, Science, Culture*, ed. George Robertson, Melinda Mash, Lisa Tickner, Jon Bird, Barry Curtis, and Tim Putnam, 146–64. London: Routledge.

———. 1996b. "Boundary Disputes: Homeostasis, Reflexivity, and the Foundations of Cybernetics." In *Virtual Realities and Their Discontents*, ed. Robert Markley, 11–37. Baltimore: Johns Hopkins University Press.

Hayles, N. Katherine. 1999. *How We Became Posthuman: Virtual Bodies in Cybernetics, Literature, and Informatics*. Chicago: University of Chicago Press.

———. 2002. *Writing Machines*. Cambridge, MA: MIT Press.

———.2005. *My Mother Was a Computer: Digital Subjects and Literary Texts*. Chicago: University of Chicago Press.

Hayot, Eric. 2005. "Moving to Norrath." *always_black*, (February 16). Available at: http://www.alwaysblack.com/?p=57 (accessed December 27, 2006).

Healy, Dave. 1997. "Cyberspace and Place: The Internet as Middle Landscape on the Electronic Frontier." In *Internet Culture*, ed. David Porter, 55–68. New York: Routledge.

Hebdige, Dick. 1979. *Subculture: The Meaning of Style*. London: Methuen.

Heeter, Carrie. 1992. "Being There: The Subjective Experience of Presence." *Presence: Teleoperators and Virtual Environments* 1, 2(Spring):262–71.

Heidegger, Martin. 1962. *Being and Time*. New York: Harper and Row.

———. 1977. "The Question Concerning Technology." In his *The Question Concerning Technology and Other Essays*, 3–35. New York: Harper and Row.

Heim, Michael. 1991. "The Erotic Ontology of Cyberspace." In *Cyberspace: First Steps*, ed. Michael Benedikt, 59–80. Cambridge, MA: MIT Press.

———. 1993. *The Metaphysics of Virtual Reality*. New York: Oxford University Press.

———. 1995. "The Design of Virtual Reality." In *Cyberspace/Cyberbodies/Cyberpunk: Cultures of Technological Embodiment*, ed. Mike Featherstone and Roger Burrows, 65–77. London: Sage.

———. 1998. *Virtual Realism*. Oxford: Oxford University Press.

Heller, Monica, ed. 1988. *Codeswitching: Anthropological and Sociolinguistic Perspectives*. Berlin: Mouton De Gruyter.

Helmreich, Stefan. 1998. *Silicon Second Nature: Culturing Artificial Life in a Digital World*. Berkeley: University of California Press.

———. 2004. "The Word for the World is Computer: Simulating Second Natures in Artificial Life." In *Growing Explanations: Historical Perspectives on the Sciences of Complexity*, ed. Norton Wise, 275–300. Durham, NC: Duke University Press.

Hemp, Paul. 2006. "Avatar-Based Marketing." *Harvard Business Review* 84, 6(June): 48–57.

Herman, Leonard. 2001. *Phoenix: the Fall and Rise of Videogames, Third Edition*. Springfield, NJ: Rolenta Press.

Herman, Andrew, Rosemary J. Coombe, and Lewis Kaye. 2006. "Your Second Life? Goodwill and the Performativity of Intellectual Property in Online Digital Gaming." *Cultural Studies* 20, 2–3(March–May):184–210.

Herz, J. C. 1997. *Joystick Nation: How Videogames Ate Our Quarters, Won Our Hearts, and Rewired Our Minds*. Boston: Little, Brown, and Co.

Hillis, Ken. 1999. *Digital Sensations: Space, Identity, and Embodiment in Virtual Reality*. Minneapolis: University of Minnesota Press.

Hiltz, Starr Roxanne, and Murray Turoff. 1978. *The Network Nation: Human Communication via Computer*. Reading, MA: Addison-Wesley.

Hine, Christine. 2000. *Virtual Ethnography*. London: Sage.

Hine, Christine. 2005. "Virtual Methods and the Sociology of Cyber-Social-Scientific Knowledge." In *Virtual Methods: Issues in Social Research on the Internet*, ed. Christine Hine, 1–13. Oxford: Berg.

Holmes, David. 1997. "Introduction: Virtual Politics—Identity and Community in Cyberspace." In *Virtual Politics: Identity and Community in Cyberspace*, ed. David Holmes, 1–25. London: Sage.

Holmes, Lowell D. 1987. *Quest for the Real Samoa: The Mead/Freeman Controversy and Beyond*. South Hadley, MA: Bergin and Garvey.

Howe, Jeff. 2006. "The Rise of Crowdsourcing." *Wired* 14, 6. Available at: http://www.wired.com/wired/archive/14.06/crowds.html (accessed January 2, 2007).

Hudson-Smith, A. 2002. "30 Days in Active Worlds: Community, Design, and Terrorism in a Virtual World." In *The Social Life of Avatars: Presence and Interaction in Shared Virtual Environments*, ed. Ralph Schroeder, 77–89. London: Springer-Verlag.

Huizinga, Johan. 1950 [1938]. *Homo Ludens: A Study of the Play-Element in Culture*. Boston: Beacon Press.

Humphreys, Sal. 2004. "Commodifying Culture: It's Not Just about the Virtual Sword." Proceedings of the Other Players conference, Copenhagen, Denmark. Available at: http://www.itu.dk/op/papers/humphreys.pdf (accessed October 27, 2006).

Ihde, Don. 2002. *Bodies in Technology*. Minneapolis: University of Minnesota Press.

Ito, Mizuko. 1997. "Virtually Embodied: The Reality of Fantasy in a Multi-User Dungeon." In *Internet Culture*, ed. David Porter, 87–109. New York: Routledge.

Ito, Mizuko, Daisuke Okabe, and Misa Matsuda, eds. 2005. *Personal, Portable, Pedestrian: Mobile Phones in Japanese Life*. Cambridge, MA: MIT Press.

Jacobson, David. 1996. "Contexts and Cues in Cyberspace: The Pragmatics of Naming in Text-based Virtual Realities." *Journal of Anthropological Research* 52, 4(Winter): 461–79.

———. 1999. "Doing Research in Cyberspace." *Field Methods* 11, 2(November):127–45.

Jakobsson, Mikael, and T.L. Taylor. 2003. "The Sopranos Meets EverQuest: Social Networking in Massively Multiplayer Online Games." *FineArt Forum* 17 (August):8. Available at: http://www.fineartforum.org/Backissues/Vol_17/faf_v17_n08/reviews/jakobsson.html (accessed March 31, 2006).

James, Clement. 2007. "Half of Second Life Users Come from Europe." *IT Week*, (May 8). Available at: http://www.itweek.co.uk/vnunet/news/2189326/half-second-lifers-come-europe (accessed May 9, 2007).

Jenkins, Henry. 2006. *Convergence Culture: Where Old and New Media Collide*. New York: New York University Press.

———. 2007. "A Second Look at Second Life." Available at: http://www.henryjenkins.org/2007/01/a_second_look_at_second_life.html (accessed February 2, 2007).

Johns, Adrian. 1998. *The Nature of the Book: Print and Knowledge in the Making*. Chicago: University of Chicago Press.

Jones, Donald E. 2006. "I, Avatar: Constructions of Self and Place in Second Life and the Technological Imagination." *Gnovis: Georgetown's Peer-Reviewed Journal of Communi-*

cation, Culture and Technology, (January 2006). Available at: http://gnovis.georgetown
.edu/articles/FA05-01-secondlife.pdf (accessed January 21, 2006).

Jones, Donald E. 2007. *Queered Virtuality: The Claiming and Making of Queer Spaces and Bodies in the User-Constructed Synthetic World of Second Life*. M.A. thesis, Georgetown University. Available at http://hdl.handle.net/1961/4293 (accessed November 6, 2007).

Jones, Quentin. 1997. "Virtual-Communities, Virtual Settlements, and Cyber-Archaeology: A Theoretical Outline." *Journal of Computer-Mediated Communication* 3, 3(December).

Jones, Steven G. 1997. "The Internet and Its Social Landscape." In *Virtual Culture: Identity and Communication in Cybersociety*, ed. Steven G. Jones, 7–35. London: Sage Publications.

———, ed. 1999. *Doing Internet Research: Critical Issues and Methods for Examining the Net*. Thousand Oaks: Sage.

Joseph, Miranda. 1998. "The Performance of Production and Consumption." *Social Text* 54(Spring):25–61.

Juul, Jesper. 2005. *Half-Real: Video Games between Real Rules and Fictional Worlds*. Cambridge, MA: MIT Press.

Keen, Andrew. 2006. "Interview with Philip Rosedale," (July 20). Available at: http://andrewkeen.typepad.com/aftertv/2006/07/interview_with_.html (accessed January 2, 2007).

Kelty, Christopher. 2005. "Geeks, Social Imaginaries, and Recursive Publics." *Cultural Anthropology* 20, 2(May):185–214.

Kendall, Lori. 2002. *Hanging Out in the Virtual Pub: Masculinities and Relationships Online*. Berkeley: University of California Press.

Kent, Steven L. 2001. *The Ultimate History of Video Games*. Roseville, CA: Prima Publishing.

Kiesler, Sara, Jane Siegel, and Timothy W. McGuire. 1984. "Social Psychological Aspects of Computer-mediated Communication." *American Psychologist* 39, 10(October): 1123–34.

King, Brad, and John Borland. 2003. *Dungeons and Dreamers: The Rise of Computer Game Culture from Geek to Chic*. New York: McGraw-Hill.

Kittler, Friedrich A. 1999. *Gramophone, Film, Typewriter*. Stanford: Stanford University Press.

Kivits, Joëlle. 2005. "Online Interviewing and the Research Relationship." In *Virtual Methods: Issues in Social Research on the Internet*, ed. Christine Hine, 35–49. Oxford: Berg.

Kolko, Beth E., Lisa Nakamura, and Gilbert B. Rodman, eds. 2000. *Race in Cyberspace*. New York: Routledge.

Kollock, Peter, and Marc A. Smith. 1999. "Communities in Cyberspace." In *Communities in Cyberspace*, ed. Marc A. Smith and Peter Kollock, 3–25. London: Routledge.

Koster, Raph. 2003. "Online World Timeline." In *Developing Online Games: An Insider's Guide*, ed. Jessica Mulligan and Bridgette Patrovsky, 437–68. Indianapolis: New Riders. Also available at: http://www.raphkoster.com/gaming/mudtimeline.shtml (accessed November 6, 2006).

Koster, Raph. 2004. *A Theory of Fun for Game Design*. Scottsdale, AZ: Paraglyph Press.

———. 2006. "The SL Cultural Gap." Available at: http://www.raphkoster.com/2006/12/13/the-sl-cultural-gap (accessed December 24, 2006).

Krueger, Myron W. 1983. *Artificial Reality*. Reading, MA: Addison-Wesley.

———. 1991. *Artificial Reality II*. Reading, MA: Addison-Wesley.

Kuper, Adam. 1996. *Anthropology and Anthropologists*. London: Routledge.

Kurzweil, Edith. 1980. *The Age of Structuralism: Lévi-Strauss to Foucault*. New York: Columbia University Press.

Kurzweil, Ray. 2005. *The Singularity is Near: When Humans Transcend Biology*. New York: Viking Press.

Kushner, David. 2003. *Masters of Doom: How Two Guys Created an Empire and Transformed Pop Culture*. New York: Random House.

———. 2004. "My Avatar, My Self." *Technology Review* 107, 3(April):50–55.

Lange, Patricia G. 2008. "Terminological Obfuscation in Online Research." In *Handbook of Computer Mediated Communication*, ed. Sigrid Kelsey and Kirk St. Amant. Hershey, PA: IGI Global.

Langer, Susanne K. 1953. *Feeling and Form: A Theory of Art*. New York: Charles Scribner's Sons.

Lapointe, MichelleMarie. 2006. "Food for Soul: Interview with Maddox Dupont." *theKonstrukt* 3, 2 (October 25). Available at: http://www.theKonstrukt.com/magz/Konstrukt3.pdf (accessed December 31, 2006).

Lastowka, F. Gregory, and Dan Hunter. 2004. "The Laws of the Virtual Worlds." *California Law Review* 92, 1(January):3–73.

———. 2006. "Virtual Worlds: A Primer." In *The State of Play: Law, Games, and Virtual Worlds*, ed. Jack Balkin and Beth Simone Noveck, 13–28. New York: New York University Press.

Latour, Bruno. 2005. *Reassembling the Social: An Introduction to Actor-Network-Theory*. Oxford: Oxford University Press.

Leap, William L., and Tom Boellstorff, eds. 2004. *Speaking in Queer Tongues: Globalization and Gay Language*. Urbana: University of Illinois Press.

LeFleur, Tulipe. 2006. "The Art of Second Life Intimacy, Part II." *Slatenight* 1, 2 (September):43. Available at: www.slatenight.com (accessed December 17, 2006).

Lessig, Lawrence. 2000. *Code and Other Laws of Cyberspace*. New York: Basic Books.

Lévi-Strauss, Claude. 1962. *Totemism*. Boston: Beacon Press.

———. 1963. *Structural Anthropology*. New York: Basic Books.

Levy, Dore Jesse. 1999. *Ideal and Actual in the Story of the Stone*. New York: Columbia University Press.

Lévy, Pierre. 1997. *Collective Intelligence: Mankind's Emerging World in Cyberspace*. New York: Plenum Trade.

———. 1998. *Becoming Virtual: Reality in the Digital Age*. New York: Plenum Trade.

———. 2001. *Cyberculture*. Minneapolis: University of Minnesota Press.

Linde, Charlotte. 1993. *Life Stories: The Creation of Coherence*. New York: Oxford University Press.

Linden, Jean. 2006. "For the Love of a New and Improved Feature Voting Tool!" (September 21). Available at: http://blog.secondlife.com/2006/09/21/for-the-love-of-a-new-and-improved-feature-voting-tool/#more-330 (accessed January 2, 2007).

Llewelyn, Gwyneth. 2004. "Beginners' Guide to Second Life." (November 10). Available at: http://gwynethllewelyn.net/articlecategory/guides-and-resources (accessed December 30, 2006).

———. 2005. "It's a Country?" (November 27). Available at: http://gwynethllewelyn.net/article53visual1layout1.html (accessed January 2, 2007).

———. 2006a. "Crowdsourcing in Second Life." (July 22). Available at: http://gwynethllewelyn.net/article76visual1layout1.html (accessed January 8, 2007).

———. 2006b. "Learning the Lesson about Copyrights." (November 16). Available at: http://gwynethllewelyn.net/article114visual1layout1.html (accessed December 31, 2006).

———. 2007a. "The Schism Around Voice: Multicasting vs. Broadcasting." (March 26). Available at: http://gwynethllewelyn.net/article147visual1layout1.html (accessed April 14, 2007).

———. 2007b. "From Welfare State to Laissez-Faire Capitalism." (June 17). Available at: http://gwynethllewelyn.net/2007/06/17/from-welfare-state-to-laissez-faire-capitalism (accessed June 20, 2007).

Lockard, Joseph. 1997. "Progressive Politics, Electronic Individualism, and the Myth of Virtual Community." In *Internet Culture*, ed. David Porter, 219–31. New York: Routledge.

Locke, John. 1690 [1980 version]. *John Locke's Second Treatise of Government*. Ed. and introd. by C. B. McPherson. Indianapolis: Hackett Publishing Company.

Lombard, Matthew, and Theresa Ditton. 1997. "At the Heart of It All: The Concept of Presence." *Journal of Computer-Mediated Communication* 3, 2(December).

Lovejoy, Arthur O. 1936. *The Great Chain of Being: a Study of the History of an Idea*. New York: Harper and Row.

Lovink, Geert. 2002. *Dark Fiber: Tracking Critical Internet Culture*. Cambridge, MA: MIT Press.

Lucy, John A. 1992. *Grammatical Categories and Cognition: A Case Study of the Linguistic Relativity Hypothesis*. Cambridge: Cambridge University Press.

Ludlow, Peter, and Mark Wallace. 2007. *The Second Life Herald: The Virtual Tabloid that Witnessed the Dawn of the Metaverse*. Cambridge, MA: MIT Press.

Lyotard, Jean François. 1991. *The Inhuman: Reflections on Time*. Trans. Geoffrey Bennington and Rachel Bowlby. Stanford: Stanford University Press.

Macpherson, C. B. 1962. *The Political Theory of Possessive Individualism: Hobbes to Locke*. Oxford: Oxford University Press.

Mageo, Jeannette Marie. 1998. *Theorizing Self in Samoa: Emotions, Genders, and Sexualities*. Ann Arbor: University of Michigan Press.

Malaby, Thomas M. 2006a. "Coding Control: Governance and Contingency in the Production of Online Worlds." *First Monday*, special issue 7. Available at: http://firstmonday.org/issues/special11_9/malaby/index.html#m2 (accessed December 15, 2006).

———. 2006b. "Parlaying Value: Capital in and beyond Virtual Worlds." *Games and Culture* 1, 2(April):141–62.

Malaby, Thomas M. 2006c. "Anti-Anti Anecdotalism." *Terra Nova*, (December 30). Available at: http://terranova.blogs.com/terra_nova/2006/12/antiantianecdot.html (accessed January 3, 2007).

———. 2006d. "Ganking the Meaning Out of Games." *Terra Nova*, (February 6). Available at: http://terranova.blogs.com/terra_nova/2006/12/antiantianecdot.html (accessed February 6, 2007).

Malinowski, Bronislaw. 1922. *Argonauts of the Western Pacific*. New York: E. P. Dutton and Co.

———. 1927. *Sex and Repression in Savage Society*. London: Routledge and Kegan Paul.

———. 1935. *Coral Gardens and Their Magic*. London: Allen and Unwin.

———. 1945 [1961 reprint]. "The New Tasks of a Modern Anthropology." In his *The Dynamics of Cultural Change*, 1–13. Westport, CT: Greenwood Press.

Manen, Esteban. 2006. "Gor for Those That Never Asked," *theKonstrukt* 3 (October 25):17–20. Available at: http://www.theKonstrukt.com/magz/Konstrukt3.pdf (accessed December 31, 2006).

Marcuse, Herbert. 1964. *One-Dimensional Man*. Boston: Beacon Press.

Markham, Annette N. 1998. *Life Online: Researching Real Experience in Virtual Space*. Walnut Creek, CA: Altamira Press.

Markley, Robert. 1996. "Boundaries: Mathematics, Alienation, and the Metaphysics of Cyberspace." In *Virtual Realities and Their Discontents*, ed. Robert Markley, 55–77. Baltimore: Johns Hopkins University Press.

Marvin, Carolyn. 1988. *When Old Technologies Were New: Thinking about Electric Communication in the Late Nineteenth Century*. Oxford: Oxford University Press.

Marx, Karl. 1976. *Capital, Vol. 1*. London: Penguin Books.

Massumi, Brian. 2002. *Parables for the Virtual: Movement, Affect, Sensation*. Durham, NC: Duke University Press.

Masterson, John T. 1994. "Ethnography of a Virtual Society, or How a Gangling, Wiry Half-Elf Found a Way to Fit In." Available at: ftp://ftp.game.org/pub/mud/text/research/ethno.txt (accessed July 7, 2006).

Maurer, Bill. 2006. "The Anthropology of Money." *Annual Review of Anthropology* 35: 15–36.

Mauss, Marcel. 1979a [1938]. "A Category of the Human Mind: the Notion of Person; the Notion of 'Self.'" In his *Sociology and Psychology: Essays by Marcel Mauss*, trans. Ben Brewster, 57–94. London: Routledge and Kegan Paul.

———. 1979b [1935]. "Body Techniques." In his *Sociology and Psychology: Essays by Marcel Mauss*, trans. Ben Brewster, 95–123. London: Routledge and Kegan Paul.

May, Timothy C. 1988 [2001 reprint]. "The Crypto Anarchist Manifesto." In *Crypto Anarchy, Cyberstates, and Pirate Utopias*, ed. Peter Ludlow, 61–63. Cambridge, MA: MIT Press.

Mazlish, Bruce. 1993. *The Fourth Discontinuity: The Co-Evolution of Humans and Machines*. New Haven: Yale University Press.

McLuhan, Marshall. 1962. *The Gutenberg Galaxy: The Making of Typographic Man*. Toronto: University of Toronto Press.

McMahan, Alison. 2003. "Immersion, Engagement, and Presence: A Method for Analyzing 3-D Video Games." In *The Video Game Theory Reader*, ed. Mark J. P. Wolf and Bernard Perron, 67–86. New York: Routledge.

McPherson, Tara. 2000. "I'll Take My Stand in Dixie-Net: White Guys, the South, and Cyberspace." In *Race in Cyberspace*, ed. Beth E. Kolko, Lisa Nakamura, and Gilbert B. Rodman, 117–31. New York: Routledge.

McRae, Shannon. 1997. "Flesh Made Word: Sex, Text, and the Virtual Body." In *Internet Culture*, ed. David Porter, 73–86. New York: Routledge.

Mead, Margaret. 1928. *Coming of Age in Samoa: A Psychological Study of Primitive Youth for Western Civilization*. New York: William Morrow and Co.

———. 1950 [2001 reprint]. "Preface to the 1950 Edition." In *Sex and Temperament in Three Primitive Societies* [first published in 1935], xxv–xxvii. New York: Perennial.

———. 1968. "Cybernetics of Cybernetics." In *Purposive Systems: Proceedings of the First Annual Symposium of the American Society for Cybernetics*, ed. Heinz von Foerster, John D. White, Larry J. Peterson, and John K. Russell, 1–11. New York: Spartan Books.

Mehrabian, Albert. 1976. *Public Places and Private Spaces: The Psychology of Work, Play, and Living Environments*. New York: Basic Books.

Meyrowitz, Joshua. 1985. *No Sense of Place: The Impact of Electronic Media on Social Behavior*. New York: Oxford University Press.

Millard, William B. 1997. "I Flamed Freud: A Case Study in Teletextual Incendiarism." In *Internet Culture*, ed. David Porter, 145–59. New York: Routledge.

Miller, Daniel. 1995. *Acknowledging Consumption: A Review of New Studies*. New York: Routledge.

Miller, Daniel, and Don Slater. 2000. *The Internet: an Ethnographic Approach*. Oxford: Berg.

Mills, Russell. 1998. "Cyber: Sexual Chat on the Internet." *Journal of Popular Culture* 32, 3(Winter):31–46.

Mindell, David A. 2002. *Between Human and Machine: Feedback, Control, and Computing before Cybernetics*. Baltimore: Johns Hopkins University Press.

Mitchell, Robert, and Phillip Thurtle, eds. 2004. *Data Made Flesh: Embodying Information*. New York: Routledge.

Mitchell, Timothy. 2002. *Rule of Experts: Egypt, Techno-Politics, Modernity*. Berkeley: University of California Press.

Mnookin, Jennifer L. 2001. "Virtual(ly) Law: The Emergence of Law in LambdaMOO." In *Crypto Anarchy, Cyberstates, and Pirate Utopias*, ed. Peter Ludlow, 245–301. Cambridge, MA: MIT Press.

Mona, Erik. 2007. "From the Basement to the Basic Set: The Early Years of *Dungeons & Dragons*." In *Second Person: Role-Playing and Story in Games and Playable Media*, ed. Pat Harrigan and Noah Wardrip-Fruin, 25–30. Cambridge, MA: MIT Press.

Morningstar, Chip, and F. Randall Farmer. 1991. "The Lessons of Lucasfilm's Habitat." In *Cyberspace: First Steps*, ed. Michael Benedikt, 273–301. Cambridge, MA: MIT Press.

Morse, Margaret. 1998. *Virtualities: Television, Media Art, and Cyberculture*. Bloomington: Indiana University Press.

Mrázek, Rudolf. 1997. "'Let Us Become Radio Mechanics': Technology and National Identity in Late-Colonial Netherlands East Indies." *Comparative Studies in Society and History* 39, 1(January):3–33.

Mulligan, Jessica, and Bridgette Patrovsky. 2003. *Developing Online Games: An Insider's Guide*. Indianapolis: New Riders.

Nakamura, Lisa. 2002. *Cybertypes: Race, Ethnicity, and Identity on the Internet*. New York: Routledge.

Nardi, Bonnie. 1984. "The Height of Her Powers: Margaret Mead's Samoa." *Feminist Studies* 10, 2(Summer):323–37.

Nardi, Bonnie, and Justin Harris. 2006. "Strangers and Friends: Collaborative Play in World of Warcraft." Proceedings of Conference on Computer-Supported Collaborative Work. Banff, Canada. New York: ACM Press.

Nardi, Bonnie, Stella Ly, and Justin Harris. 2007. "Learning Conversations in World of Warcraft." Proceedings of Hawaii International Conference on Systems Science. January. Big Island, Hawaii.

Nayar, Pramod K. 2004. *Virtual Worlds: Culture and Politics in the Age of Cybertechnology*. New Delhi: Sage Publications.

Neva, Prokofy. 2005. "The Memory Palace." *Second Thoughts*, (November 9). Available at: http://secondthoughts.typepad.com/second_thoughts/2005/11/the_memory_pala .html (accessed February 19, 2007).

———. 2006a. "The Real Awful Stuff." *Second Thoughts*, (December 26). Available at: http://secondthoughts.typepad.com/second_thoughts/griefers_scammers_criminals /index.html (accessed December 27, 2006).

———. 2006b. "Island vs. Mainland." *Second Thoughts*, (October 29). Available at: http:// secondthoughts.typepad.com/second_thoughts/current_affairs/index.html (accessed November 26, 2006).

———. 2006c. "A Coup in Second Life." *Second Thoughts*, (September 16). Available at: http://secondthoughts.typepad.com/second_thoughts/2006/09/index.html (accessed September 20, 2006).

———. 2006d. "FIC-o-Pedia." *Second Thoughts*, (March 21). Available at: http://second thoughts.typepad.com/second_thoughts/2006/03/ficopedia.html (accessed January 7, 2007).

———. 2007a. "Ageplay or Pageplay? War Vet Camps New Virtual Capitol Hill." *Second Life Herald*, (January 4). Available at: http://www.secondlifeherald.com/slh/2007/01/ page_play_or_ag.html (accessed January 5, 2007).

———. 2007b. "'How many Grateful Dead Concerts?' 'Zero.'" *Second Thoughts*, (June 14). Available at: http://secondthoughts.typepad.com/second_thoughts/2007/06/how_ many_gratef.html (accessed June 20, 2007).

———. 2007c. "The Medicis of Second Life." *Second Life Herald*, (March 26). Available at: http://www.secondlifeherald.com/slh/2007/03/the_medicis_of_.html (accessed March 29, 2007).

Nguyen, D. T., and J. Alexander. 1996. "The Coming of Cyberspacetime and the End of the Polity." In *Cultures of Internet: Virtual Spaces, Real Histories, Living Bodies*, ed. Rob Shields, 99–124. London: Sage.

Nino, Tateru. 2006. "New World Numbers." *New World Notes*, (November 16). Available at: http://nwn.blogs.com/nwn/2006/11/new_world_numbe.html (accessed January 3, 2007).

Norman, John. 1978. *Beasts of Gor*. New York: DAW Books.

O'Farrell, Mary Ann, and Lynne Vallone, eds. 1999. *Virtual Gender: Fantasies of Subjectivity and Embodiment*. Ann Arbor: University of Michigan Press.

Oldenberg, Ray. 1989. *The Great Good Place*. New York: Marlowe & Company.

Ondrejka (Linden), Cory R. 2004a. "Escaping the Gilded Cage: User Created Content and Building the Metaverse." Available at: http://papers.ssrn.com/sol3/papers.cfm?abstract_id=538362 (accessed December 1, 2004).

———. 2004b. "Living on the Edge: Digital Worlds Which Embrace the Real World." Available at: http://ssrn.com/abstract=555661 (accessed December 1, 2004).

———. 2004c. "A Piece of Place: Modeling the Digital on the Real in Second Life." Available at: http://papers.ssrn.com/sol3/papers.cfm?abstract_id=555883 (accessed December 1, 2004).

———. 2004d. "Aviators, Moguls, Fashionistas, and Barons: Economics and Ownership in Second Life." Available at: http://papers.ssrn.com/sol3/papers.cfm?abstract_id=614663 (accessed January 1, 2007).

———. 2006a. "Finding Common Ground in New Worlds." *Games and Culture* 1, 1(January):111–15.

———. 2006b. "Use of CopyBot and Similar Tools a ToS Violation." (November 14). Avaliable at: http://blog.secondlife.com/2006/11/14/use-of-copybot-and-similar-tools-a-tos-violation (accessed December 31, 2006).

Ong, Walter. 1982. *Orality and Literacy: the Technologizing of the Word*. London: Methuen.

Orans, Martin. 1996. *Not Even Wrong: Margaret Mead, Derek Freeman, and the Samoans*. Novato, CA: Chandler and Sharp Publishers, Inc.

Orgad, Shani. 2005. "From Online to Offline and Back: Moving from Online to Offline Relationships with Research Informants." In *Virtual Methods: Issues in Social Research on the Internet*, ed. Christine Hine, 51–65. Oxford: Berg.

Ortner, Sherry. 1974a. "Is Female to Male as Nature Is to Culture?" In *Woman, Culture, and Society*, ed. Michelle Rosaldo and Louise Lamphere, 67–87. Stanford: Stanford University Press.

———. 1996. "So, *Is* Female to Male as Nature Is to Culture?" In her *Making Gender: The Politics and Erotics of Culture*, 173–80. Boston: Beacon Press.

———. 2006. *Anthropology and Social Theory: Culture, Power, and the Acting Subject*. Durham, NC: Duke University Press.

Paasonen, Susanna. 2002. *Figures of Fantasy: Women, Cyberdiscourse, and the Popular Internet*. Turku: Turun Yliopisto.

Paccagnella, Luciano. 1997. "Getting the Seats of Your Pants Dirty: Strategies for Ethnographic Research on Virtual Communities." *Journal of Computer-Mediated Communication* 3, 1(June).

Papert, Seymour. 1980. *Mindstorms: Children, Computers, and Powerful Ideas*. New York: Basic Books.

Pearce, Celia. 1997. *The Interactive Book: A Guide to the Interactive Revolution*. New York: Penguin Putnam.

———. 2006a. *Playing Ethnography: A Study of Emergent Behaviour in Online Games and Virtual Worlds*. Ph.D. Thesis: SMARTlab Centre, Central Saint Martins College of Art and Design, University of the Arts, London.

———. 2006b. "Productive Play: Game Culture from the Bottom Up." *Games and Culture* 1, 1(January):17-24.

———. 2007. "Communities of Play: The Social Construction of Identity in Persistent Online Game Worlds." In *Second Person: Role-Playing and Story in Games and Playable Media*, ed. Pat Harrigan and Noah Wardrip-Fruin, 311–17. Cambridge, MA: MIT Press.

Pettus, Jason. 2006. "Edgeplay." *In the Grid* 1(October):16–24. Available at: http://www.jasonpettus.com/inthegrid/itg01us.pdf (accessed December 24, 2006).

Plant, Sadie. 1995. "The Future Looms: Weaving Women and Cybernetics." In *Cyberspace/Cyberbodies/Cyberpunk: Cultures of Technological Embodiment*, ed. Mike Featherstone and Roger Burrows, 45–64. London: Sage.

———. 1996. "Connectionism and the Posthumanities." In *Beyond the Book: Theory, Culture, and the Politics of Cyberspace*, ed. Warren Chernaik, Marilyn Deegan, and Andrew Gibson, 33–41. Oxford: Office for Humanities Communication.

———. 1997. *Zeros + Ones: Digital Women + The New Technoculture*. London: Fourth Estate.

Plato. 1991. *The Republic: The Complete and Unabridged Jowett Translation*. New York: Vintage Books.

Poole, Steven. 2000. *Trigger Happy: The Aesthetics of Videogames*. London: Fourth Estate.

Poovey, Mary. 2001. "For Everything Else, There's . . ." *Social Research* 68, 2(Summer): 397–426.

Popper, Karl. 1979. *Objective Knowledge: An Evolutionary Approach*. Oxford: Clarendon Press.

Poster, Mark. 1990. *The Mode of Information: Poststructuralism and Social Context*. Cambridge: Polity Press.

———. 1996. "Postmodern Virtualities." In *FutureNatural: Nature, Science, Culture*, ed. George Robertson, Melinda Mash, Lisa Tickner, Jon Bird, Barry Curtis, and Tim Putnam, 183–202. London: Routledge.

———. 1998. "Virtual Ethnicity: Tribal Identity in an Age of Global Communications." In *CyberSociety 2.0: Revisiting Computer-Mediated Communication and Community*, ed. Steven G. Jones, 184–211. Thousand Oaks, CA: Sage Publications.

———. 1999. "Theorizing Virtual Reality: Baudrillard and Derrida." In *Cyberspace Textuality: Computer Technology and Literary Theory*, ed. Marie-Laure Ryan, 42–60. Bloomington: Indiana University Press.

———. 2001. *The Information Subject*. Amsterdam: G+B Arts International.

———. 2006. *Information Please: Culture and Politics in the Age of Digital Machines*. Durham, NC: Duke University Press.

Pottage, Alain. 2001. "Persons and Things: An Ethnographic Analogy." *Economy and Society* 30, 1(February):112–38.

Purdy, Jedediah S. 2001. "The God of the Digerati." In *Crypto Anarchy, Cyberstates, and Pirate Utopias*, ed. Peter Ludlow, 353–62. Cambridge, MA: MIT Press.

Rabinow, Paul. 2003. *Anthropos Today: Reflections on Modern Equipment*. Princeton: Princeton University Press.

Radcliffe-Brown, A. R. 1952. "On Social Structure" (originally published in 1940). In his *Structure and Function in Primitive* Society, 188–204. New York: Free Press.

Rafael, Vicente. 2003. "The Cell Phone and the Crowd: Messianic Politics in the Contemporary Philippines." *Public Culture* 15, 3(Fall):399–425.

Redfield, Peter. 2000. *Space in the Tropics: From Convicts to Rockets in French Guiana*. Berkeley: University of California Press.

Redfield, Robert. 1955. *The Little Community: Viewpoints for the Study of a Human Whole*. Chicago: University of Chicago Press.

Reed, Adam. 2005. "'My Blog Is Me': Texts and Persons in UK Online Journal Culture (and Anthropology)." *Ethnos* 70, 2(June):220–42.

Reid, Elizabeth M. 1996. "Text-based Virtual Realities: Identity and the Cyborg Body." In *High Noon on the Electronic Frontier: Conceptual Issues in Cyberspace*, ed. Peter Ludlow, 327–45. Cambridge, MA: MIT Press.

———. 1999. "Hierarchy and Power: Social Control in Cyberspace." In *Communities in Cyberspace*, ed. Marc A. Smith and Peter Kollock, 107–33. London: Routledge.

Relph, Edward. 1976. *Place and Placelessness*. London: Pion Limited.

Reuters [Pasick], Adam. 2006. "Anshe Chung Battles 'PR Hype' with Some of Her Own." *Reuters*, (November 29). Available at: http://secondlife.reuters.com/stories/2006/11/29/anshe-chung-battles-pr-hype-with-some-of-her-own (accessed December 26, 2006).

———. 2007. "Gauging the Second Life Hype Cycle." *Reuters*, (January 2). Available at: http://secondlife.reuters.com/stories/2007/01/02/gauging-the-second-life-hype-cycle (accessed January 2, 2007).

Reynolds, Ren. 2006. "Countdown to SL Backlash." Available at: http://terranova.blogs.com/terra_nova/2006/12/countdown_to_ba.html#comments (accessed January 1, 2007).

Rheingold, Howard. 1991. *Virtual Reality*. New York: Simon and Schuster.

———. 2000. *The Virtual Community: Homesteading on the Electronic Frontier*. Cambridge, MA: MIT Press.

Rice, Eric. 2006. "RIAA-styled Rage in Second Life–by Everyday People." (November 13). Available at: http://www.ericrice.com/blog/?p=199 (accessed December 31, 2006).

Rifkin, Jeremy. 1987. *Time Wars: The Primary Conflict in Human History*. New York: Henry Holt and Company.

Riles, Annelise. 2000. *The Network Inside Out*. Ann Arbor: University of Michigan Press.

Roberts, Lynne D., and Malcolm R. Parks. 1999. "The Social Geography of Gender-Switching in Virtual Environments on the Internet." *Information, Communication, and Society* 2, 4(December):521–40.

Robinett, Warren. 2003. "Foreword." In *The Video Game Theory Reader*, ed. Mark J. P. Wolf and Bernard Perron, vii–xix. New York: Routledge.

Rodríguez, Juana Maria. 2003. *Queer Latinidad: Identity Practices, Discursive Spaces*. New York: New York University Press.

Rofel, Lisa. 2007. *Desiring China: Experiments in Neoliberalism, Sexuality, and Public Culture*. Durham, NC: Duke University Press.

Ronell, Avital. 1989. *The Telephone Book: Technology, Schizophrenia, Electric Speech*. Lincoln: University of Nebraska Press.

Ropolyi, Laszlo. 2001. "Virtuality and Plurality." In *Virtual Reality: Cognitive Foundations, Technological Issues, and Philosophical Implications*, ed. Alexander Riegler, Markus F. Peschl, Karl Edlinger, Gunther Fleck, and Walter Feigl, 167–87. Frankfurt: Peter Lang.

Rosenberg, Michael S. 1992. "Virtual Reality: Reflections of Life, Dreams, and Technology: An Ethnography of a Computer Society." Available at: http://www.eff.org/Net_culture/MOO_MUD_IRC/rosenberg_vr_reflections.paper (accessed July 10, 2006).

Rubin, Gayle. 1993. "Thinking Sex: Notes for a Radical Theory of the Politics of Sexuality." In *The Lesbian and Gay Studies Reader*, ed. Henry Abelove, Michele Aina Barale, and David M. Halperin, 3–44. New York: Routledge.

Rudnytsky, Peter L. 1993. "Introduction." In *Transitional Objects and Potential Spaces: Literary Uses of D. W. Winnicott*, ed. Peter L. Rudnytsky, xi–xxii. New York: Columbia University Press.

Ruhleder, Karen. 2000. "The Virtual Ethnographer: Fieldwork in Distributed Electronic Environments." *Field Methods* 12, 1(February):3–17.

Rutsky, R. L. 1999. *High Techne: Art and Aesthetics from the Machine Age to the Posthuman*. Minneapolis: University of Minnesota Press.

Rutter, Jason, and Gregory W. H. Smith. 2005. "Ethnographic Presence in a Nebulous Setting." In *Virtual Methods: Issues in Social Research on the Internet*, ed. Christine Hine, 81–92. Oxford: Berg.

Ryan, Marie-Laure. 1991. *Possible Worlds, Artificial Intelligence, and Narrative Theory*. Bloomington: Indiana University Press.

———. 1999. *Cyberspace Textuality: Computer Technology and Literary Theory*. Bloomington: Indiana University Press.

Rymaszewski, Michael, Wagner James Au, Mark Wallace, Catherine Winters, Cory Ondrejka, and Benjamin Batstone-Cunningham. 2007. *Second Life: The Official Guide*. Hoboken, NJ: John Wiley and Sons.

Salen, Katie, and Eric Zimmerman. 2004. *Rules of Play: Game Design Fundamentals*. Cambridge, MA: MIT Press.

Sapir, Edward. 1949. *Edward Sapir: Selected Writings in Language, Culture, and Personality*. Ed. David G. Mandelbaum. Berkeley: University of California Press.

Schaap, Frank. 2002. *The Words that Took Us There: Ethnography in a Virtual Reality*. Amersterdam: Aksant Academic Publishers.

Schechner, Richard. 1988. "Playing." *Play and Culture* 1, 1(January):3–20.

Schroeder, Ralph. 1996. *Possible Worlds: The Social Dynamic of Virtual Reality Technology*. Boulder: Westview Press.

———. 2002. "Social Interaction in Virtual Environments: Key Issues, Common Themes, and a Framework for Research." In *The Social Life of Avatars: Presence and Interaction in Shared Virtual Environments*, ed. Ralph Schroeder, 1–18. London: Springer-Verlag.

Schroeder, Ralph. 2006. "Being There Together and the Future of Connected Presence." *Presence* 15, 4(August):438–54.

Schroeder, Ralph, Noel Heather, and Raymond M. Lee. 1998. "The Sacred and the Virtual: Religion in Multi-User Virtual Reality." *Journal of Computer Mediated Communication* 4, 2(December). Available at: http://jcmc.indiana.edu/vol4/issue2/schroeder .html (accessed October 27, 2006).

Schubert, Damion. 2003. "The Lighter Side of Meridian 59's History." In *Developing Online Games: An Insider's Guide*, ed. Jessica Mulligan and Bridgette Patrovsky, 361–71. Indianapolis: New Riders.

Schuemie, Martijn J., Peter van der Straaten, Merel Krijn, and Charles A.P.G. van der Mast. 2001. "Research on Presence in Virtual Reality: A Survey." *CyberPsychology and Behavior* 4, 2(April):183–201.

Schwartz, Hillel. 1996. *The Culture of the Copy: Striking Likenesses, Unreasonable Facsimiles*. New York: Zone Books.

Scott, James C. 1998. *Seeing Like a State: How Certain Schemes to Improve the Human Condition Have Failed*. New Haven: Yale University Press.

Scott, James C., John Tehranian, and Jeremy Mathias. 2002. "The Production of Legal Identities Proper to States: The Case of the Permanent Family Surname." *Comparative Studies in Society and History* 44, 1(January):4–44.

Semuels, Alana. 2007. "Virtual Loses its Virtues." *Los Angeles Times*, (February 22). Available at: http://www.latimes.com/entertainment/news/la-fi-second22feb22,1,4841916, full.story?coll=la-headlines-entnews (accessed February 25, 2007).

Shah, Rawn, and Jim Romine. 1995. *Playing MUDS on the Internet*. New York: John Wiley and Sons.

Shapiro, Andrew L. 1999. *The Control Revolution: How the Internet is Putting Individuals in Charge and Changing the World We Know*. New York: PublicAffairs.

Shankman, Paul. 1996. "The History of Samoan Sexual Conduct and the Mead-Freeman Controversy." *American Anthropologist* 98, 3 (September):555–67.

Shelley, Mary Wollstonecraft. 2007 [1818]. *Frankenstein, or, The Modern Prometheus*. New York: Pearson Longman.

Shirky, Clay. 2006. "Second Life: What are the Real Numbers?" *Many-to-Many*, (December 12). Available at: http://many.corante.com/archives/2006/12/12/second_life_ what_are_the_real_numbers.php (accessed December 24, 2006).

———. 2007. "Second Life, Games, and Virtual Worlds." *Many-to-Many*, (January 29). Available at: http://many.corante.com/archives/2007/01/29/second_life_games_ and _virtual_worlds.php (accessed February 1, 2007).

Silverstone, Roger. 1999. *Why Study the Media?* London: Sage.

Sipress, Alan. 2006. "Where Real Money Meets Virtual Reality, the Jury is Still Out." *Washington Post*, (December 26). Available at: http://www.washingtonpost.com/wp -dyn/content/article/2006/12/25/AR2006122500635.html (accessed January 2, 2007).

Smith, Anna DuVal. 1999. "Problems of Conflict Management in Virtual Communities." In *Communities in Cyberspace*, ed. Marc A. Smith and Peter Kollock, 134–63. London: Routledge.

Smith, Brian Cantwell. 1996. *On the Origin of Objects*. Cambridge, MA: MIT Press.

Smith, Marc A. 1999. "Invisible Crowds in Cyberspace: Mapping the Social Structure of the Usenet." In *Communities in Cyberspace*, ed. Marc A. Smith and Peter Kollock, 195–219. London: Routledge.

Smith, Neil. 1996. "The Production of Nature." In *FutureNatural: Nature, Science, Culture*, ed. George Robertson, Melinda Mash, Lisa Tickner, Jon Bird, Barry Curtis, and Tim Putnam, 35–54. London: Routledge.

Spence, Jonathan D. 1984. *The Memory Palace of Matteo Ricci*. New York: Viking Press.

Spengler, Oswald. 1932. *Man and Technics: A Contribution to a Philosophy of Life*. New York: Knopf.

Spivak, Gayatri Chakravorty. 1988. "Can the Subaltern Speak?" In *Marxism and the Interpretation of Culture*, ed. Cary Nelson and Lawrence Grossberg, 271–313. Urbana: University of Illinois Press.

Stein, Jeremy. 1999. "The Telephone: Its Social Shaping and Public Negotiation in Late Nineteenth- and Early Twentieth-Century London." In *Virtual Geographies: Bodies, Space, and Relations*, ed. Mike Crang, Phil Crang, and Jon May, 44–62. London: Routledge.

Stein, Joel. 2006. "My So-Called Second Life." *Time* 168, 26 (December 25):40–41, 76–77.

Steinkuehler, Constance, and Dimitri Williams. 2006. "Where Everybody Knows Your (Screen) Name: Online Games as 'Third Places.'" *Journal of Computer-Mediated Communication* 11, 4, article 1. Available at: http://jcmc.indiana.edu/vol11/issue4/steinkuehler.html (accessed October 27, 2006).

Stephenson, Neal. 1993. *Snow Crash*. New York: Bantam Books.

Sterling, Bruce. 1992. *The Hacker Crackdown: Law and Disorder on the Electronic Frontier*. New York: Bantam Books.

———. 2005. *Shaping Things*. Cambridge, MA: MIT Press.

Sterne, Jonathan. 2003. *The Audible Past: Cultural Origins of Sound Reproduction*. Durham, NC: Duke University Press.

Steuer, Jonathan. 1992. "Defining Virtual Reality: Dimensions Determining Telepresence." *Journal of Communication* 42, 4(Autumn):73–93.

Stiegler, Bernard. 1998. *Technics and Time, 1: The Fault of Epimetheus*. Stanford: Stanford University Press.

Stocking, George W., Jr. 1974. "The Basic Assumptions of Boasian Anthropology." In his *The Franz Boas Reader*, 1–20. Chicago: University of Chicago Press.

Stone, Allucquère Rosanne. 1991. "Will the Real Body Please Stand Up? Boundary Stories about Virtual Cultures." In *Cyberspace: First Steps*, ed. Michael Benedikt, 81–118. Cambridge, MA: MIT Press.

———. 1995. *The War of Desire and Technology at the Close of the Mechanical Age*. Boston: MIT Press.

Strathern, Marilyn. 1985. "Discovering 'Social Control.'" *Journal of Law and Society* 12, 2 (Summer):111–34.

———. 1988. *The Gender of the Gift: Problems with Women and Problems with Society in Melanesia*. Berkeley: University of California Press.

Strathern, Marilyn. 1991. *Partial Connections*. Savage, MD: Rowman and Littlefield Publishers, Inc.

———. 1992. *Reproducing the Future: Anthropology, Kinship, and the New Reproductive Technologies*. New York: Routledge.

———. 1996. "Cutting the Network." *Journal of the Royal Anthropological Institute* 2, 3 (September):517–35.

———. 1999. *Property, Substance, and Effect: Anthropological Essays on Persons and Things*. London: The Athlone Press.

———. 2002. "Abstraction and Decontextualization: An Anthropological Comment." In *Virtual Society? Technology, Cyberbole, Reality*, ed. Steve Woolgar, 302–13. Oxford: Oxford University Press.

———. 2004. *Commons and Borderlands: Working Papers on Interdisciplinarity, Accountability, and the Flow of Knowledge*. Wantage: Sean Kingston Publishing.

Suits, Bernard. 1978. *The Grasshopper: Games, Life, and Utopia*. Edinburgh: Scottish Academic Press.

Suler, John. 1996. "The Psychology of Cyberspace." Available at: http://www.rider.edu/users/suler/psycyber/psycyber.html (accessed October 27, 2006).

Sullivan, Andrew. 1995. *Virtually Normal: An Argument about Homosexuality*. New York: A. A. Knopf.

Sundén, Jenny. 2003. *Material Virtualities: Approaching Online Textual Embodiment*. New York: Peter Lang.

Sveningsson, Malin. 2002. "Cyberlove: Creating Romanic Relationships on the Net." In *Digital Borderlands: Cultural Studies of Identity and Interactivity on the Internet*, ed. Johan Fornäs, Kajsa Klein, Martina Ladendorf, Jenny Sundén, and Malin Sveningsson, 48–78. New York: Peter Lang.

Takashi, Tao. 2006. "The CopyBot Controversy." (November 15). Available at: http://taotakashi.wordpress.com/2006/11/15/the-copybot-controversy (accessed December 31, 2006).

Talin. 2003. "Managing Deviant Behavior in Online Worlds." In *Developing Online Games: An Insider's Guide*, ed. Jessica Mulligan and Bridgette Patrovsky, 347–60. Indianapolis: New Riders.

Taylor, T. L. 2002. "Living Digitally: Embodiment in Virtual Worlds." In *The Social Life of Avatars: Presence and Interaction in Shared Virtual Environments*, ed. Ralph Schroeder, 40–62. London: Springer-Verlag.

———. 2006a. *Play Between Worlds: Exploring Online Game Culture*. Cambridge, MA: MIT Press.

———. 2006b. "Beyond Management: Considering Participatory Design and Governance in Player Culture." *First Monday*, special issue 7. Available at: http://firstmonday.org/issues/special11_9/taylor (accessed December 15, 2006).

Tepper, Michele. 1997. "Usenet Communities and the Cultural Politics of Information." In *Internet Culture*, ed. David Porter, 39–54. New York: Routledge.

Teriman, Daniel. 2006. "Phony Kids, Virtual Sex." *CNet*, (April 12). Available at: http://news.com.com/Phony+kids,+virtual+sex/2100-1043_3-6060132.html (accessed April 24, 2006).

Thomas, Douglas. 2005. "Power, Play and Performance: Studying Virtual Worlds." Paper presented at the Society for the Social Studies of Science conference, (October 21). Pasadena, California.

Tilgher, Adriano. 1930. *Homo Faber: Work through the Ages*. Introds. by Ronald Gross and Dorothy Canfield Fisher. Chicago: Henry Regnery Company.

Toffler, Alvin. 1980. *The Third Wave*. New York: Bantam Books.

Tolkien, J.R.R. 1966. "On Fairy Stories." In his *The Tolkien Reader*, 3–84. New York: Ballantine Books.

Tomas, David. 1991. "Old Rituals for New Space: *Rites de Passage* and William Gibson's Cultural Model of Cyberspace." In *Cyberspace: First Steps*, ed. Michael Benedikt, 31–47. Cambridge, MA: MIT Press.

———. 1995. "Feedback and Cybernetics: Reimagining the Body in the Age of the Cyborg." In *Cyberspace/Cyberbodies/Cyberpunk: Cultures of Technological Embodiment*, ed. Mike Featherstone and Roger Burrows, 21–43. London: Sage.

Towell, John, and Elizabeth Towell. 1997. "Presence in Text-Based Networked Virtual Environments or 'MUDS'." *Presence: Teleoperators and Virtual Environments* 6, 5(October):590–95.

Trilling, Lionel. 1971. *Sincerity and Authenticity*. Cambridge, MA: Harvard University Press.

Tuan, Yi-Fu. 1977. *Space and Place: The Perspective of Experience*. Minneapolis: University of Minnesota Press.

Turkle, Sherry. 1984. *The Second Self: Computers and the Human Spirit*. New York: Simon and Schuster.

———. 1995. *Life on the Screen: Identity in the Age of the Internet*. New York: Simon and Schuster.

———. 1997. "Constructions and Reconstructions of Self in Virtual Reality: Playing in the MUDs." In *Culture of the Internet*, ed. Sara Kiesler, 143–55. Mahwah, NJ: Lawrence Erlbaum Associates.

Turner, Fred. 2006. *From Counterculture to Cyberculture: Stewart Brand, the Whole Earth Network, and the Rise of Digital Utopianism*. Chicago: University of Chicago Press.

Turner, Phil, and Susan Turner. 2006. "Place, Sense of Place, and Presence." *Presence* 15, 2(April):204–17.

Turner, Victor Witter. 1982. *From Ritual to Theatre: The Human Seriousness of Play*. New York: Performing Arts Journal Publications.

Tylor, Edward Burnett. 1871. *Primitive Culture, Volume 1: The Origins of Culture*. New York: Harper and Row.

Vaid, Urvashi. 1996. *Virtual Equality: The Mainstreaming of Gay and Lesbian Liberation*. New York: Anchor Books.

Vaihinger, Hans. 1924. *Philosophy of the As If: A System of the Theoretical, Practical and Religious Fictions of Mankind*. London: Routledge and Kegan Paul.

Van Gelder, Lindsey. 1991 [1985]. "The Strange Case of the Electronic Lover." In *Computerization and Controversy: Value Conflicts and Social Choices*, ed. Charles Dunlop and Rob Kling, 364–75. Boston: Academic Press.

Vasseleu, Cathryn. 1997. "Virtual Bodies/Virtual Worlds." In *Virtual Politics: Identity and Community in Cyberspace*, ed. David Holmes, 46–58. London: Sage.

Veblen, Thorstein. 1899 [1994]. *The Theory of the Lesiure Class*. New York: Dover Publications.

———. 1921. *The Engineers and the Price System*. New York: B. W. Huebsch.

Venera, Chaos. 2006. "Time for Democracy?" *theKonstrukt* 5 (November 27):8–9. Available at: http://www.theKonstrukt.com/magz/Konstrukt5.pdf (accessed December 31, 2006).

Vinge, Vernor. 2001 [1981]. "True Names." In *True Names by Vernor Vinge and the Opening of the Cyberspace Frontier*, ed. James Frenkel, 241–330. New York: Tom Doherty Associates.

Virilio, Paul. 1994. *The Vision Machine*. Bloomington: Indiana University Press.

von Neumann, John, and Oskar Morgenstern. 1944. *Theory of Games and Economic Behavior*. Princeton: Princeton University Press.

Wagner, Roy. 2001. *An Anthropology of the Subject: Holographic Worldview in New Guinea and its Meaning and Significance for the World of Anthropology*. Berkeley: University of California Press.

Wakeford, Nina. 1999. "Gender and the Landscapes of Computing in an Internet Café." In *Virtual Geographies: Bodies, Space, and Relations*, ed. Mike Crang, Phil Crang, and Jon May, 178–201. London: Routledge.

———. 2000. "Cyberqueer." In *The Cybercultures Reader*, ed. David Bell and Barbara M. Kennedy, 403–15. London: Routledge.

Wallace, Mark. 2006. "Philip Rosedale: Boy Hacker." *3pointD.com*, (August 23). Available at: http://www.3pointd.com/20060823/philip-rosedale-boy-hacker (accessed January 2, 2007).

Walsh, Tony. 2005. "SL's Tringo Hits RL Markets." *Clickable Culture*, (March 3). Available at: http://secretlair.com/index.php?/clickableculture/entry/sls_tringo_hits_rl_markets (accessed December 31, 2006).

———. 2007. "'Second Life' Through a Hype-Cycle Lens." *Clickable Culture*, (January 1). Available at: http://www.secretlair.com/index.php?/clickableculture/entry/second_life_through_a_hype_cycle_lens (accessed January 7, 2007).

Walzer, Michael. 1987. *Interpretation and Social Criticism*. Cambridge, MA: Harvard University Press.

Wark, McKenzie. 2007. *Gamer Theory*. Cambridge, MA: Harvard University Press.

Wardrip-Fruin, Noah, and Pat Harrigan, eds. 2004. *First Person: New Media as Story, Performance, and Game*. Cambridge, MA: MIT Press.

Weber, Aimee, Kimberly Rufer-Bach, and Richard Platel. 2007. *Creating Your World: The Official Guide to Advanced Content Creation for Second Life*. Hoboken, NJ: Sybex.

Weber, Max. 1992 [1930]. *The Protestant Ethic and the Spirit of Capitalism*. London: Routledge.

Weheliye, Alexander. 2002. "'Feenin': Posthuman Voices in Contemporary Black Popular Music." *Social Text* 20, 2(Summer):21–47.

Weiner, Annette B. 1983. "Ethnographic Determinism: Samoa and the Margaret Mead Controversy." *American Anthropologist* 85, 4(December):909–18.

Weinstone, Ann. 2004. *Avatar Bodies: A Tantra for Posthumanism*. Minneapolis: University of Minnesota Press.

Wellman, Barry, and Milena Gulia. 1999. "Virtual Communities as Communities: Net Surfers Don't Ride Alone." In *Communities in Cyberspace*, ed. Marc A. Smith and Peter Kollock, 167–94. London: Routledge.

Wertheim, Margaret. 1999. *The Pearly Gates of Cyberspace: A History of Space from Dante to the Internet*. New York: W. W. Norton and Co.

Weschler, Lawrence. 1995. *Mr. Wilson's Cabinet of Wonder: Pronged Ants, Horned Humans, Mice on Toast, and Other Marvels of Jurassic Technology*. New York: Vintage Books.

Weston, Kath. 1997. "The Virtual Anthropologist." In *Anthropological Locations: Boundaries and Grounds of a Field Science*, ed. Akhil Gupta and James Ferguson, 163–84. Berkeley: University of California Press.

White, Brian A. 2007. *Second Life: A Guide to Your Virtual World*. Indianapolis: Que Publishing.

White, Michele. 2006. *The Body and the Screen: Theories of Internet Spectatorship*. Cambridge, MA: MIT Press.

Whorf, Benjamin Lee. 1956. *Language, Thought, and Reality: Selected Writings of Benjamin Lee Whorf*. Ed. John B. Carroll. Cambridge, MA: MIT Press.

Wiener, Norbert. 1948. *Cybernetics: or Control and Communication in the Animal and the Machine*. New York: John Wiley and Sons.

Wilbur, Shawn P. 1997. "An Archaeology of Cyberspaces: Virtuality, Community, Identity." In *Internet Culture*, ed. David Porter, 5–22. New York: Routledge.

Williams, Tad. 1996. *Otherland: Volume One, City of Golden Shadow*. New York: Daw Books.

Winnicott, D. W. 1993 [1967]. "The Location of Cultural Experience." In *Transitional Objects and Potential Spaces: Literary Uses of D.W. Winnicott*, ed. Peter L. Rudnytsky, 3–12. New York: Columbia University Press.

Wise, Patricia. 1997. "Always Already Virtual: Feminist Politics in Cyberspace." In *Virtual Politics: Identity and Community in Cyberspace*, ed. David Holmes, 179–96. London: Sage.

Witte, Deeeep. 2006. "So You Want to Go to Gor?" *Slatenight* 1, 2(August):10. Available at: http://www.slatenight.com (accessed December 17, 2006).

Wittel, Andreas. 2001. "Toward a Network Sociality." *Theory, Culture and Society* 18, 6(December):51–76.

Wolf, Mark J. P. 2001. "Space in the Video Game." In *The Medium of the Video Game*, ed. Mark J. P. Wolf, 51–75. Austin: University of Texas Press.

Wolf, Mark J. P., and Bernard Perron. 2003. "Introduction." In *The Video Game Theory Reader*, ed. Mark J. P. Wolf and Bernard Perron, 1–11. New York: Routledge.

Woolley, Benjamin. 1992. *Virtual Worlds: A Journey in Hype and Hyperreality*. Oxford: Blackwell.

Xueqin, Cao. 1973. *The Story of the Stone, or the Dream of the Red Chamber (Vol. 1, The Golden Days)*. New York: Penguin Classics.

Yanagisako, Sylvia Junko. 2002. *Producing Culture and Capital: Family Firms in Italy*. Princeton: Princeton University Press.

Yee, Nick. 2002. "Ariadne—Understanding MMORPG Addiction." Avaliable at: http://www.nickyee.com/hub/addiction/home.htm (accessed December 23, 2006).

———. 2004. "Addiction." The Daedalus Project, (July 9). Available at: http://www.nickyee.com/daedalus/archives/000818.php (accessed December 23, 2006).

———. 2005. "Problematic Usage." The Daedalus Project, (May 10). Available at: http://www.nickyee.com/daedalus/archives/001336.php (accessed December 23, 2006).

———. 2006a. "The Demographics, Motivations and Derived Experiences of Users of Massively-Multiuser Online Graphical Environments." *Presence Teleoperators and Virtual Environments* 15, 3(June):309–29.

———. 2006b. "The Labor of Fun: How Video Games Blur the Boundaries of Work and Play." *Games and Culture* 1, 1(January):68–71.

———. 2006c. "A New Disorder is Born." The Daedalus Project, (January 3). Available at: http://www.nickyee.com/daedalus/archives/001494.php (accessed December 23, 2006).

———. 2007. The Proteus Effect: Behavioral Modification Via Transformations of Digital Self-Representation. Ph.D. Dissertation, Department of Communications, Stanford University, June.

Yee, Nick, Jeremy N. Bailenson, Mark Urbanek, Francis Chang, and Dan Merget. 2007. "The Unbearable Lightness of Being Digital: The Persistence of Nonverbal Social Norms in Online Virtual Environments." *CyberPsychology and Behavior* 10, 1(February):115–21.

Young, Kimberly S. 1998. *Caught in the Net: How to Recognize the Signs of Internet Addiction, and a Winning Strategy for Recovery.* New York: John Wiley and Sons.

Yu, Anthony C. 1997. *Rereading the Stone: Desire and the Making of Fiction in Dream of the Red Chamber.* Princeton: Princeton University Press.

Zaretsky, Eli. 1976. *Capitalism, the Family, and Personal Life.* New York: Harper and Row.

Zhai, Philip. 1998. *Get Real: A Philosophical Adventure in Virtual Reality.* Lanham, MD: Rowman and Littlefield Publishers, Inc.

Zhan, Mei. 2001. "Does It Take A Miracle? Negotiating Knowledges, Identities, and Communities of Traditional Chinese Medicine." *Cultural Anthropology* 16, 4(November):453–80.

Žižek, Slavoj. 1992. "From Virtual Reality to the Virtualization of Reality." In *On Justifying the Hypothetical Nature of Art and the Non-identicality Within the Object World,* ed. Peter Weibel, 127–36. Austin: University of Texas Press. Köln: Buchhandlung Walther König.

Ihde, Don, 135
Imagined Communities (Anderson), 24
immersion, social, 112, *113,* 113–16, 263n28
ims (instant messages), 13, 108, 110, 117, 146, 152–54, 252
inequality, 25, 221, 225–29, 234–35, 270nn23, 24
Internet, 35, 39, 49–50, 176
The Internet: An Ethnographic Approach (Miller and Slater), 62
interviews, methodology and, 4, 16, 76–78, 260n5
intimacy: chat and, 117, 160; friendship and, 156, 159–60; ims and, 153–54; language and, 151; love and, 166, 170; partners and, 166, 171, 266n17; selfhood and, 151, 156; sexuality and, 157, 160; virtual worlds and, 156–57, 178. *See also* family; love; sexuality
inventory feature, 9–11, *10,* 14–15, 98, 152
islands feature, 13, 94, 217, 261n6, 268nn11–12
Ito, Mizuko, 35, 54, 127, 132, 134, 189, 258n3

Jacey controversy, 190–91, *191*
Jacobson, David, 69, 151, 167
Jakobsson, Mikael, 54, 126, 157, 183, 186, 226
James, Clement, 255n4, 264n18
Jenkins, Henry, 54, 207
JennyMUSH, 189
Joan/Alex controversy, 120, 142
Johns, Adrian, 30
Jones, Donald E., 129, 134
Jones, Quentin, 54
Jones, Steven G., 54, 91
Joseph, Miranda, 209
Juul, Jesper, 54

Kay, Alan, 32
Kaye, Lewis, 54, 214
Kelty, Christopher, 58, 220
Kendall, Lori, 53, 54, 62, 79, 85, 103, 108, 123, 139, 144, 185, 226, 260n7
Kent, Steven L., 47, 49, 242
Kiesler, Sara, 266n6
Kim, Taeyong, 20
kindness, 186–87, 195. *See also* altruism
King, Brad, 38, 52
Kittler, Friedrich A., 36
Kivits, Joëlle, 85

knowledge: techne vs., 25, 55–56, 59, 66, 67, 166, 240
Koivisto, Elina M. I., 194
Kolko, Beth E., 54, 144
Kollock, Peter, 50, 53, 226, 259n18
Koster, Ralph, 7, 48, 50, 51, 184, 189, 245, 259n17, 268n6
Krueger, Myron, 37, 42–47, *44, 45, 46,* 129
Kuper, Adam, 255n2
Kurzweil, Ray, 237
Kushner, David, 11, 17, 48, 129

labor: creationist capitalism and, 210, 219; fashion design and, 8, 73, 108, 213; as leisure activity, 213; money and, 211–12; restrictions and, 12, 212, 214–15, 231; service labor and, 215; textures and, 98, 213, 268n9. *See also* commodity economies
lag, 98, 101–6, 127, 192, 252, 262nn19–20, 22, 268n9
Lakoff, Andrew, 56
LambdaMOO, 51, 53, 188–89, 261n14, 263n2
land ownership: auctions and, 94; banning and, 95, 96, 196, 222, 234, 261n6, 265n9; dwell/traffic and, 95, 253, 261n11, 262n26; history of, 216, 268n11; islands and, 13, 94, 217, 261n6, 268nn11–12; land barons and, 216–17; life course and, 126; sandboxes and, 99; tiering fee and, 9, 127, 184, 213, 215–16, 227, 268n11; value of land and, 94–95, 231–32, 261n7, 261nn8, 10; virtual made real and, 215. *See also* building feature
landscapes, 92–94, 96, 261nn5, 6
Lange, Patricia, 17, 57
Langer, Susanne K., 57
language: American English, 85, 154–56; body language of avatars, 130–31; codeswitching and, 154, 265n4; computer programs and, 151; intimacy and, 151; linguistic component of sexuality, 160–61; Linden Scripting Language, 50, 98, 214; multiple languages in SL, 155–56, 198, 267n16; text predominance and, 151, 152; thoughts shaped by, 231; virtual nature of, 151; virtual worlds and, 54. *See also* chat feature; ims; voice capabilities
Lanier, Jaron, 256–57n16
Lastowka, F. Gregory, 48, 50, 51, 206, 214
Latour, Bruno, 19, 100, 149, 247